THE SIMPSONS™

HOLIDAY HUMDINGER

Perennial
Currents

An Imprint of HarperCollins*Publishers*

Dedicated to Snowball I:

As this snow sculpture thaws on the first warm day,
so will our hearts melt whenever we think of you.

THE SIMPSONS™ HOLIDAY HUMDINGER

Copyright © 1994, 1995, 2000, 2003 & 2004 by
Bongo Entertainment, Inc. and Matt Groening Productions, Inc. All rights reserved.

Printed in the United States of America.
No part of this book may be used or reproduced in any manner whatsoever
without written permission except in the case of brief quotations
embodied in critical articles and reviews. For information address
HarperCollins Publishers Inc.,
10 East 53rd Street, New York, NY 10022.

HarperCollins books may be purchased for educational, business, or sales
promotional use. For information please write:
Special Markets Department,
HarperCollins Publishers Inc.,
10 East 53rd Street, New York, NY 10022.

FIRST EDITION
ISBN 0-06-072338-6

04 05 06 07 08 09 RRD 10 9 8 7 6 5 4 3 2 1

Publisher: Matt Groening
Creative Director: Bill Morrison
Managing Editor: Terry Delegeane
Director of Operations: Robert Zaugh
Special Projects Art Director: Serban Cristescu
Art Director: Nathan Kane
Production Manager: Christopher Ungar
Production/Design: Karen Bates, Art Villanueva
Production Assistance: Chia-Hsien Jason Ho, Mike Rote
Editorial Assistance: Sherri Smith, Nathan Hamill
Legal Guardian: Susan A. Grode

Book Concepts and Design: Serban Cristescu

Contributing Artists:
Karen Bates, Tim Bavington, John Costanza, Isabelle Cristescu, Serban Cristescu, Luis Escobar,
Stephanie Gladden, Nathan Kane, William Mahaney, Bill Morrison, Kevin M. Newman, Phil Ortiz, Mike Rote,
Howard Shum, Steve Steere Jr., Chris Ungar, Art Villanueva

Contributing Writers:
Ian Boothby, Paul Dini, Scott M. Gimple, Jason Grode, Bill Morrison, Gail Simone, Mary Trainor

HarperCollins Editors: Susan Weinberg, Kate Travers

Special Thanks to:
Pete Benson, N. Vyolet Diaz, Deanna MacLellan, Mili Smythe, and Ursula Wendel

TABLE OF CONTENTS

BEST INTRO EVER!

Salutations from the Captain's chair of the Android's Dungeon, Springfield's world-renowned comic book shop and the finest purveyor of sport cards and sci-fi/fantasy collectibles in the tri-city area. (Nerts to you, Frodo's of Shelbyville!)

While recently engaged in a spirited discourse with my online role-playing group, the subject of the impending holidays reared its head. The question put before The Continuum was, in a wintertime scenario, which frost-bound character would you be? Predictably many opted for the heroic demeanor of Iceman, or the cold-hearted villainy of Mr. Freeze or even the innocuous japery of Chilly Willy. While Frink 8.5 (the fool) remained unshakable in his position that Captain Cold is a far superior evil-doer than Mr. Freeze (oh please) and The Internet King staunchly defended some nobody named Mr. Plow, I remained steadfast in my conviction that the greatest of all winter characters is the one and only Santa Claus.

Yes, I truly envy that jolly old soul. Why, his ready access to eggnog and gingerbread alone secures him the top spot in my price guide. And let us not forget his happy little helpers. Imagine, if your Muggle brain will let you, commanding legions of elf-lackeys to fashion the rarest of treasures for your personal collection. If I were blessed with the power of the Clausinator, crates of banned missile-launching Boba Fett action figures would line my workshop. I'd use Fantasia animation cels as place mats and wipe doughnut sprinkles from my mouth with Joe DiMaggio baseball cards.

Most wondrous of all, I would have my sprightly drones faithfully re-create classics of graphic storytelling long out of print. Classics like the merry tales contained herein. You hold in your unworthy hands **The Simpsons Holiday Humdinger**, a compilation of seasonal glee from our favorite family's Christmases past. Any one of these now priceless books would cost you a fortune on the back issue market, if you could find them (and rest assured you can't), but thanks to the magic of the Yuletide season, they are yours merely for the wishing, and of course, the $14.95 marked on the back cover.

Now heat up the cocoa, break out the cookies, assemble your friends (super or otherwise), and enjoy this diverting selection of holiday frippery.

And don't forget the Dungeon's Post-Xmas Clearance Sale 11 A.M. to 9 P.M. on Dec. 26th. All seasonal merchandise 40% off! (No refunds or exchanges.)

Comic Book Guy

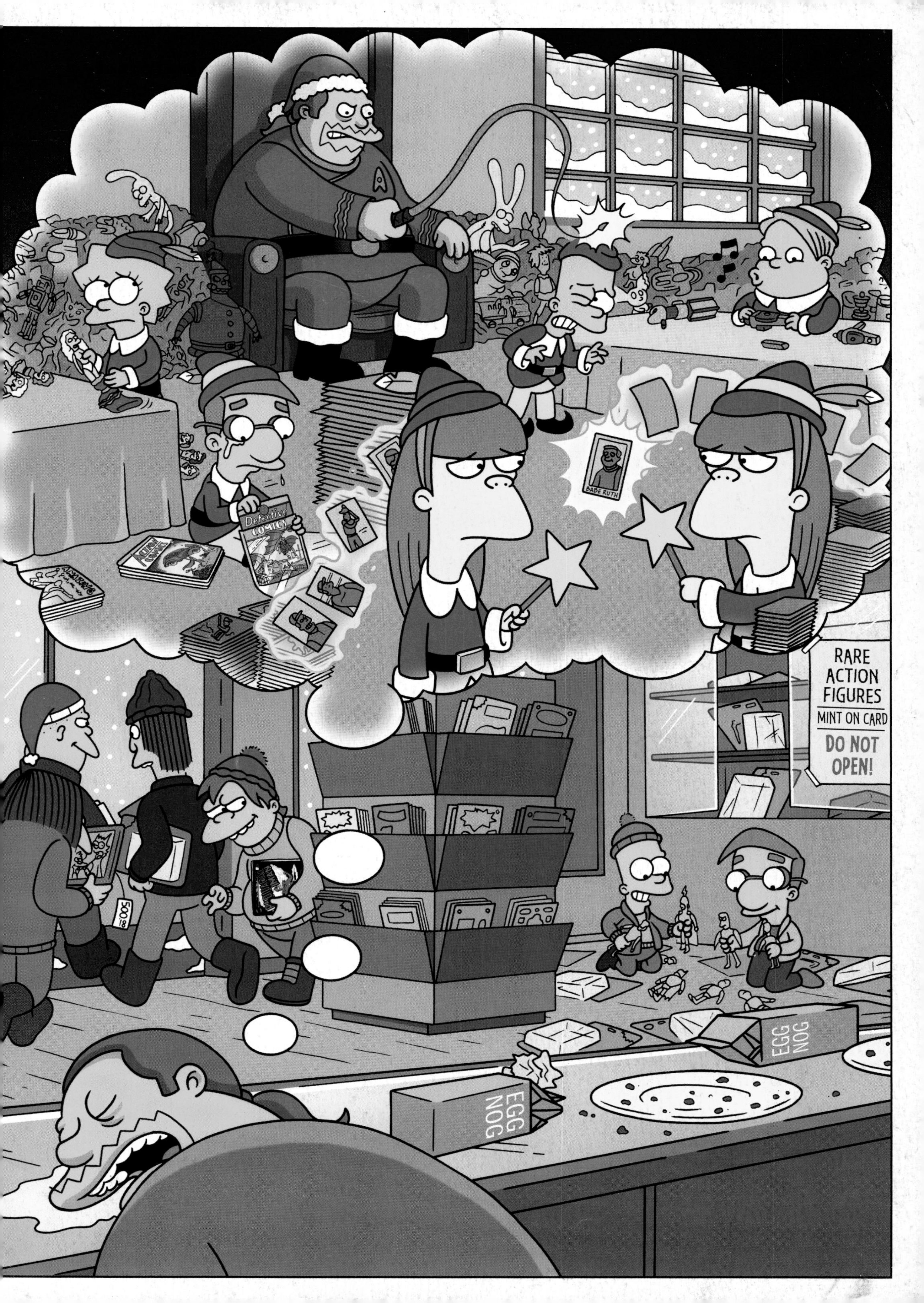

Detective COMICS
ACTION COMICS
BABE RUTH
RARE ACTION FIGURES
MINT ON CARD
DO NOT OPEN!
EGG NOG
EGG NOG

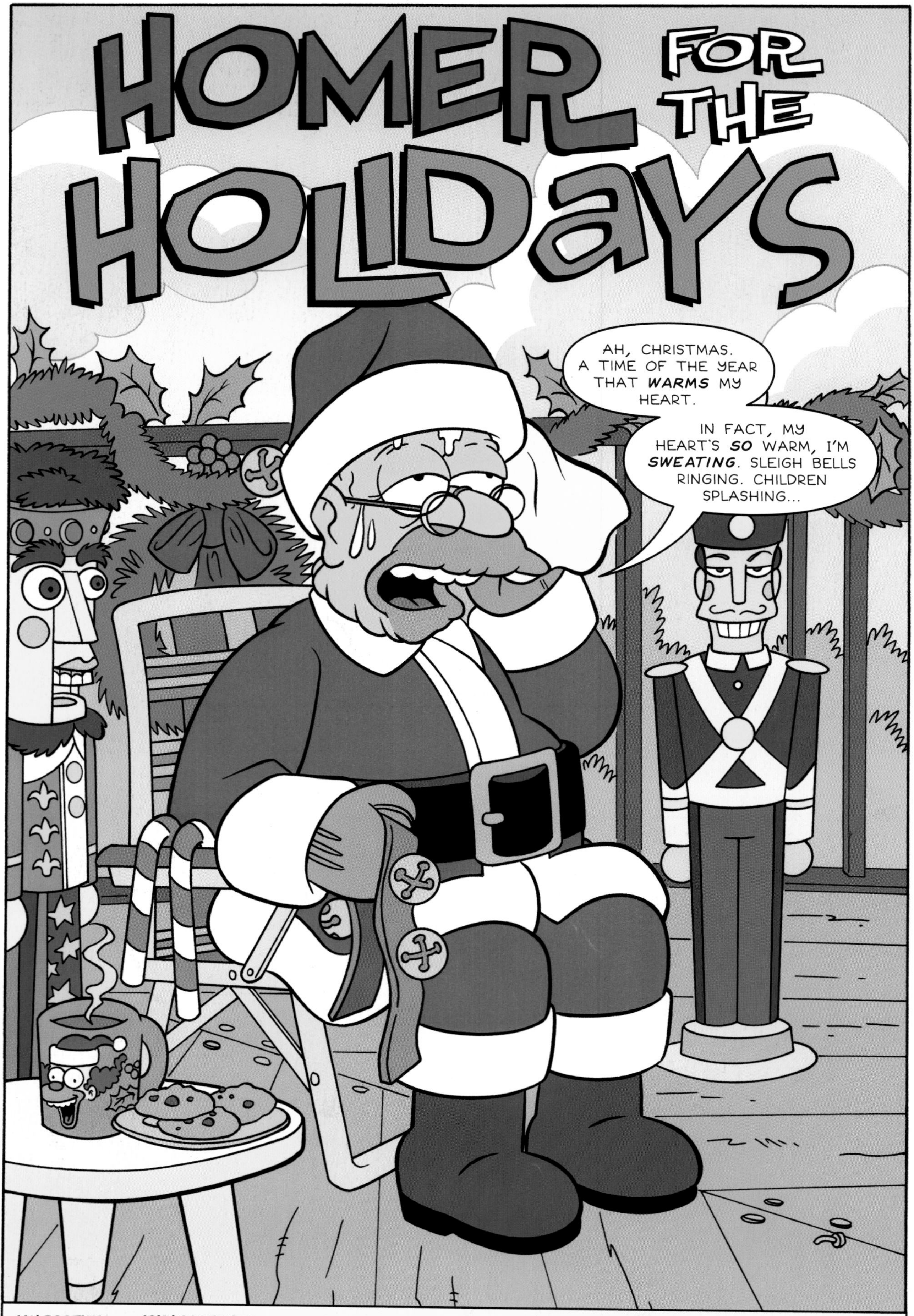
HOMER FOR THE HOLIDAYS
AH, CHRISTMAS. A TIME OF THE YEAR THAT WARMS MY HEART.
IN FACT, MY HEART'S SO WARM, I'M SWEATING. SLEIGH BELLS RINGING. CHILDREN SPLASHING...

IAN BOOTHBY script · JOHN COSTANZA pencils · HOWARD SHUM inks · ART VILLANUEVA colors · KAREN BATES letters · BILL MORRISON editor · MATT GROENING nutcracker

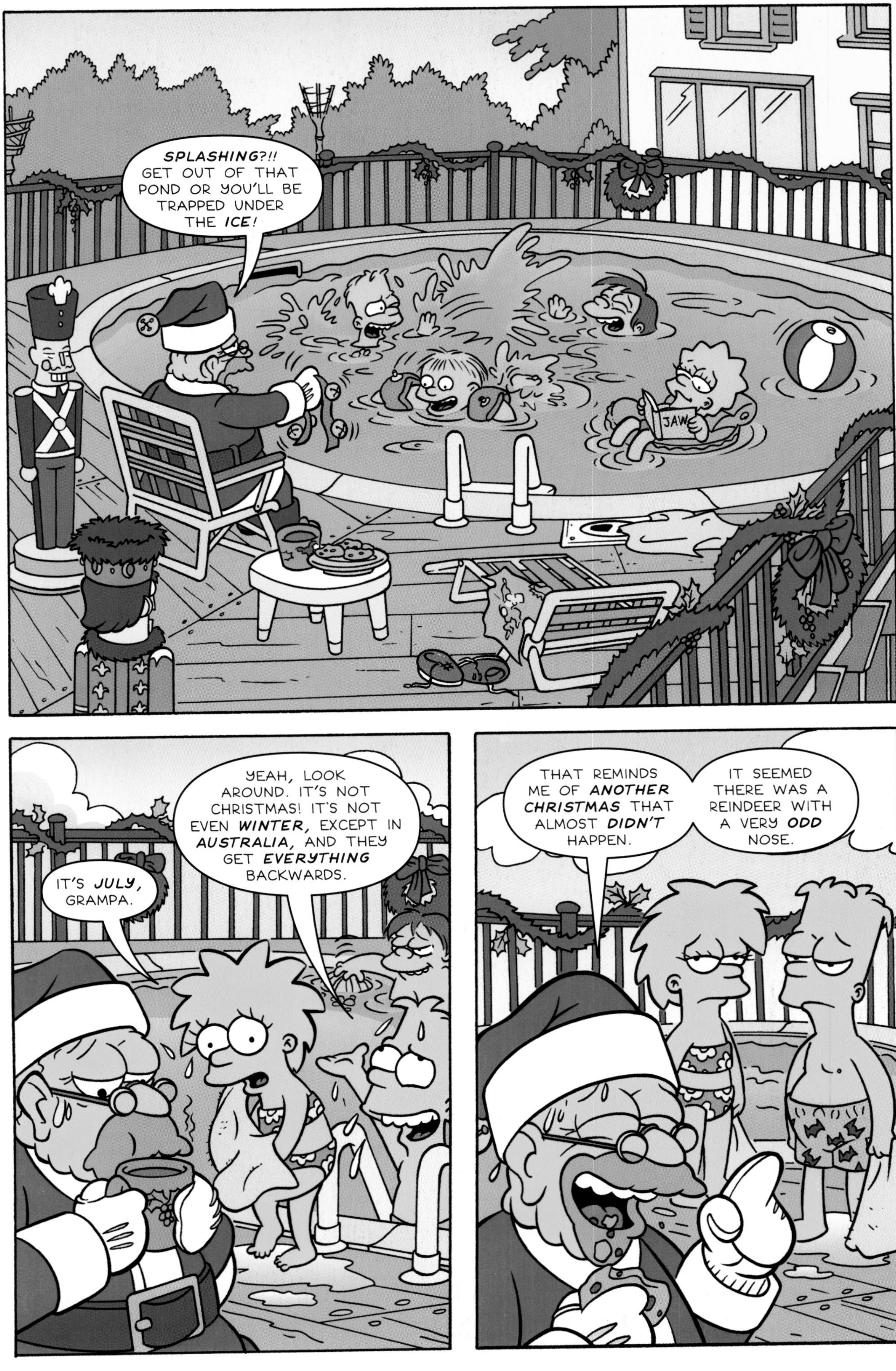

SPLASHING?!! GET OUT OF THAT POND OR YOU'LL BE TRAPPED UNDER THE ICE!
JAW
IT'S JULY, GRAMPA.
YEAH, LOOK AROUND. IT'S NOT CHRISTMAS! IT'S NOT EVEN WINTER, EXCEPT IN AUSTRALIA, AND THEY GET EVERYTHING BACKWARDS.
THAT REMINDS ME OF ANOTHER CHRISTMAS THAT ALMOST DIDN'T HAPPEN.
IT SEEMED THERE WAS A REINDEER WITH A VERY ODD NOSE.

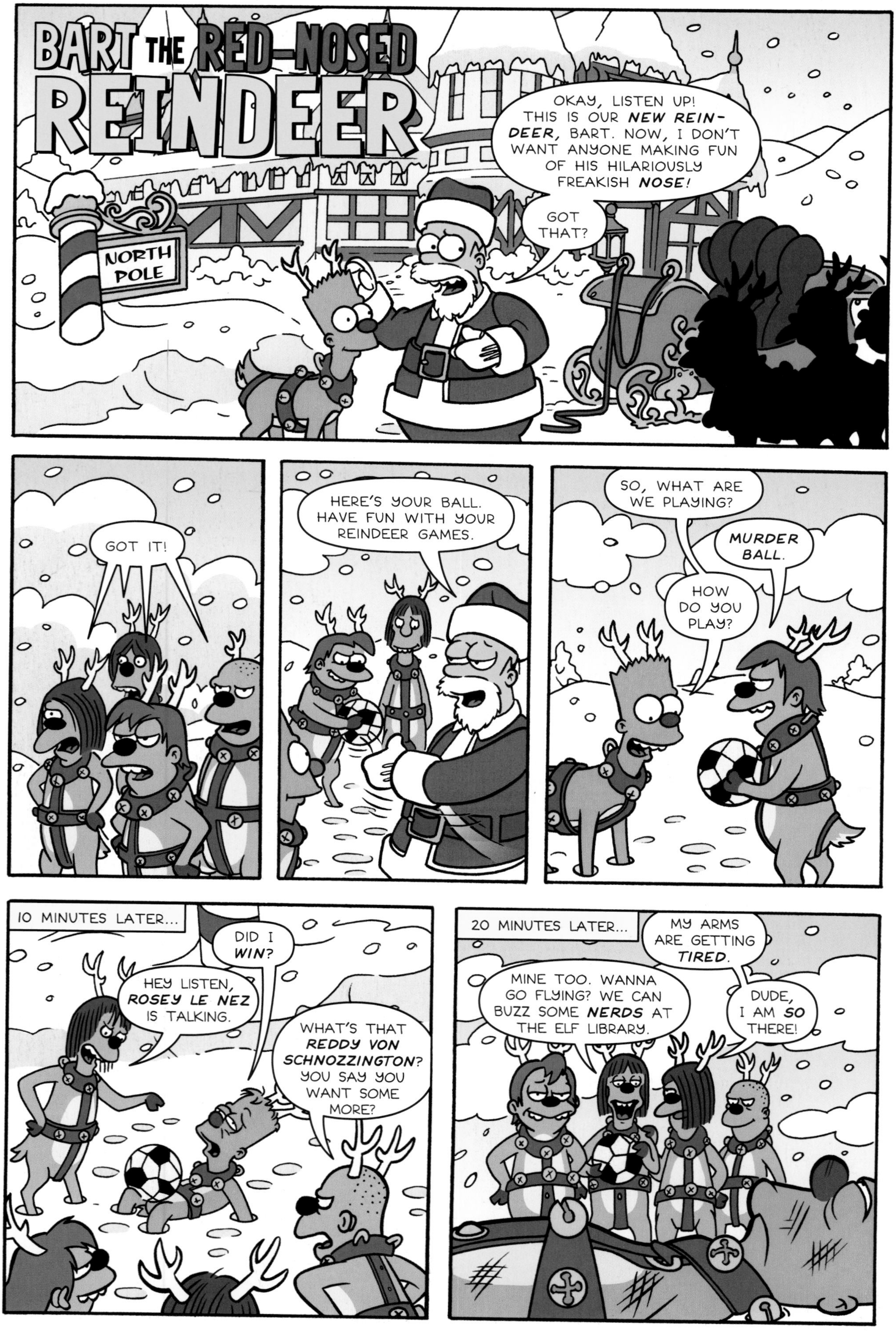
BART THE RED-NOSED REINDEER
NORTH POLE
OKAY, LISTEN UP! THIS IS OUR NEW REINDEER, BART. NOW, I DON'T WANT ANYONE MAKING FUN OF HIS HILARIOUSLY FREAKISH NOSE!
GOT THAT?
GOT IT!
HERE'S YOUR BALL. HAVE FUN WITH YOUR REINDEER GAMES.
SO, WHAT ARE WE PLAYING?
MURDER BALL.
HOW DO YOU PLAY?
10 MINUTES LATER...
DID I WIN?
HEY LISTEN, ROSEY LE NEZ IS TALKING.
WHAT'S THAT REDDY VON SCHNOZZINGTON? YOU SAY YOU WANT SOME MORE?
20 MINUTES LATER...
MY ARMS ARE GETTING TIRED.
MINE TOO. WANNA GO FLYING? WE CAN BUZZ SOME NERDS AT THE ELF LIBRARY.
DUDE, I AM SO THERE!

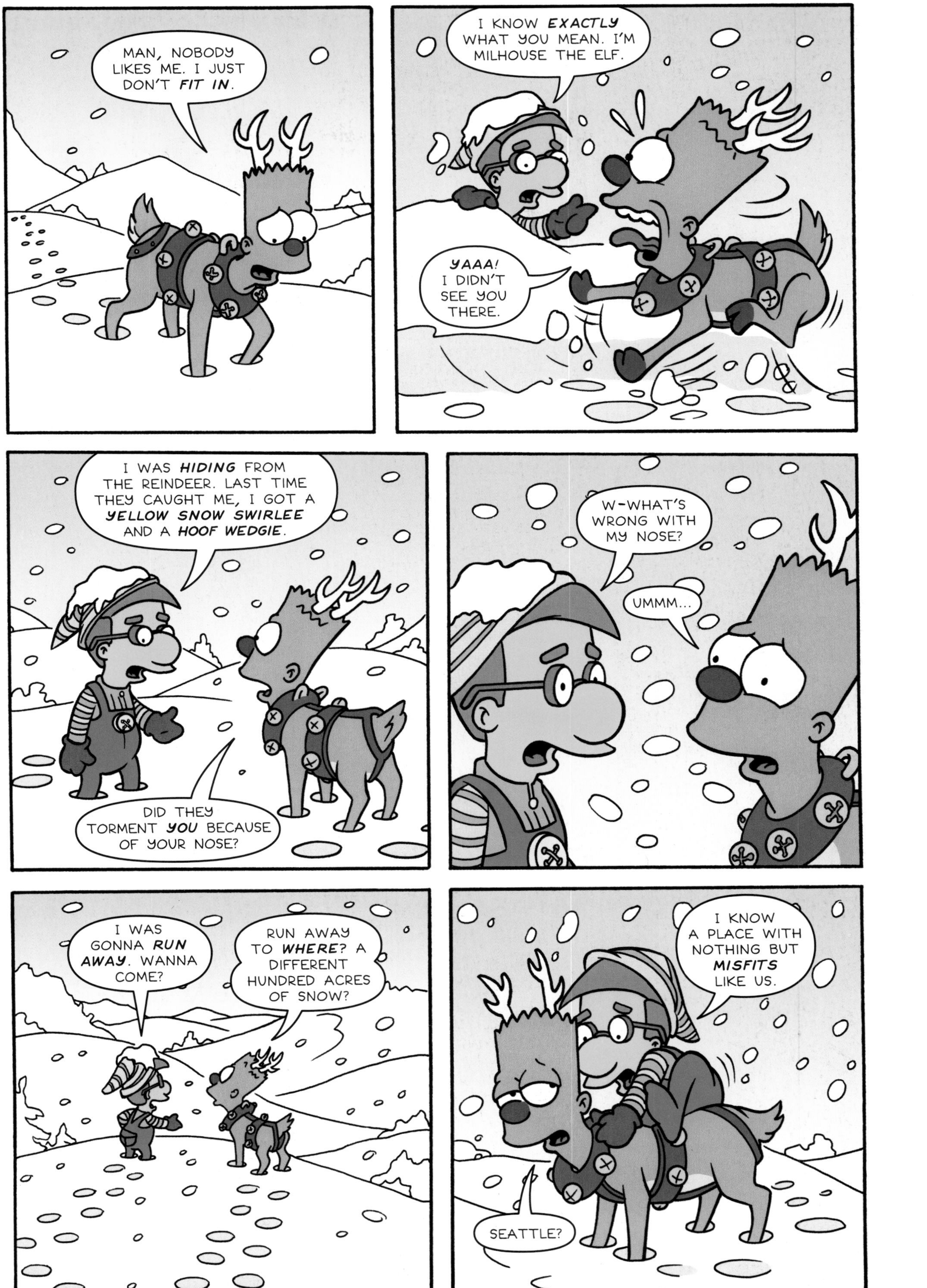
MAN, NOBODY LIKES ME. I JUST DON'T FIT IN.
I KNOW EXACTLY WHAT YOU MEAN. I'M MILHOUSE THE ELF.
YAAA! I DIDN'T SEE YOU THERE.
I WAS HIDING FROM THE REINDEER. LAST TIME THEY CAUGHT ME, I GOT A YELLOW SNOW SWIRLEE AND A HOOF WEDGIE.
DID THEY TORMENT YOU BECAUSE OF YOUR NOSE?
W-WHAT'S WRONG WITH MY NOSE?
UMMM...
I WAS GONNA RUN AWAY. WANNA COME?
RUN AWAY TO WHERE? A DIFFERENT HUNDRED ACRES OF SNOW?
I KNOW A PLACE WITH NOTHING BUT MISFITS LIKE US.
SEATTLE?

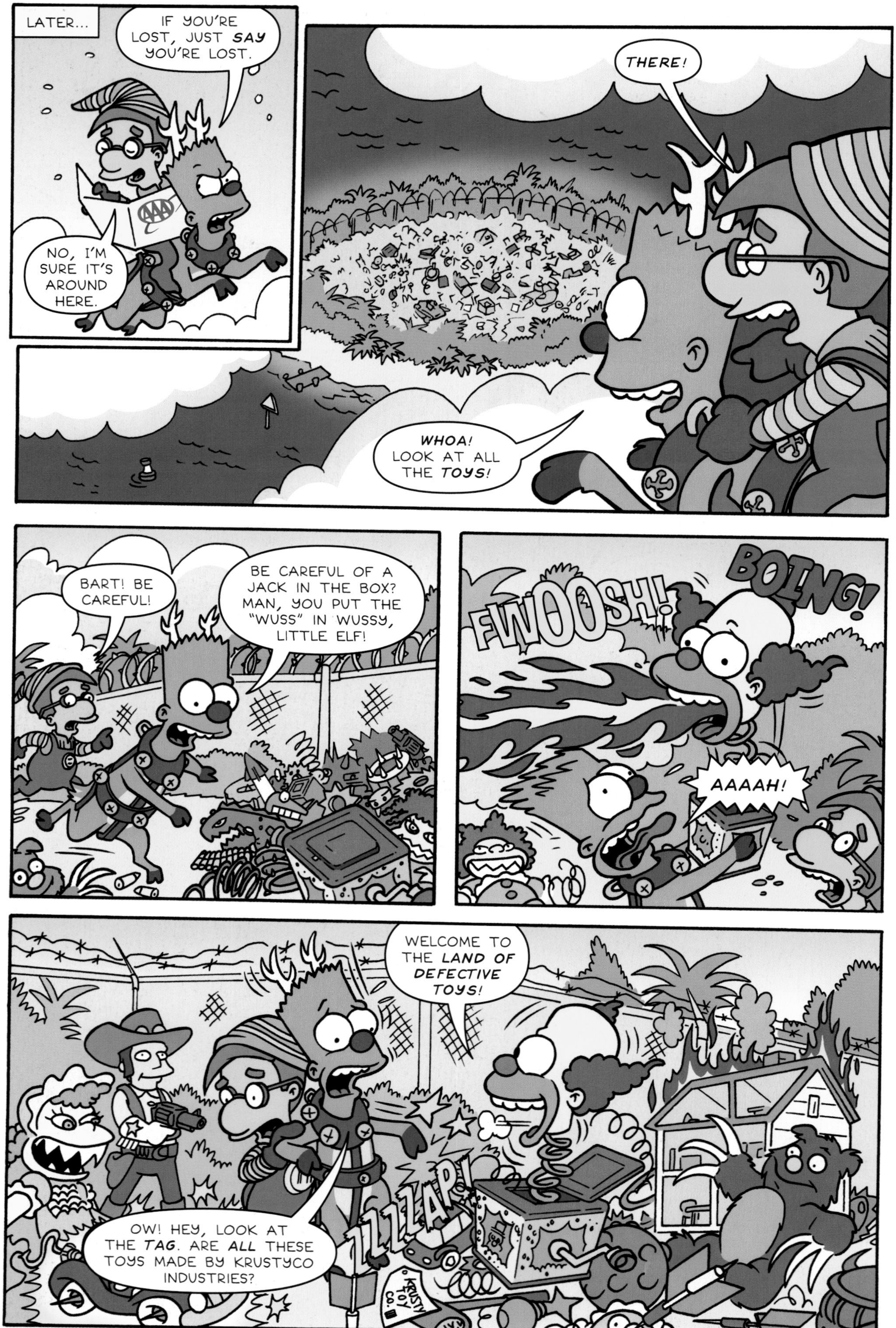
LATER...
IF YOU'RE LOST, JUST SAY YOU'RE LOST.
NO, I'M SURE IT'S AROUND HERE.
THERE!
WHOA! LOOK AT ALL THE TOYS!
BART! BE CAREFUL!
BE CAREFUL OF A JACK IN THE BOX? MAN, YOU PUT THE "WUSS" IN WUSSY, LITTLE ELF!
FWOOSH!
BOING!
AAAAH!
WELCOME TO THE LAND OF DEFECTIVE TOYS!
ZZZZAP!
OW! HEY, LOOK AT THE TAG. ARE ALL THESE TOYS MADE BY KRUSTYCO INDUSTRIES?
KRUSTY TOY CO.

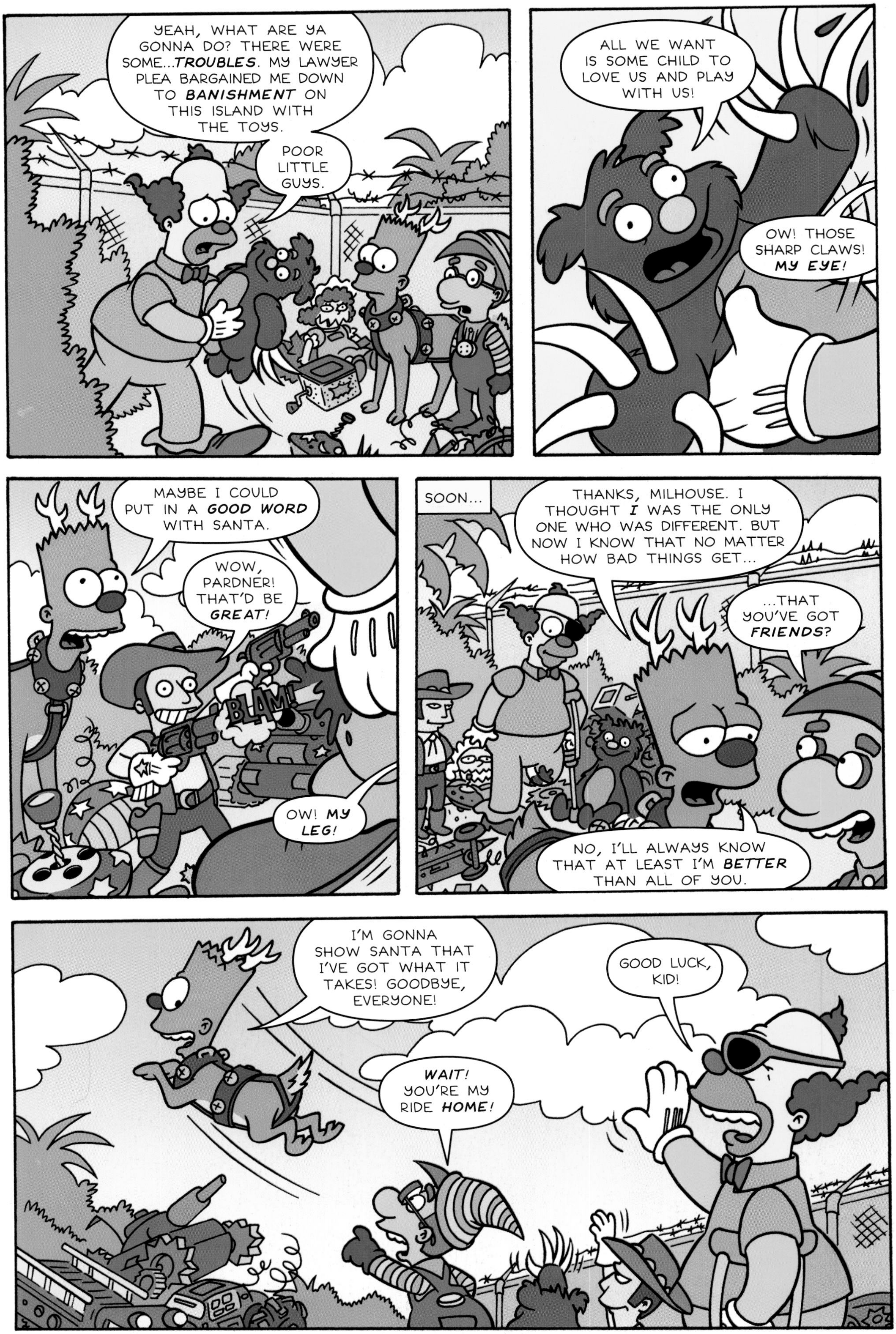
YEAH, WHAT ARE YA GONNA DO? THERE WERE SOME...**TROUBLES**. MY LAWYER PLEA BARGAINED ME DOWN TO **BANISHMENT** ON THIS ISLAND WITH THE TOYS.
POOR LITTLE GUYS.
ALL WE WANT IS SOME CHILD TO LOVE US AND PLAY WITH US!
OW! THOSE SHARP CLAWS! **MY EYE!**
MAYBE I COULD PUT IN A **GOOD WORD** WITH SANTA.
WOW, PARDNER! THAT'D BE **GREAT**!
BLAM!
OW! **MY LEG!**
SOON...
THANKS, MILHOUSE. I THOUGHT **I** WAS THE ONLY ONE WHO WAS DIFFERENT. BUT NOW I KNOW THAT NO MATTER HOW BAD THINGS GET...
...THAT YOU'VE GOT **FRIENDS**?
NO, I'LL ALWAYS KNOW THAT AT LEAST I'M **BETTER** THAN ALL OF YOU.
I'M GONNA SHOW SANTA THAT I'VE GOT WHAT IT TAKES! GOODBYE, EVERYONE!
GOOD LUCK, KID!
WAIT! YOU'RE MY RIDE **HOME!**

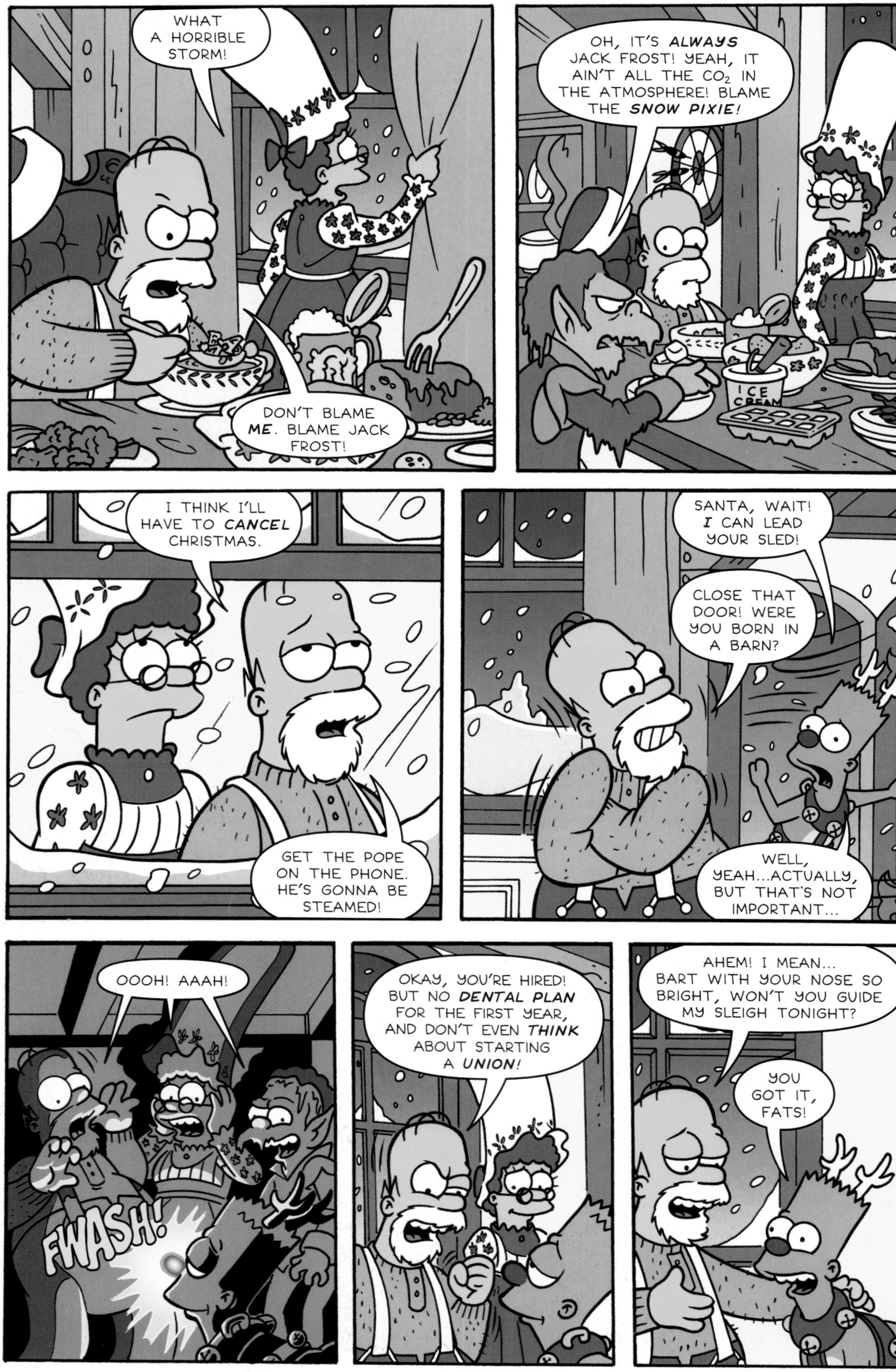
WHAT A HORRIBLE STORM!
DON'T BLAME ME. BLAME JACK FROST!
OH, IT'S ALWAYS JACK FROST! YEAH, IT AIN'T ALL THE CO_2 IN THE ATMOSPHERE! BLAME THE SNOW PIXIE!
ICE CREAM
I THINK I'LL HAVE TO CANCEL CHRISTMAS.
GET THE POPE ON THE PHONE. HE'S GONNA BE STEAMED!
SANTA, WAIT! I CAN LEAD YOUR SLED!
CLOSE THAT DOOR! WERE YOU BORN IN A BARN?
WELL, YEAH...ACTUALLY, BUT THAT'S NOT IMPORTANT...
OOOH! AAAH!
FWASH!
OKAY, YOU'RE HIRED! BUT NO DENTAL PLAN FOR THE FIRST YEAR, AND DON'T EVEN THINK ABOUT STARTING A UNION!
AHEM! I MEAN... BART WITH YOUR NOSE SO BRIGHT, WON'T YOU GUIDE MY SLEIGH TONIGHT?
YOU GOT IT, FATS!

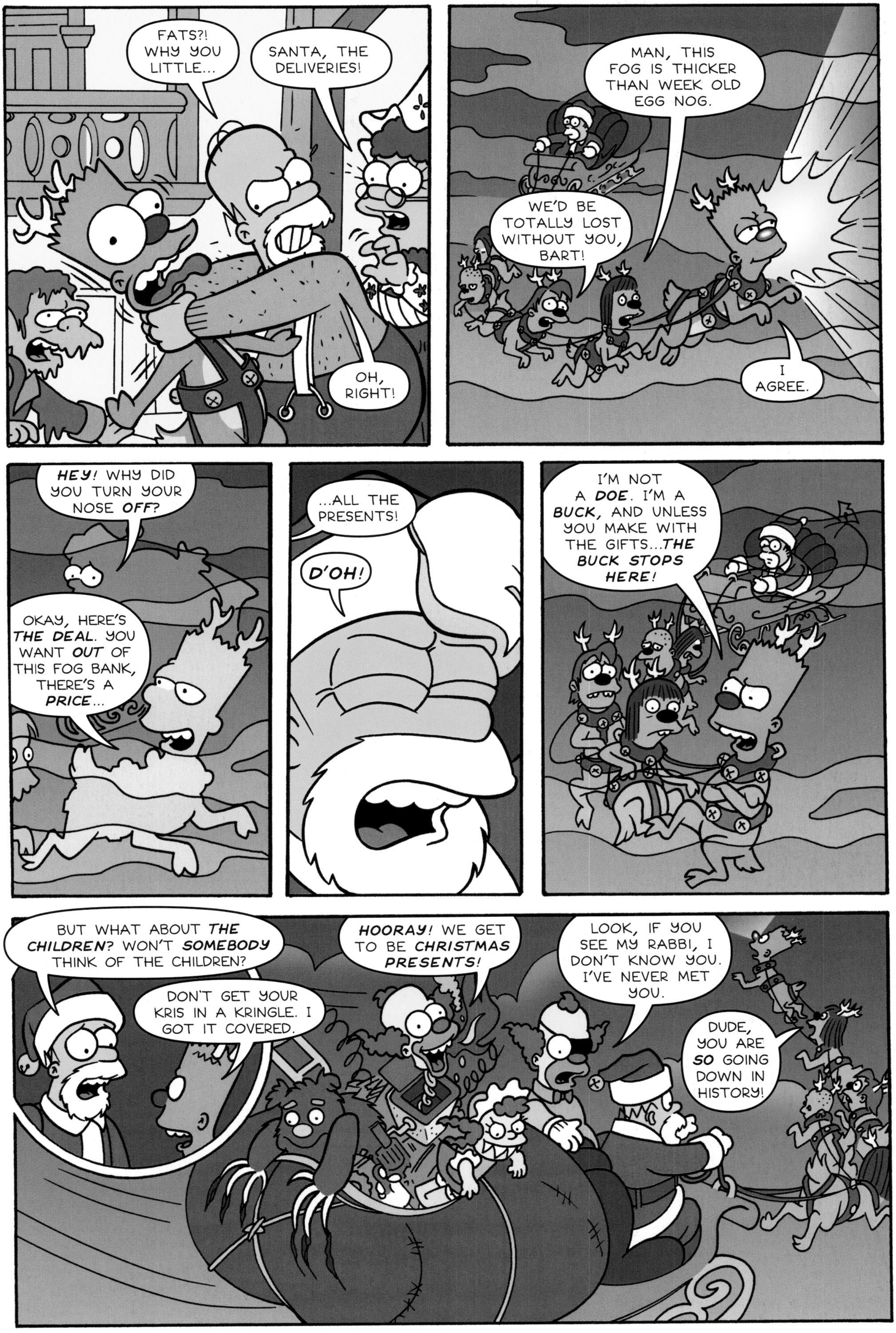
FATS?! WHY YOU LITTLE...
SANTA, THE DELIVERIES!
OH, RIGHT!
MAN, THIS FOG IS THICKER THAN WEEK OLD EGG NOG.
WE'D BE TOTALLY LOST WITHOUT YOU, BART!
I AGREE.
HEY! WHY DID YOU TURN YOUR NOSE OFF?
OKAY, HERE'S THE DEAL. YOU WANT OUT OF THIS FOG BANK, THERE'S A PRICE...
...ALL THE PRESENTS!
D'OH!
I'M NOT A DOE. I'M A BUCK, AND UNLESS YOU MAKE WITH THE GIFTS...THE BUCK STOPS HERE!
BUT WHAT ABOUT THE CHILDREN? WON'T SOMEBODY THINK OF THE CHILDREN?
DON'T GET YOUR KRIS IN A KRINGLE. I GOT IT COVERED.
HOORAY! WE GET TO BE CHRISTMAS PRESENTS!
LOOK, IF YOU SEE MY RABBI, I DON'T KNOW YOU. I'VE NEVER MET YOU.
DUDE, YOU ARE SO GOING DOWN IN HISTORY!

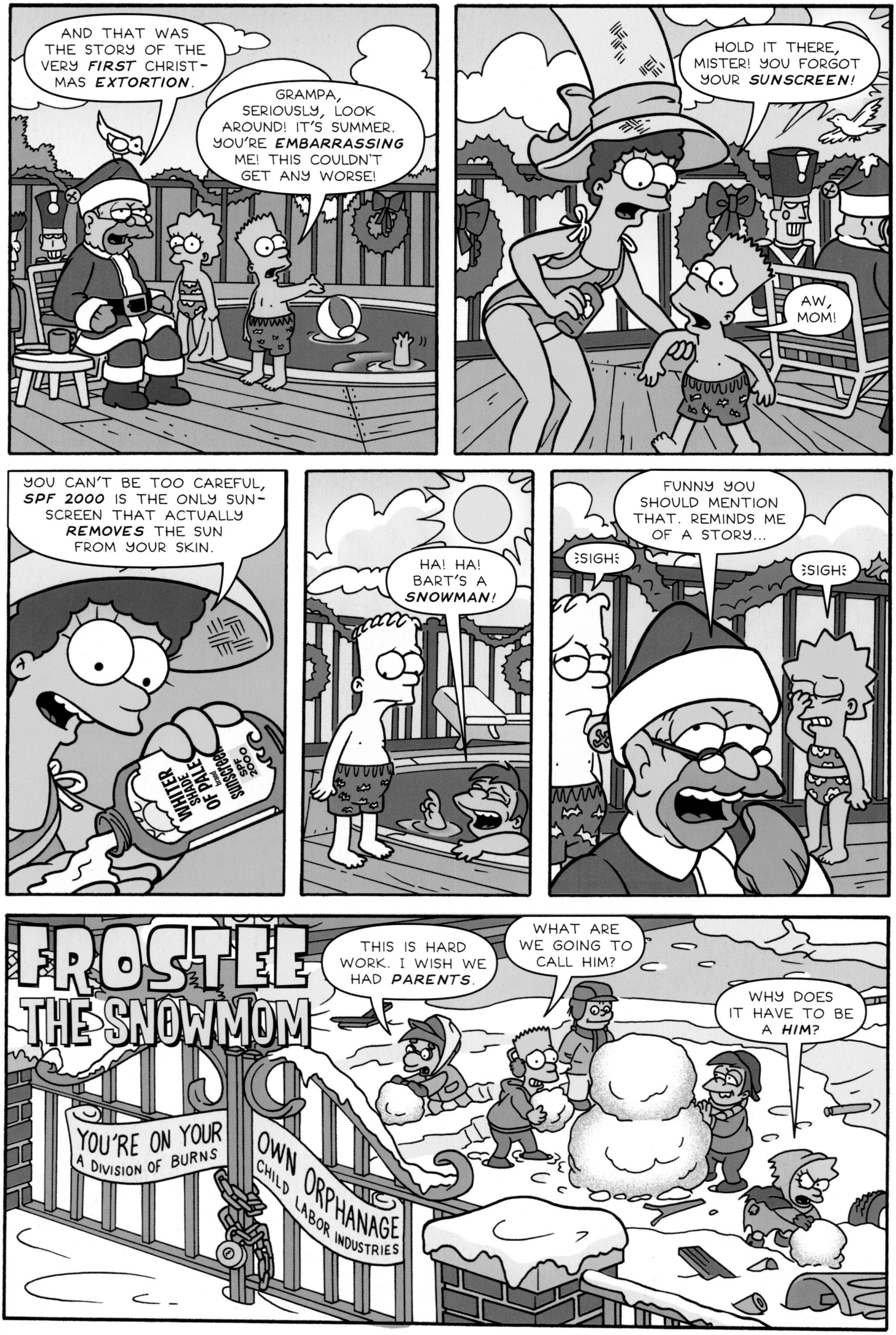
AND THAT WAS THE STORY OF THE VERY FIRST CHRISTMAS EXTORTION.
GRAMPA, SERIOUSLY, LOOK AROUND! IT'S SUMMER. YOU'RE EMBARRASSING ME! THIS COULDN'T GET ANY WORSE!
HOLD IT THERE, MISTER! YOU FORGOT YOUR SUNSCREEN!
AW, MOM!
YOU CAN'T BE TOO CAREFUL, SPF 2000 IS THE ONLY SUNSCREEN THAT ACTUALLY REMOVES THE SUN FROM YOUR SKIN.
WHITER SHADE OF PALE brand SUNSCREEN SPF 2000
HA! HA! BART'S A SNOWMAN!
FUNNY YOU SHOULD MENTION THAT. REMINDS ME OF A STORY...
SIGH
SIGH
FROSTEE THE SNOWMOM
THIS IS HARD WORK. I WISH WE HAD PARENTS.
WHAT ARE WE GOING TO CALL HIM?
WHY DOES IT HAVE TO BE A HIM?
YOU'RE ON YOUR OWN ORPHANAGE
A DIVISION OF BURNS CHILD LABOR INDUSTRIES

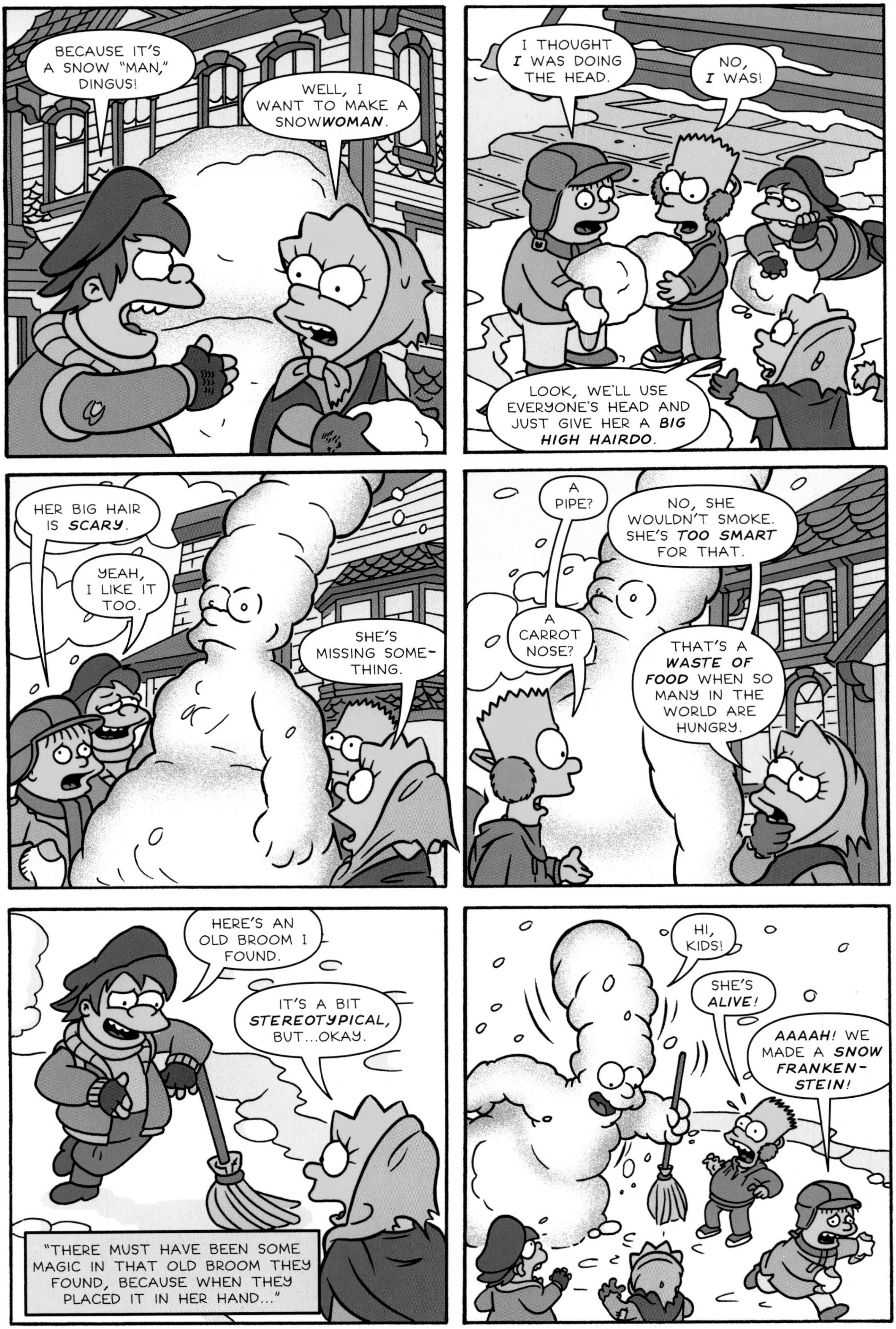
BECAUSE IT'S A SNOW "MAN," DINGUS!
WELL, I WANT TO MAKE A SNOW**WOMAN**.
I THOUGHT *I* WAS DOING THE HEAD.
NO, *I* WAS!
LOOK, WE'LL USE EVERYONE'S HEAD AND JUST GIVE HER A ***BIG HIGH HAIRDO***.
HER BIG HAIR IS ***SCARY***.
YEAH, I LIKE IT TOO.
SHE'S MISSING SOME-THING.
A PIPE?
NO, SHE WOULDN'T SMOKE. SHE'S ***TOO SMART*** FOR THAT.
A CARROT NOSE?
THAT'S A ***WASTE OF FOOD*** WHEN SO MANY IN THE WORLD ARE HUNGRY.
HERE'S AN OLD BROOM I FOUND.
IT'S A BIT ***STEREOTYPICAL***, BUT...OKAY.
"THERE MUST HAVE BEEN SOME MAGIC IN THAT OLD BROOM THEY FOUND, BECAUSE WHEN THEY PLACED IT IN HER HAND..."
HI, KIDS!
SHE'S ***ALIVE***!
AAAAH! WE MADE A ***SNOW FRANKEN-STEIN!***

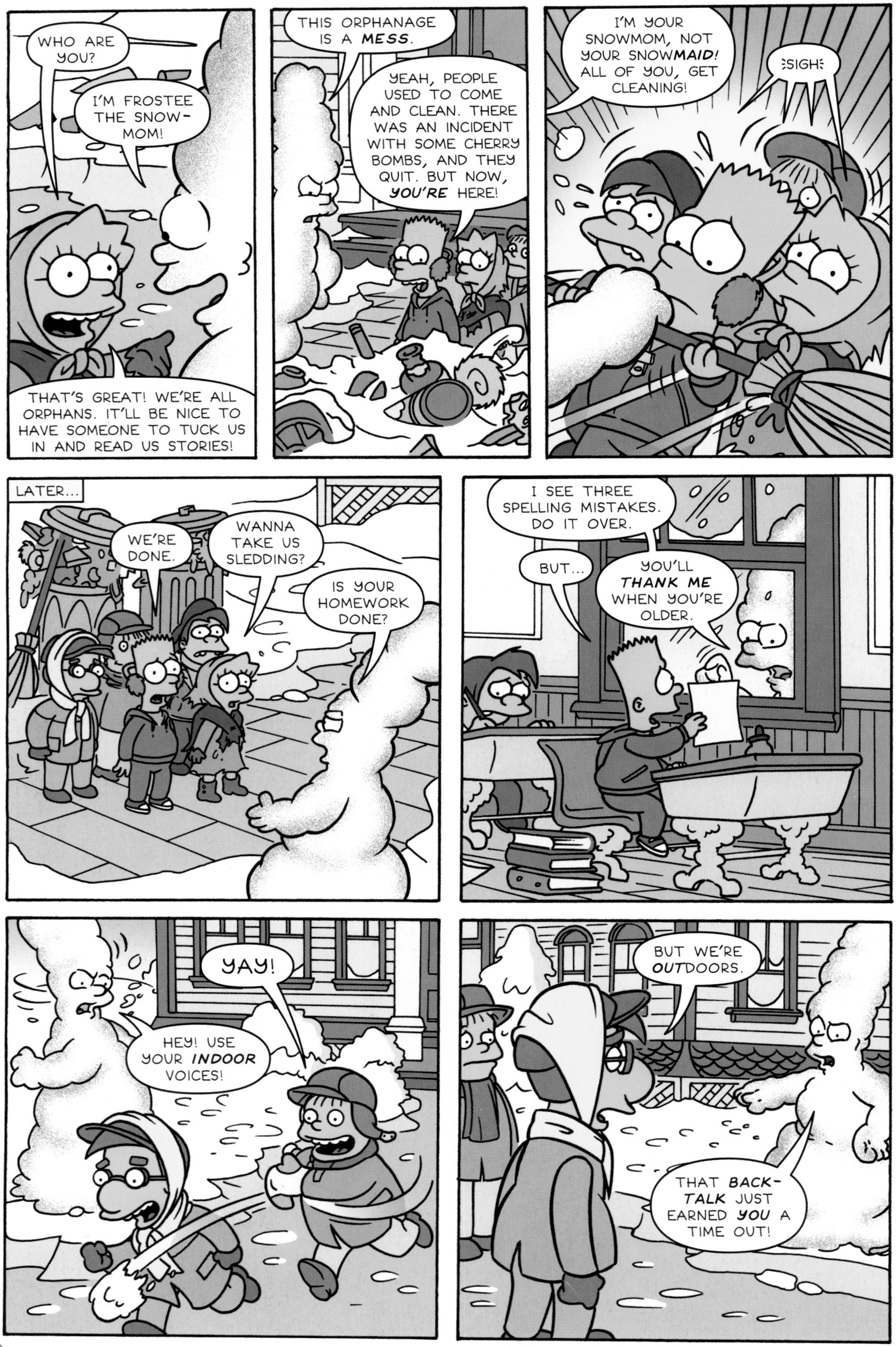
WHO ARE YOU?
I'M FROSTEE THE SNOW-MOM!
THAT'S GREAT! WE'RE ALL ORPHANS. IT'LL BE NICE TO HAVE SOMEONE TO TUCK US IN AND READ US STORIES!
THIS ORPHANAGE IS A MESS.
YEAH, PEOPLE USED TO COME AND CLEAN. THERE WAS AN INCIDENT WITH SOME CHERRY BOMBS, AND THEY QUIT. BUT NOW, YOU'RE HERE!
I'M YOUR SNOWMOM, NOT YOUR SNOWMAID! ALL OF YOU, GET CLEANING!
SIGH
LATER...
WE'RE DONE.
WANNA TAKE US SLEDDING?
IS YOUR HOMEWORK DONE?
I SEE THREE SPELLING MISTAKES. DO IT OVER.
BUT...
YOU'LL THANK ME WHEN YOU'RE OLDER.
YAY!
HEY! USE YOUR INDOOR VOICES!
BUT WE'RE OUTDOORS.
THAT BACK-TALK JUST EARNED YOU A TIME OUT!

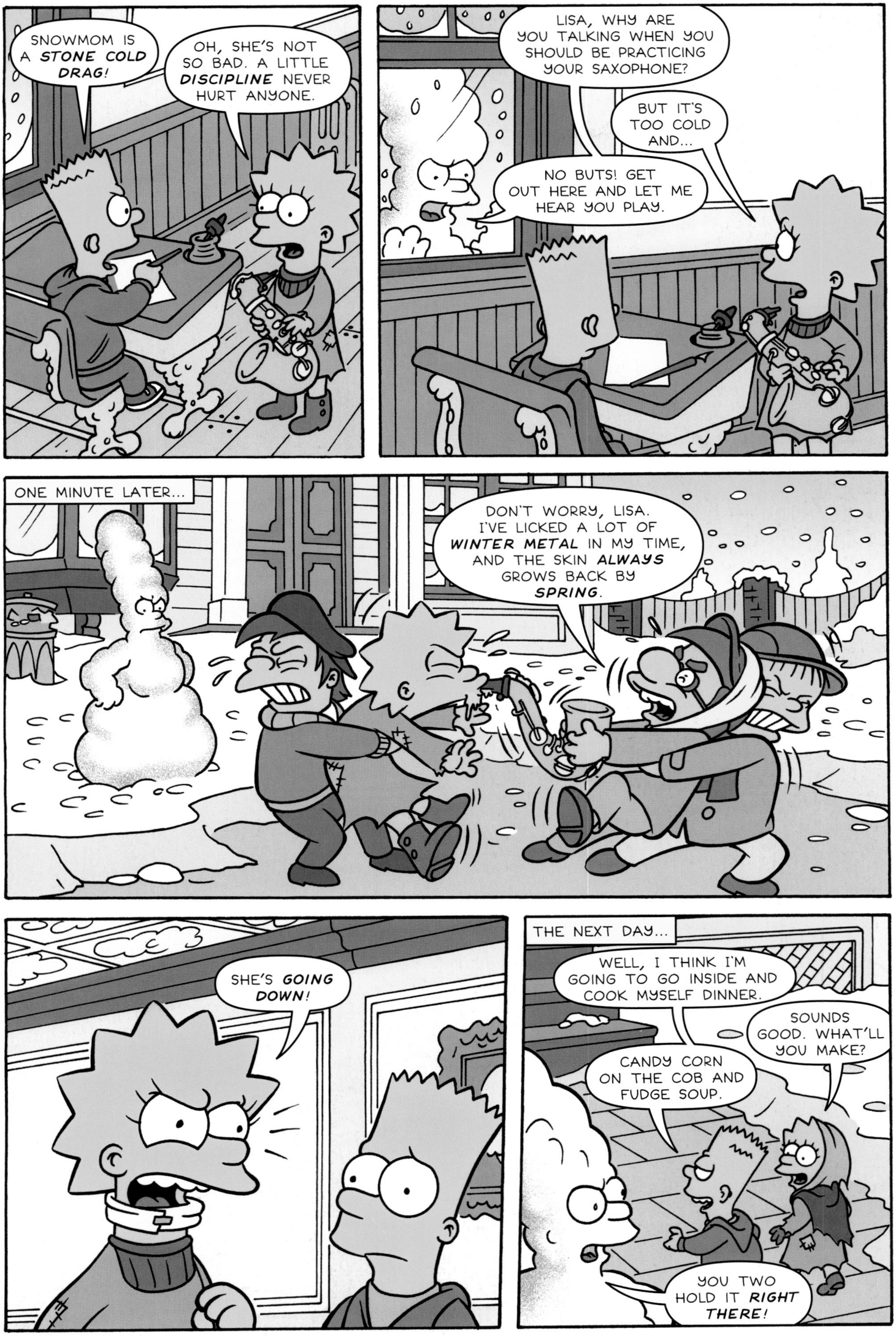

SNOWMOM IS A **STONE COLD DRAG**!
OH, SHE'S NOT SO BAD. A LITTLE **DISCIPLINE** NEVER HURT ANYONE.
LISA, WHY ARE YOU TALKING WHEN YOU SHOULD BE PRACTICING YOUR SAXOPHONE?
BUT IT'S TOO COLD AND...
NO BUTS! GET OUT HERE AND LET ME HEAR YOU PLAY.
ONE MINUTE LATER...
DON'T WORRY, LISA. I'VE LICKED A LOT OF **WINTER METAL** IN MY TIME, AND THE SKIN **ALWAYS** GROWS BACK BY **SPRING**.
SHE'S **GOING DOWN**!
THE NEXT DAY...
WELL, I THINK I'M GOING TO GO INSIDE AND COOK MYSELF DINNER.
SOUNDS GOOD. WHAT'LL YOU MAKE?
CANDY CORN ON THE COB AND FUDGE SOUP.
YOU TWO HOLD IT **RIGHT THERE**!

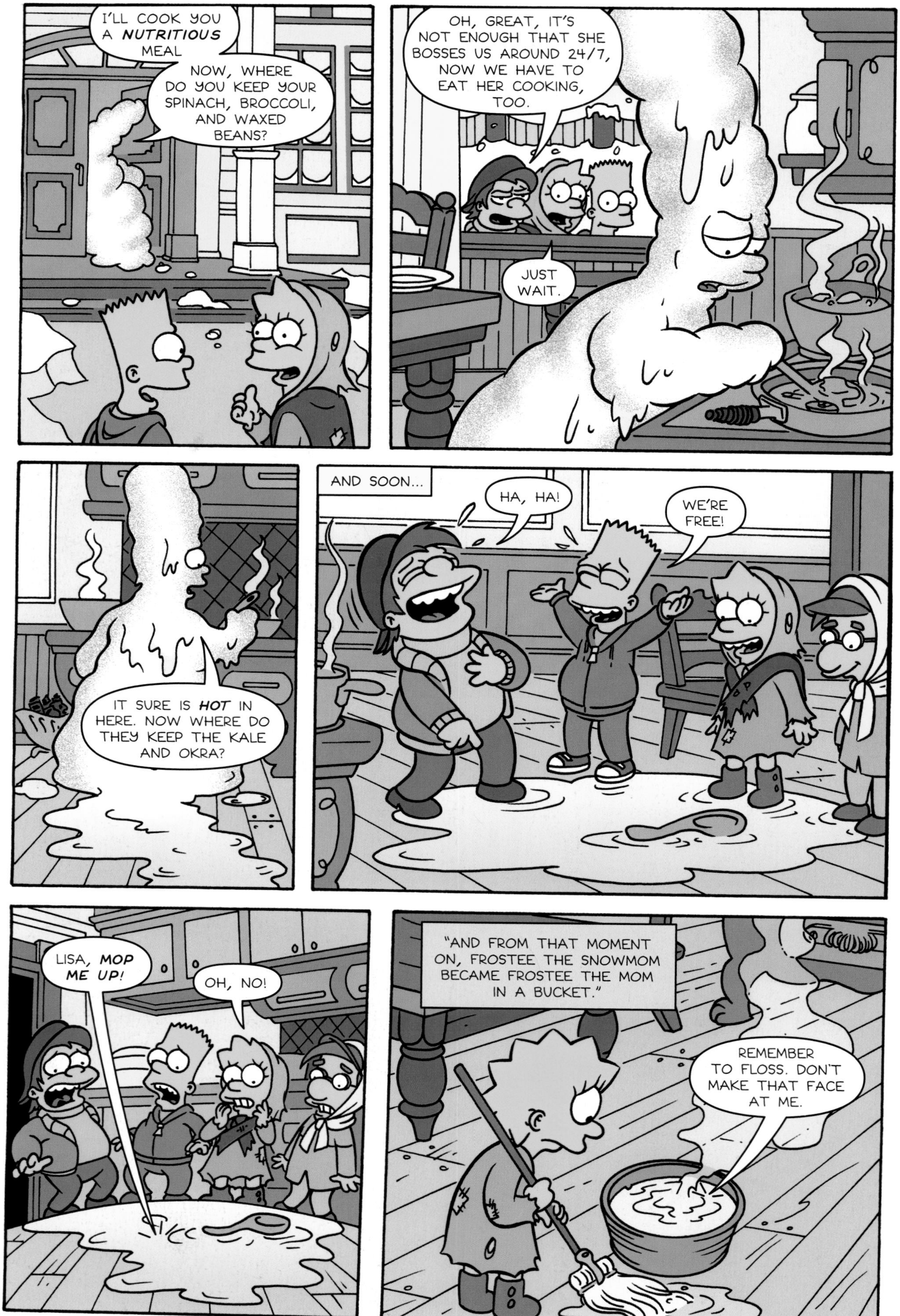
I'LL COOK YOU A **NUTRITIOUS** MEAL
NOW, WHERE DO YOU KEEP YOUR SPINACH, BROCCOLI, AND WAXED BEANS?
OH, GREAT, IT'S NOT ENOUGH THAT SHE BOSSES US AROUND 24/7, NOW WE HAVE TO EAT HER COOKING, TOO.
JUST WAIT.
IT SURE IS **HOT** IN HERE. NOW WHERE DO THEY KEEP THE KALE AND OKRA?
AND SOON...
HA, HA!
WE'RE FREE!
LISA, **MOP ME UP**!
OH, NO!
"AND FROM THAT MOMENT ON, FROSTEE THE SNOWMOM BECAME FROSTEE THE MOM IN A BUCKET."
REMEMBER TO FLOSS. DON'T MAKE THAT FACE AT ME.

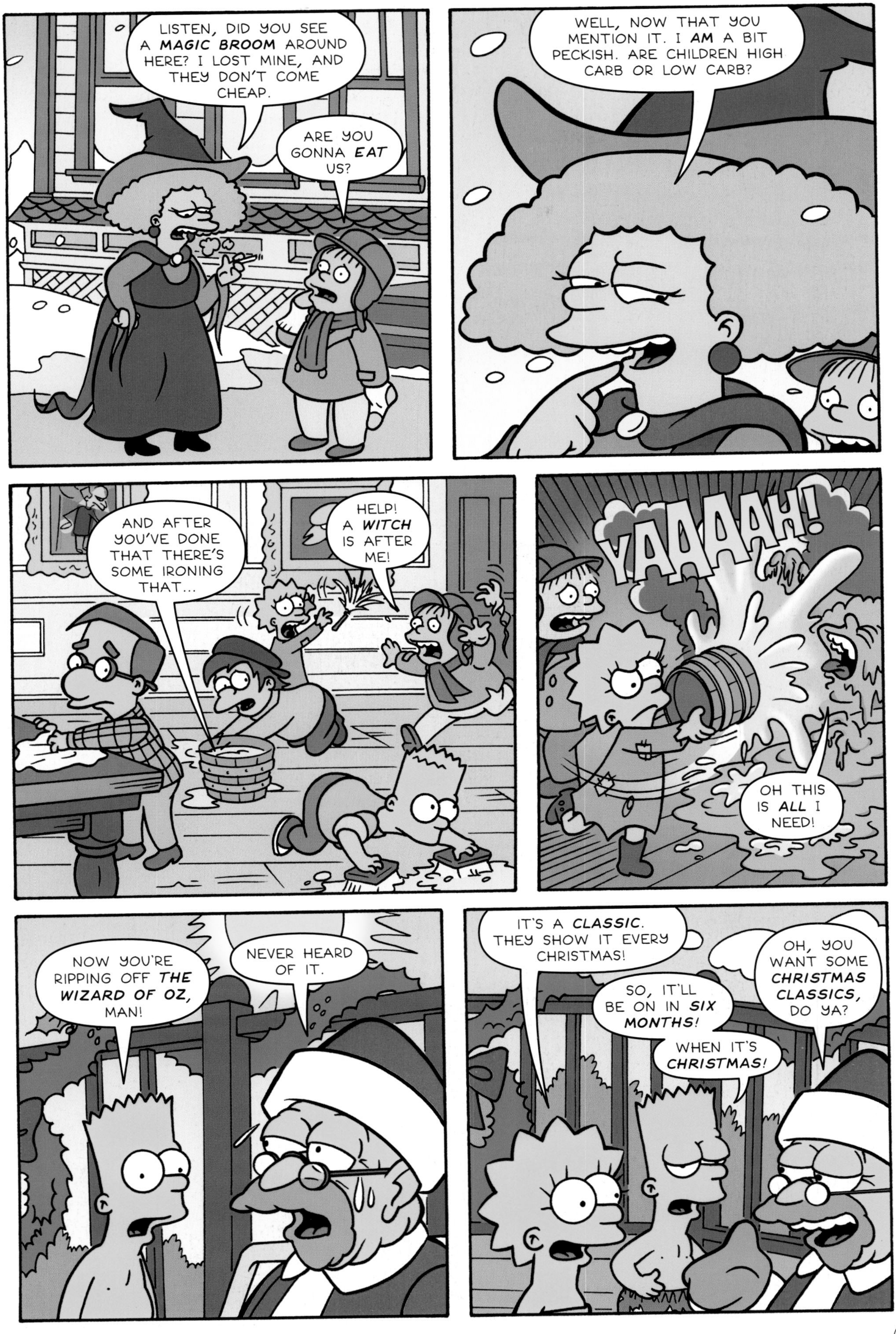

LISTEN, DID YOU SEE A MAGIC BROOM AROUND HERE? I LOST MINE, AND THEY DON'T COME CHEAP.
ARE YOU GONNA EAT US?
WELL, NOW THAT YOU MENTION IT. I AM A BIT PECKISH. ARE CHILDREN HIGH CARB OR LOW CARB?
AND AFTER YOU'VE DONE THAT THERE'S SOME IRONING THAT...
HELP! A WITCH IS AFTER ME!
YAAAAH!
OH THIS IS ALL I NEED!
NOW YOU'RE RIPPING OFF THE WIZARD OF OZ, MAN!
NEVER HEARD OF IT.
IT'S A CLASSIC. THEY SHOW IT EVERY CHRISTMAS!
SO, IT'LL BE ON IN SIX MONTHS!
WHEN IT'S CHRISTMAS!
OH, YOU WANT SOME CHRISTMAS CLASSICS, DO YA?

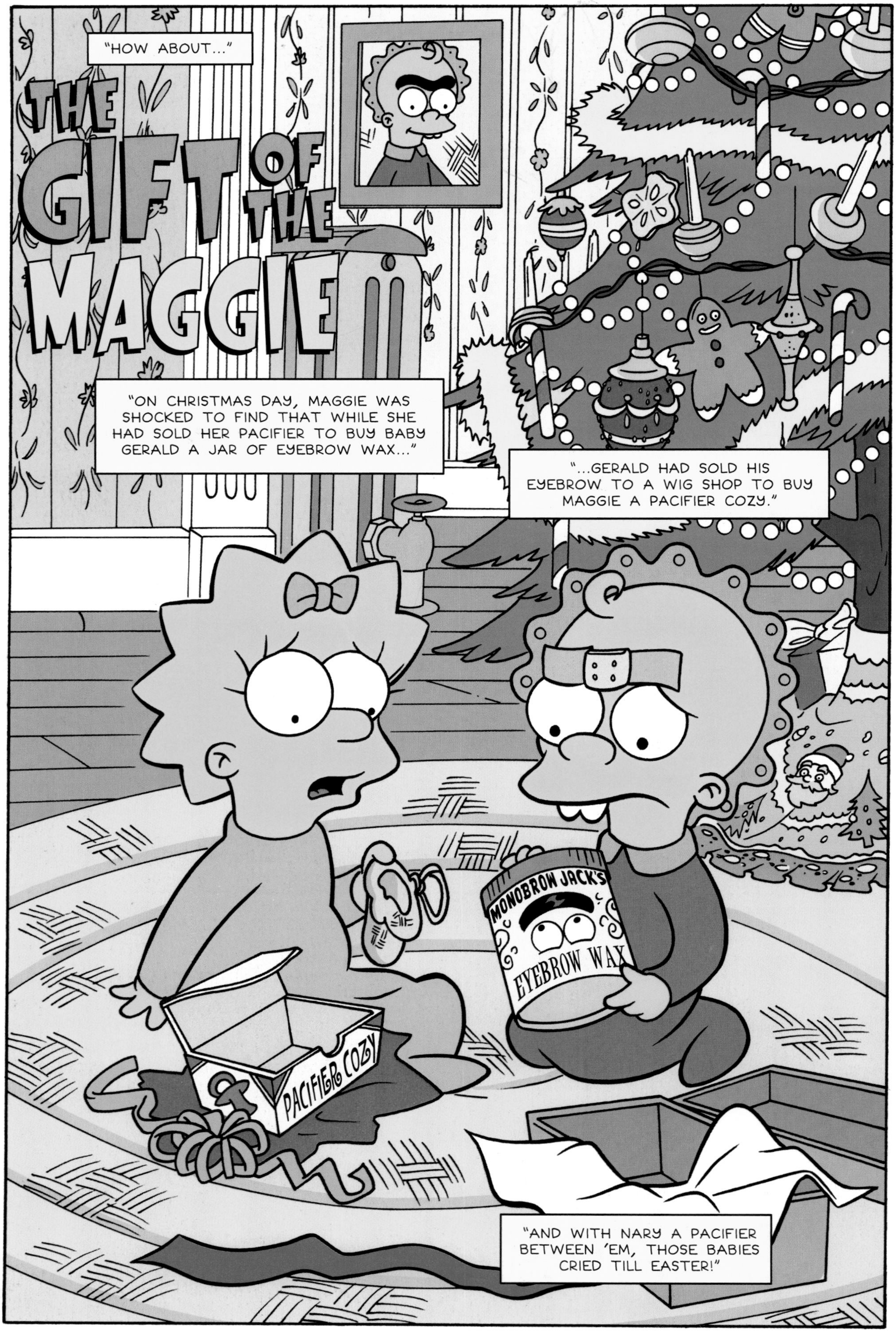

"HOW ABOUT..."
THE GIFT OF THE MAGGIE
"ON CHRISTMAS DAY, MAGGIE WAS SHOCKED TO FIND THAT WHILE SHE HAD SOLD HER PACIFIER TO BUY BABY GERALD A JAR OF EYEBROW WAX..."
"...GERALD HAD SOLD HIS EYEBROW TO A WIG SHOP TO BUY MAGGIE A PACIFIER COZY."
MONOBROW JACK'S EYEBROW WAX
PACIFIER COZY
"AND WITH NARY A PACIFIER BETWEEN 'EM, THOSE BABIES CRIED TILL EASTER!"

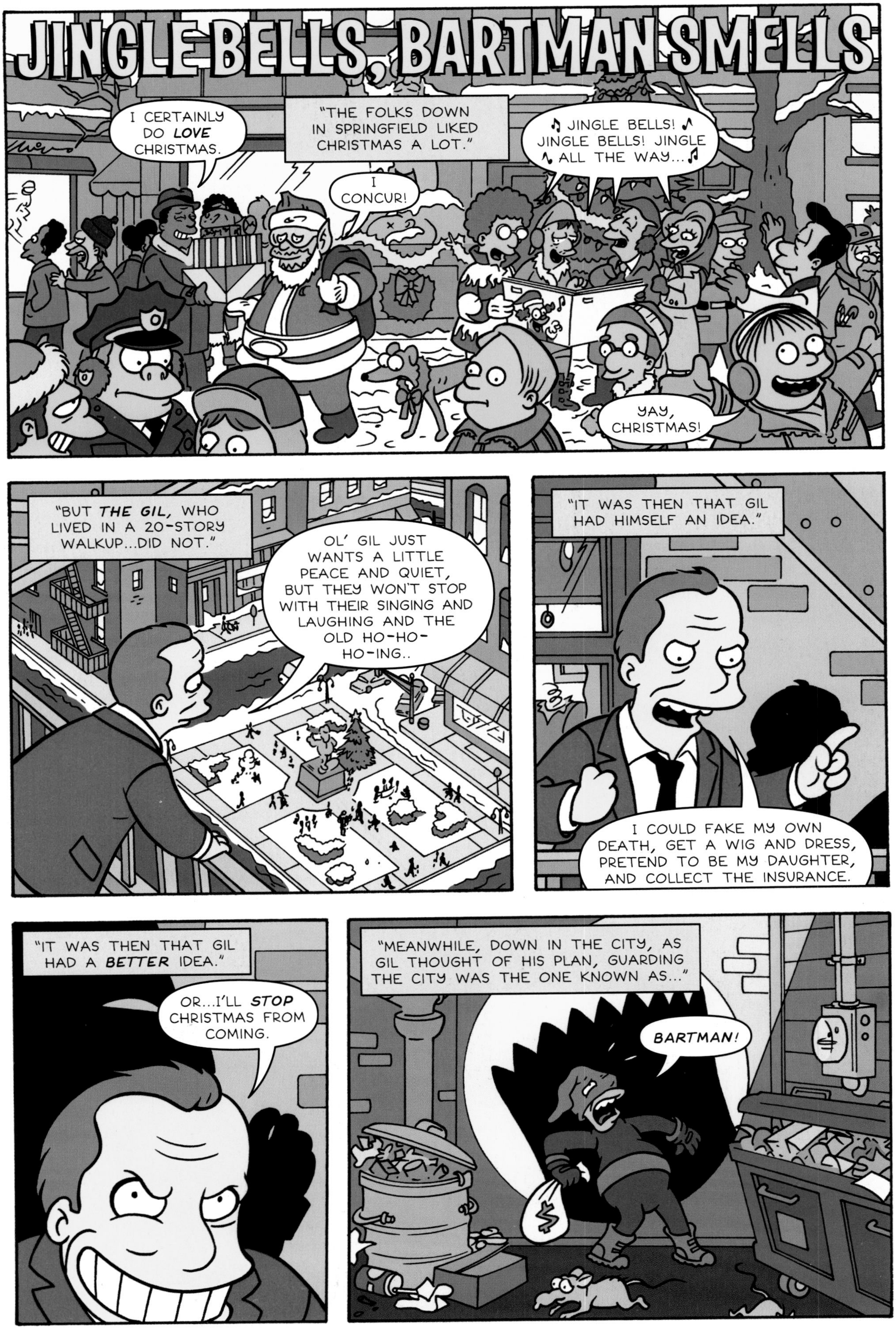
JINGLE BELLS, BARTMAN SMELLS
I CERTAINLY DO LOVE CHRISTMAS.
"THE FOLKS DOWN IN SPRINGFIELD LIKED CHRISTMAS A LOT."
I CONCUR!
♫ JINGLE BELLS! ♪ JINGLE BELLS! JINGLE ♪ ALL THE WAY... ♫
YAY, CHRISTMAS!
"BUT THE GIL, WHO LIVED IN A 20-STORY WALKUP...DID NOT."
OL' GIL JUST WANTS A LITTLE PEACE AND QUIET, BUT THEY WON'T STOP WITH THEIR SINGING AND LAUGHING AND THE OLD HO-HO-HO-ING..
"IT WAS THEN THAT GIL HAD HIMSELF AN IDEA."
I COULD FAKE MY OWN DEATH, GET A WIG AND DRESS, PRETEND TO BE MY DAUGHTER, AND COLLECT THE INSURANCE.
"IT WAS THEN THAT GIL HAD A BETTER IDEA."
OR...I'LL STOP CHRISTMAS FROM COMING.
"MEANWHILE, DOWN IN THE CITY, AS GIL THOUGHT OF HIS PLAN, GUARDING THE CITY WAS THE ONE KNOWN AS..."
BARTMAN!

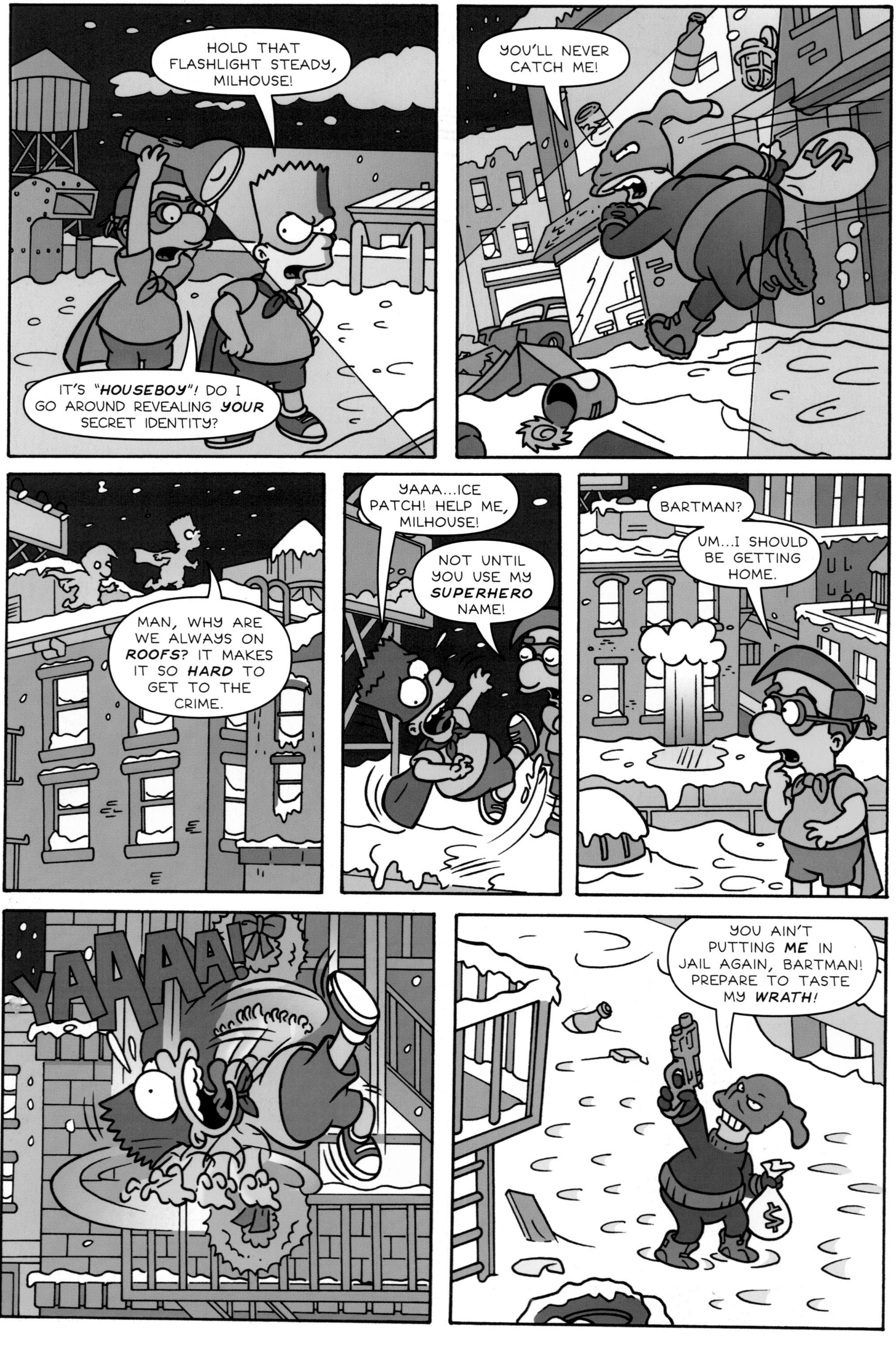
HOLD THAT FLASHLIGHT STEADY, MILHOUSE!
IT'S "HOUSEBOY"! DO I GO AROUND REVEALING YOUR SECRET IDENTITY?
YOU'LL NEVER CATCH ME!
MAN, WHY ARE WE ALWAYS ON ROOFS? IT MAKES IT SO HARD TO GET TO THE CRIME.
YAAA...ICE PATCH! HELP ME, MILHOUSE!
NOT UNTIL YOU USE MY SUPERHERO NAME!
BARTMAN?
UM...I SHOULD BE GETTING HOME.
YAAAA!
YOU AIN'T PUTTING ME IN JAIL AGAIN, BARTMAN! PREPARE TO TASTE MY WRATH!

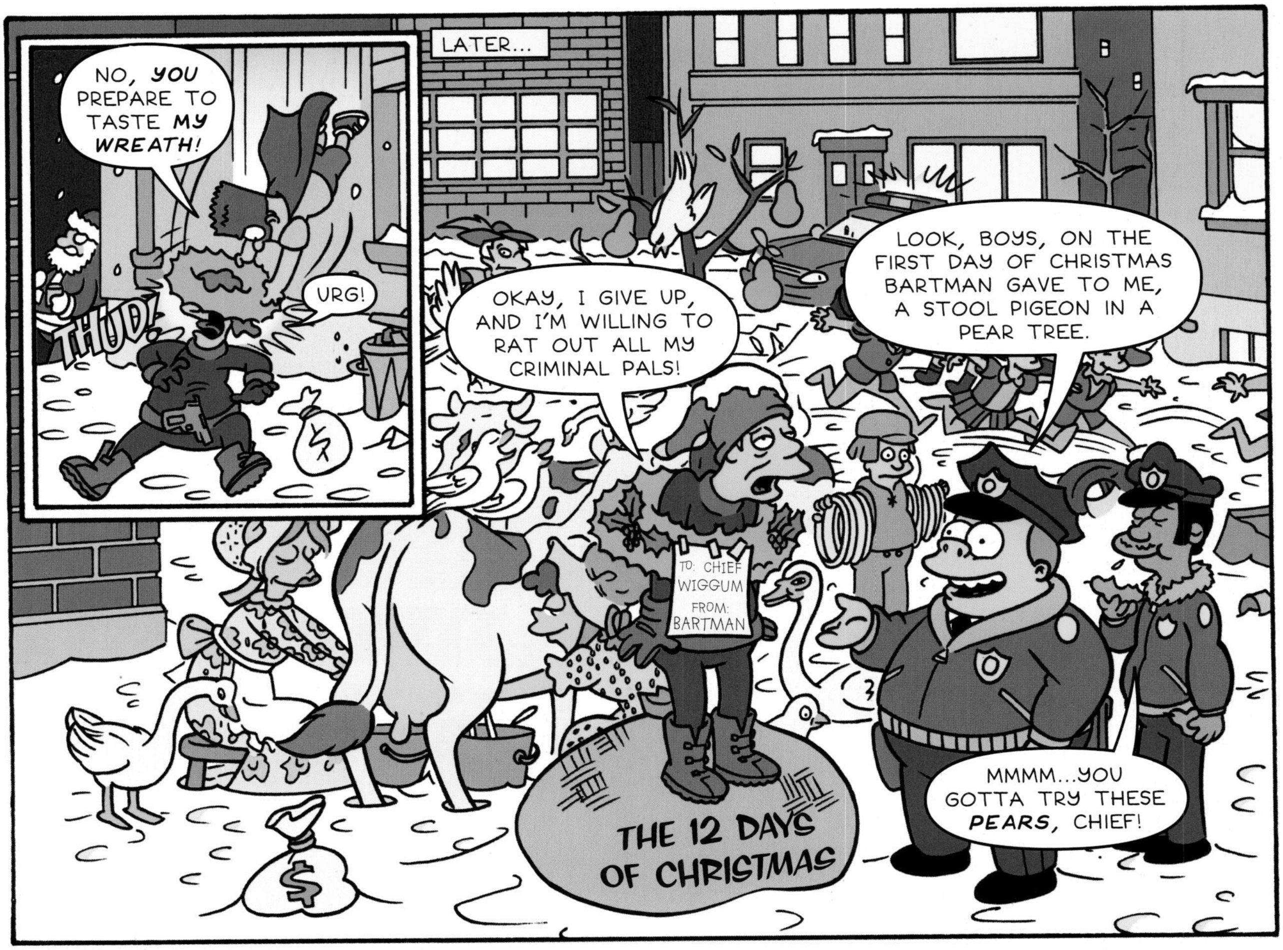
NO, YOU PREPARE TO TASTE MY WREATH!
URG!
THUD!
LATER...
OKAY, I GIVE UP, AND I'M WILLING TO RAT OUT ALL MY CRIMINAL PALS!
LOOK, BOYS, ON THE FIRST DAY OF CHRISTMAS BARTMAN GAVE TO ME, A STOOL PIGEON IN A PEAR TREE.
TO: CHIEF WIGGUM FROM: BARTMAN
MMMM...YOU GOTTA TRY THESE PEARS, CHIEF!
THE 12 DAYS OF CHRISTMAS

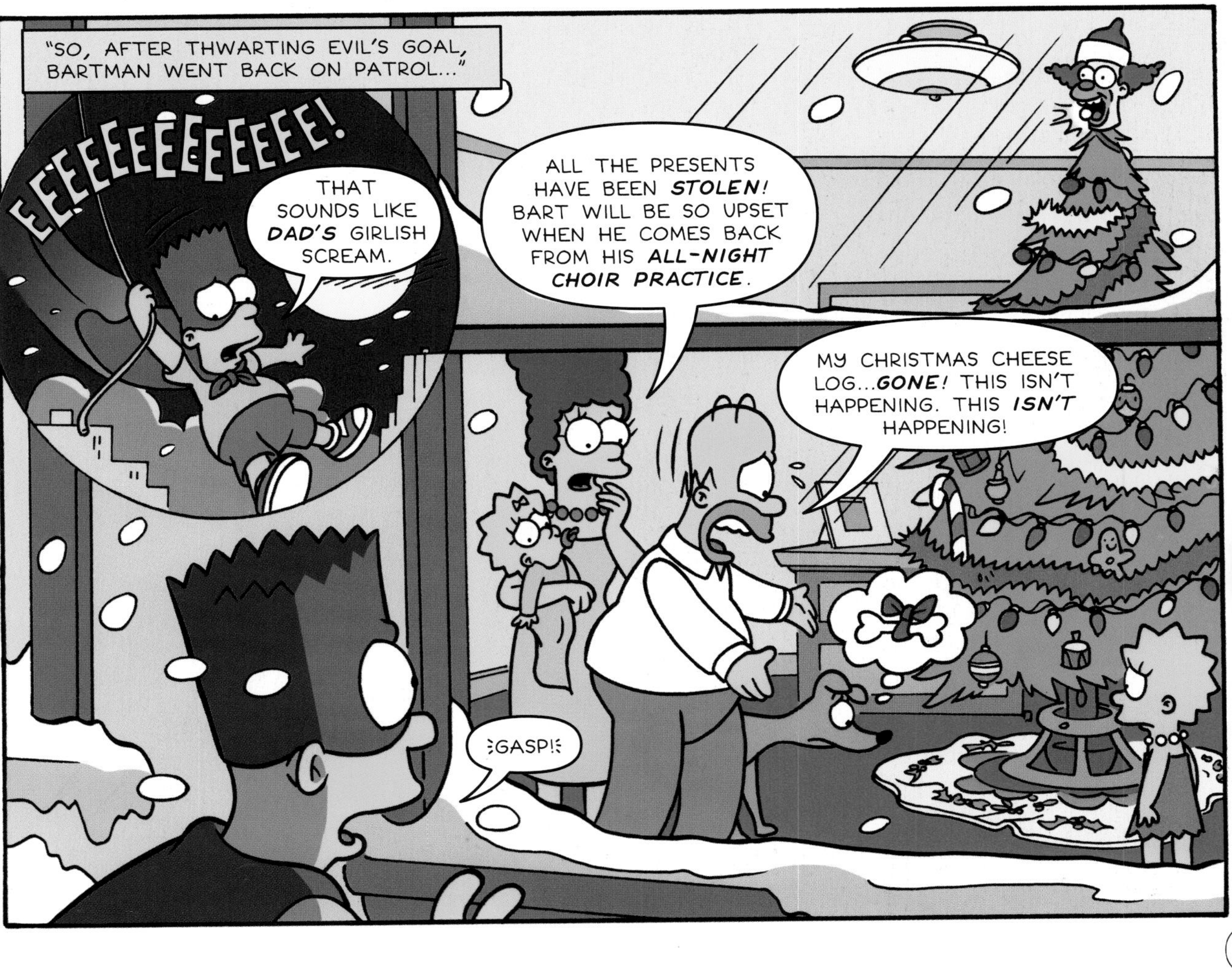
"SO, AFTER THWARTING EVIL'S GOAL, BARTMAN WENT BACK ON PATROL..."
EEEEEEEEEEEEE!
THAT SOUNDS LIKE DAD'S GIRLISH SCREAM.
ALL THE PRESENTS HAVE BEEN STOLEN! BART WILL BE SO UPSET WHEN HE COMES BACK FROM HIS ALL-NIGHT CHOIR PRACTICE.
MY CHRISTMAS CHEESE LOG...GONE! THIS ISN'T HAPPENING. THIS ISN'T HAPPENING!
GASP!

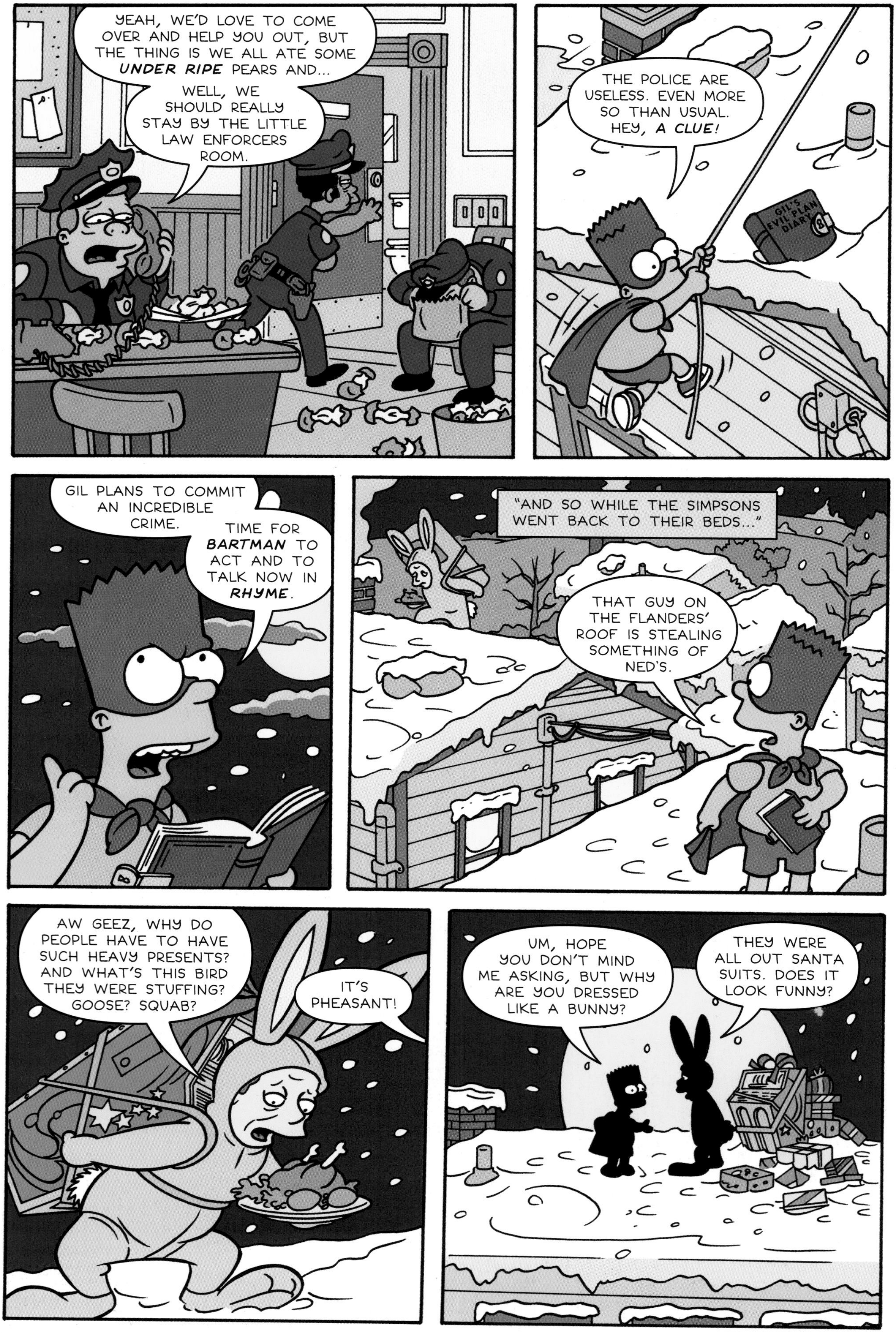
YEAH, WE'D LOVE TO COME OVER AND HELP YOU OUT, BUT THE THING IS WE ALL ATE SOME UNDER RIPE PEARS AND...
WELL, WE SHOULD REALLY STAY BY THE LITTLE LAW ENFORCERS ROOM.
THE POLICE ARE USELESS. EVEN MORE SO THAN USUAL. HEY, A CLUE!
GIL'S EVIL PLAN DIARY
GIL PLANS TO COMMIT AN INCREDIBLE CRIME.
TIME FOR BARTMAN TO ACT AND TO TALK NOW IN RHYME.
"AND SO WHILE THE SIMPSONS WENT BACK TO THEIR BEDS..."
THAT GUY ON THE FLANDERS' ROOF IS STEALING SOMETHING OF NED'S.
AW GEEZ, WHY DO PEOPLE HAVE TO HAVE SUCH HEAVY PRESENTS? AND WHAT'S THIS BIRD THEY WERE STUFFING? GOOSE? SQUAB?
IT'S PHEASANT!
UM, HOPE YOU DON'T MIND ME ASKING, BUT WHY ARE YOU DRESSED LIKE A BUNNY?
THEY WERE ALL OUT SANTA SUITS. DOES IT LOOK FUNNY?

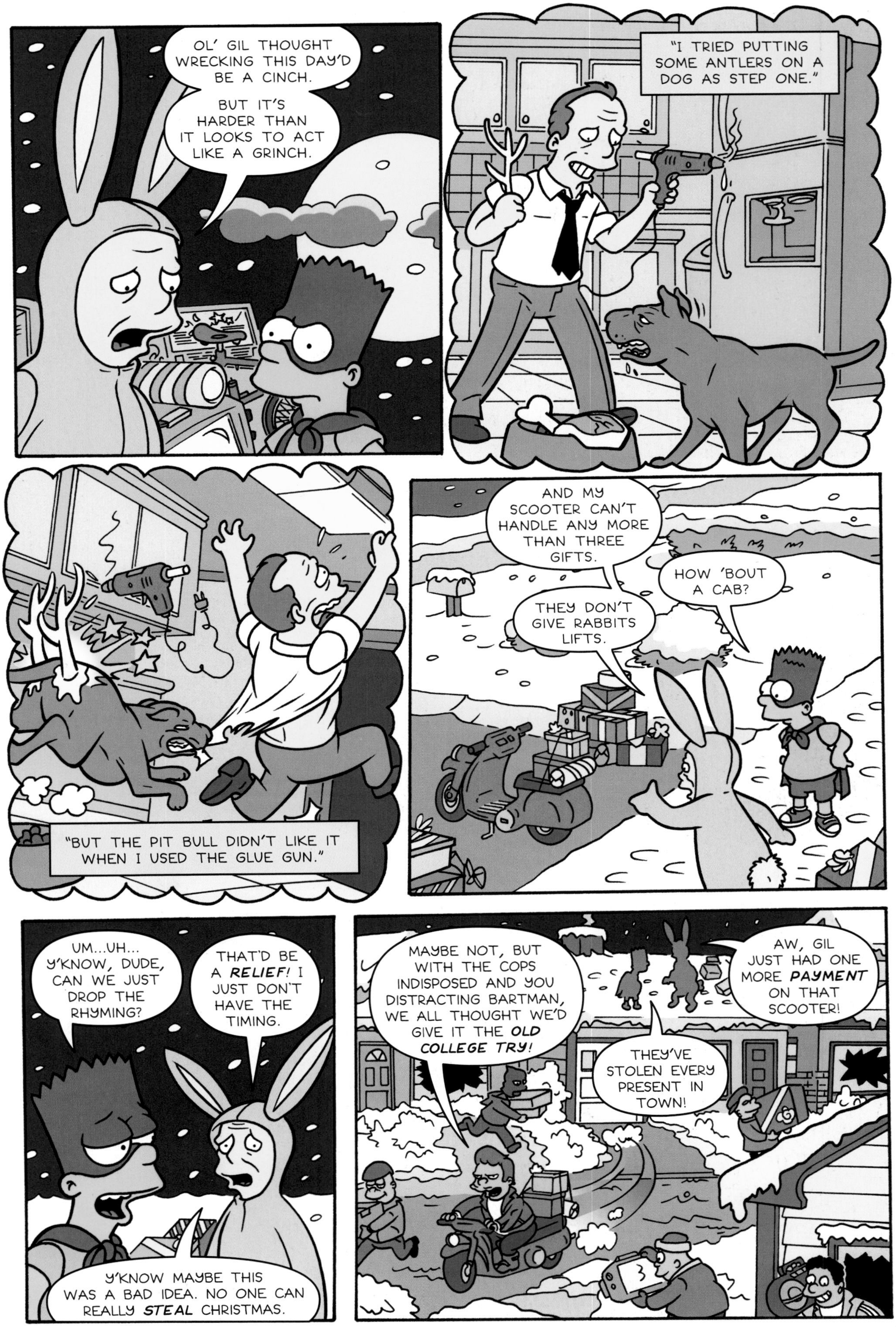
OL' GIL THOUGHT WRECKING THIS DAY'D BE A CINCH.
BUT IT'S HARDER THAN IT LOOKS TO ACT LIKE A GRINCH.
"I TRIED PUTTING SOME ANTLERS ON A DOG AS STEP ONE."
"BUT THE PIT BULL DIDN'T LIKE IT WHEN I USED THE GLUE GUN."
AND MY SCOOTER CAN'T HANDLE ANY MORE THAN THREE GIFTS.
HOW 'BOUT A CAB?
THEY DON'T GIVE RABBITS LIFTS.
UM...UH... Y'KNOW, DUDE, CAN WE JUST DROP THE RHYMING?
THAT'D BE A RELIEF! I JUST DON'T HAVE THE TIMING.
Y'KNOW MAYBE THIS WAS A BAD IDEA. NO ONE CAN REALLY STEAL CHRISTMAS.
MAYBE NOT, BUT WITH THE COPS INDISPOSED AND YOU DISTRACTING BARTMAN, WE ALL THOUGHT WE'D GIVE IT THE OLD COLLEGE TRY!
AW, GIL JUST HAD ONE MORE PAYMENT ON THAT SCOOTER!
THEY'VE STOLEN EVERY PRESENT IN TOWN!

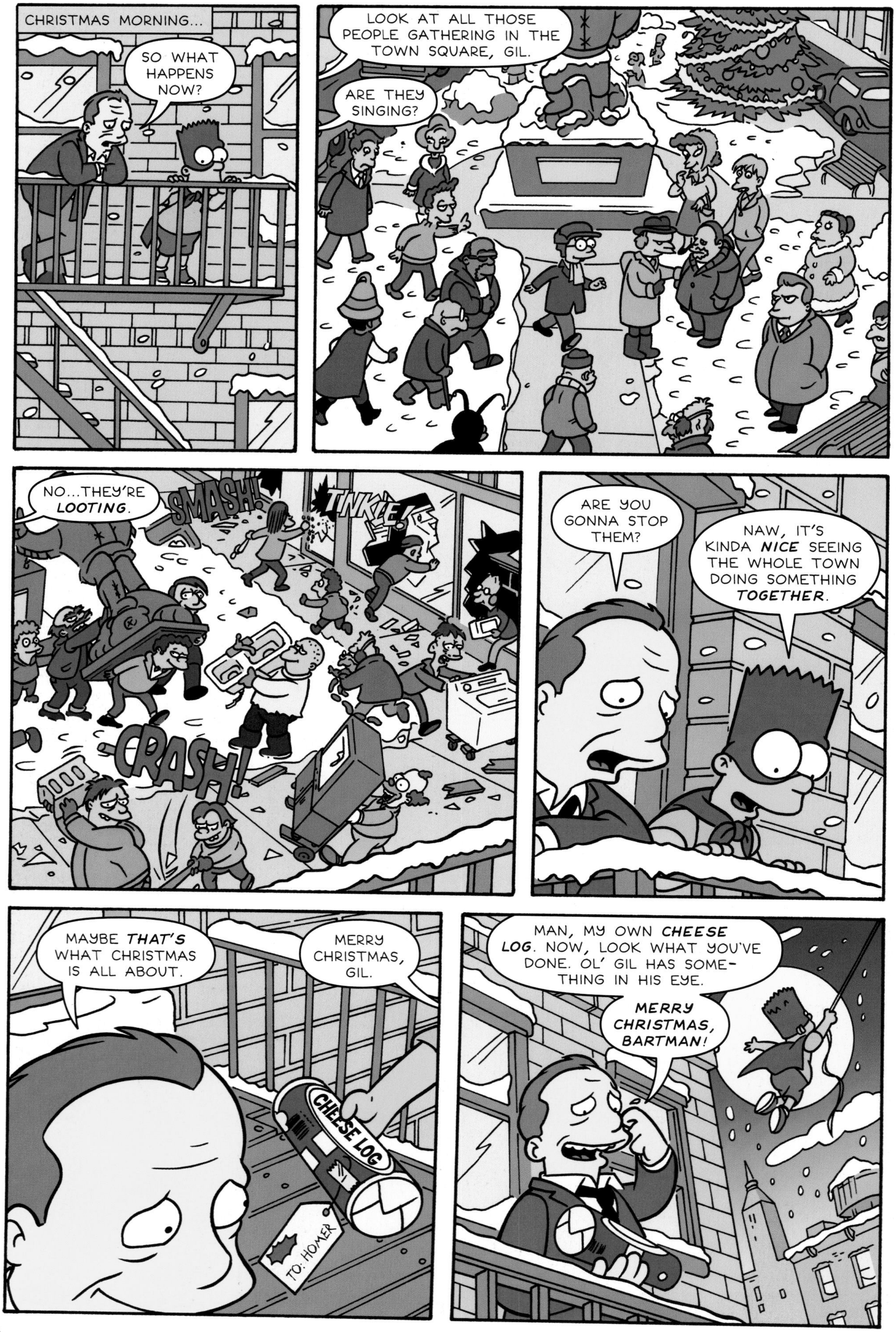
CHRISTMAS MORNING...
SO WHAT HAPPENS NOW?
LOOK AT ALL THOSE PEOPLE GATHERING IN THE TOWN SQUARE, GIL.
ARE THEY SINGING?
NO...THEY'RE *LOOTING*.
SMASH!
TINKLE!
CRASH!
ARE YOU GONNA STOP THEM?
NAW, IT'S KINDA **NICE** SEEING THE WHOLE TOWN DOING SOMETHING ***TOGETHER***.
MAYBE *THAT'S* WHAT CHRISTMAS IS ALL ABOUT.
MERRY CHRISTMAS, GIL.
CHEESE LOG
TO: HOMER
MAN, MY OWN **CHEESE LOG**. NOW, LOOK WHAT YOU'VE DONE. OL' GIL HAS SOME-THING IN HIS EYE.
MERRY CHRISTMAS, BARTMAN!

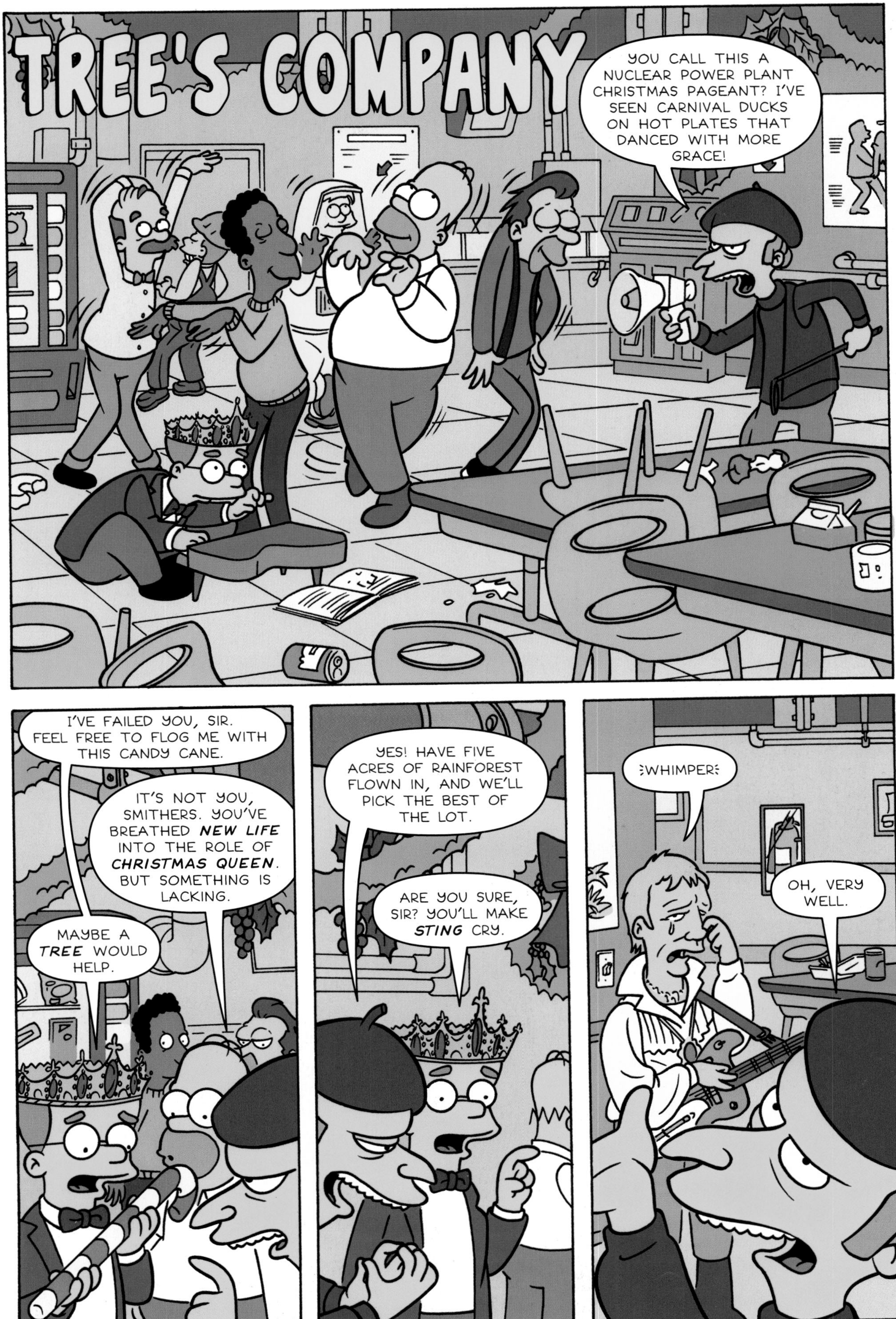
TREE'S COMPANY
YOU CALL THIS A NUCLEAR POWER PLANT CHRISTMAS PAGEANT? I'VE SEEN CARNIVAL DUCKS ON HOT PLATES THAT DANCED WITH MORE GRACE!
I'VE FAILED YOU, SIR. FEEL FREE TO FLOG ME WITH THIS CANDY CANE.
IT'S NOT YOU, SMITHERS. YOU'VE BREATHED NEW LIFE INTO THE ROLE OF CHRISTMAS QUEEN. BUT SOMETHING IS LACKING.
MAYBE A TREE WOULD HELP.
YES! HAVE FIVE ACRES OF RAINFOREST FLOWN IN, AND WE'LL PICK THE BEST OF THE LOT.
ARE YOU SURE, SIR? YOU'LL MAKE STING CRY.
WHIMPER
OH, VERY WELL.

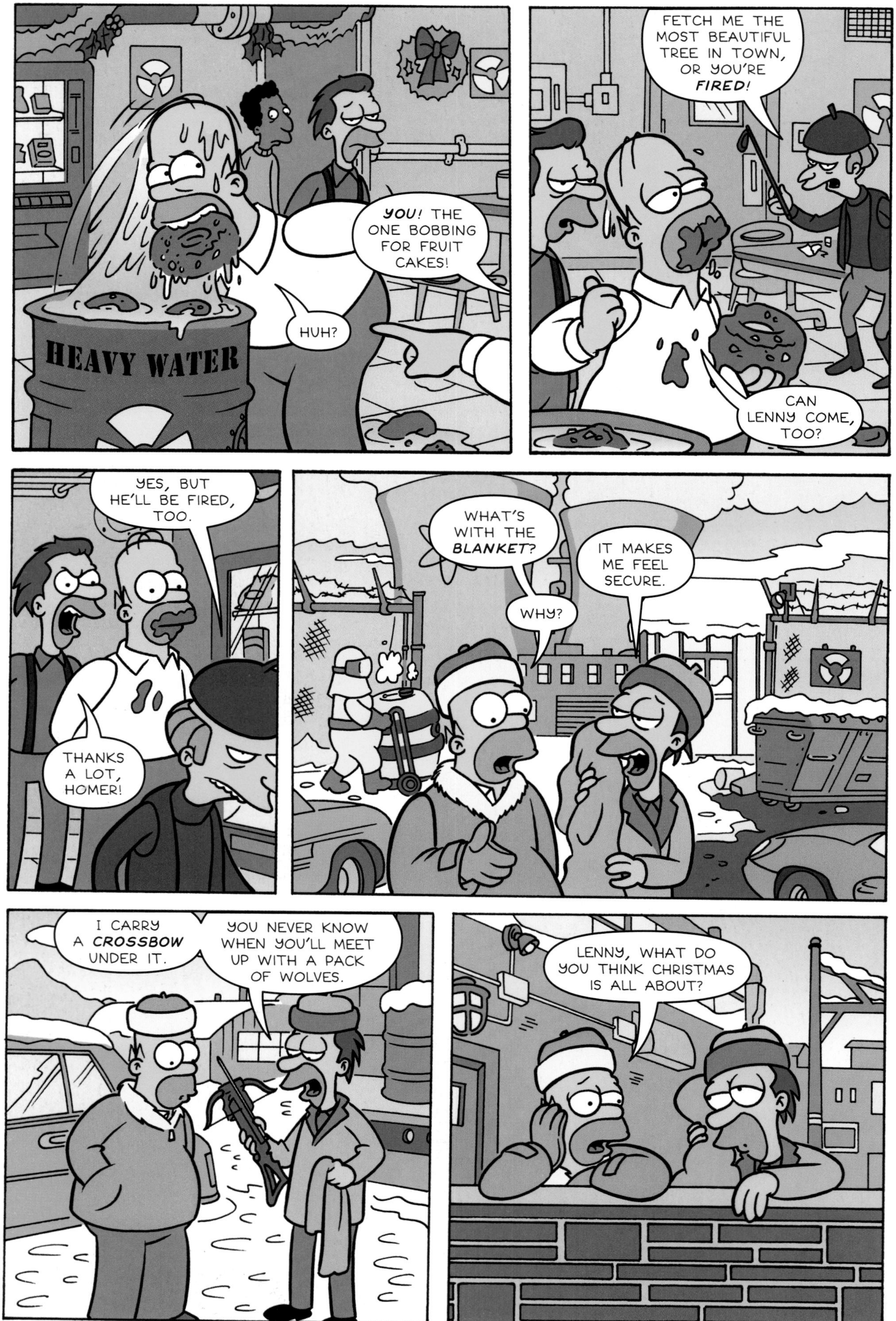
YOU! THE ONE BOBBING FOR FRUIT CAKES!
HUH?
HEAVY WATER
FETCH ME THE MOST BEAUTIFUL TREE IN TOWN, OR YOU'RE FIRED!
CAN LENNY COME, TOO?
YES, BUT HE'LL BE FIRED, TOO.
THANKS A LOT, HOMER!
WHAT'S WITH THE BLANKET?
WHY?
IT MAKES ME FEEL SECURE.
I CARRY A CROSSBOW UNDER IT.
YOU NEVER KNOW WHEN YOU'LL MEET UP WITH A PACK OF WOLVES.
LENNY, WHAT DO YOU THINK CHRISTMAS IS ALL ABOUT?

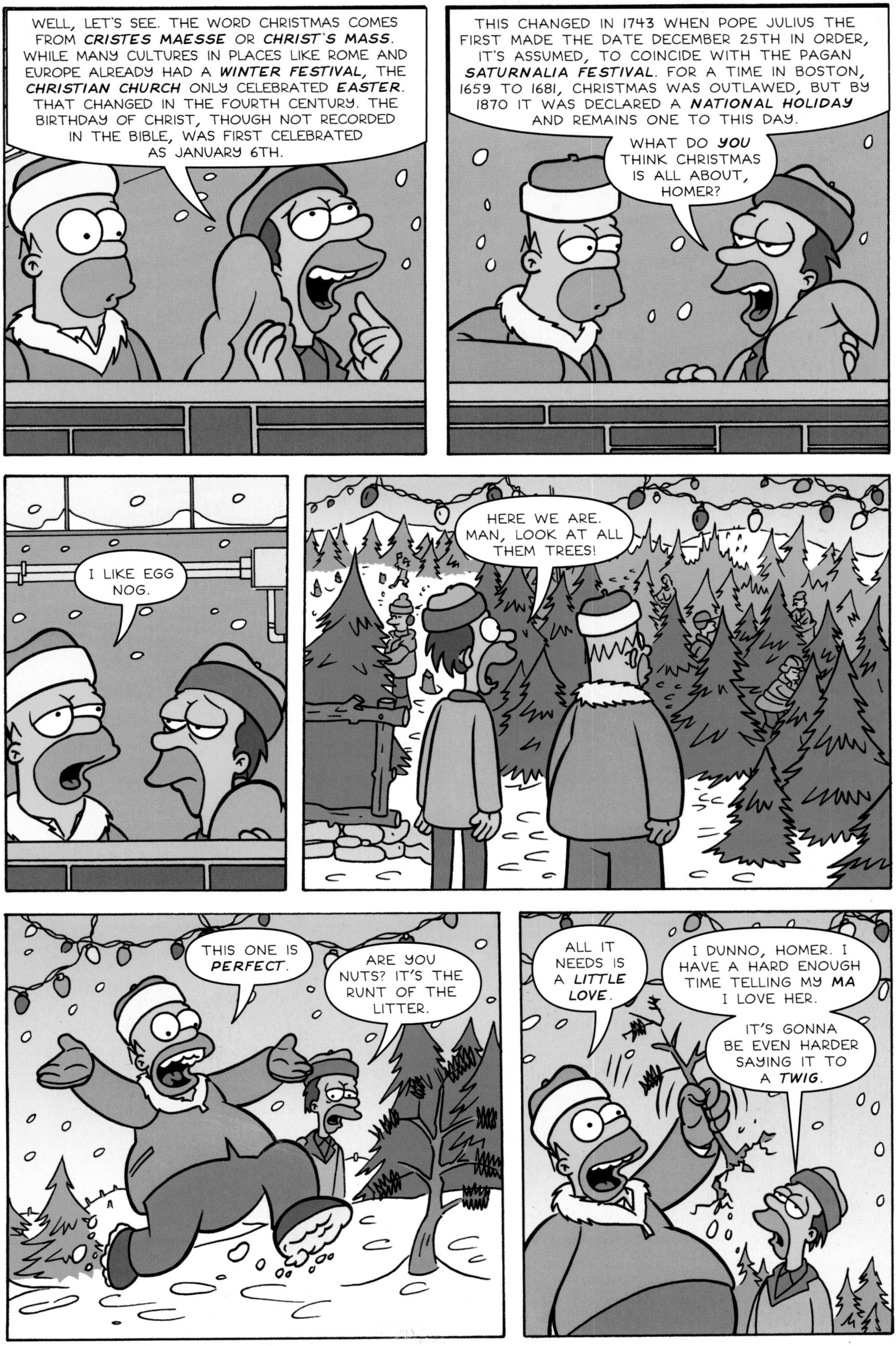
WELL, LET'S SEE. THE WORD CHRISTMAS COMES FROM CRISTES MAESSE OR CHRIST'S MASS. WHILE MANY CULTURES IN PLACES LIKE ROME AND EUROPE ALREADY HAD A WINTER FESTIVAL, THE CHRISTIAN CHURCH ONLY CELEBRATED EASTER. THAT CHANGED IN THE FOURTH CENTURY. THE BIRTHDAY OF CHRIST, THOUGH NOT RECORDED IN THE BIBLE, WAS FIRST CELEBRATED AS JANUARY 6TH.
THIS CHANGED IN 1743 WHEN POPE JULIUS THE FIRST MADE THE DATE DECEMBER 25TH IN ORDER, IT'S ASSUMED, TO COINCIDE WITH THE PAGAN SATURNALIA FESTIVAL. FOR A TIME IN BOSTON, 1659 TO 1681, CHRISTMAS WAS OUTLAWED, BUT BY 1870 IT WAS DECLARED A NATIONAL HOLIDAY AND REMAINS ONE TO THIS DAY.
WHAT DO YOU THINK CHRISTMAS IS ALL ABOUT, HOMER?
I LIKE EGG NOG.
HERE WE ARE. MAN, LOOK AT ALL THEM TREES!
THIS ONE IS PERFECT.
ARE YOU NUTS? IT'S THE RUNT OF THE LITTER.
ALL IT NEEDS IS A LITTLE LOVE.
I DUNNO, HOMER. I HAVE A HARD ENOUGH TIME TELLING MY MA I LOVE HER.
IT'S GONNA BE EVEN HARDER SAYING IT TO A TWIG.

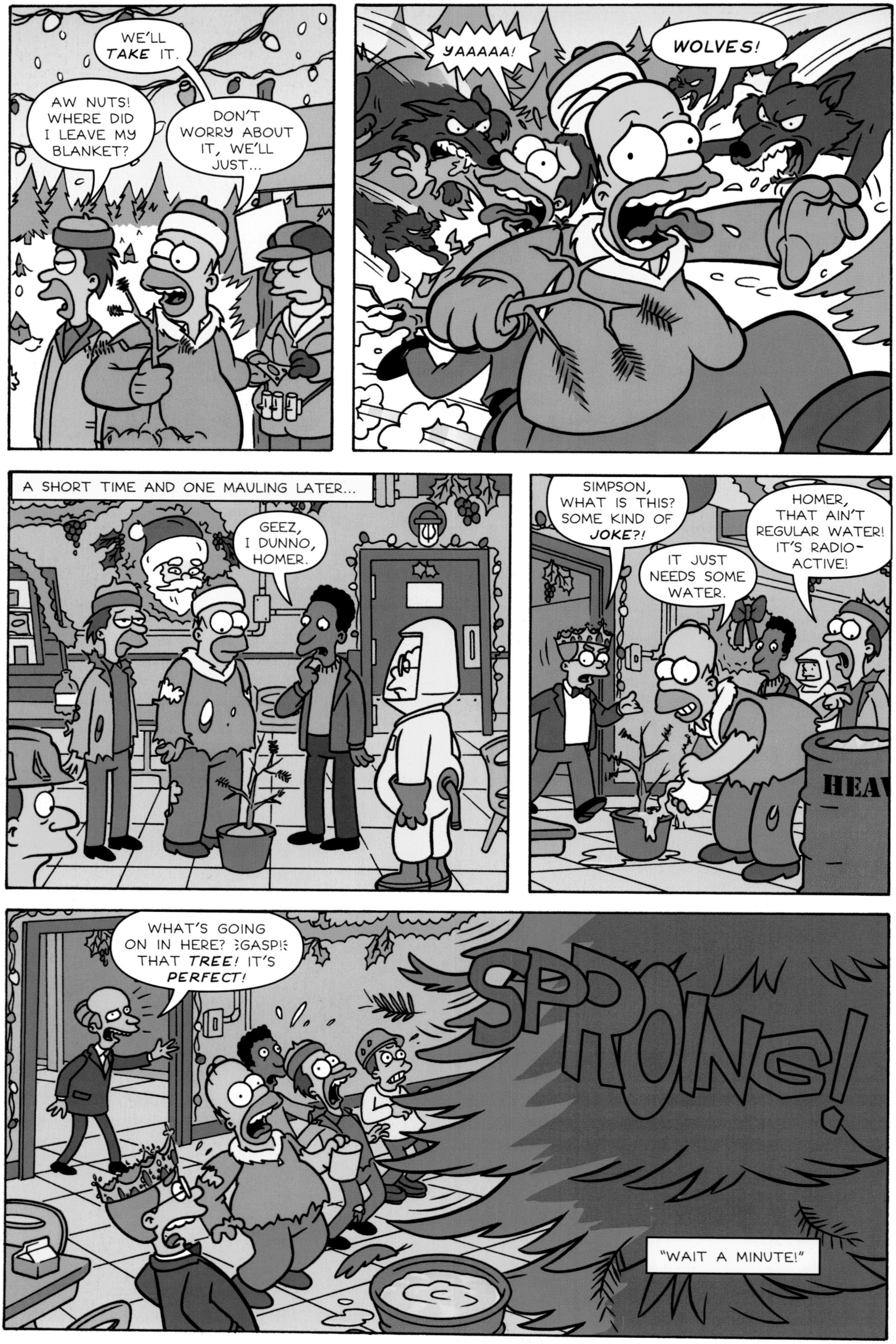
AW NUTS! WHERE DID I LEAVE MY BLANKET?
WE'LL *TAKE* IT.
DON'T WORRY ABOUT IT, WE'LL JUST...
YAAAAA!
WOLVES!
A SHORT TIME AND ONE MAULING LATER...
GEEZ, I DUNNO, HOMER.
SIMPSON, WHAT IS THIS? SOME KIND OF *JOKE?!*
IT JUST NEEDS SOME WATER.
HOMER, THAT AIN'T REGULAR WATER! IT'S RADIO-ACTIVE!
HEAV
WHAT'S GOING ON IN HERE? :GASP!: THAT *TREE!* IT'S *PERFECT!*
SPROING!
"WAIT A MINUTE!"

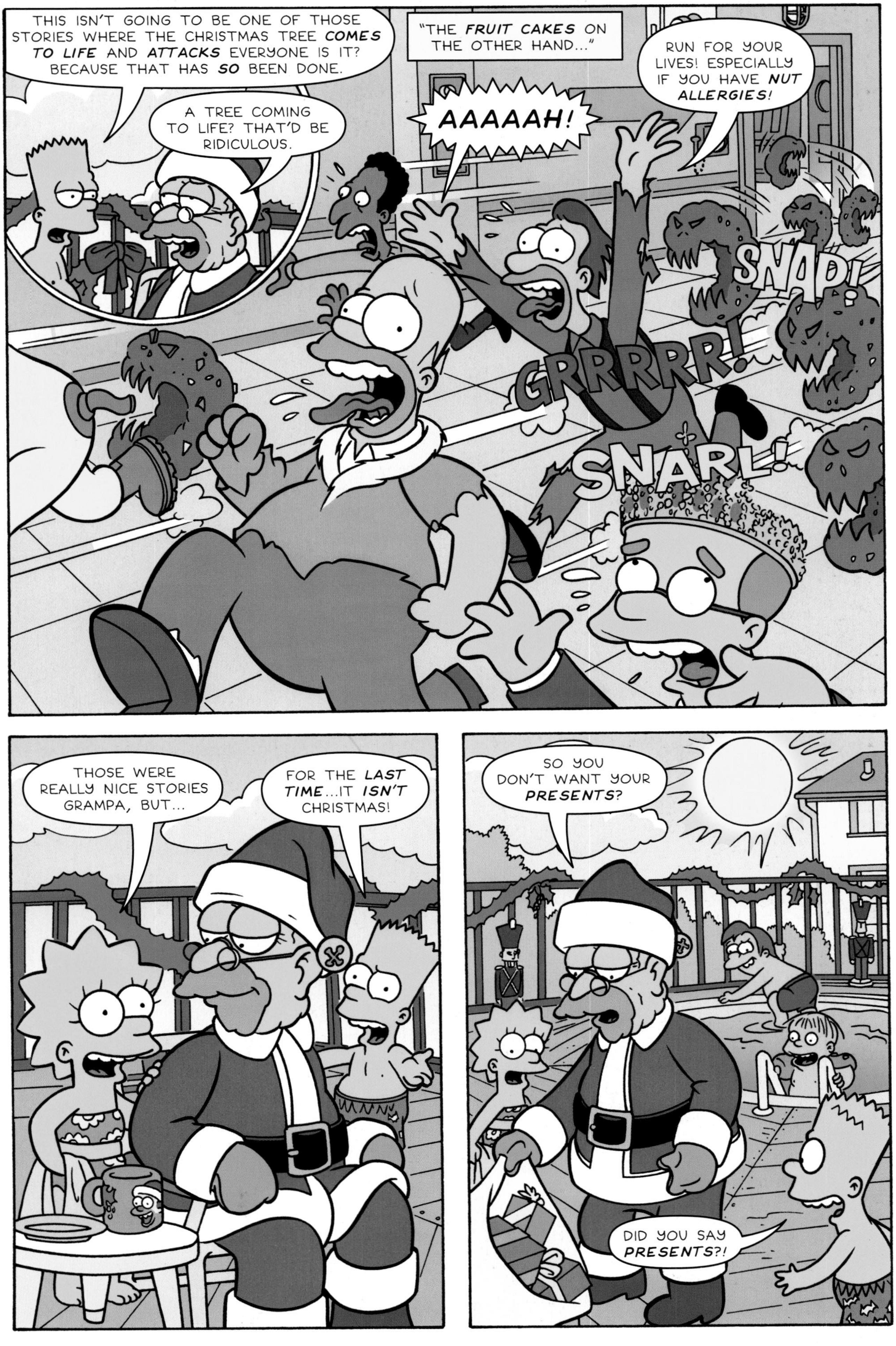

THIS ISN'T GOING TO BE ONE OF THOSE STORIES WHERE THE CHRISTMAS TREE **COMES TO LIFE** AND **ATTACKS** EVERYONE IS IT? BECAUSE THAT HAS **SO** BEEN DONE.
A TREE COMING TO LIFE? THAT'D BE RIDICULOUS.
"THE **FRUIT CAKES** ON THE OTHER HAND..."
AAAAAH!
RUN FOR YOUR LIVES! ESPECIALLY IF YOU HAVE **NUT ALLERGIES!**
SNAP!
GRRRRR!
SNARL!
THOSE WERE REALLY NICE STORIES GRAMPA, BUT...
FOR THE **LAST TIME**...IT **ISN'T** CHRISTMAS!
SO YOU DON'T WANT YOUR **PRESENTS**?
DID YOU SAY **PRESENTS**?!

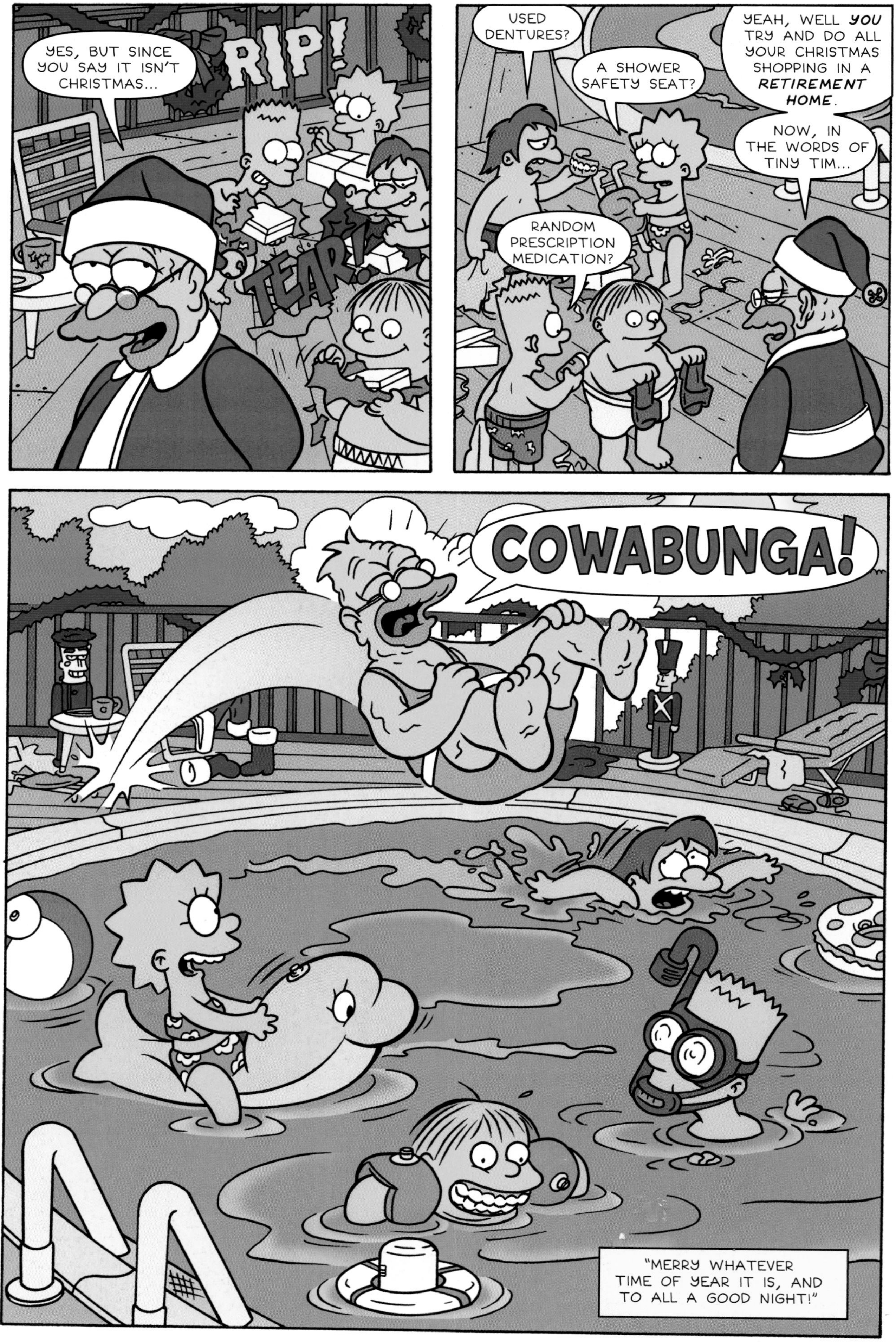
YES, BUT SINCE YOU SAY IT ISN'T CHRISTMAS...
RIP!
TEAR!
USED DENTURES?
A SHOWER SAFETY SEAT?
RANDOM PRESCRIPTION MEDICATION?
YEAH, WELL YOU TRY AND DO ALL YOUR CHRISTMAS SHOPPING IN A RETIREMENT HOME.
NOW, IN THE WORDS OF TINY TIM...
COWABUNGA!
"MERRY WHATEVER TIME OF YEAR IT IS, AND TO ALL A GOOD NIGHT!"

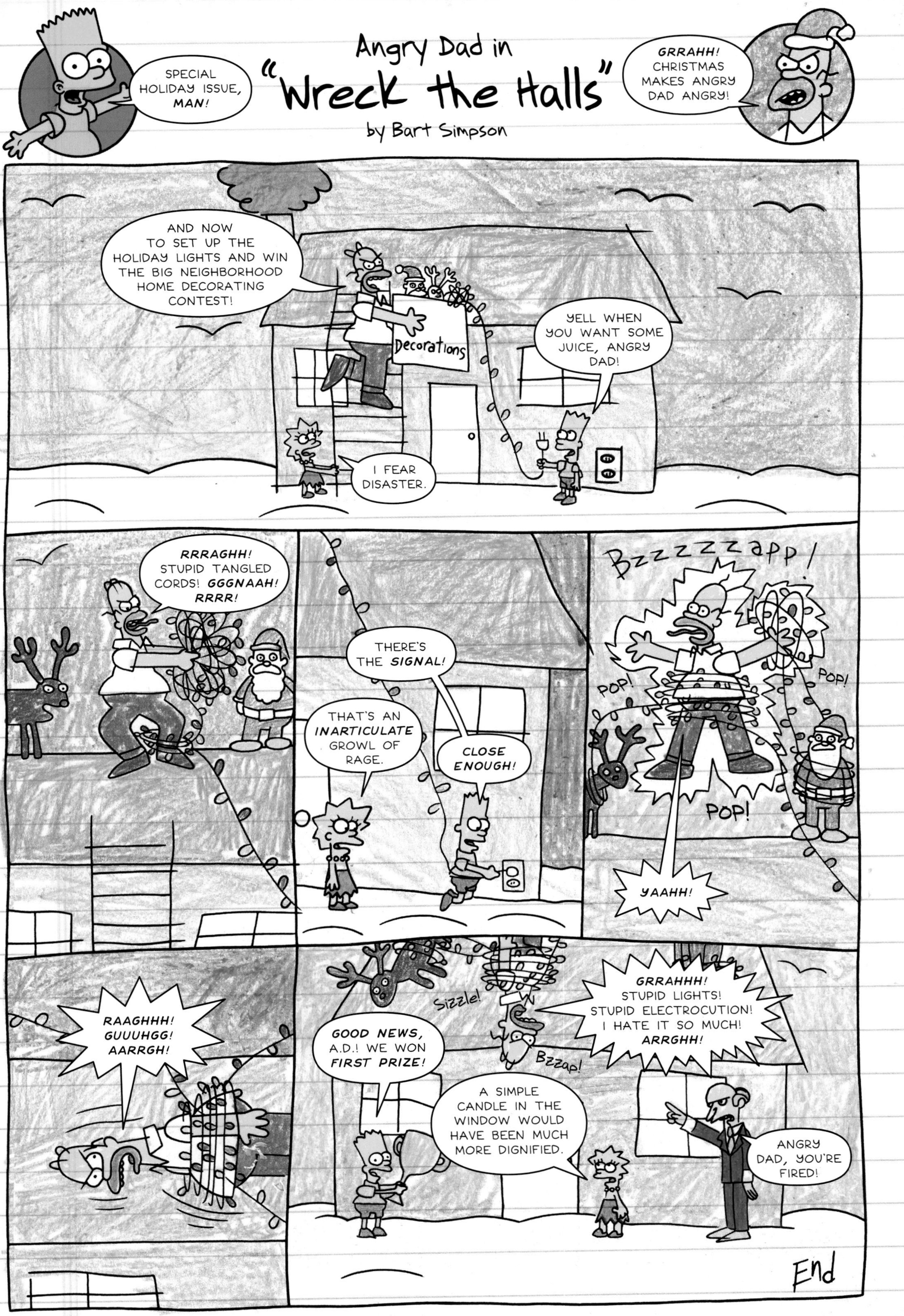
Angry Dad in
"Wreck the Halls"
by Bart Simpson
SPECIAL HOLIDAY ISSUE, MAN!
GRRAHH! CHRISTMAS MAKES ANGRY DAD ANGRY!
AND NOW TO SET UP THE HOLIDAY LIGHTS AND WIN THE BIG NEIGHBORHOOD HOME DECORATING CONTEST!
Decorations
YELL WHEN YOU WANT SOME JUICE, ANGRY DAD!
I FEAR DISASTER.
RRRAGHH! STUPID TANGLED CORDS! GGGNAAH! RRRR!
THERE'S THE SIGNAL!
THAT'S AN INARTICULATE GROWL OF RAGE.
CLOSE ENOUGH!
Bzzzzzzapp!
POP!
POP!
POP!
YAAHH!
RAAGHHH! GUUUHGG! AARRGH!
Sizzle!
Bzzap!
GRRAHHH! STUPID LIGHTS! STUPID ELECTROCUTION! I HATE IT SO MUCH! ARRGHH!
GOOD NEWS, A.D.! WE WON FIRST PRIZE!
A SIMPLE CANDLE IN THE WINDOW WOULD HAVE BEEN MUCH MORE DIGNIFIED.
ANGRY DAD, YOU'RE FIRED!
End

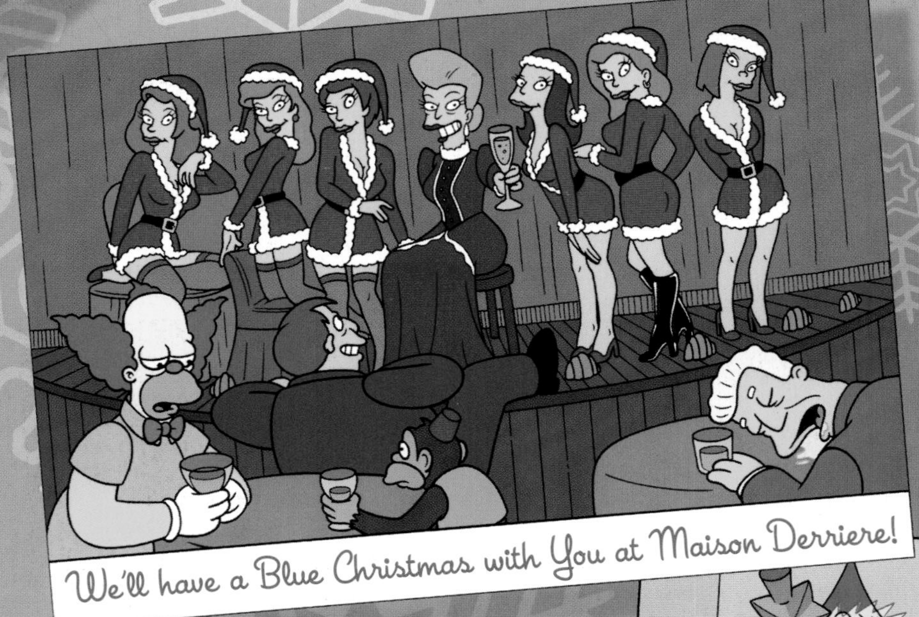
We'll have a Blue Christmas with You at Maison Derriere!

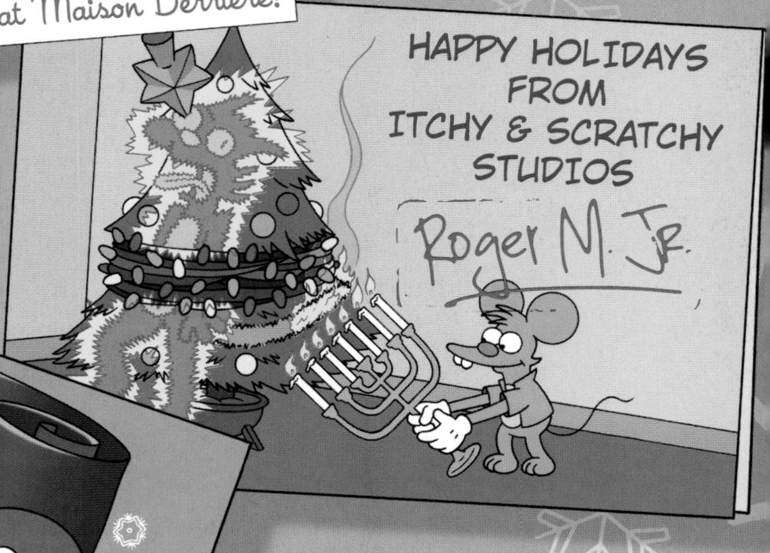
HAPPY HOLIDAYS
FROM
ITCHY & SCRATCHY
STUDIOS
Roger M. Jr.

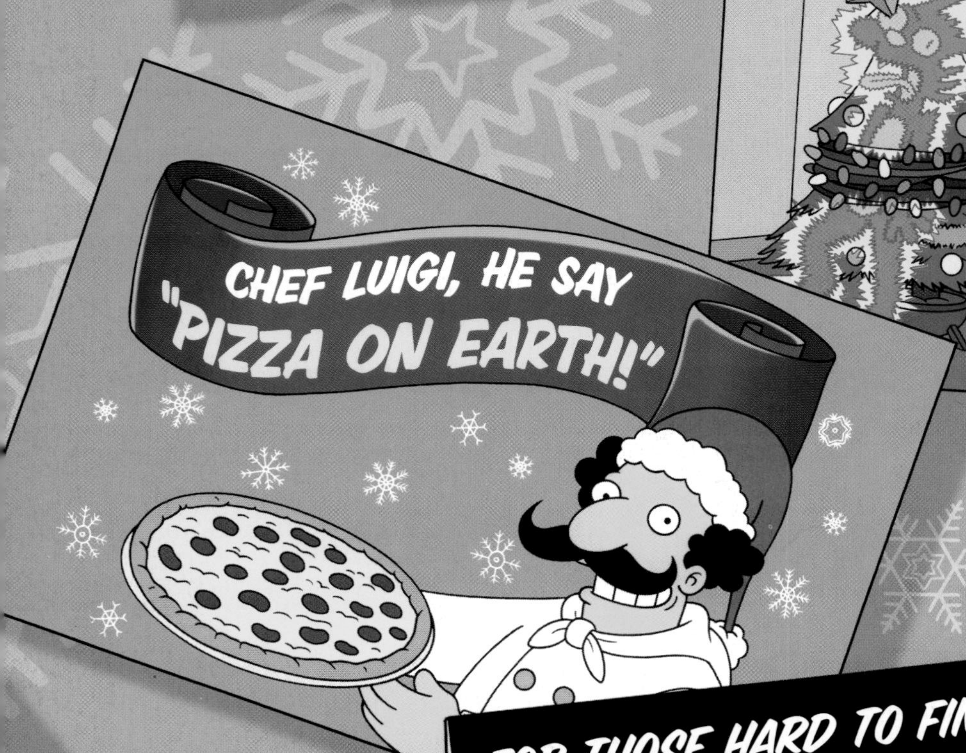
CHEF LUIGI, HE SAY
"PIZZA ON EARTH!"

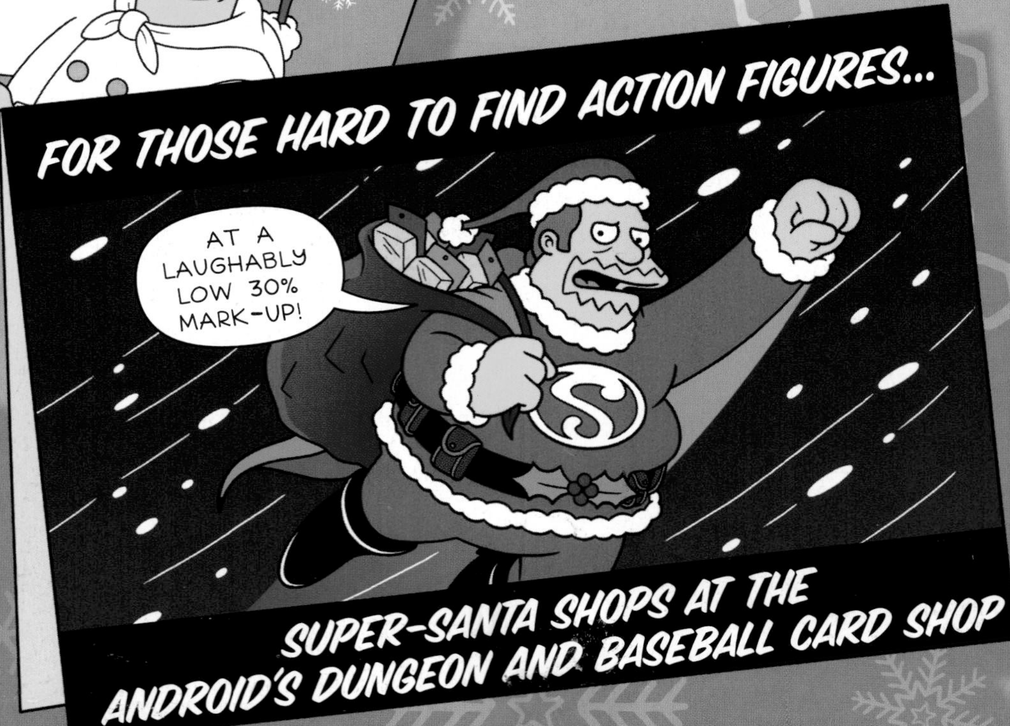
FOR THOSE HARD TO FIND ACTION FIGURES...
AT A LAUGHABLY LOW 30% MARK-UP!
SUPER-SANTA SHOPS AT THE
ANDROID'S DUNGEON AND BASEBALL CARD SHOP

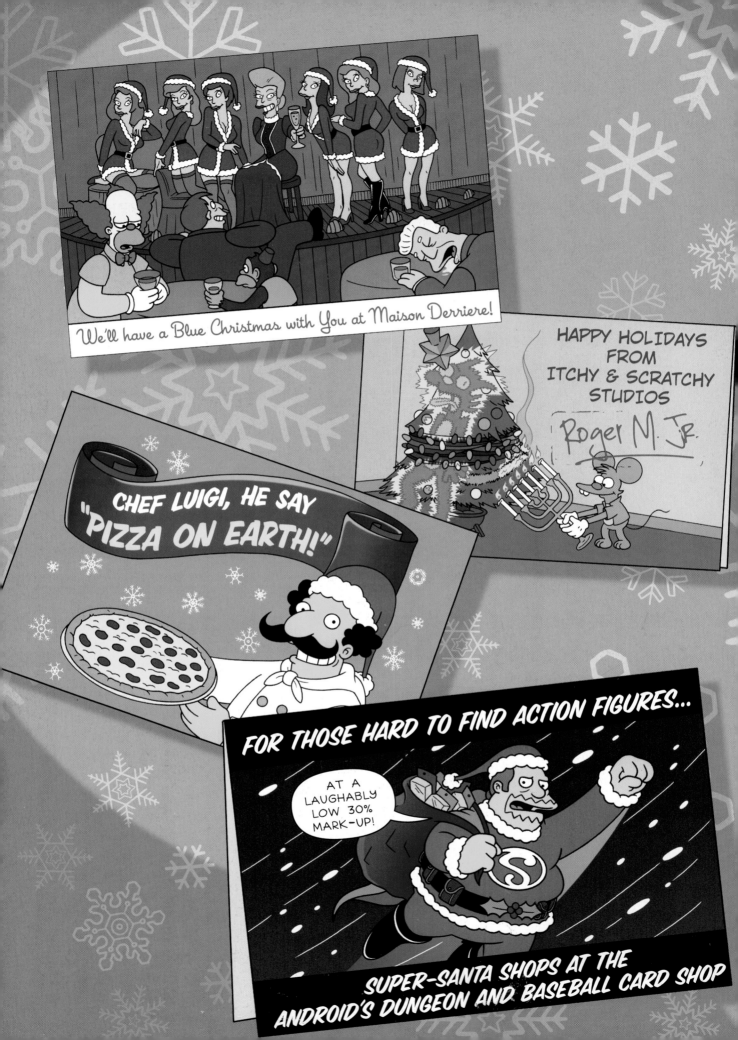

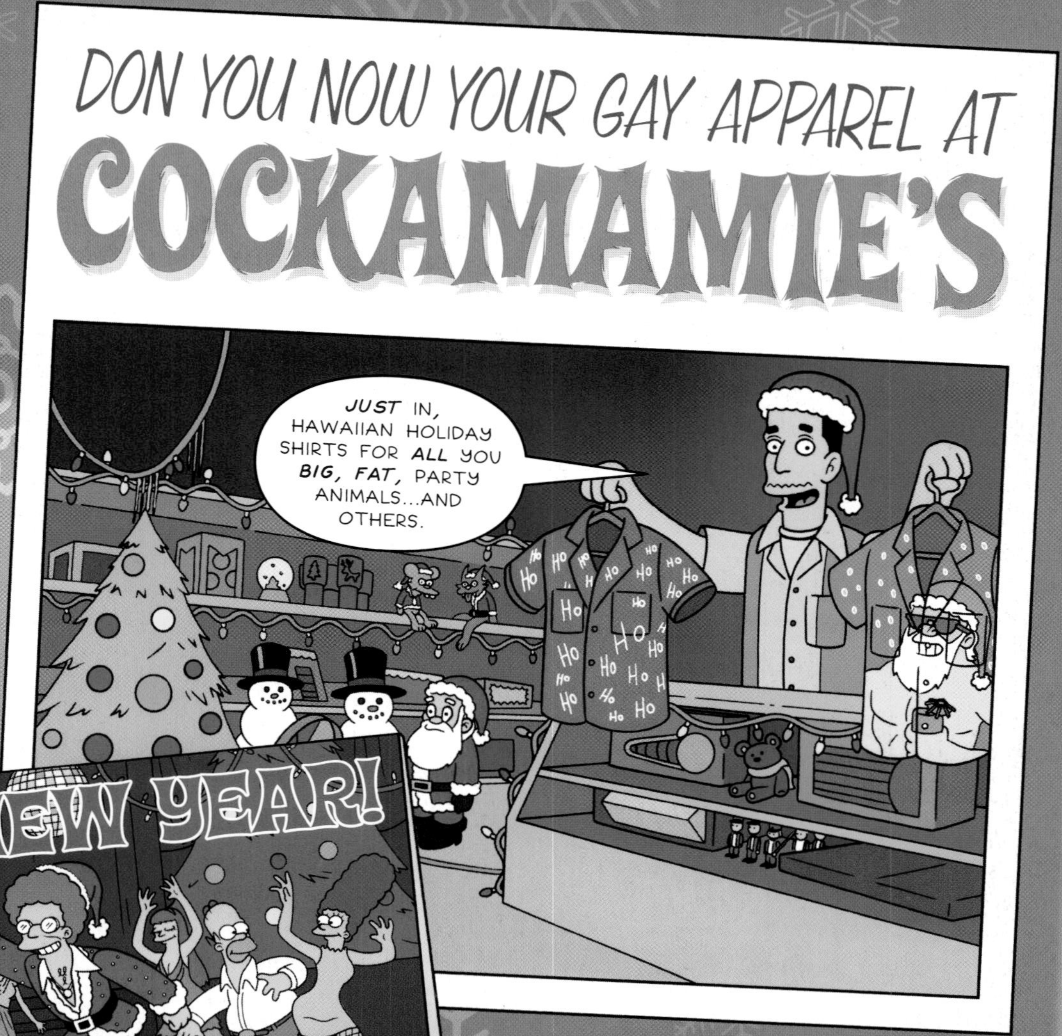
DON YOU NOW YOUR GAY APPAREL AT
COCKAMAMIE'S
JUST IN, HAWAIIAN HOLIDAY SHIRTS FOR ALL YOU BIG, FAT, PARTY ANIMALS...AND OTHERS.

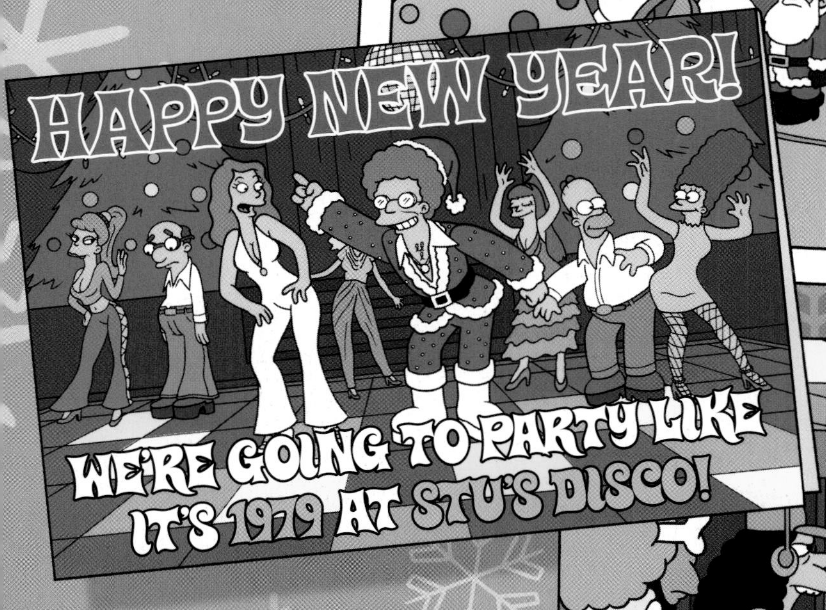
HAPPY NEW YEAR!
WE'RE GOING TO PARTY LIKE IT'S 1979 AT STU'S DISCO!

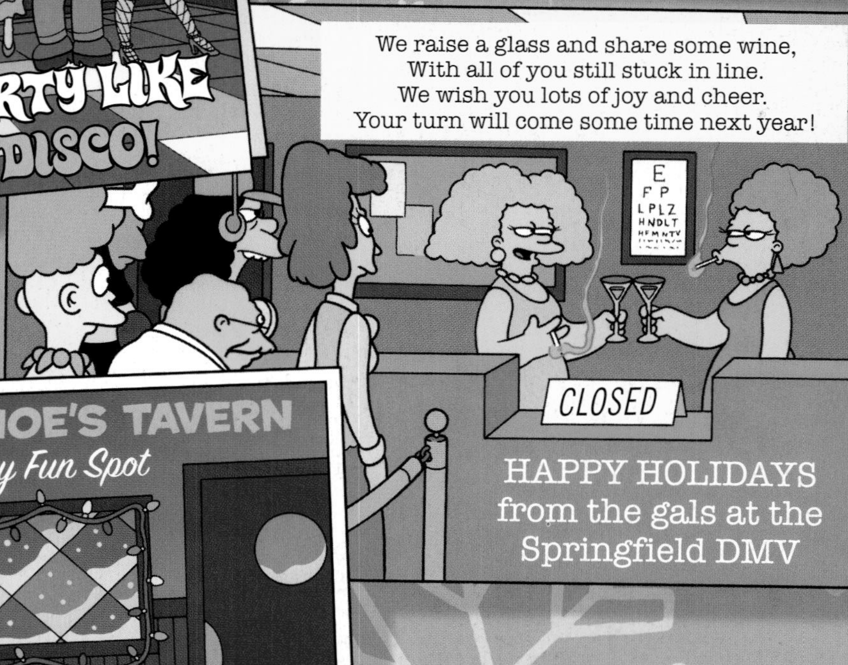
We raise a glass and share some wine,
With all of you still stuck in line.
We wish you lots of joy and cheer.
Your turn will come some time next year!
CLOSED
HAPPY HOLIDAYS from the gals at the Springfield DMV

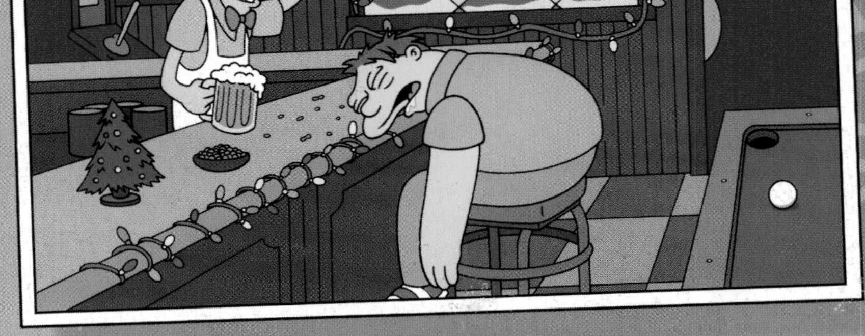
GREETINGS FROM MOE'S TAVERN
Your One Stop Holiday Fun Spot

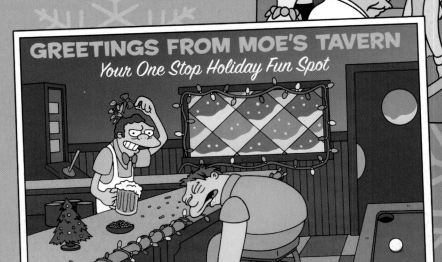

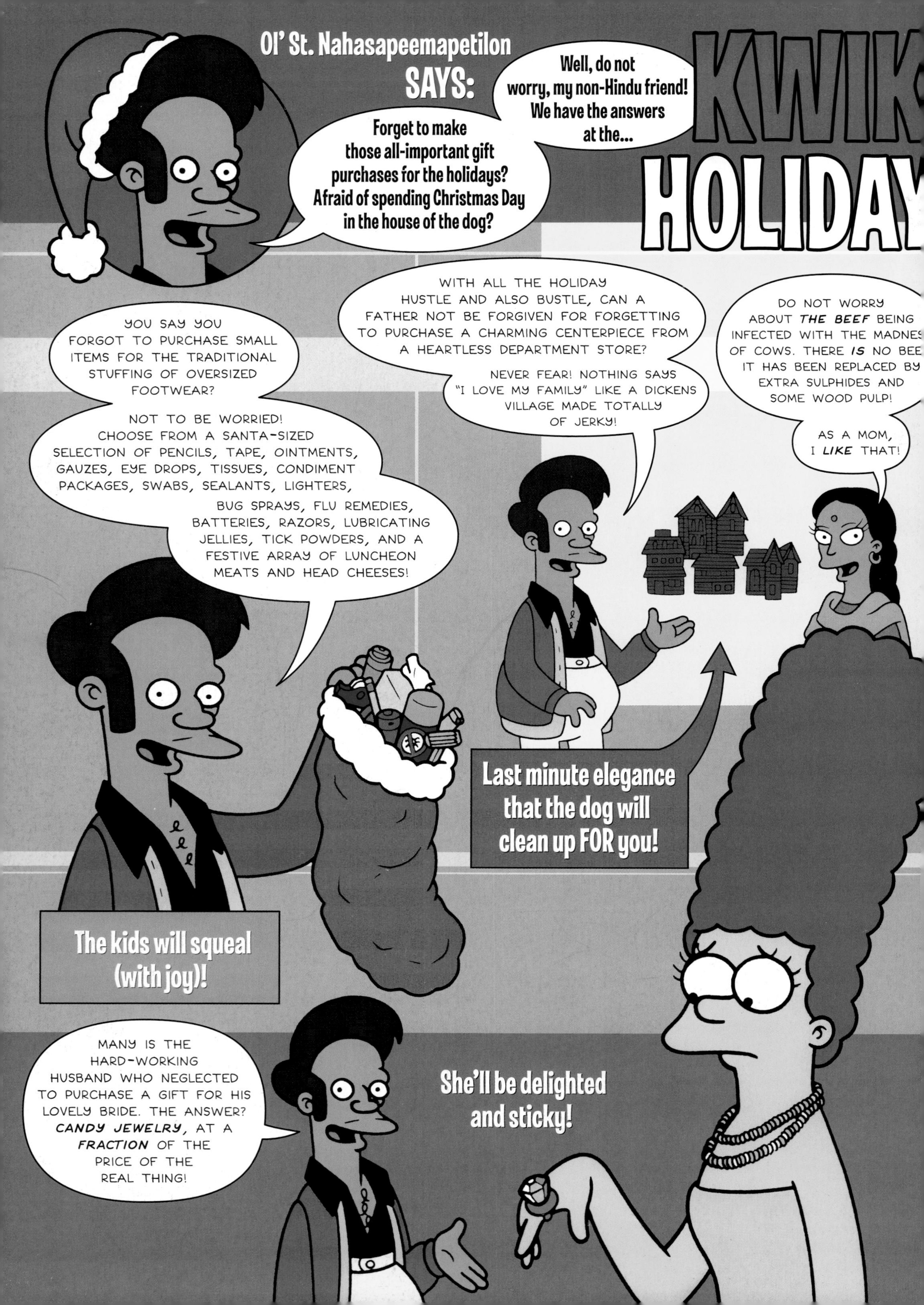

Ol' St. Nahasapeemapetilon SAYS:
Forget to make those all-important gift purchases for the holidays? Afraid of spending Christmas Day in the house of the dog?
Well, do not worry, my non-Hindu friend! We have the answers at the...
KWIK
HOLIDAY
YOU SAY YOU FORGOT TO PURCHASE SMALL ITEMS FOR THE TRADITIONAL STUFFING OF OVERSIZED FOOTWEAR?
NOT TO BE WORRIED! CHOOSE FROM A SANTA-SIZED SELECTION OF PENCILS, TAPE, OINTMENTS, GAUZES, EYE DROPS, TISSUES, CONDIMENT PACKAGES, SWABS, SEALANTS, LIGHTERS,
BUG SPRAYS, FLU REMEDIES, BATTERIES, RAZORS, LUBRICATING JELLIES, TICK POWDERS, AND A FESTIVE ARRAY OF LUNCHEON MEATS AND HEAD CHEESES!
The kids will squeal (with joy)!
WITH ALL THE HOLIDAY HUSTLE AND ALSO BUSTLE, CAN A FATHER NOT BE FORGIVEN FOR FORGETTING TO PURCHASE A CHARMING CENTERPIECE FROM A HEARTLESS DEPARTMENT STORE?
NEVER FEAR! NOTHING SAYS "I LOVE MY FAMILY" LIKE A DICKENS VILLAGE MADE TOTALLY OF JERKY!
Last minute elegance that the dog will clean up FOR you!
DO NOT WORRY ABOUT *THE BEEF* BEING INFECTED WITH THE MADNES OF COWS. THERE *IS* NO BEE IT HAS BEEN REPLACED BY EXTRA SULPHIDES AND SOME WOOD PULP!
AS A MOM, I *LIKE* THAT!
MANY IS THE HARD-WORKING HUSBAND WHO NEGLECTED TO PURCHASE A GIFT FOR HIS LOVELY BRIDE. THE ANSWER? *CANDY JEWELRY*, AT A *FRACTION* OF THE PRICE OF THE REAL THING!
She'll be delighted and sticky!

E-MART LAST MINUTE GIFT SPEND-O-RAMA!

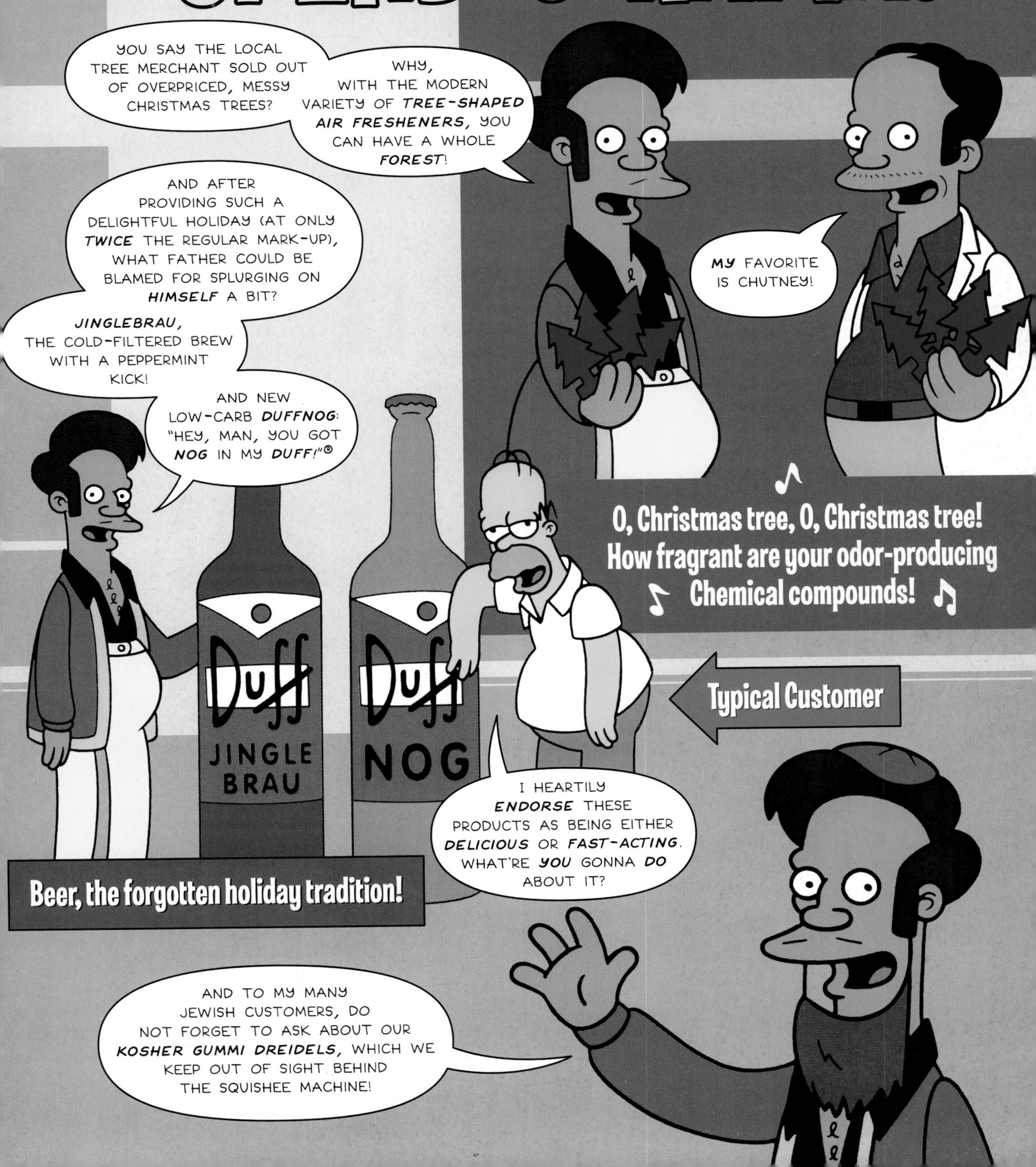

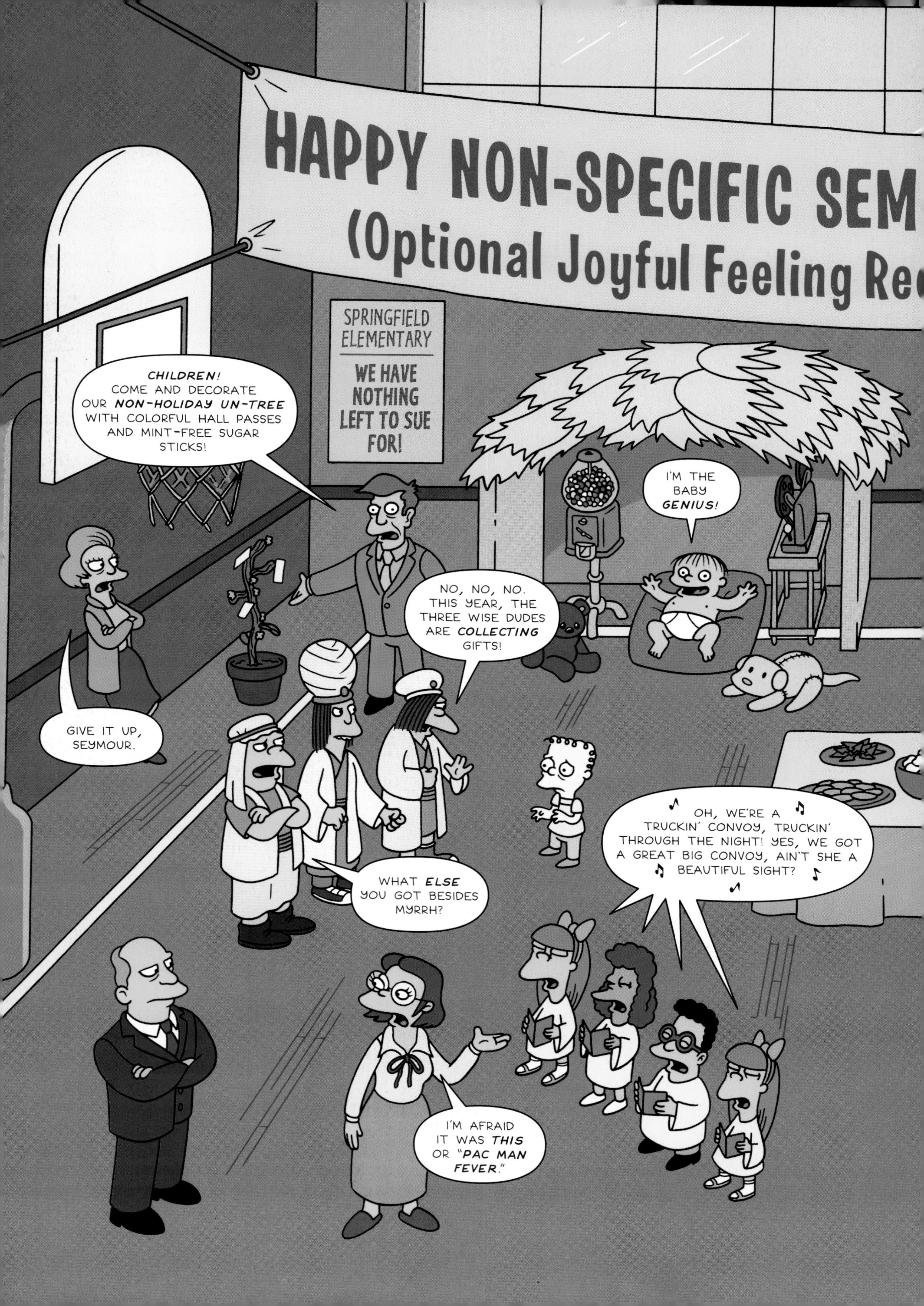
HAPPY NON-SPECIFIC SEM
(Optional Joyful Feeling Re
SPRINGFIELD ELEMENTARY
WE HAVE NOTHING LEFT TO SUE FOR!
CHILDREN! COME AND DECORATE OUR NON-HOLIDAY UN-TREE WITH COLORFUL HALL PASSES AND MINT-FREE SUGAR STICKS!
GIVE IT UP, SEYMOUR.
I'M THE BABY GENIUS!
NO, NO, NO. THIS YEAR, THE THREE WISE DUDES ARE COLLECTING GIFTS!
WHAT ELSE YOU GOT BESIDES MYRRH?
♪ OH, WE'RE A TRUCKIN' CONVOY, TRUCKIN' THROUGH THE NIGHT! YES, WE GOT A GREAT BIG CONVOY, AIN'T SHE A BEAUTIFUL SIGHT? ♪
I'M AFRAID IT WAS THIS OR "PAC MAN FEVER."

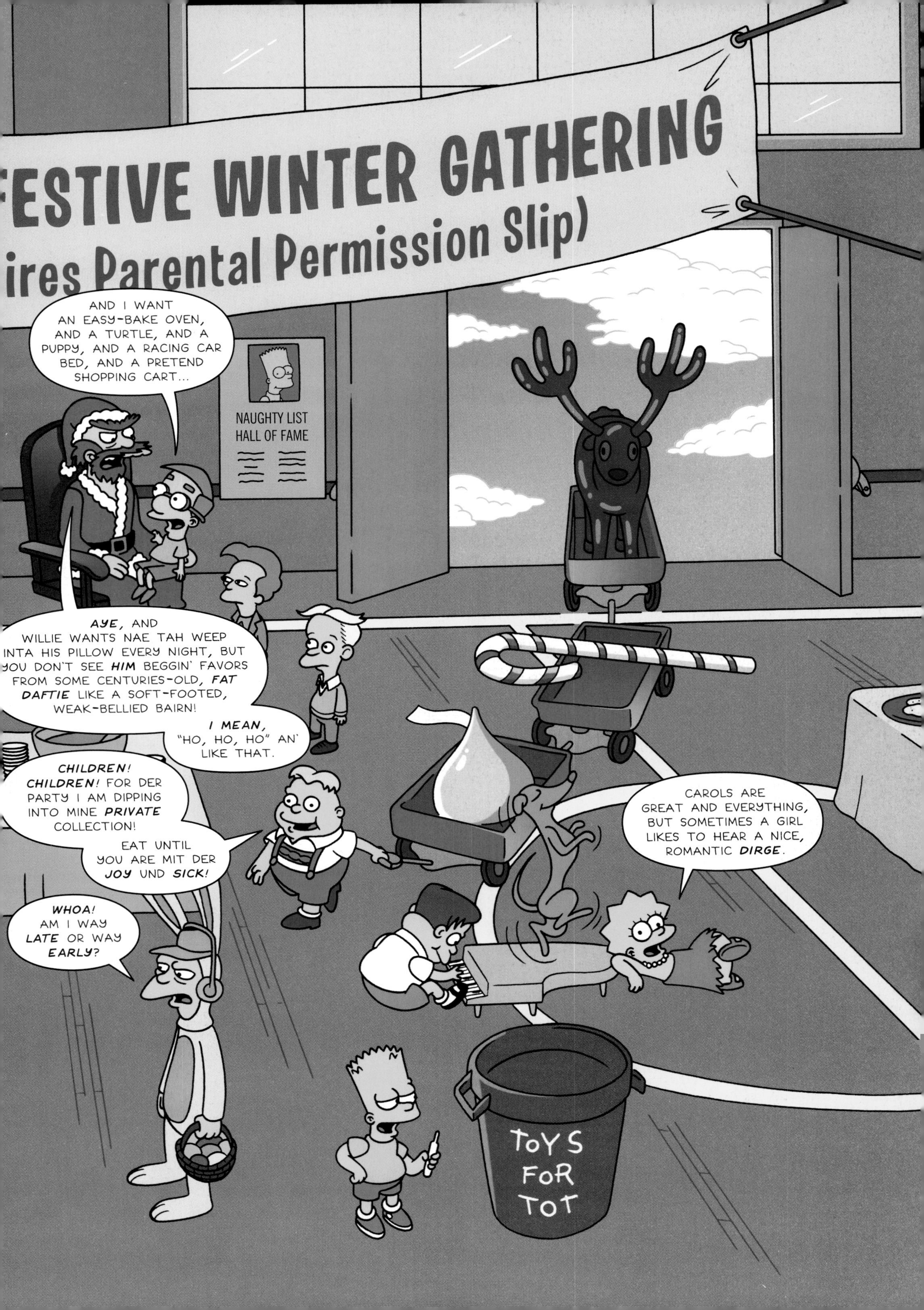
FESTIVE WINTER GATHERING
ires Parental Permission Slip)
AND I WANT AN EASY-BAKE OVEN, AND A TURTLE, AND A PUPPY, AND A RACING CAR BED, AND A PRETEND SHOPPING CART...
NAUGHTY LIST HALL OF FAME
AYE, AND WILLIE WANTS NAE TAH WEEP INTA HIS PILLOW EVERY NIGHT, BUT YOU DON'T SEE HIM BEGGIN' FAVORS FROM SOME CENTURIES-OLD, FAT DAFTIE LIKE A SOFT-FOOTED, WEAK-BELLIED BAIRN!
I MEAN, "HO, HO, HO" AN' LIKE THAT.
CHILDREN! CHILDREN! FOR DER PARTY I AM DIPPING INTO MINE PRIVATE COLLECTION!
EAT UNTIL YOU ARE MIT DER JOY UND SICK!
CAROLS ARE GREAT AND EVERYTHING, BUT SOMETIMES A GIRL LIKES TO HEAR A NICE, ROMANTIC DIRGE.
WHOA! AM I WAY LATE OR WAY EARLY?
TOYS FOR TOT

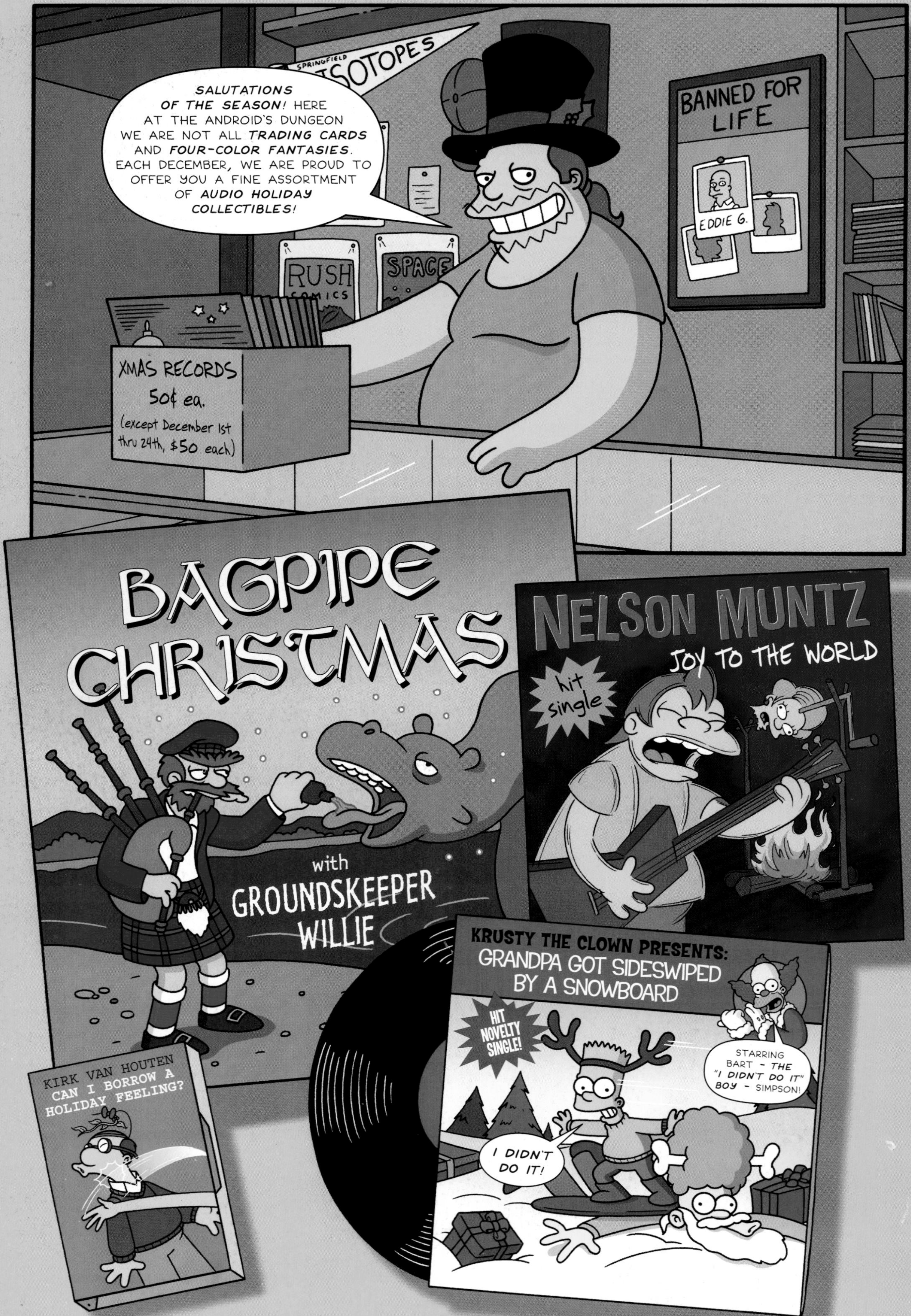

SPRINGFIELD ISOTOPES
SALUTATIONS OF THE SEASON! HERE AT THE ANDROID'S DUNGEON WE ARE NOT ALL TRADING CARDS AND FOUR-COLOR FANTASIES. EACH DECEMBER, WE ARE PROUD TO OFFER YOU A FINE ASSORTMENT OF AUDIO HOLIDAY COLLECTIBLES!
BANNED FOR LIFE
EDDIE G.
RUSH COMICS
SPACE
XMAS RECORDS 50¢ ea. (except December 1st thru 24th, $50 each)
BAGPIPE CHRISTMAS
with GROUNDSKEEPER WILLIE
NELSON MUNTZ
JOY TO THE WORLD
hit single
KRUSTY THE CLOWN PRESENTS:
GRANDPA GOT SIDESWIPED BY A SNOWBOARD
HIT NOVELTY SINGLE!
STARRING BART - THE "I DIDN'T DO IT" BOY - SIMPSON!
I DIDN'T DO IT!
KIRK VAN HOUTEN
CAN I BORROW A HOLIDAY FEELING?

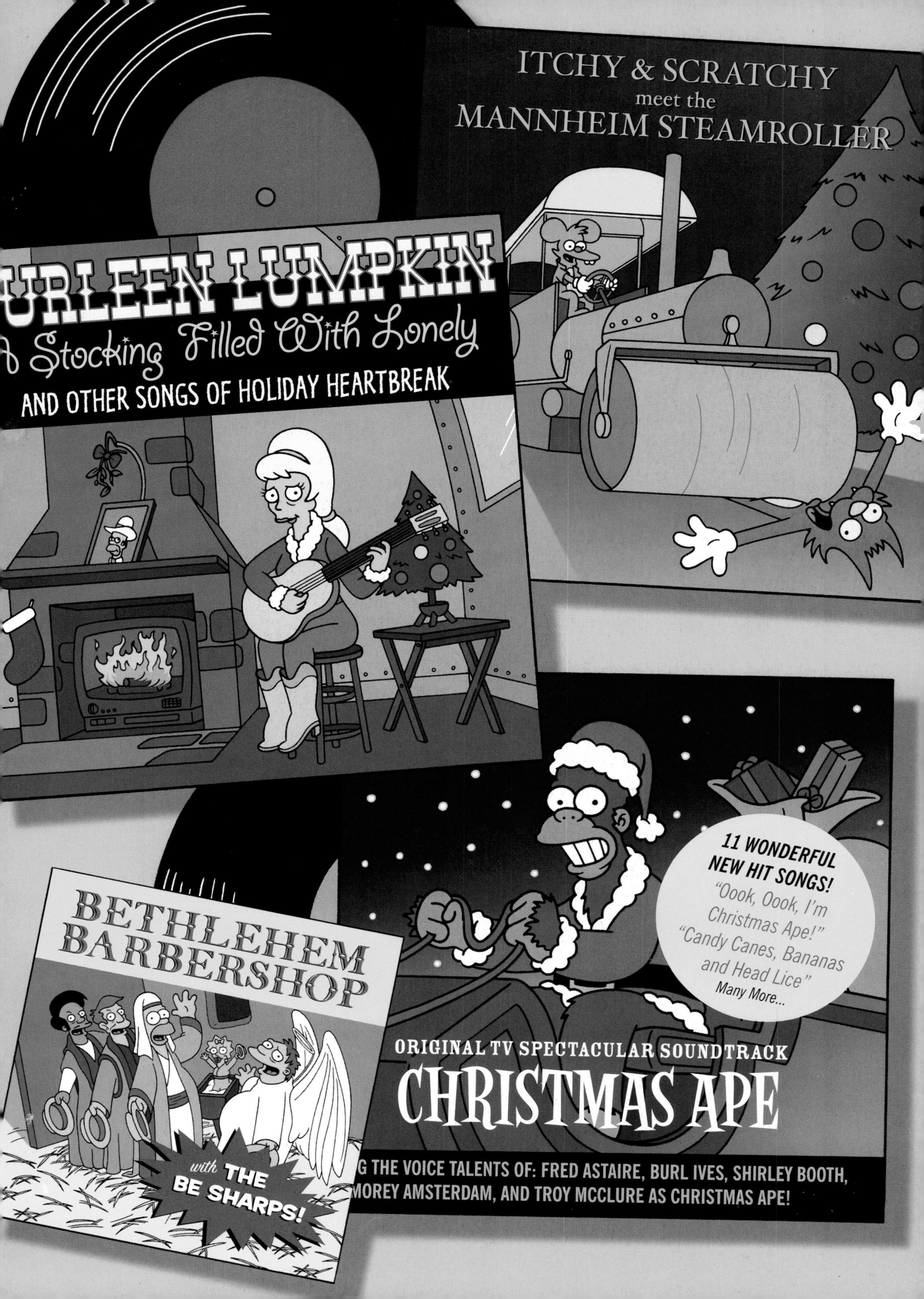
ITCHY & SCRATCHY
meet the
MANNHEIM STEAMROLLER
URLEEN LUMPKIN
Stocking Filled With Lonely
AND OTHER SONGS OF HOLIDAY HEARTBREAK
11 WONDERFUL
NEW HIT SONGS!
"Oook, Oook, I'm
Christmas Ape!"
"Candy Canes, Bananas
and Head Lice"
Many More...
ORIGINAL TV SPECTACULAR SOUNDTRACK
CHRISTMAS APE
G THE VOICE TALENTS OF: FRED ASTAIRE, BURL IVES, SHIRLEY BOOTH,
MOREY AMSTERDAM, AND TROY MCCLURE AS CHRISTMAS APE!
BETHLEHEM
BARBERSHOP
with THE
BE SHARPS!

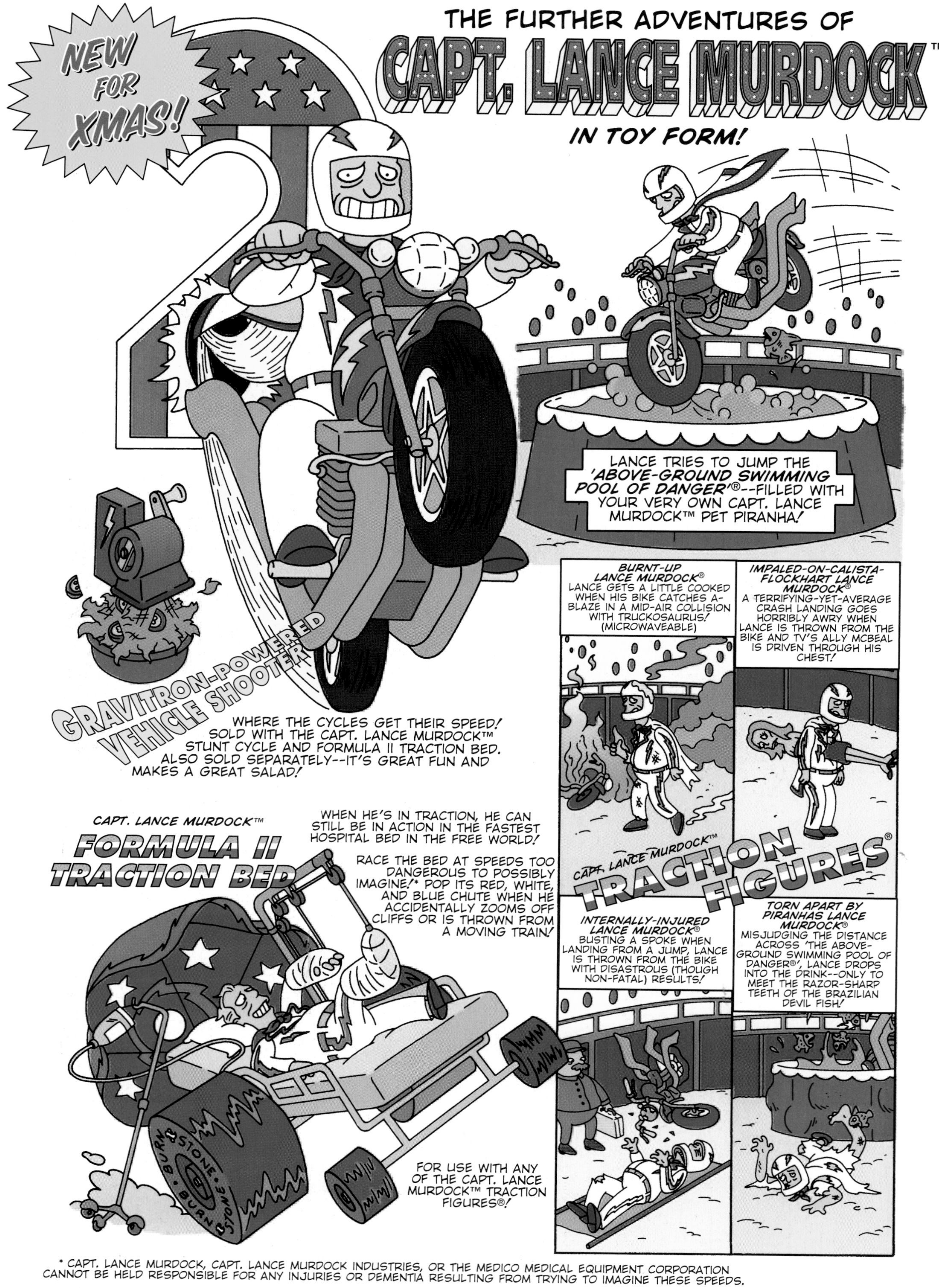

NEW FOR XMAS!
THE FURTHER ADVENTURES OF
CAPT. LANCE MURDOCK™
IN TOY FORM!
LANCE TRIES TO JUMP THE 'ABOVE-GROUND SWIMMING POOL OF DANGER'®--FILLED WITH YOUR VERY OWN CAPT. LANCE MURDOCK™ PET PIRANHA!
GRAVITRON-POWERED VEHICLE SHOOTER
WHERE THE CYCLES GET THEIR SPEED! SOLD WITH THE CAPT. LANCE MURDOCK™ STUNT CYCLE AND FORMULA II TRACTION BED. ALSO SOLD SEPARATELY--IT'S GREAT FUN AND MAKES A GREAT SALAD!
CAPT. LANCE MURDOCK™
FORMULA II TRACTION BED
WHEN HE'S IN TRACTION, HE CAN STILL BE IN ACTION IN THE FASTEST HOSPITAL BED IN THE FREE WORLD!
RACE THE BED AT SPEEDS TOO DANGEROUS TO POSSIBLY IMAGINE!* POP ITS RED, WHITE, AND BLUE CHUTE WHEN HE ACCIDENTALLY ZOOMS OFF CLIFFS OR IS THROWN FROM A MOVING TRAIN!
BURN STONE
FOR USE WITH ANY OF THE CAPT. LANCE MURDOCK™ TRACTION FIGURES®!
BURNT-UP LANCE MURDOCK®
LANCE GETS A LITTLE COOKED WHEN HIS BIKE CATCHES A-BLAZE IN A MID-AIR COLLISION WITH TRUCKOSAURUS! (MICROWAVEABLE)
IMPALED-ON-CALISTA-FLOCKHART LANCE MURDOCK®
A TERRIFYING-YET-AVERAGE CRASH LANDING GOES HORRIBLY AWRY WHEN LANCE IS THROWN FROM THE BIKE AND TV'S ALLY MCBEAL IS DRIVEN THROUGH HIS CHEST!
CAPT. LANCE MURDOCK™
TRACTION FIGURES®
INTERNALLY-INJURED LANCE MURDOCK®
BUSTING A SPOKE WHEN LANDING FROM A JUMP, LANCE IS THROWN FROM THE BIKE WITH DISASTROUS (THOUGH NON-FATAL) RESULTS!
TORN APART BY PIRANHAS LANCE MURDOCK®
MISJUDGING THE DISTANCE ACROSS 'THE ABOVE-GROUND SWIMMING POOL OF DANGER®', LANCE DROPS INTO THE DRINK--ONLY TO MEET THE RAZOR-SHARP TEETH OF THE BRAZILIAN DEVIL FISH!

* CAPT. LANCE MURDOCK, CAPT. LANCE MURDOCK INDUSTRIES, OR THE MEDICO MEDICAL EQUIPMENT CORPORATION CANNOT BE HELD RESPONSIBLE FOR ANY INJURIES OR DEMENTIA RESULTING FROM TRYING TO IMAGINE THESE SPEEDS.

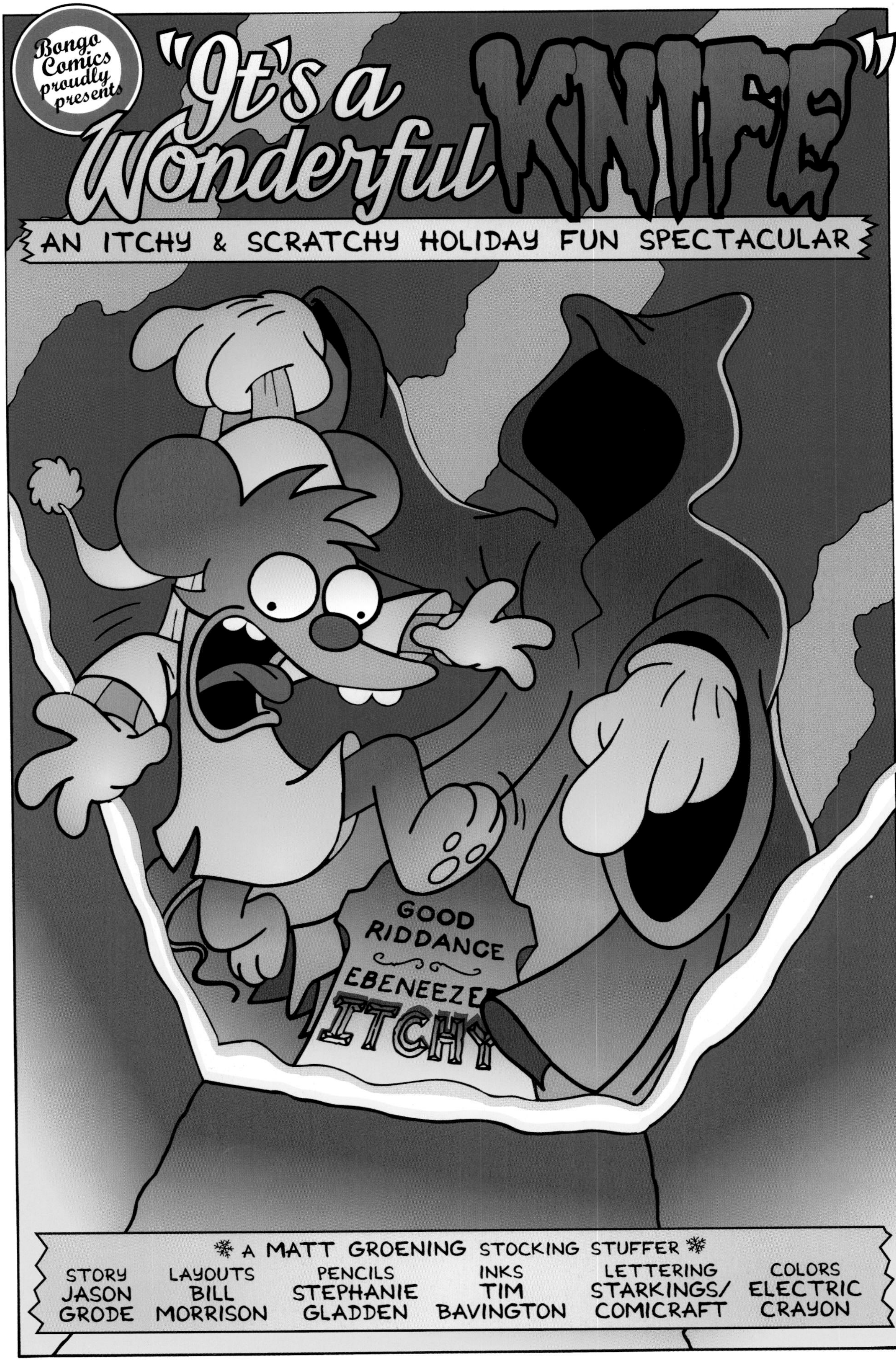

Bongo Comics proudly presents
"It's a Wonderful KNIFE"
AN ITCHY & SCRATCHY HOLIDAY FUN SPECTACULAR
GOOD RIDDANCE
EBENEEZER ITCHY
A MATT GROENING STOCKING STUFFER
STORY JASON GRODE
LAYOUTS BILL MORRISON
PENCILS STEPHANIE GLADDEN
INKS TIM BAVINGTON
LETTERING STARKINGS/ COMICRAFT
COLORS ELECTRIC CRAYON

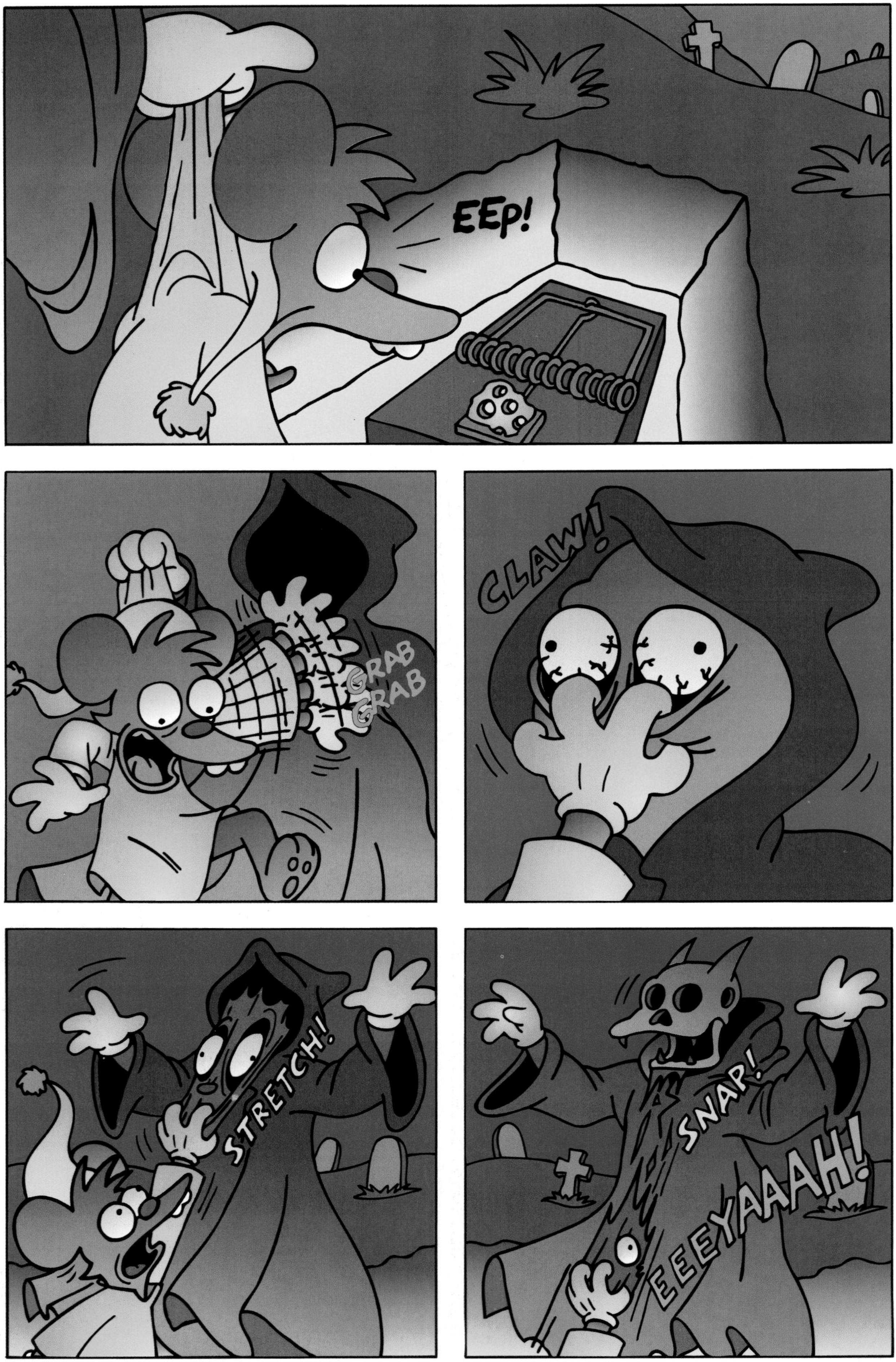
EEp!
GRAB
GRAB
CLAW!
STRETCH!
SNAP!
EEEYAAAH!

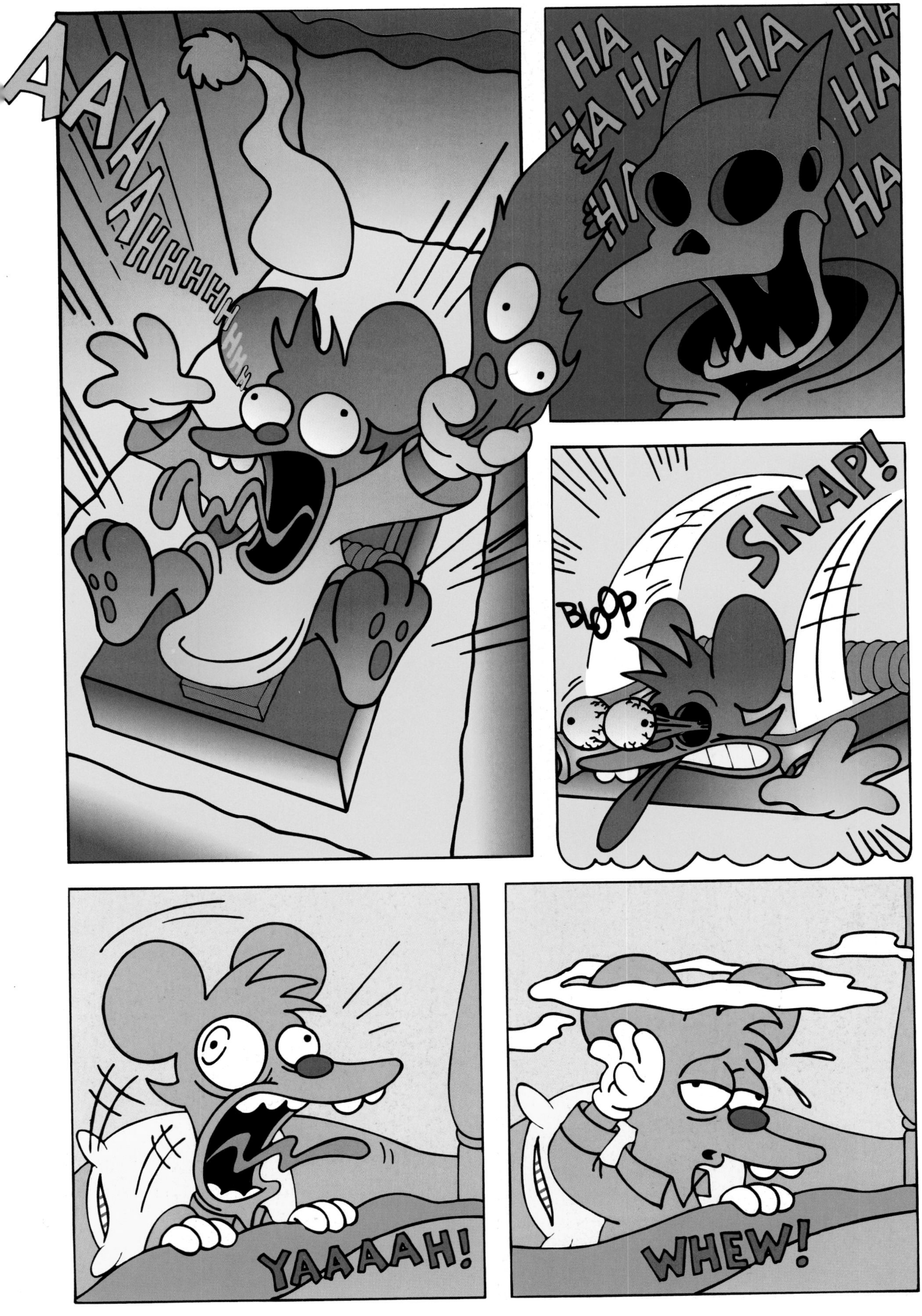

AAAAAHHHHHHHHHH
HA HA HA HA HA HA HA HA HA
SNAP!
BLOOP
YAAAAH!
WHEW!

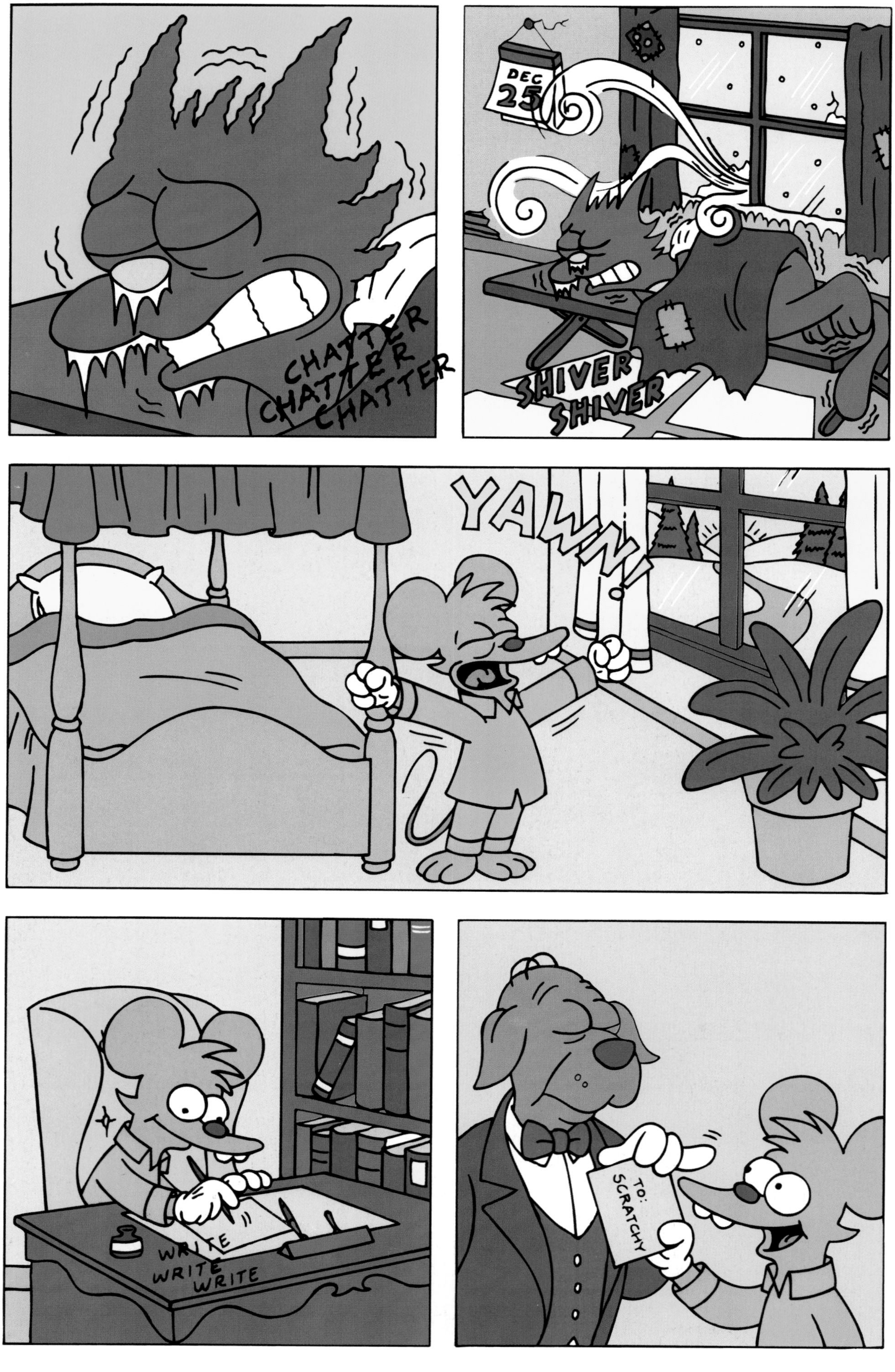
CHATTER
CHATTER
CHATTER
DEC 25
SHIVER
SHIVER
YAWN!
WRITE
WRITE
WRITE
TO:
SCRATCHY

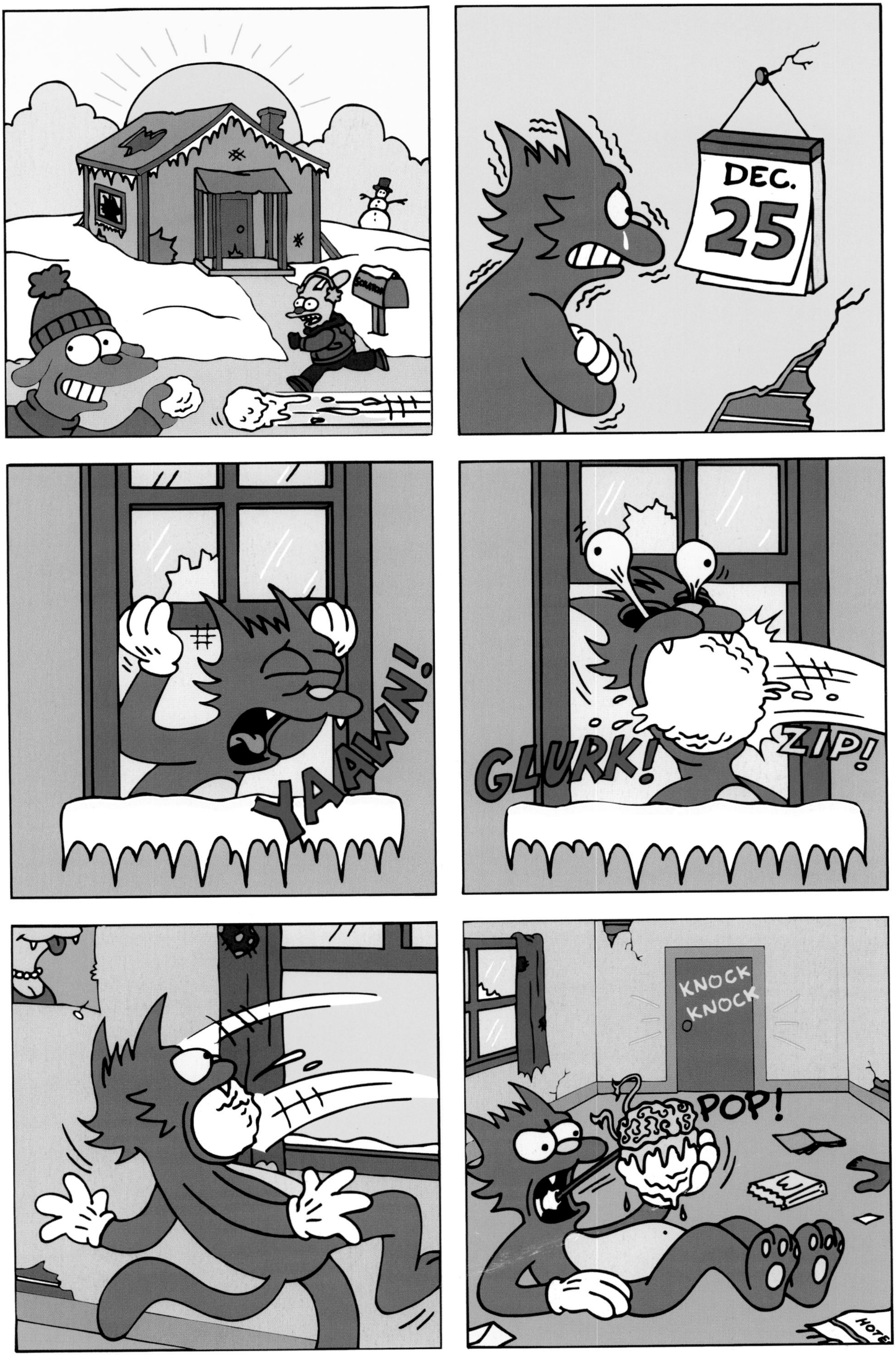
DEC.
25
YAAWN!
GLURK!
ZIP!
KNOCK
KNOCK
POP!

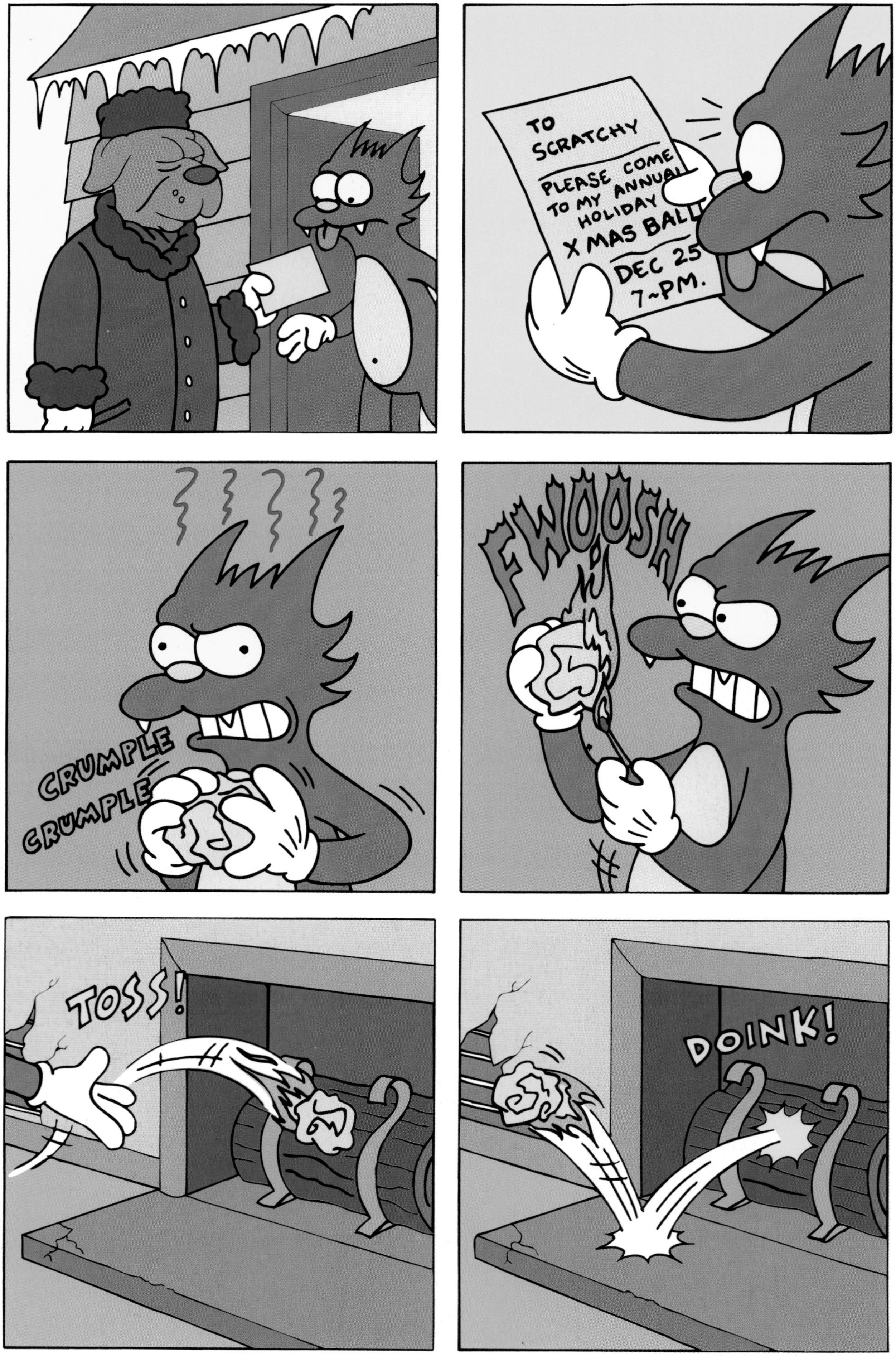
TO SCRATCHY
PLEASE COME TO MY ANNUAL HOLIDAY
XMAS BALL
DEC 25 7~PM.
CRUMPLE
CRUMPLE
FWOOSH
TOSS!
DOINK!

ZIP!

FWOOOOOSH!

YAAAAAAHH!

PAT PAT PAT PAT PAT PAT PAT PAT

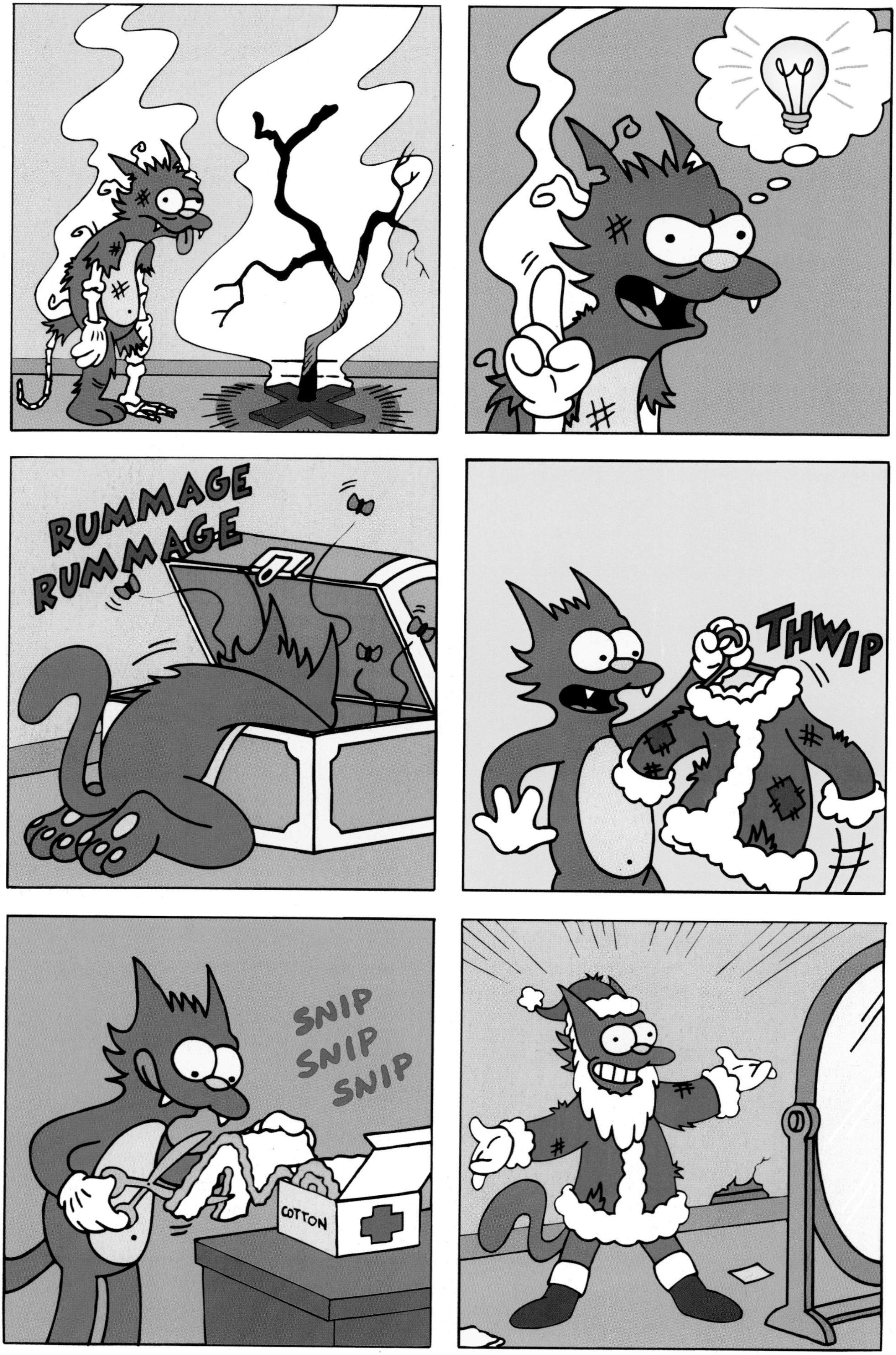
RUMMAGE
RUMMAGE
THWIP
SNIP
SNIP
SNIP
COTTON

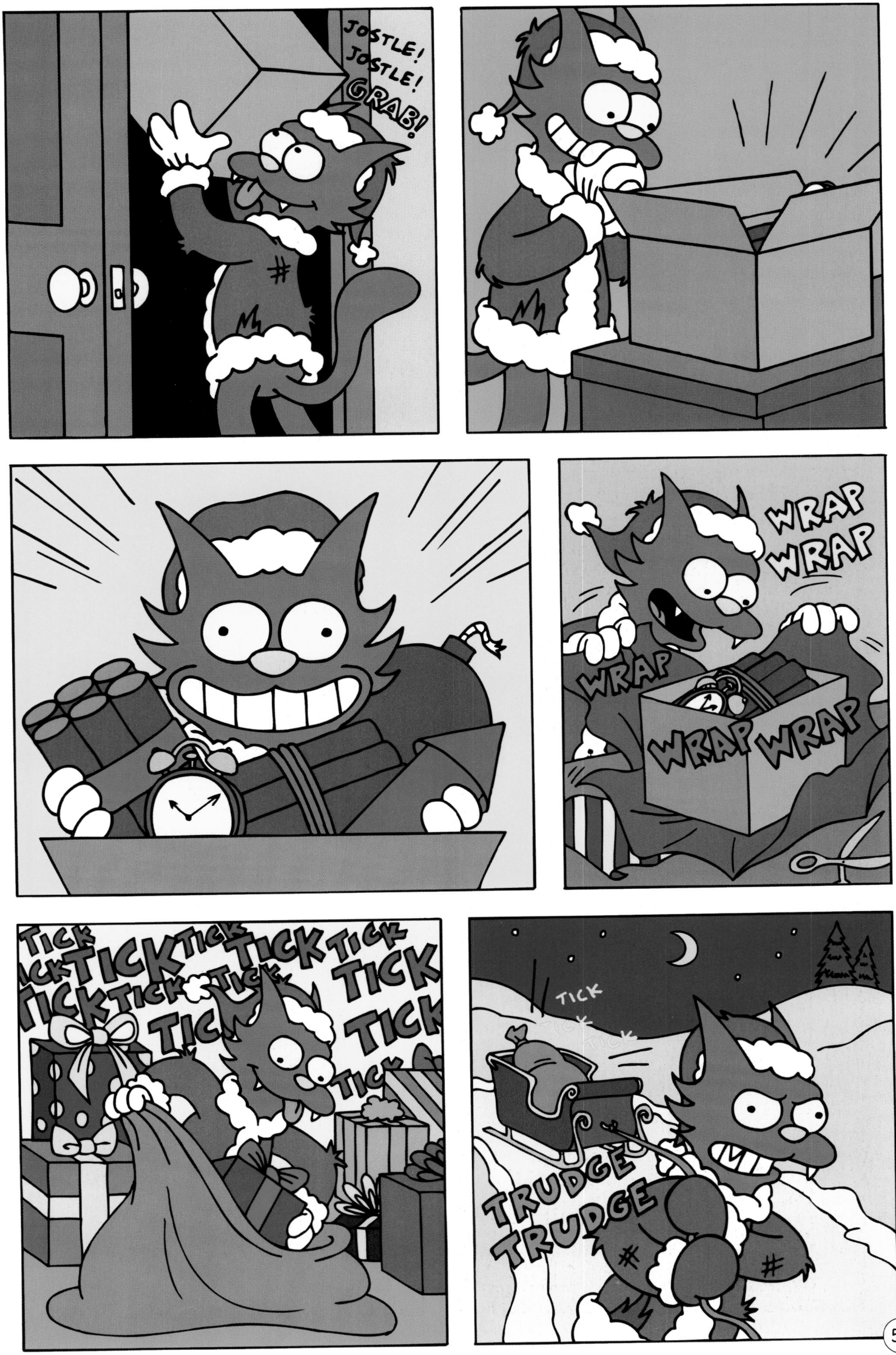
JOSTLE! JOSTLE!
GRAB!
WRAP WRAP
WRAP
WRAP WRAP
TICK TICK TICK TICK TICK TICK TICK TICK TICK TICK TICK TICK
TICK TICK TICK
TRUDGE TRUDGE

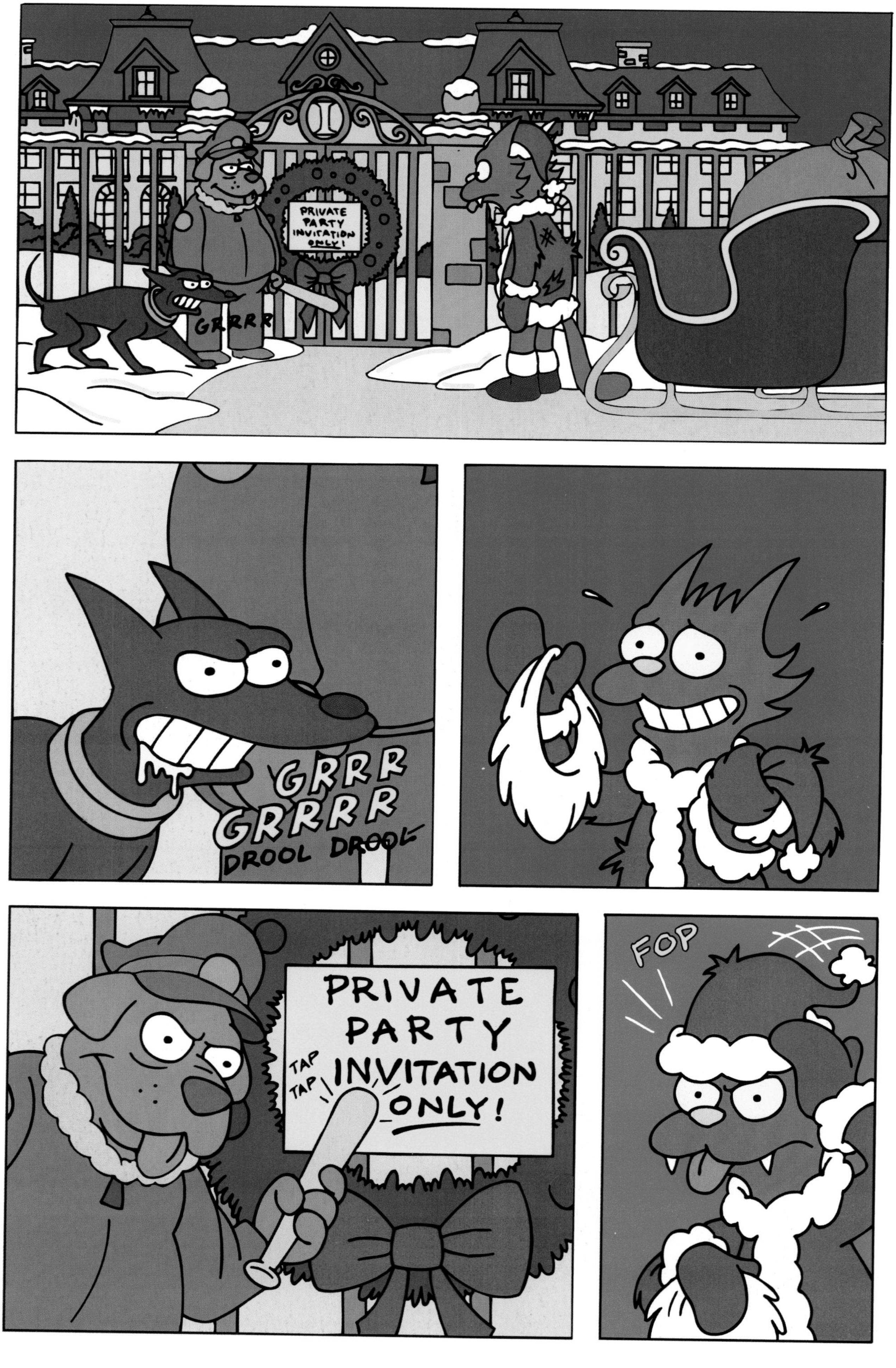
PRIVATE PARTY INVITATION ONLY!
GRRRR
GRRR
GRRRR
DROOL DROOL
TAP
TAP
PRIVATE PARTY INVITATION ONLY!
FOP

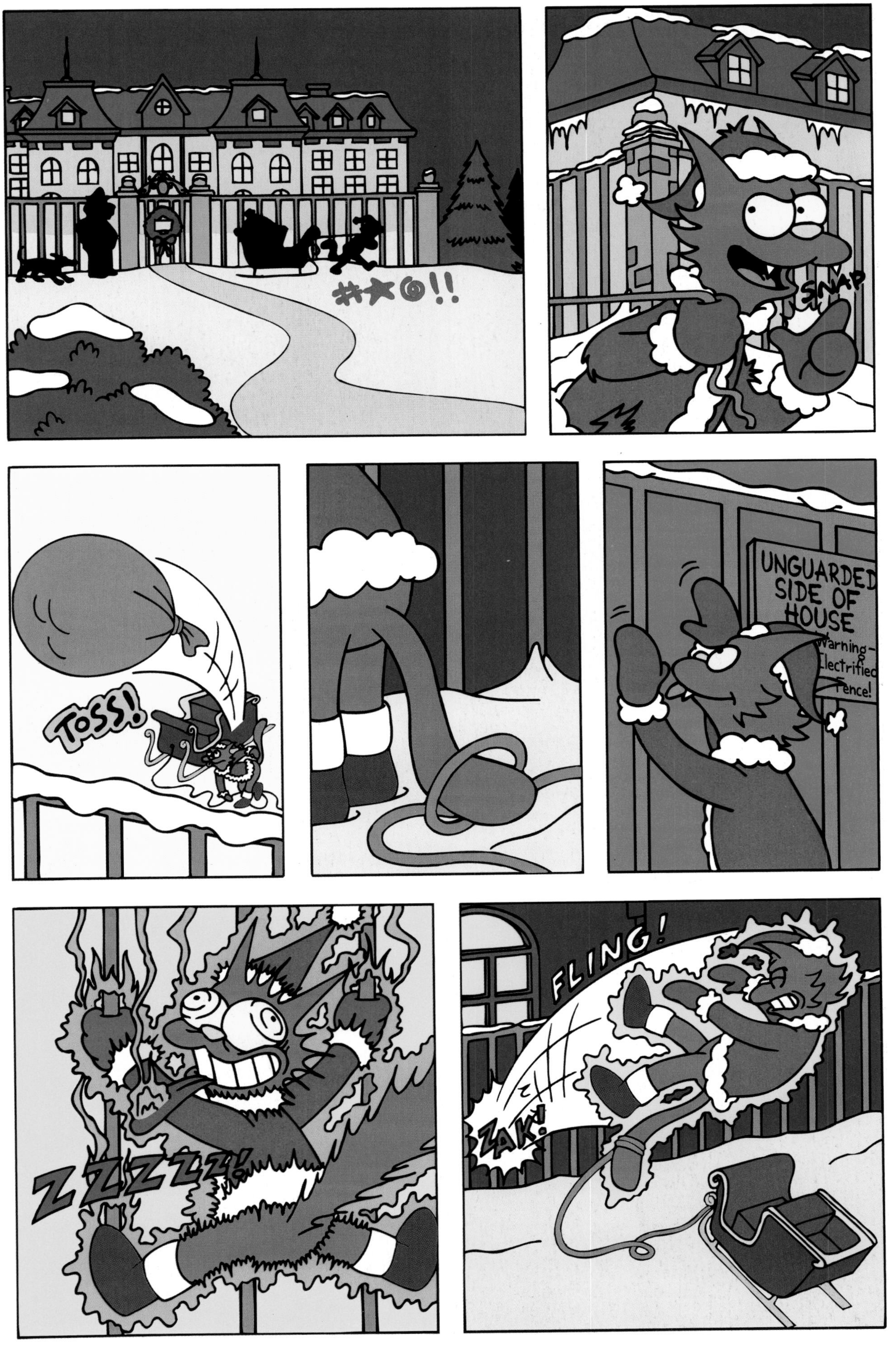

#★@!!
SNAP
TOSS!
UNGUARDED SIDE OF HOUSE
Warning- Electrified Fence!
ZZZZZZ!
FLING!
ZAK!

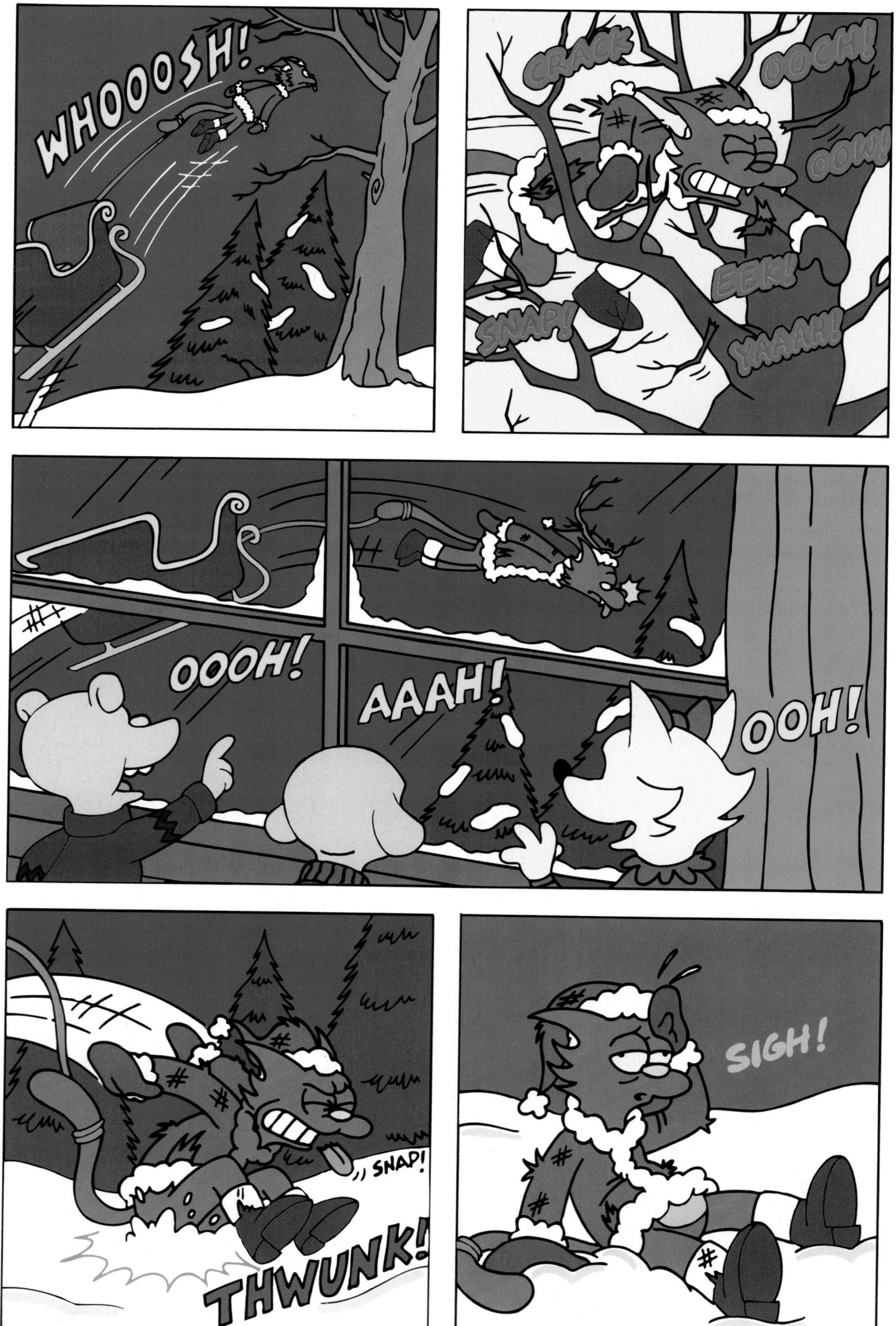
WHOOOSH!
CRACK
OOCH!
OOW!
EEK!
SNAP!
YAAAH!
OOOH!
AAAH!
OOH!
SNAP!
THWUNK!
SIGH!

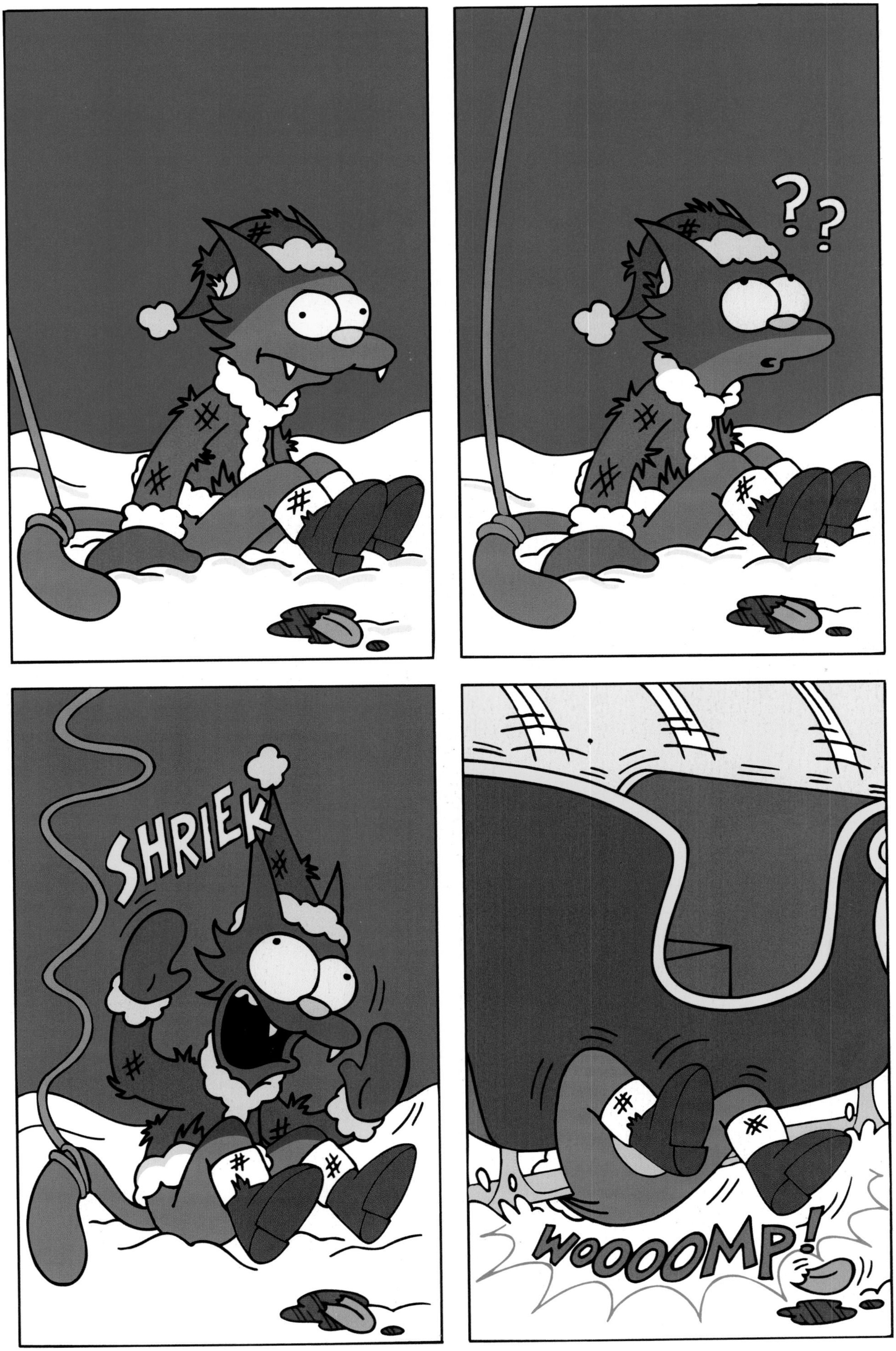
??
SHRIEK
WOOOOOMP!

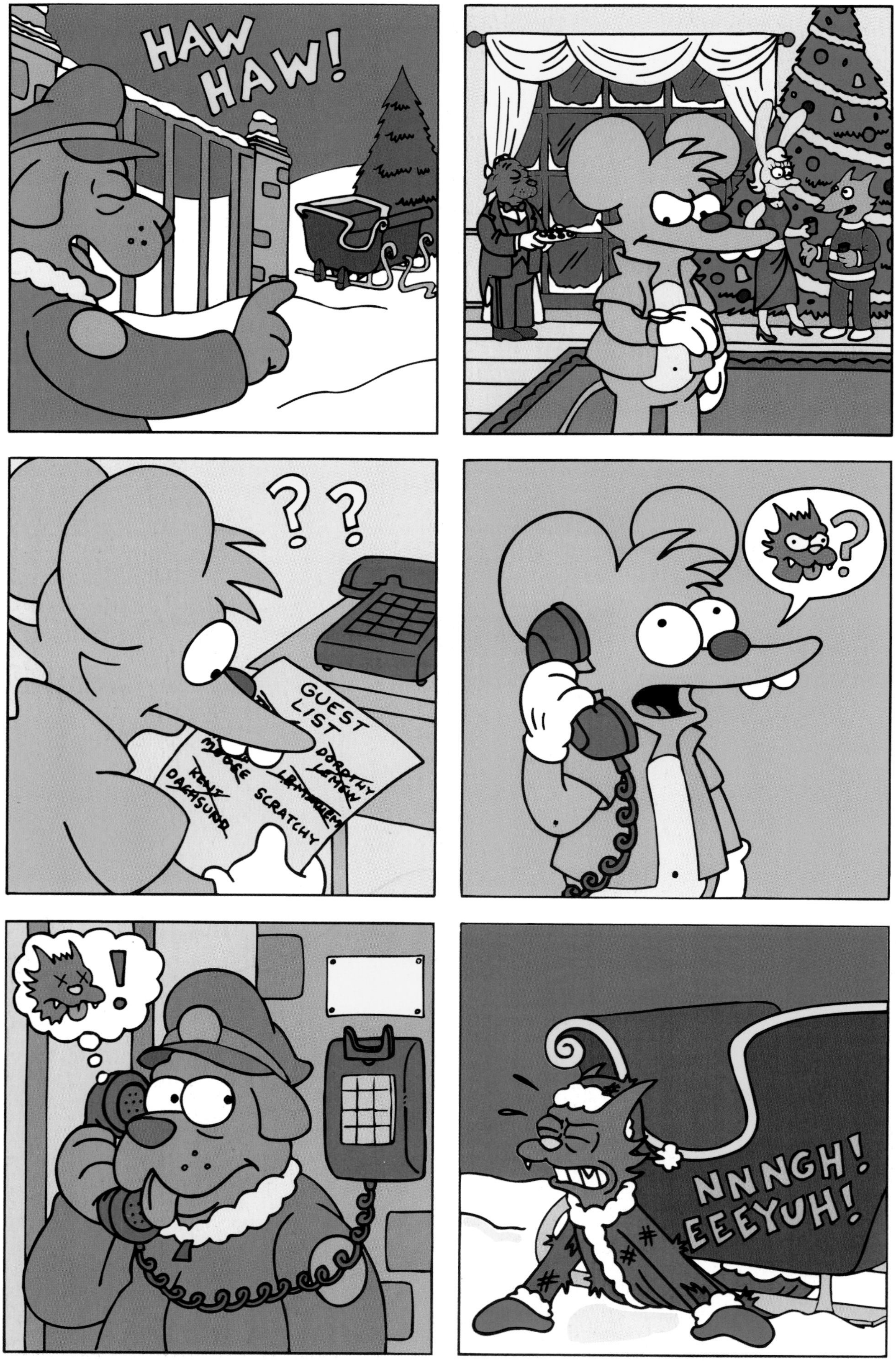
HAW HAW!
??
GUEST LIST
SCRATCHY
?
!
NNNGH! EEEYUH!

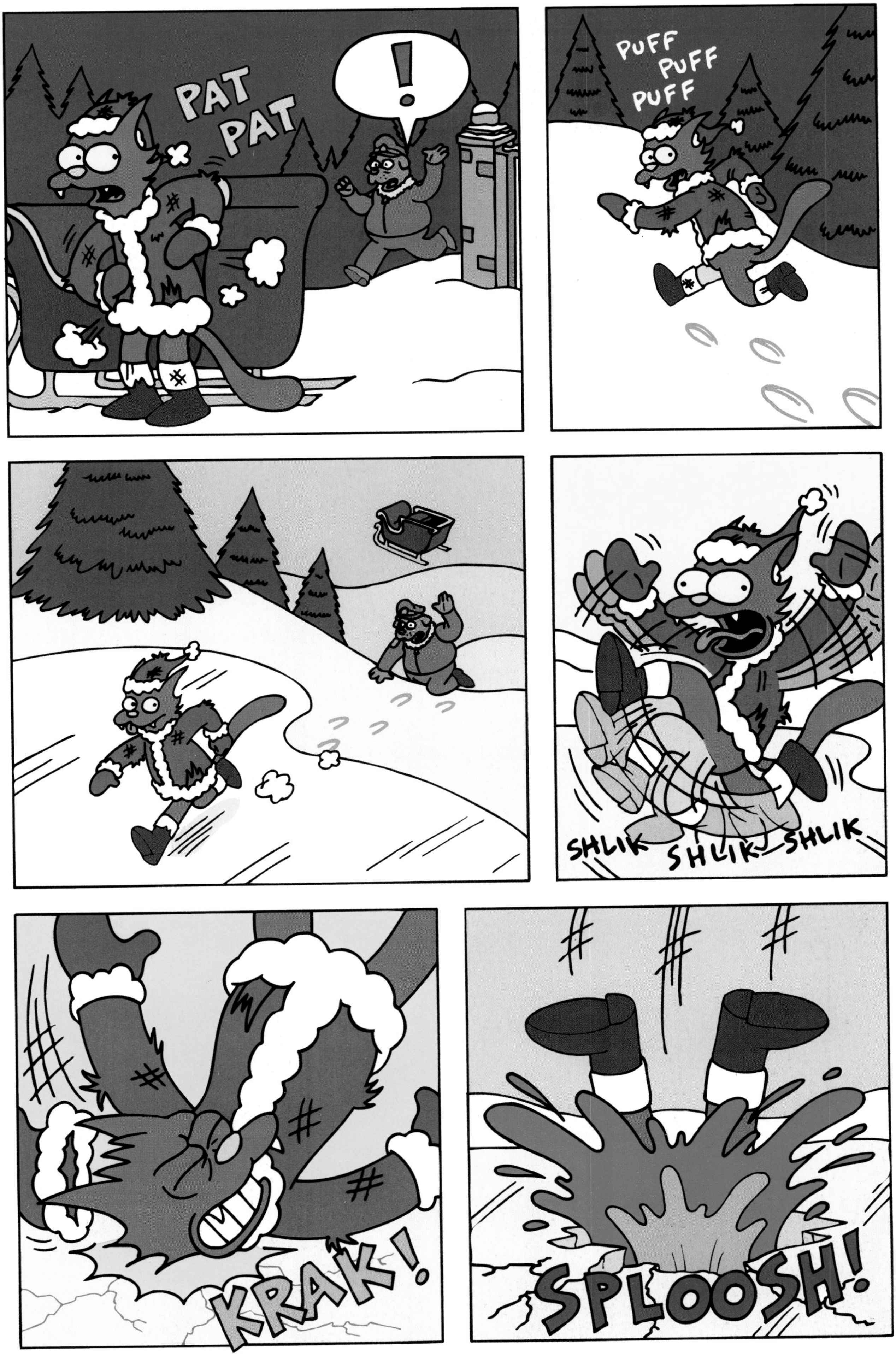
PAT
PAT
!
PUFF
PUFF
PUFF
SHLIK SHLIK SHLIK
KRAK!
SPLOOSH!

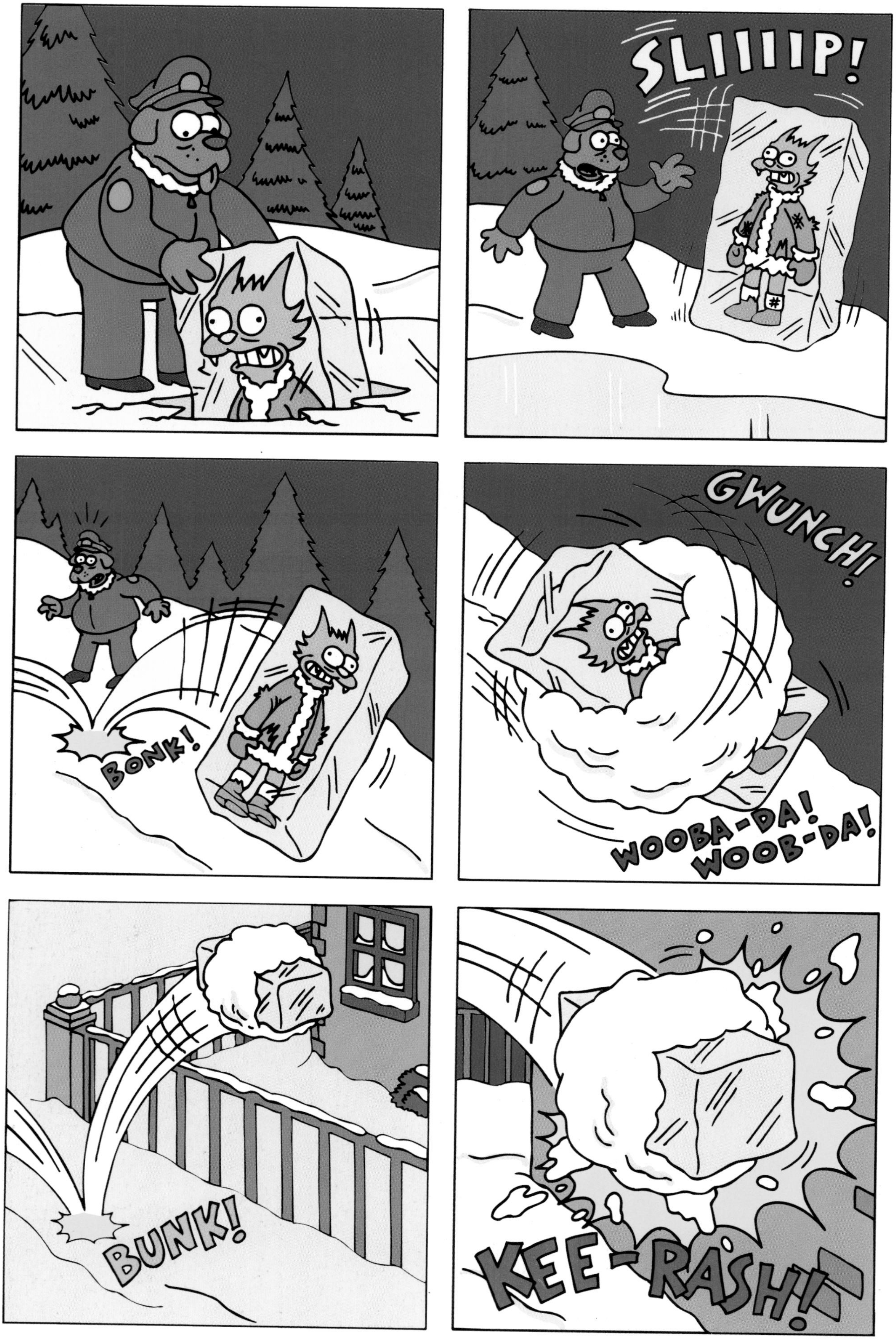
SLIIIIP!
BONK!
GWUNCH!
WOOBA-DA! WOOB-DA!
BUNK!
KEE-RASH!

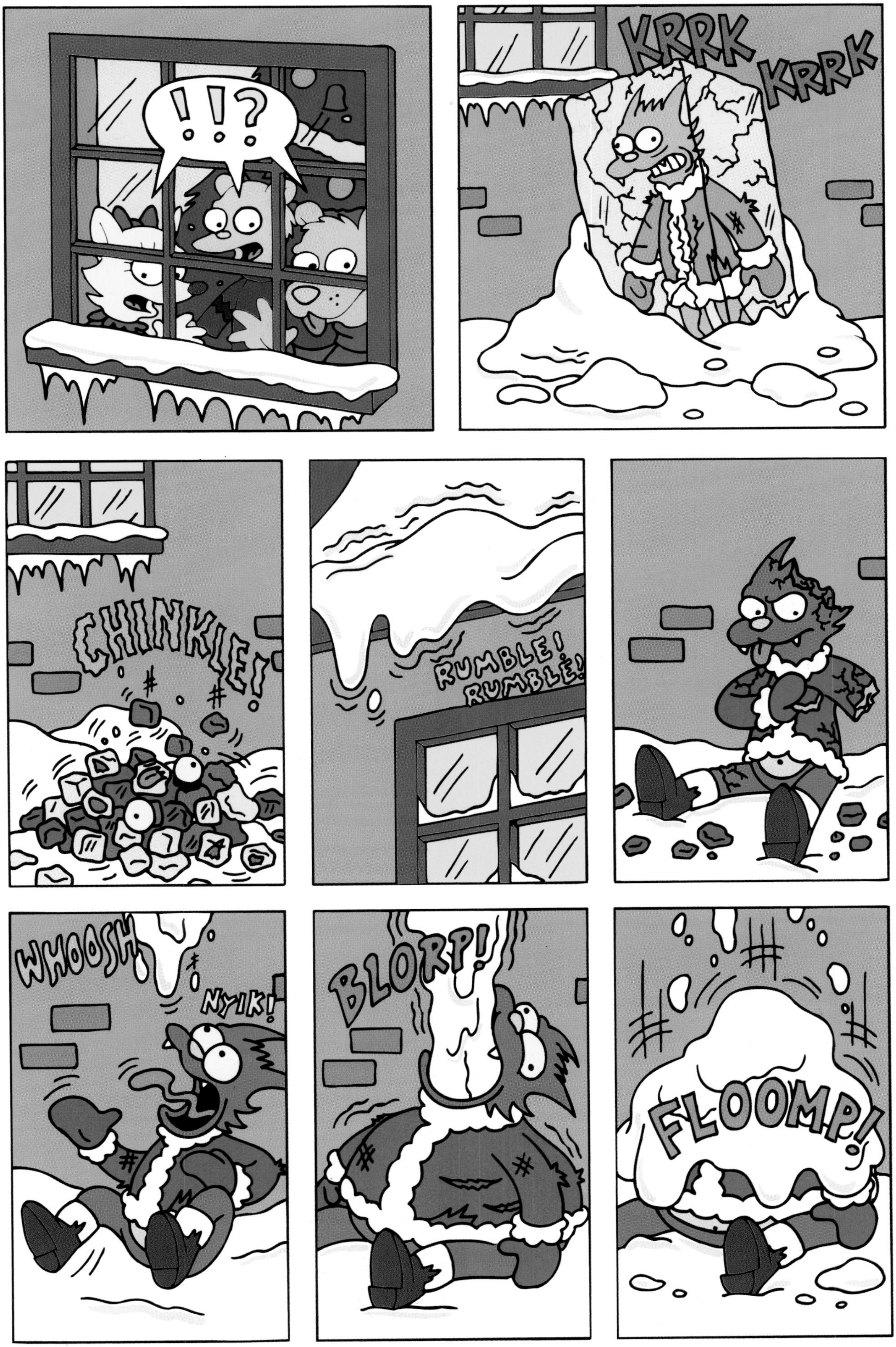
!!?
KRRK KRRK
CHINKLE!
RUMBLE! RUMBLE!
WHOOSH
NYIK!
BLORP!
FLOOMP!

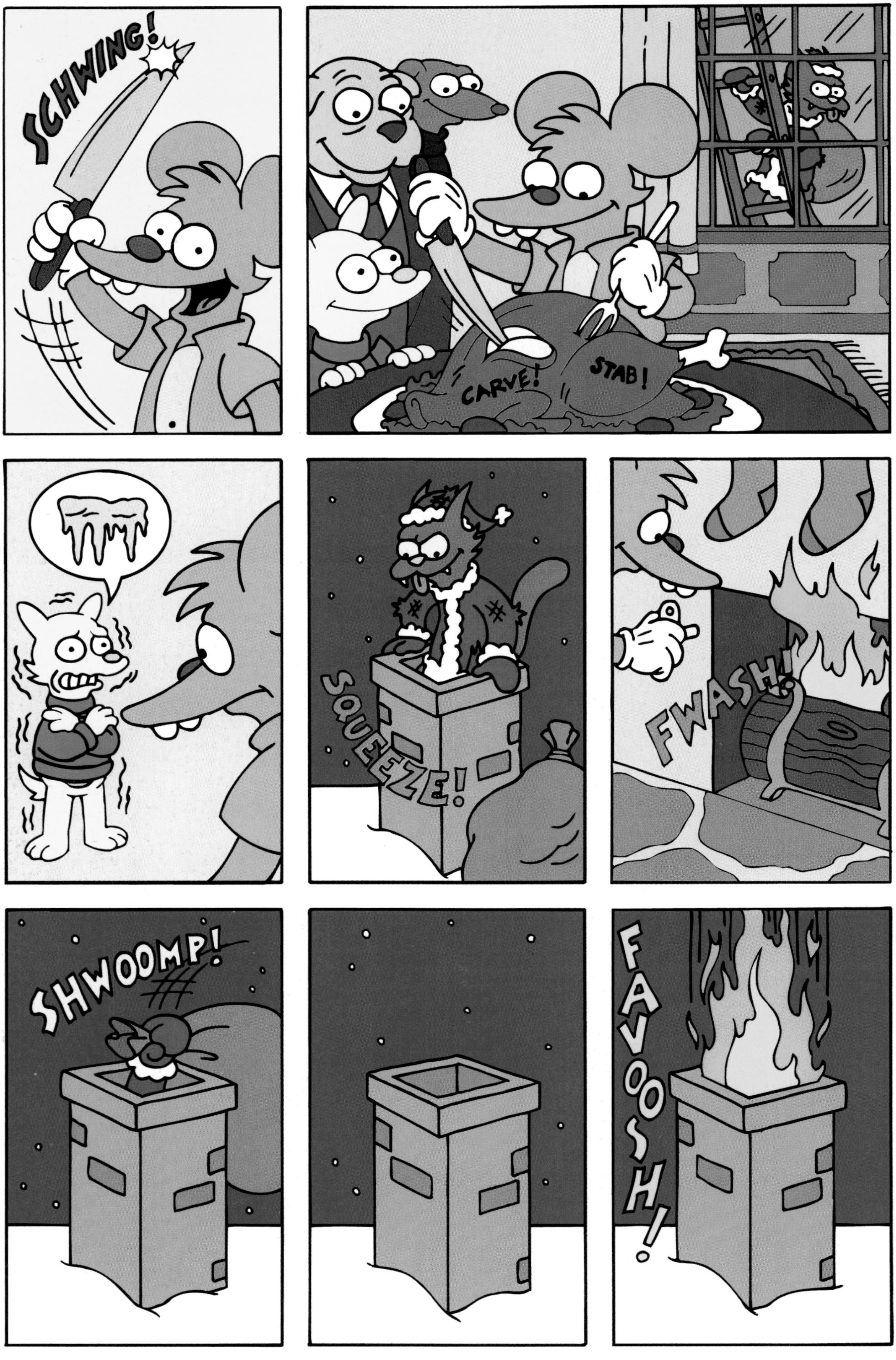
SCHWING!
CARVE!
STAB!
SQUEEEZE!
FWASH!
SHWOOMP!
FAVOOSH!

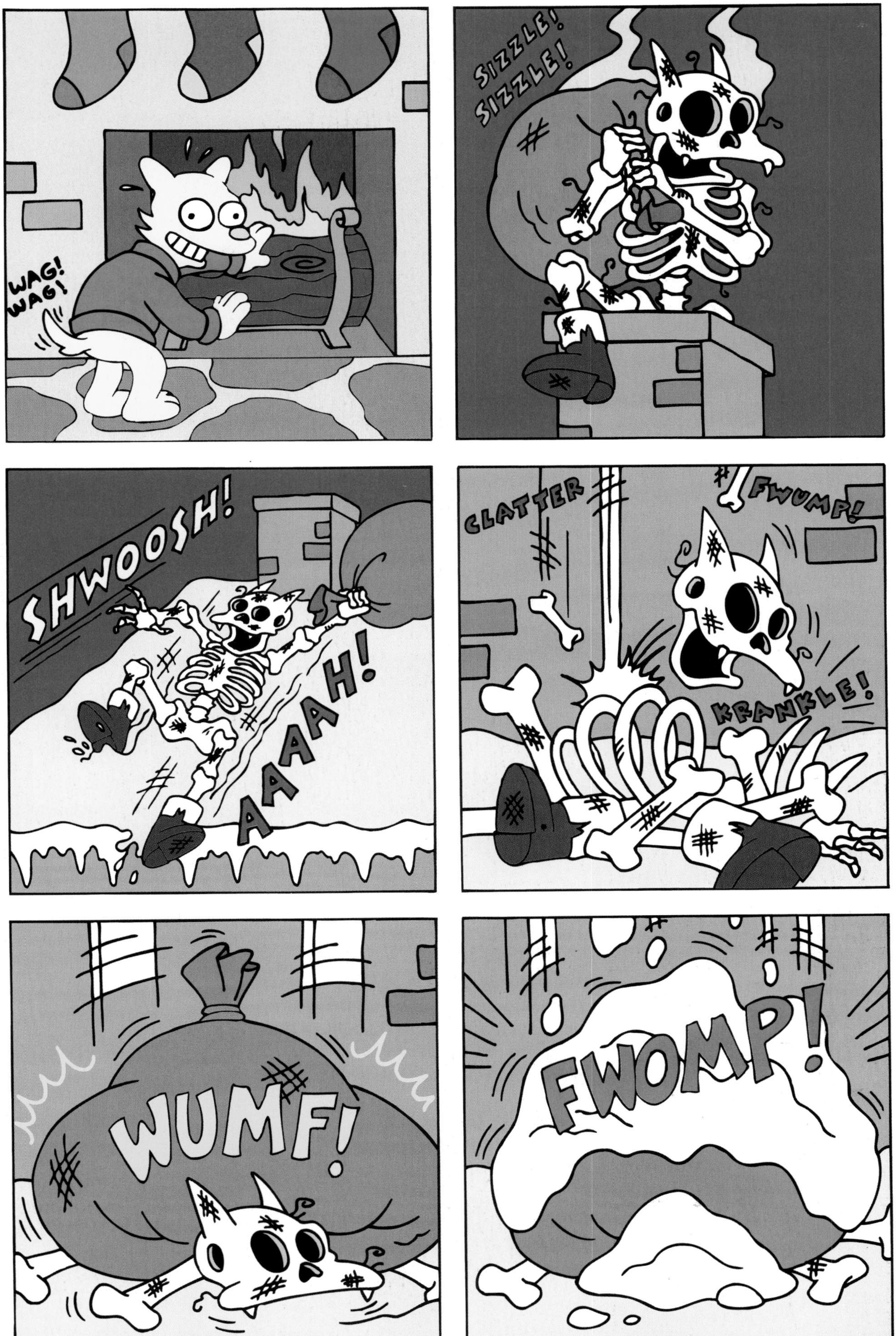

WAG!
WAG!
SIZZLE!
SIZZLE!
SHWOOSH!
AAAAH!
CLATTER
FWUMP!
KRANKLE!
WUMF!
FWOMP!

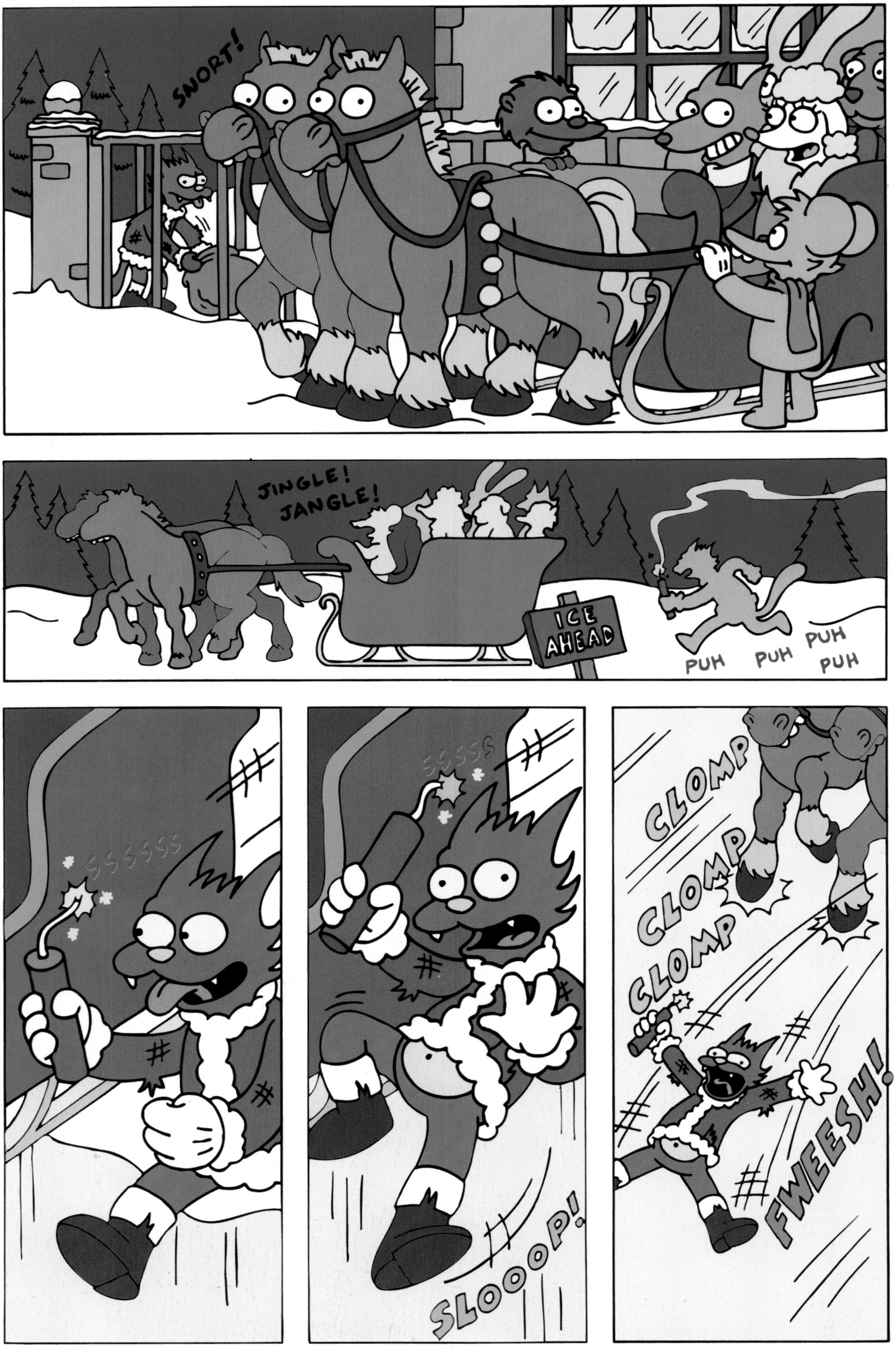
SNORT!
JINGLE! JANGLE!
ICE AHEAD
PUH PUH PUH PUH
SSSSSS
SSSSS
SLOOOP!
CLOMP
CLOMP
CLOMP
CLOMP
FWEESH!

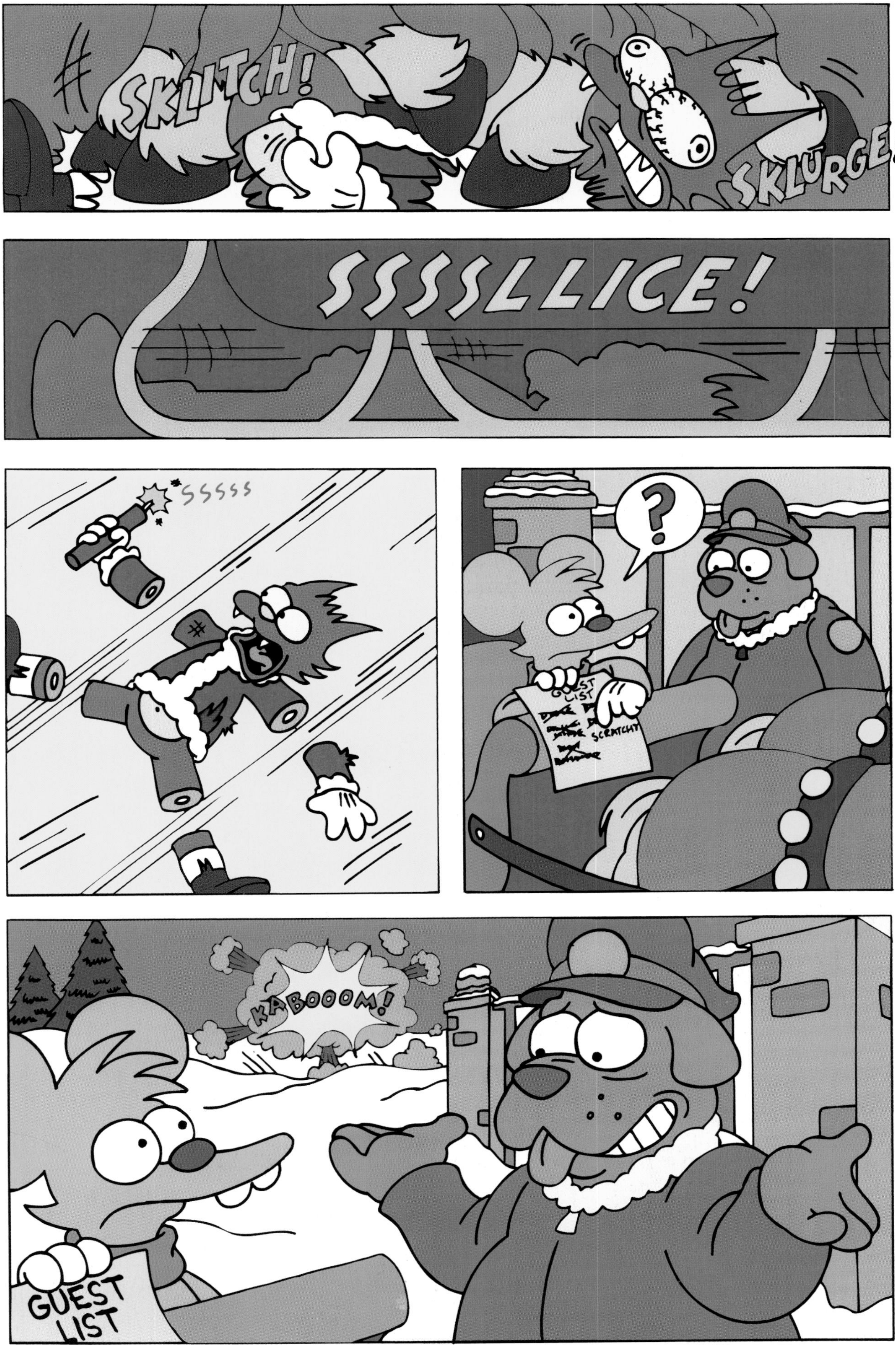
SKLITCH!
SKLURGE!
SSSSLLICE!
SSSSS
?
GUEST LIST
SCRATCHY
KABOOOM!
GUEST LIST

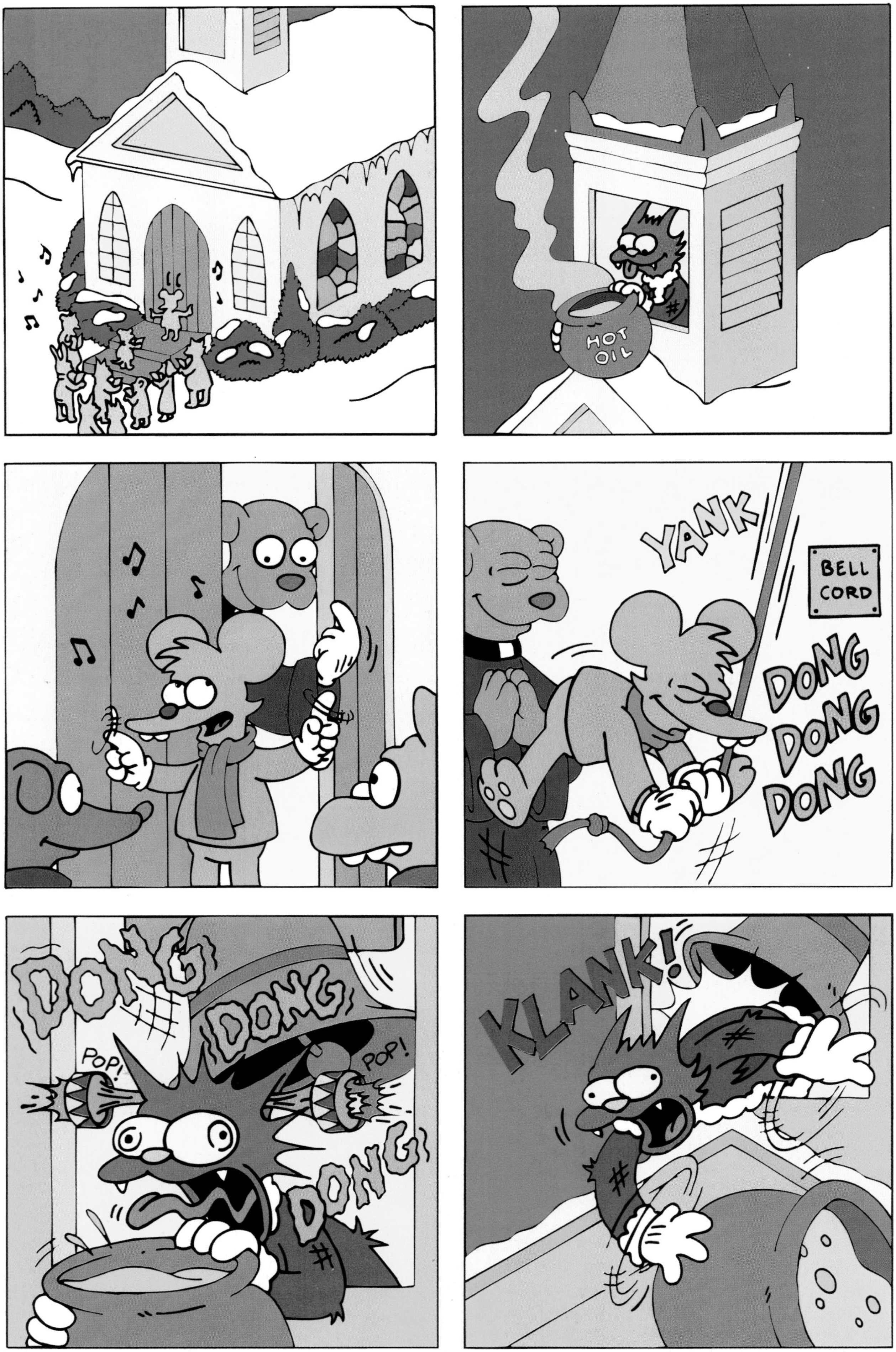
HOT OIL
YANK
BELL CORD
DONG
DONG
DONG
DONG
DONG
POP!
POP!
DONG
DONG
KLANK!

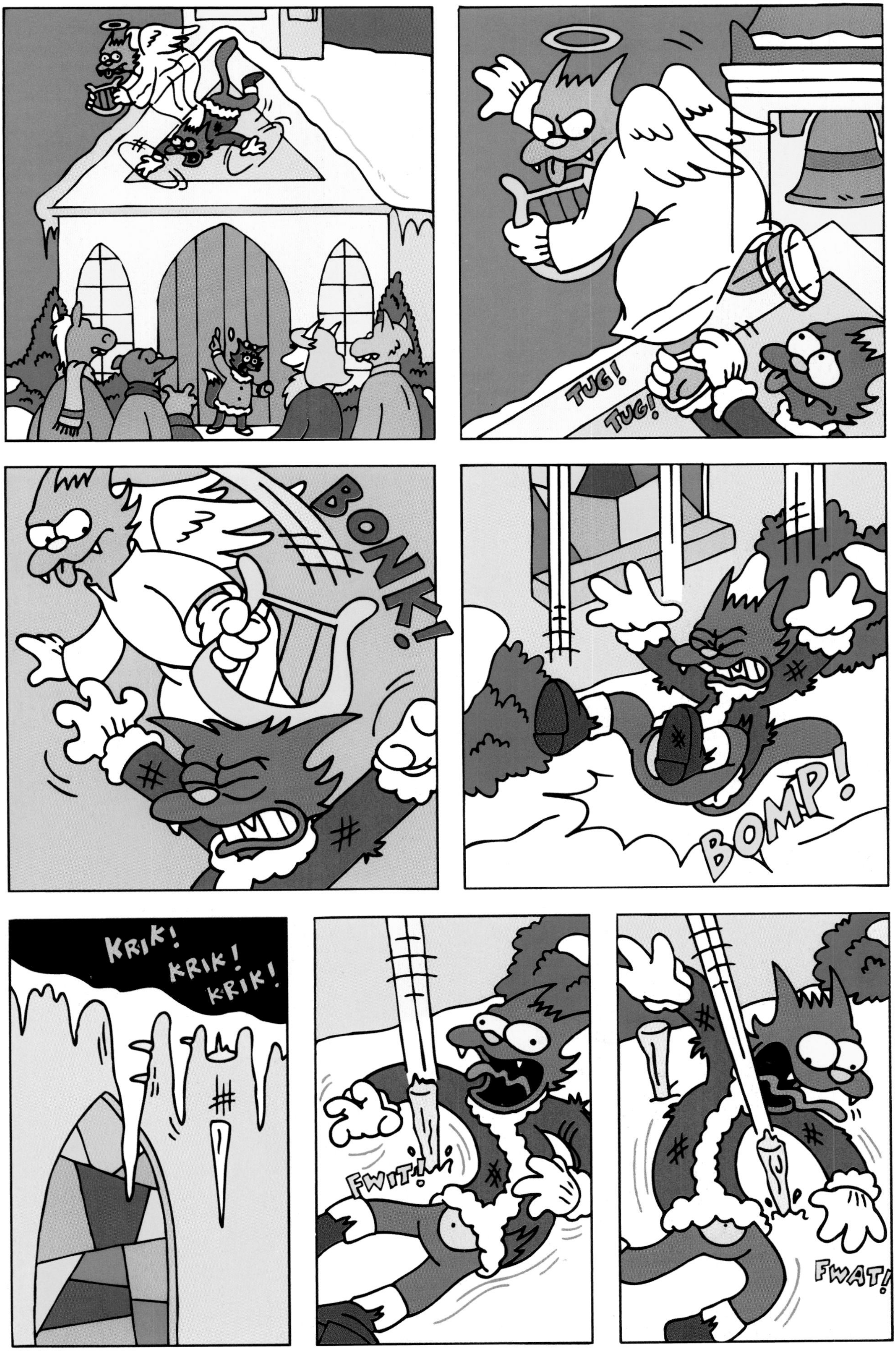
TUG!
TUG!
BONK!
BOMP!
KRIK!
KRIK!
KRIK!
FWIT!
FWAT!

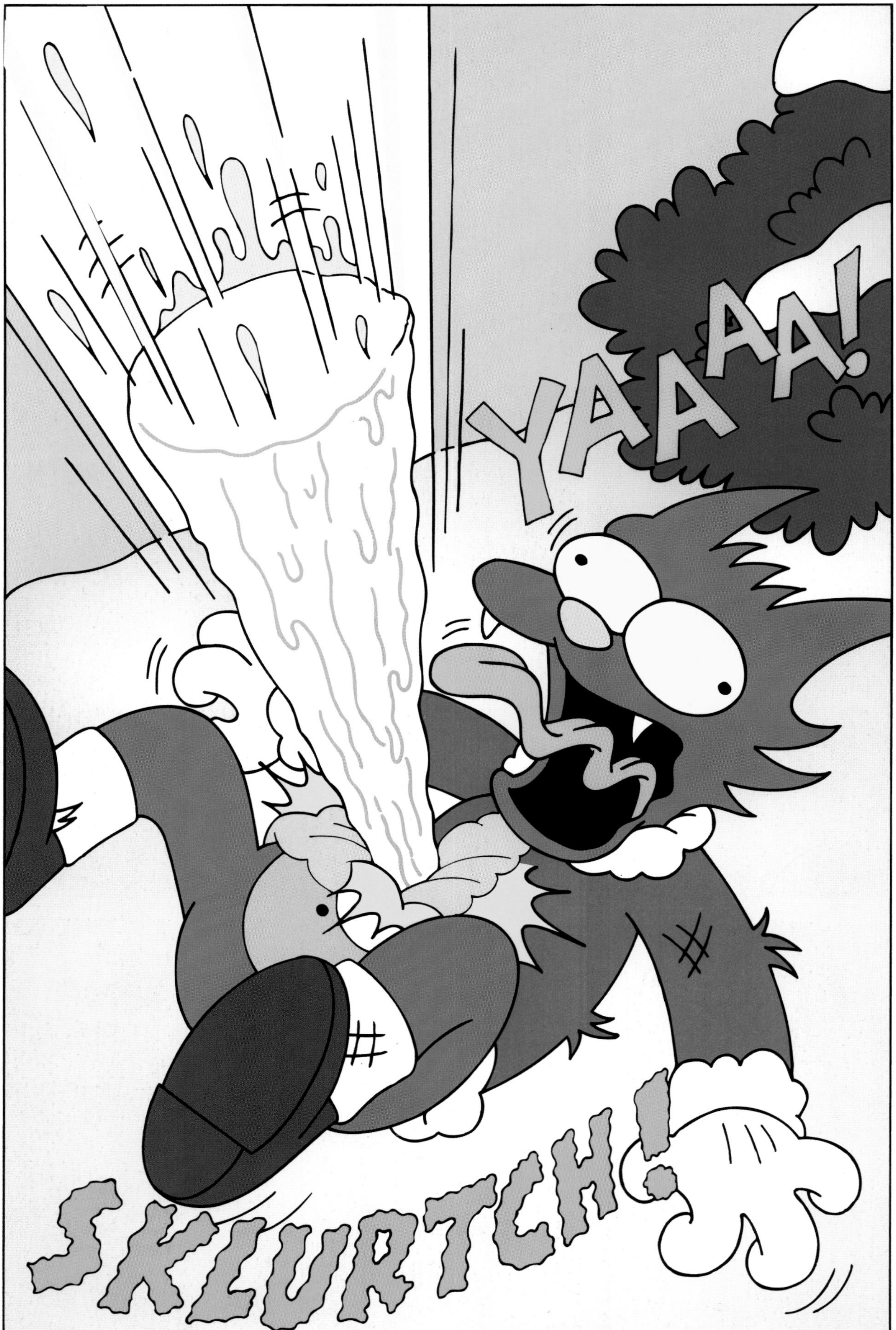
YAAAAA!
SKLURTCH!

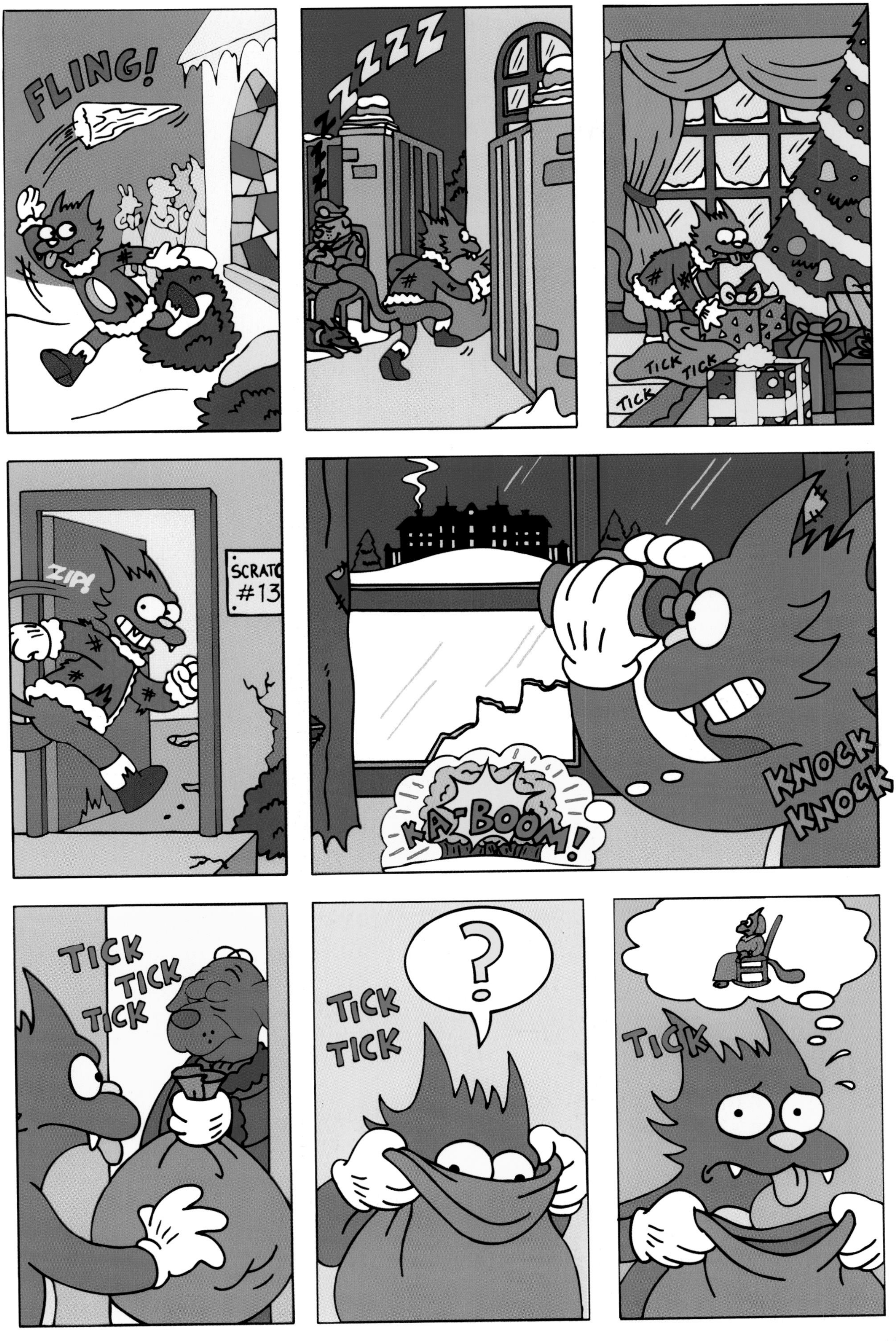
FLING!
ZZZZZZZ
TICK
TICK
TICK
ZIP!
SCRATC
#13
KNOCK
KNOCK
KA-BOOM!
TICK
TICK
TICK
TICK
TICK
?
TICK

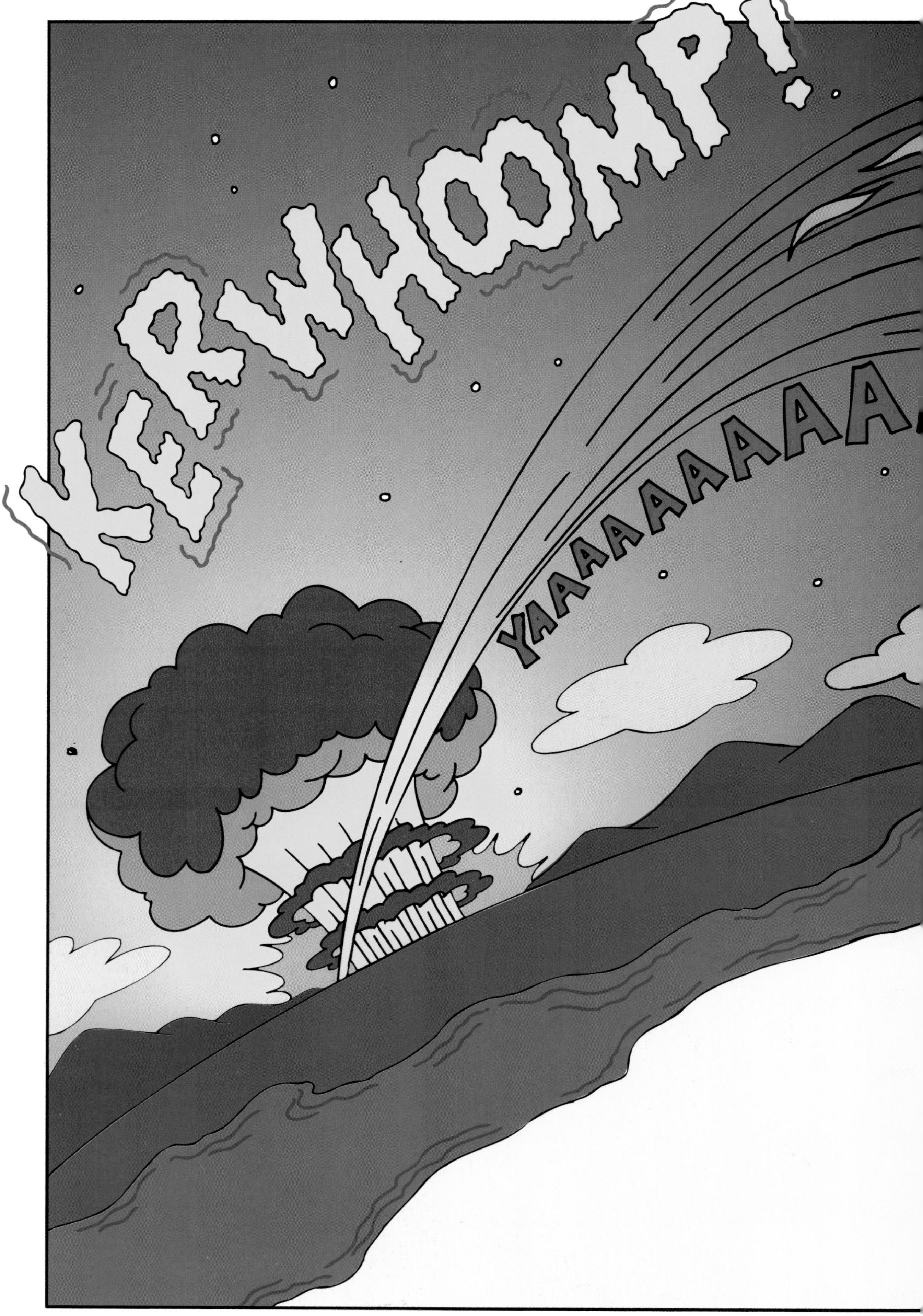
KERWHOOMP!
YAAAAAAAAAA

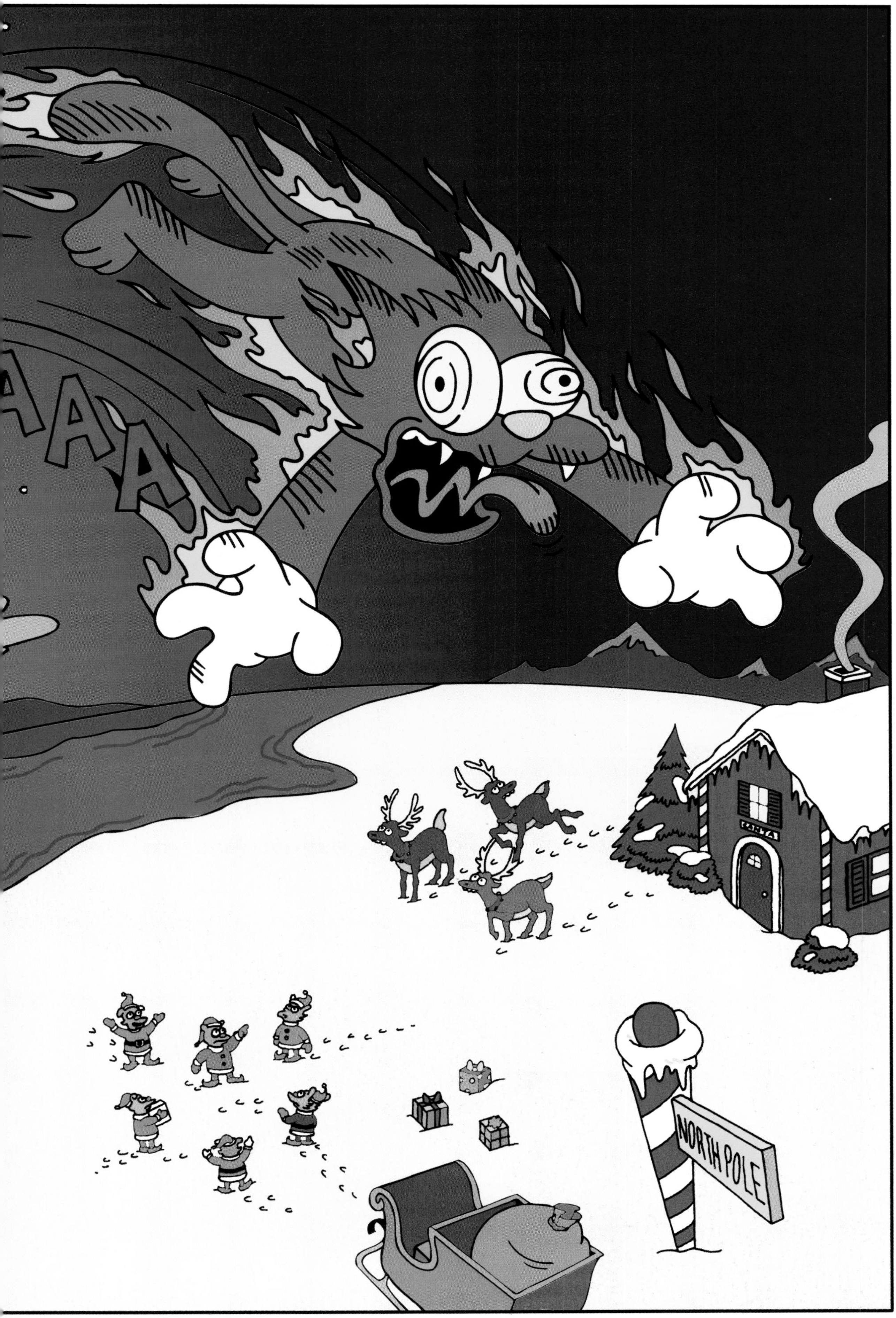
AAAA
SANTA
NORTH POLE

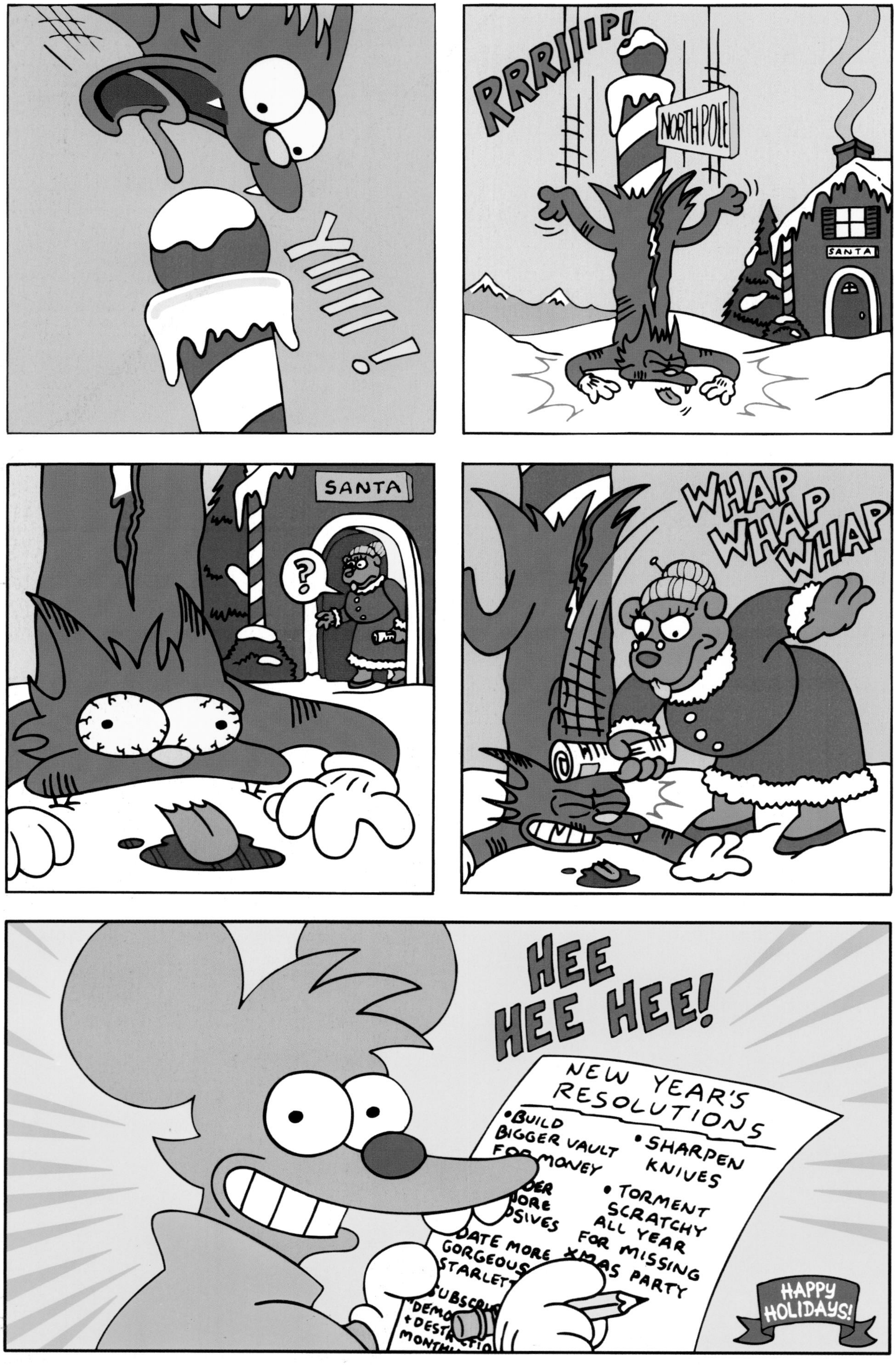
YIIIII!
RRRIIIIP!
NORTH POLE
SANTA
SANTA
?
WHAP
WHAP
WHAP
HEE
HEE HEE!
NEW YEAR'S
RESOLUTIONS
•BUILD
BIGGER VAULT
•SHARPEN
KNIVES
•TORMENT
SCRATCHY
ALL YEAR
FOR MISSING
XMAS PARTY
HAPPY
HOLIDAYS!

reetings, lucky friends, family, patients, former patients, future patients, gauze suppliers, pharmaceutical junket coordinators, nosy mailmen, and Consuela, the best housekeeper in Springfield! Just why are you so lucky? Well, you have just received...

R. JULIUS HIBBERT'S FAMILY PRACTICE KWANZAA LETTER!

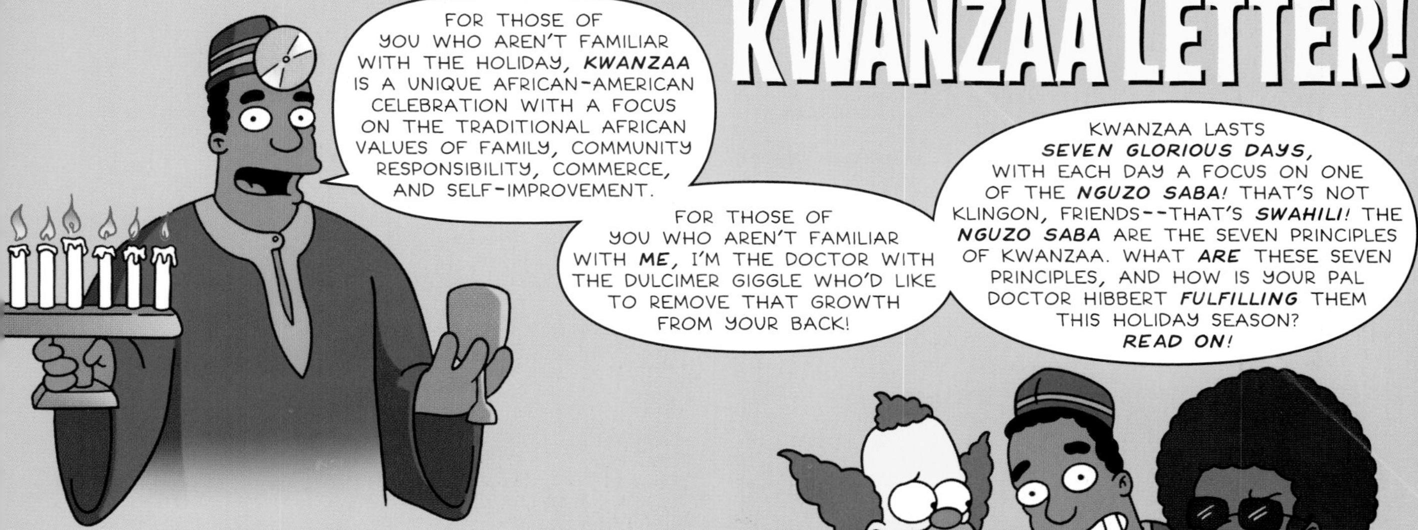
FOR THOSE OF YOU WHO AREN'T FAMILIAR WITH THE HOLIDAY, *KWANZAA* IS A UNIQUE AFRICAN-AMERICAN CELEBRATION WITH A FOCUS ON THE TRADITIONAL AFRICAN VALUES OF FAMILY, COMMUNITY RESPONSIBILITY, COMMERCE, AND SELF-IMPROVEMENT.
FOR THOSE OF YOU WHO AREN'T FAMILIAR WITH *ME*, I'M THE DOCTOR WITH THE DULCIMER GIGGLE WHO'D LIKE TO REMOVE THAT GROWTH FROM YOUR BACK!
KWANZAA LASTS *SEVEN GLORIOUS DAYS*, WITH EACH DAY A FOCUS ON ONE OF THE *NGUZO SABA*! THAT'S NOT KLINGON, FRIENDS--THAT'S *SWAHILI*! THE *NGUZO SABA* ARE THE SEVEN PRINCIPLES OF KWANZAA. WHAT *ARE* THESE SEVEN PRINCIPLES, AND HOW IS YOUR PAL DOCTOR HIBBERT *FULFILLING* THEM THIS HOLIDAY SEASON? *READ ON*!

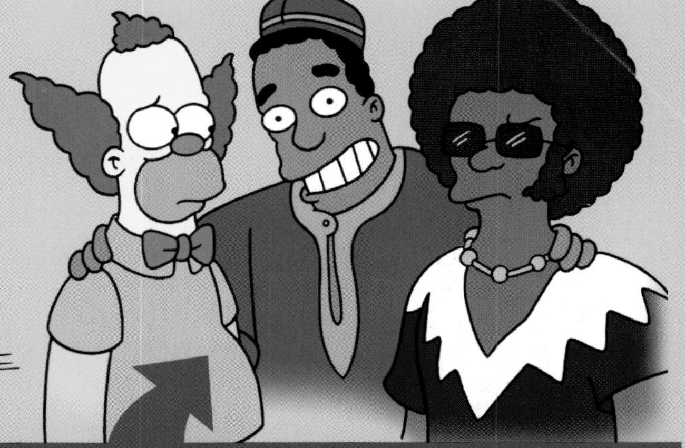

Umoja (Unity)

The first principle of Kwanzaa is to strive for and maintain **unity.** In the spirit of this day, I got **Krusty the Clown** to finally make amends with his estranged sidekick, **Sideshow Raheem.** They're currently in development on what's sure to be a hilarious new UPN sitcom called **"Clizzy in Da Hizzy."**

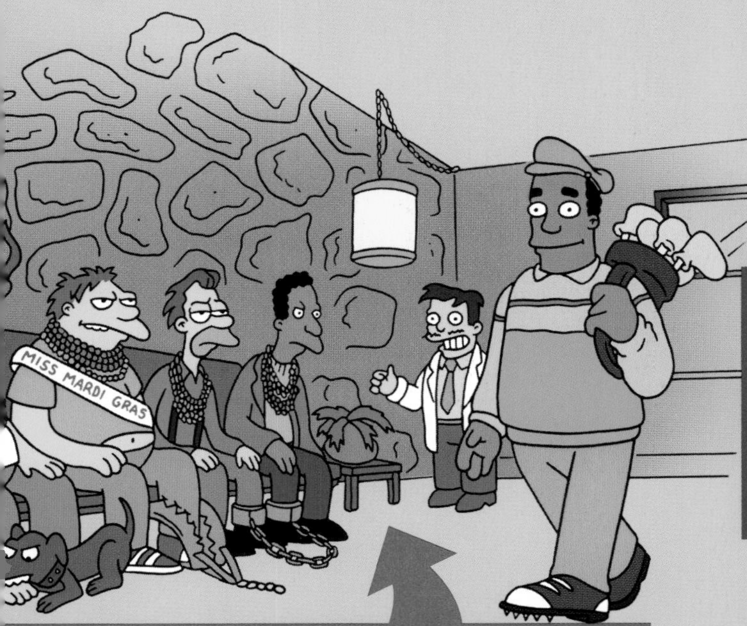
MISS MARDI GRAS

ujichagulia (Self-Determination)

e second principle of Kwanzaa is **self-determination.** On Day Two, **etermined** that I'd rather play golf than work at the Springfield ot Clinic.

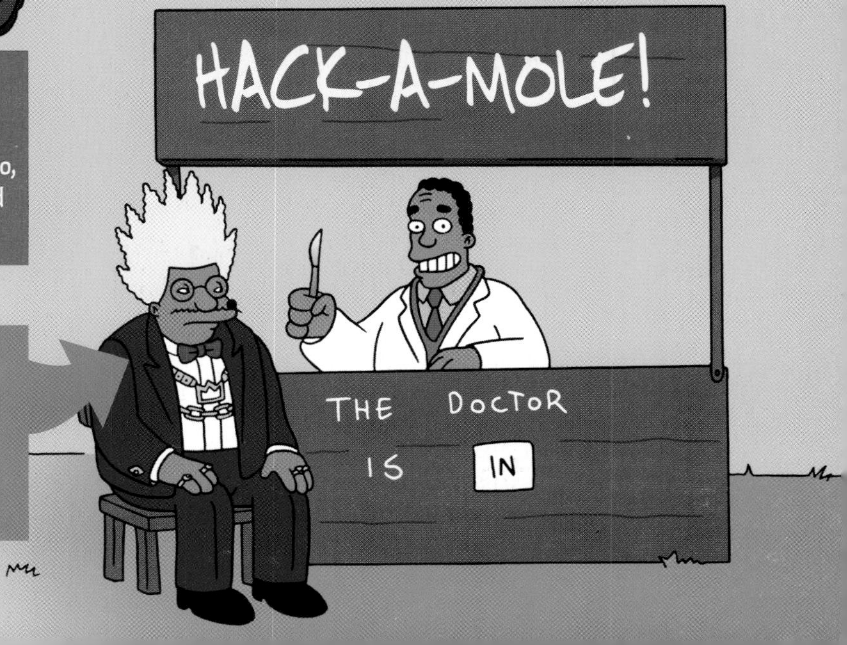
HACK-A-MOLE!
THE DOCTOR IS IN

jima (Collective Work and Responsibility)

e principle of **Ujima** is about making our fellow man's problems **r own**, and to solve them **together**. That's why I held "Free Mole noval Day" at the Springfield Mall on Day Three.

Doc Hibbert's GOOD-TIME SWEATER EXPERIENCE

Ujamaa (Cooperative Economics)

Ujamaa encourages African-Americans to open our own stores and to patronize them. That's why I finally fulfilled my lifelong dream of opening a first-class sweaterteria. Like what you see? That's Alpaca hair, purchased from my cousin's herd! The tags were sewn by a fraternity at Grambling State! Cornell West designed our new collection of turtlenecks! See, we scratch each other's back, and I mean **literally!** Some of these babies are 100% wool!

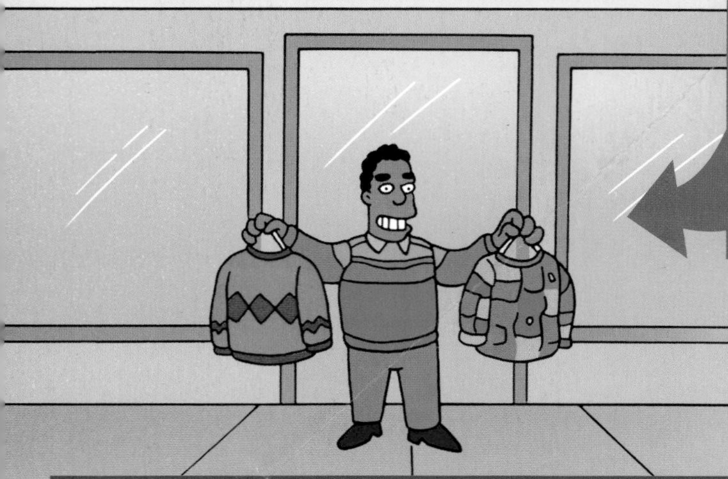

Nia (Purpose)

The fifth day of Kwanzaa has to do with **setting personal goals**—and recognizing how they fit into the community. That's why I'm involving elderly Springfielders in my weight training program. Right now, I'm up to twenty reps of Hans Moleman. This time next month, I hope to be doing dead lifts of Abraham Simpson, who, thanks to my biweekly efforts in the emergency room, continues to be very much alive.

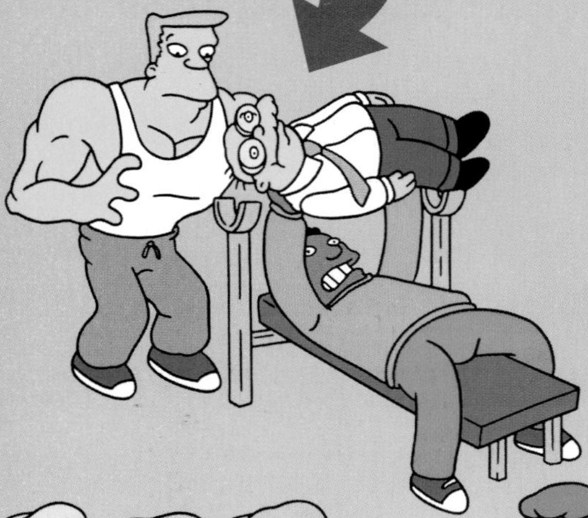

Kumba (Creativity)

Day Six of Kwanzaa celebrates **Kumba**, or **creativity**. To celebrate, I baked the family a sweet potato pie in the shape of Africa, which I served à la Mode-agascar.

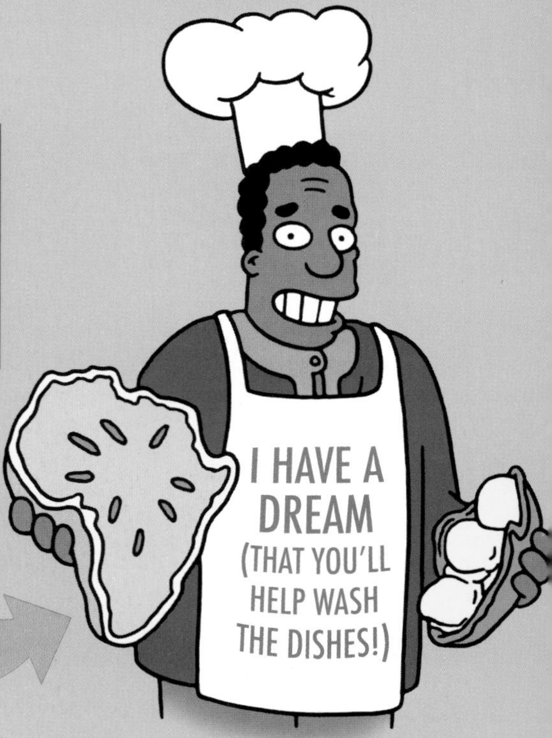
I HAVE A DREAM (THAT YOU'LL HELP WASH THE DISHES!)

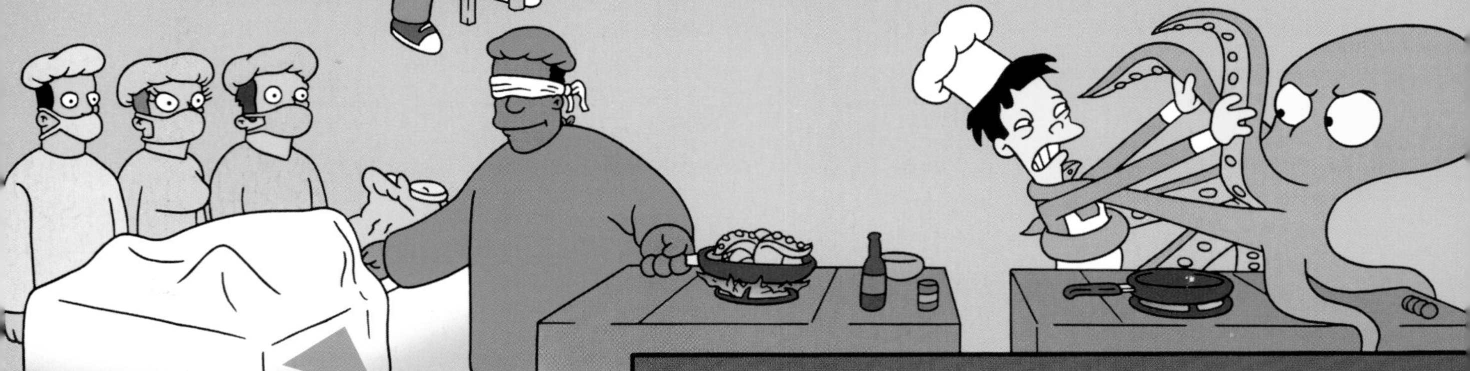

Imani (Faith)

Imani is about ascending to a new level of greatness for our people and all humankind by **believing** in ourselves, both individually and as a whole. It is **faith** that is the focus of this final day of Kwanzaa. So I challenged Iron Chef Japanese to a duel while removing Jasper's gallbladder **blindfolded!**

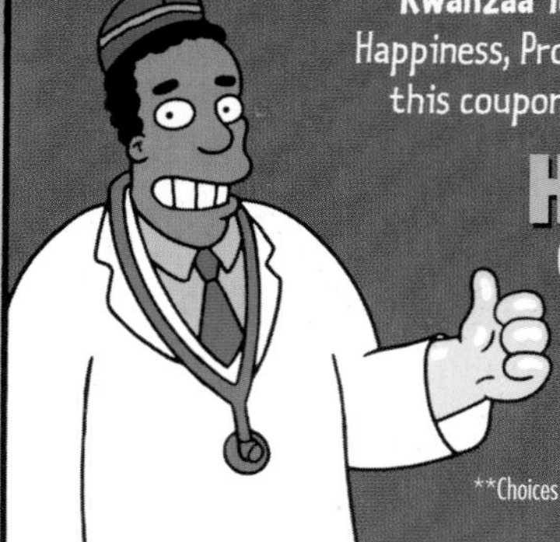

Kwanzaa Yenu Iwe Na Heri! (May your Kwanzaa be one of Happiness, Prosperity, and Goodness!) To that end, please take this coupon, with my compliments and Kwanzaa blessings!

HAPPY HOLIDAYS!

Good for one ***FREE*** OBJECT EXTRACTION*, DECORATIVE WOUND STITCH**, or CAUTERIZATION!

EXPIRES: St. Patrick's Day, 2005.

*Extracted objects become the property of Dr. Julius Hibbert M.D.

**Choices include skull, Pac-Man, "Kilroy was here" cartoon, dollar sign, and Van Halen symbol. Other designs require upgrade.

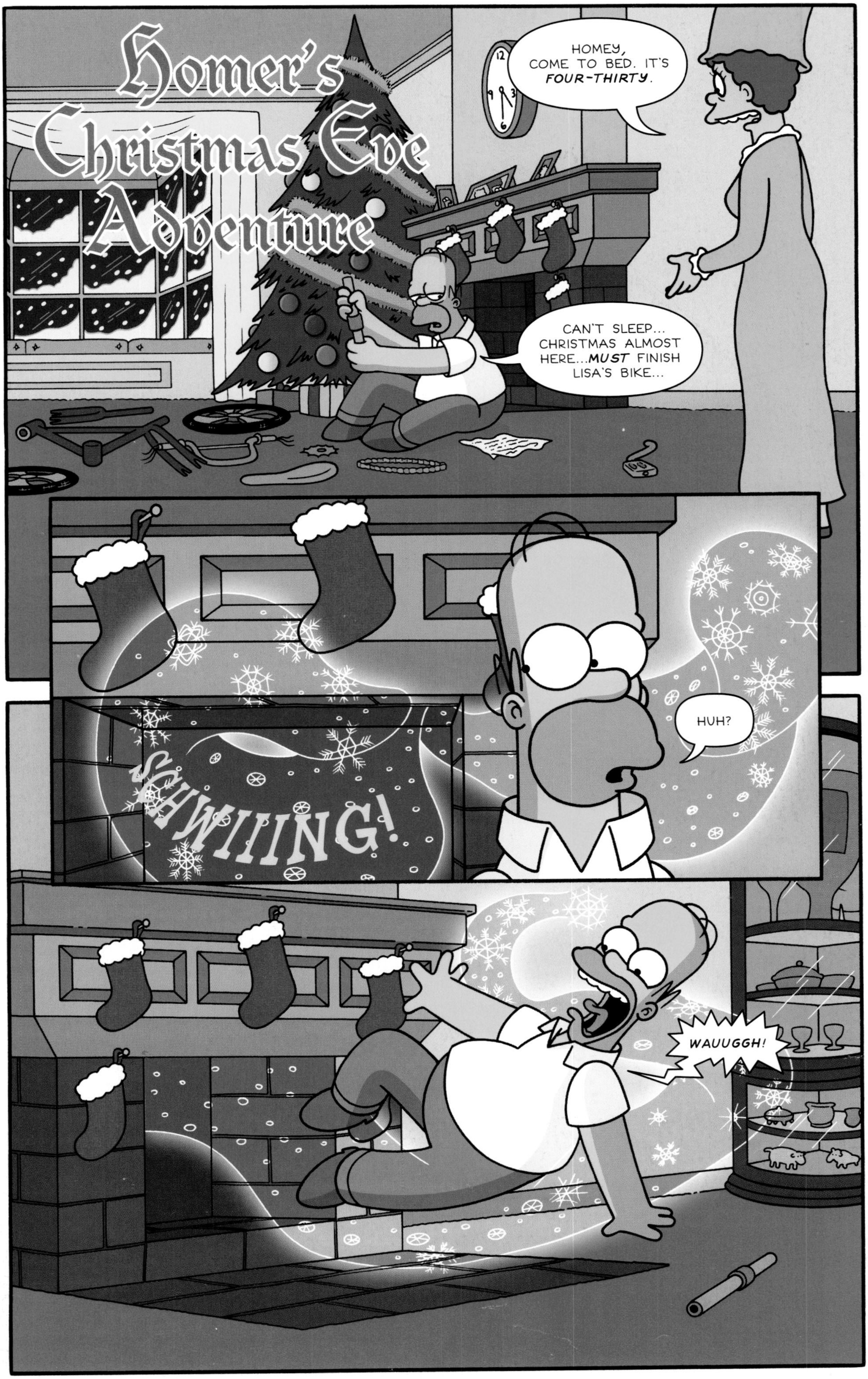
Homer's Christmas Eve Adventure
HOMEY, COME TO BED. IT'S FOUR-THIRTY.
CAN'T SLEEP... CHRISTMAS ALMOST HERE...MUST FINISH LISA'S BIKE...
SCHWIIING!
HUH?
WAUUGGH!

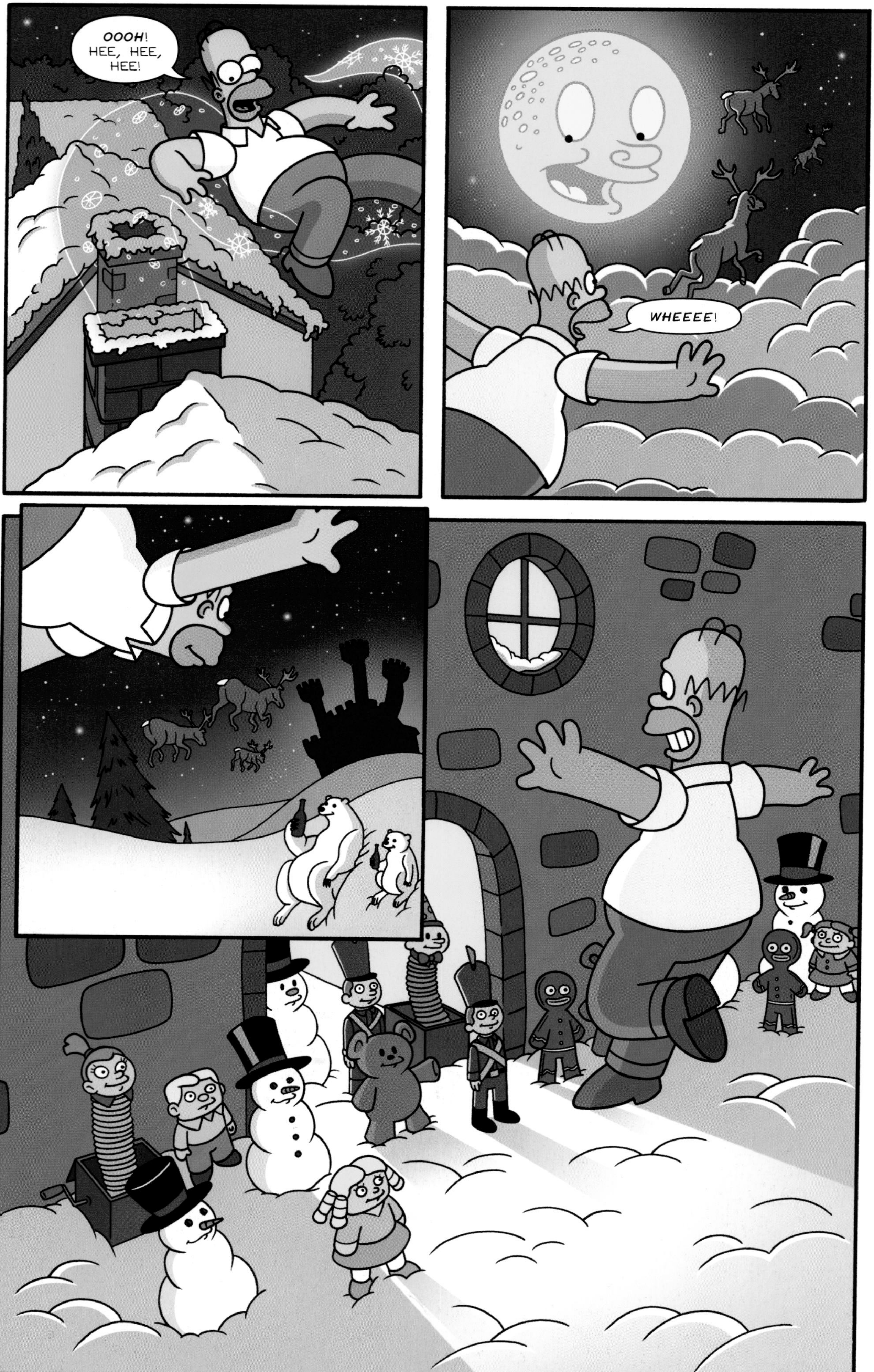

OOOH! HEE, HEE, HEE!
WHEEEE!

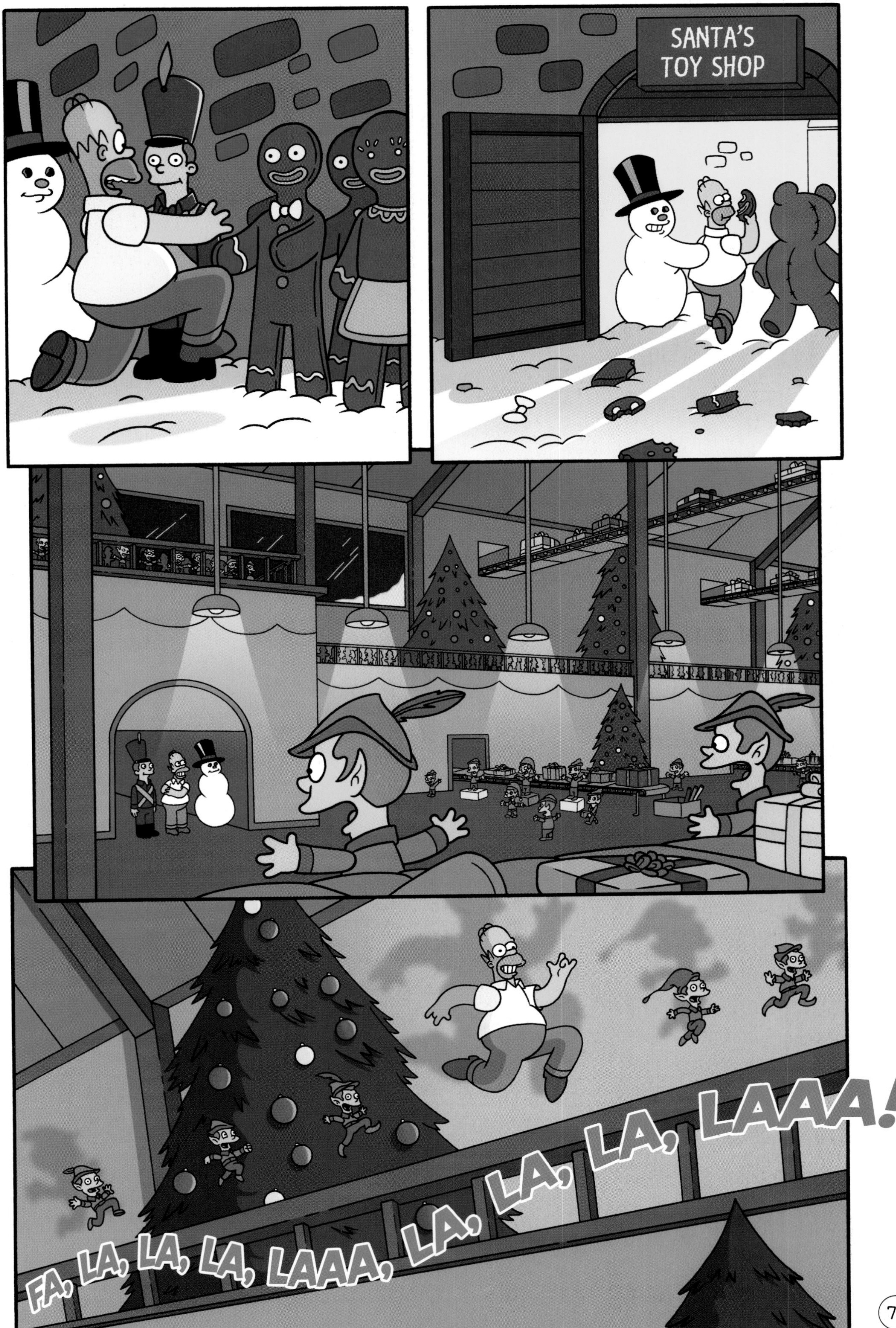
SANTA'S TOY SHOP
FA, LA, LA, LA, LAAA, LA, LA, LA, LAAA!

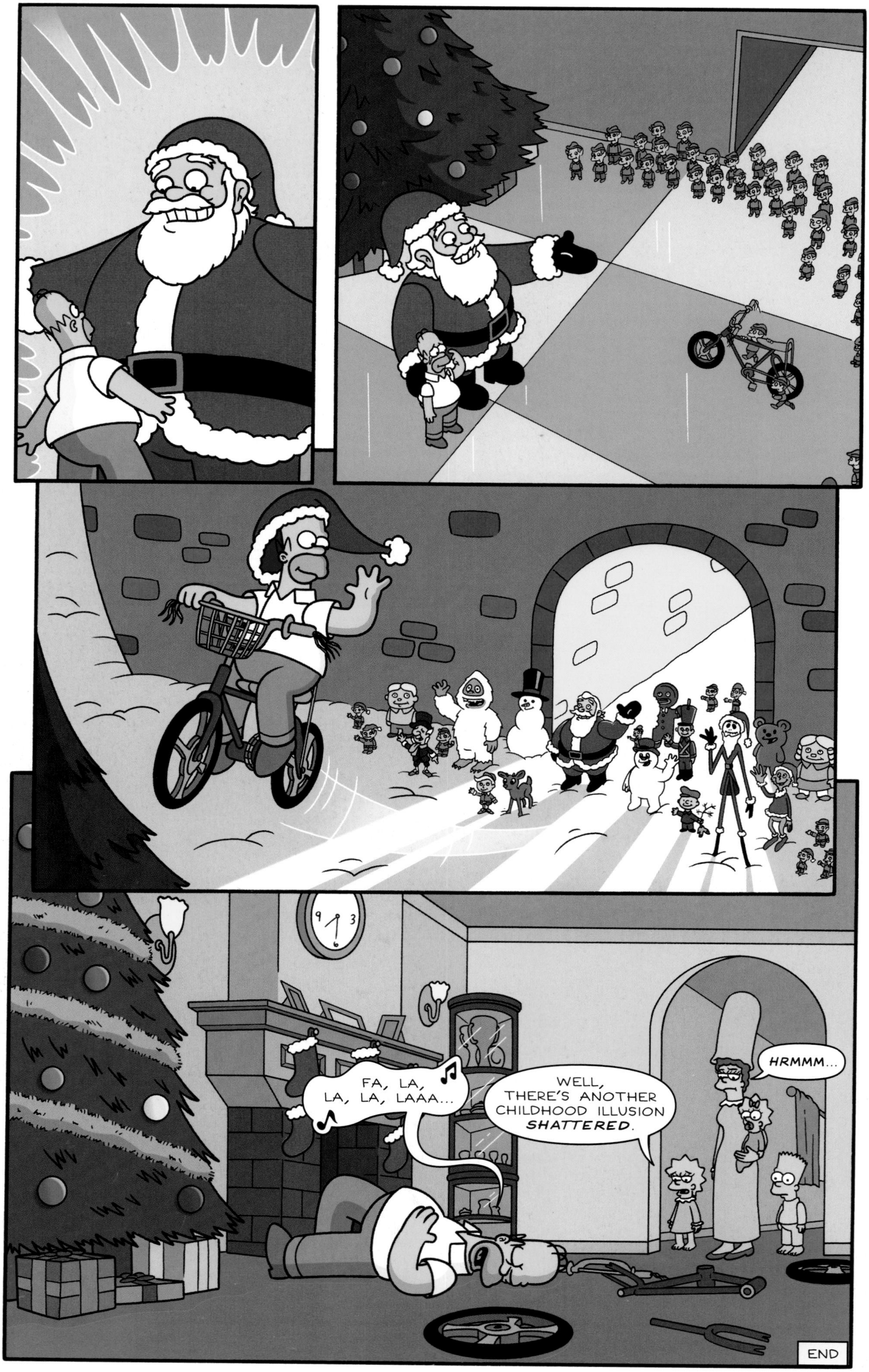
FA, LA,
LA, LA, LAAA...
WELL,
THERE'S ANOTHER
CHILDHOOD ILLUSION
SHATTERED.
HRMMM...
END

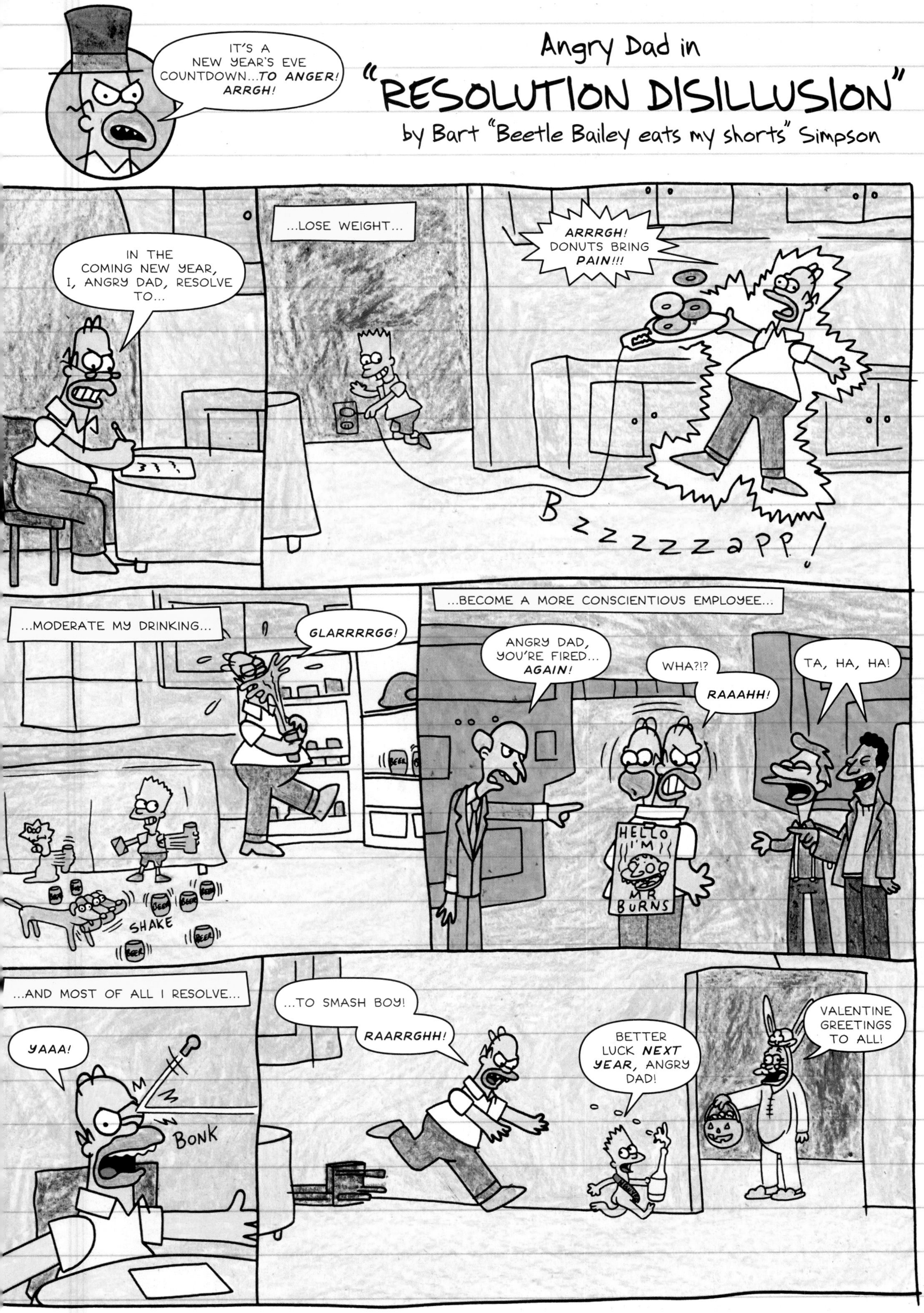
IT'S A NEW YEAR'S EVE COUNTDOWN...TO ANGER! ARRGH!
Angry Dad in
"RESOLUTION DISILLUSION"
by Bart "Beetle Bailey eats my shorts" Simpson
IN THE COMING NEW YEAR, I, ANGRY DAD, RESOLVE TO...
...LOSE WEIGHT...
ARRRGH! DONUTS BRING PAIN!!!
BZZZZZZAPP!
...MODERATE MY DRINKING...
GLARRRRGG!
SHAKE
...BECOME A MORE CONSCIENTIOUS EMPLOYEE...
ANGRY DAD, YOU'RE FIRED... AGAIN!
WHA?!?
RAAAHH!
TA, HA, HA!
HELLO I'M MR BURNS
...AND MOST OF ALL I RESOLVE...
YAAA!
BONK
...TO SMASH BOY!
RAARRGHH!
BETTER LUCK NEXT YEAR, ANGRY DAD!
VALENTINE GREETINGS TO ALL!

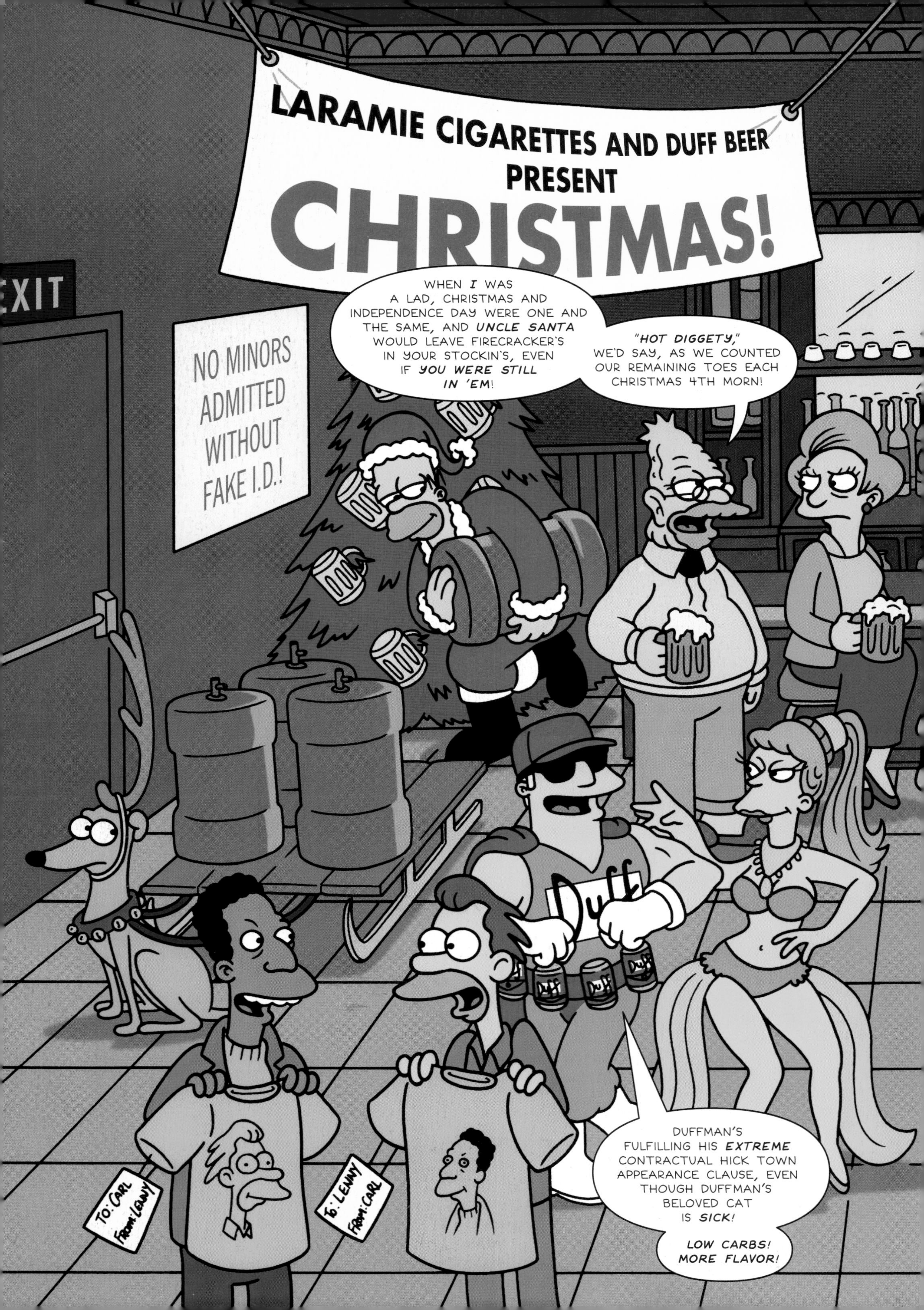
LARAMIE CIGARETTES AND DUFF BEER PRESENT CHRISTMAS!
EXIT
NO MINORS ADMITTED WITHOUT FAKE I.D.!
WHEN I WAS A LAD, CHRISTMAS AND INDEPENDENCE DAY WERE ONE AND THE SAME, AND UNCLE SANTA WOULD LEAVE FIRECRACKER'S IN YOUR STOCKIN'S, EVEN IF YOU WERE STILL IN 'EM!
"HOT DIGGETY," WE'D SAY, AS WE COUNTED OUR REMAINING TOES EACH CHRISTMAS 4TH MORN!
Duff
TO: CARL FROM: LENNY
To: LENNY FROM: CARL
DUFFMAN'S FULFILLING HIS EXTREME CONTRACTUAL HICK TOWN APPEARANCE CLAUSE, EVEN THOUGH DUFFMAN'S BELOVED CAT IS SICK!
LOW CARBS! MORE FLAVOR!

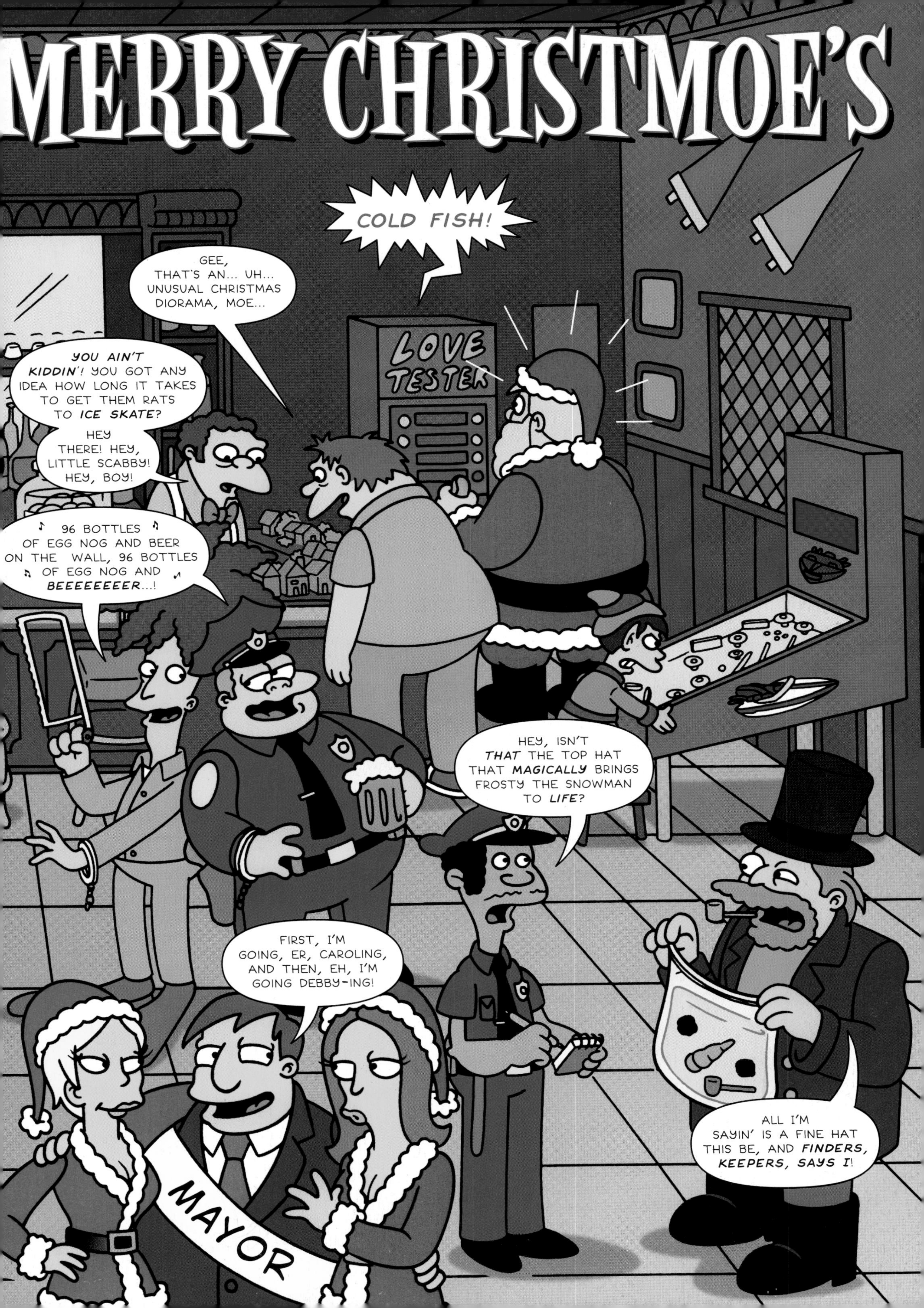
MERRY CHRISTMOE'S
COLD FISH!
GEE, THAT'S AN... UH... UNUSUAL CHRISTMAS DIORAMA, MOE...
YOU AIN'T KIDDIN'! YOU GOT ANY IDEA HOW LONG IT TAKES TO GET THEM RATS TO ICE SKATE?
HEY THERE! HEY, LITTLE SCABBY! HEY, BOY!
LOVE TESTER
♪ 96 BOTTLES ♪ OF EGG NOG AND BEER ON THE WALL, 96 BOTTLES ♪ OF EGG NOG AND ♪ BEEEEEEEER...!
HEY, ISN'T THAT THE TOP HAT THAT MAGICALLY BRINGS FROSTY THE SNOWMAN TO LIFE?
FIRST, I'M GOING, ER, CAROLING, AND THEN, EH, I'M GOING DEBBY-ING!
ALL I'M SAYIN' IS A FINE HAT THIS BE, AND FINDERS, KEEPERS, SAYS I!
MAYOR

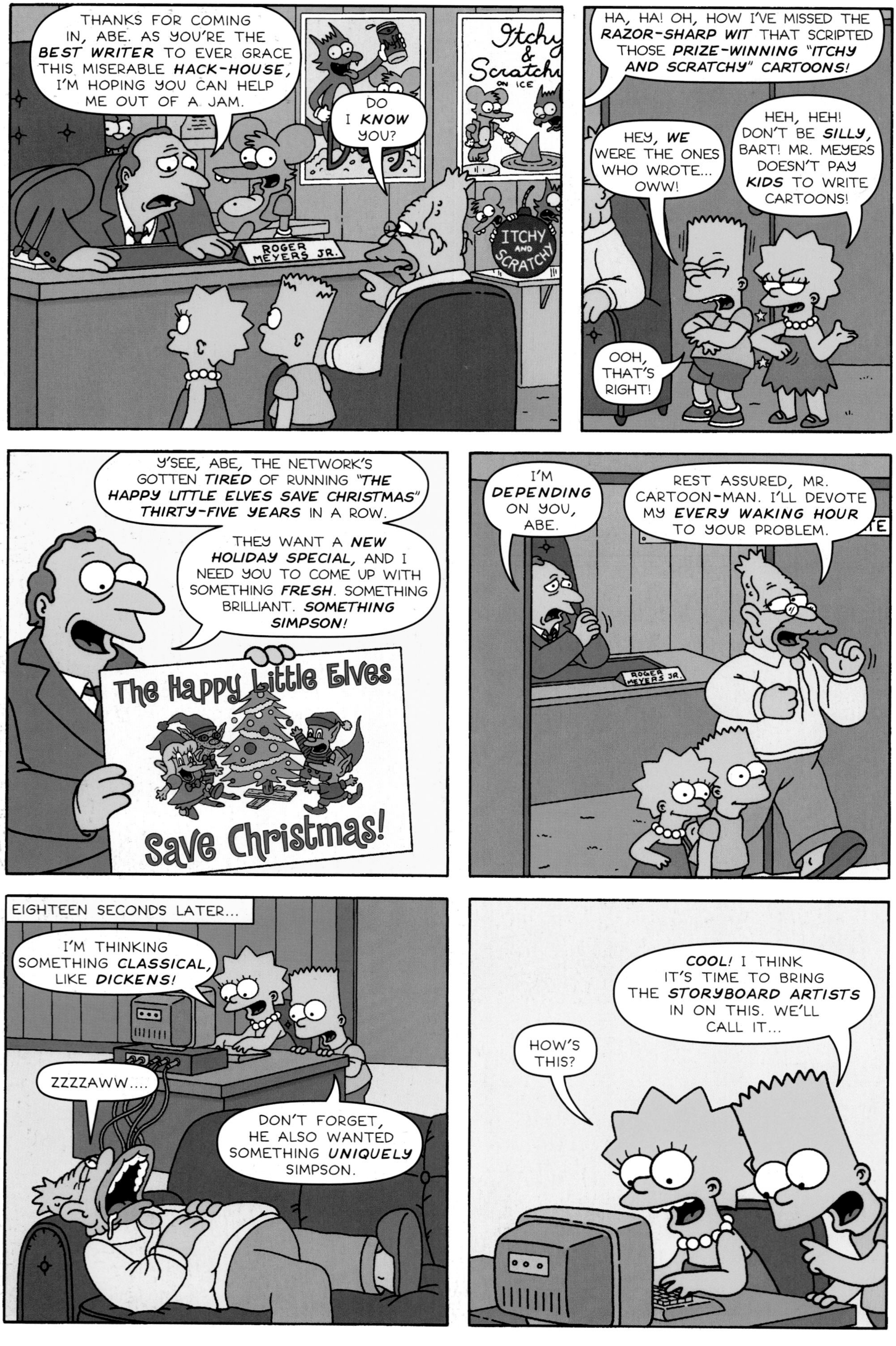
THANKS FOR COMING IN, ABE. AS YOU'RE THE BEST WRITER TO EVER GRACE THIS MISERABLE HACK-HOUSE, I'M HOPING YOU CAN HELP ME OUT OF A JAM.
DO I KNOW YOU?
Itchy & Scratchy ON ICE
ROGER MEYERS JR.
ITCHY AND SCRATCHY
HA, HA! OH, HOW I'VE MISSED THE RAZOR-SHARP WIT THAT SCRIPTED THOSE PRIZE-WINNING "ITCHY AND SCRATCHY" CARTOONS!
HEY, WE WERE THE ONES WHO WROTE... OWW!
HEH, HEH! DON'T BE SILLY, BART! MR. MEYERS DOESN'T PAY KIDS TO WRITE CARTOONS!
OOH, THAT'S RIGHT!
Y'SEE, ABE, THE NETWORK'S GOTTEN TIRED OF RUNNING "THE HAPPY LITTLE ELVES SAVE CHRISTMAS" THIRTY-FIVE YEARS IN A ROW.
THEY WANT A NEW HOLIDAY SPECIAL, AND I NEED YOU TO COME UP WITH SOMETHING FRESH. SOMETHING BRILLIANT. SOMETHING SIMPSON!
The Happy Little Elves Save Christmas!
I'M DEPENDING ON YOU, ABE.
REST ASSURED, MR. CARTOON-MAN. I'LL DEVOTE MY EVERY WAKING HOUR TO YOUR PROBLEM.
ROGER MEYERS JR.
EIGHTEEN SECONDS LATER...
I'M THINKING SOMETHING CLASSICAL, LIKE DICKENS!
ZZZZAWW....
DON'T FORGET, HE ALSO WANTED SOMETHING UNIQUELY SIMPSON.
HOW'S THIS?
COOL! I THINK IT'S TIME TO BRING THE STORYBOARD ARTISTS IN ON THIS. WE'LL CALL IT...

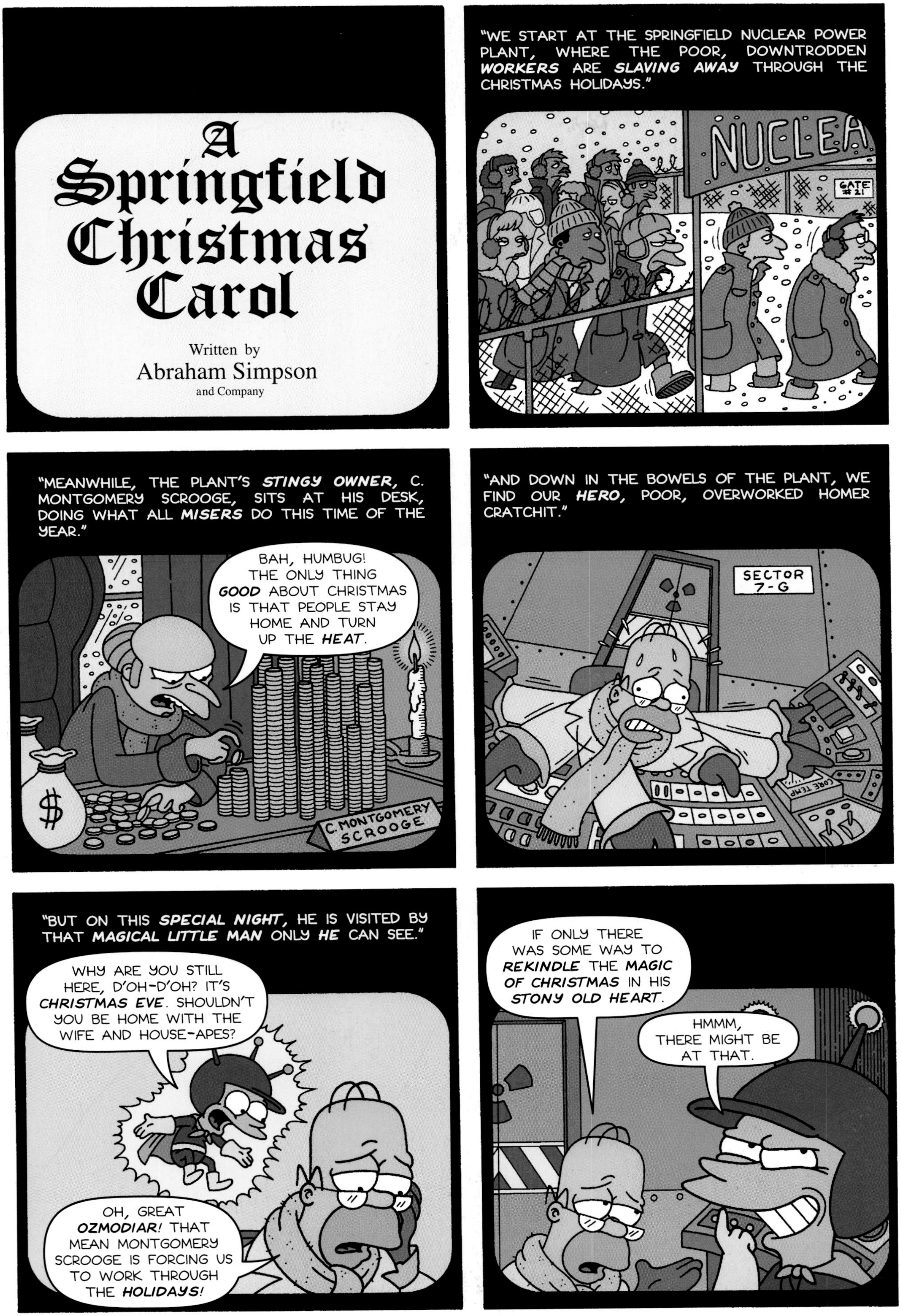
A Springfield Christmas Carol
Written by
Abraham Simpson
and Company
"WE START AT THE SPRINGFIELD NUCLEAR POWER PLANT, WHERE THE POOR, DOWNTRODDEN WORKERS ARE SLAVING AWAY THROUGH THE CHRISTMAS HOLIDAYS."
NUCLEA
GATE #21
"MEANWHILE, THE PLANT'S STINGY OWNER, C. MONTGOMERY SCROOGE, SITS AT HIS DESK, DOING WHAT ALL MISERS DO THIS TIME OF THE YEAR."
BAH, HUMBUG! THE ONLY THING GOOD ABOUT CHRISTMAS IS THAT PEOPLE STAY HOME AND TURN UP THE HEAT.
$
C. MONTGOMERY SCROOGE
"AND DOWN IN THE BOWELS OF THE PLANT, WE FIND OUR HERO, POOR, OVERWORKED HOMER CRATCHIT."
SECTOR 7-G
CORE TEMP
"BUT ON THIS SPECIAL NIGHT, HE IS VISITED BY THAT MAGICAL LITTLE MAN ONLY HE CAN SEE."
WHY ARE YOU STILL HERE, D'OH-D'OH? IT'S CHRISTMAS EVE. SHOULDN'T YOU BE HOME WITH THE WIFE AND HOUSE-APES?
OH, GREAT OZMODIAR! THAT MEAN MONTGOMERY SCROOGE IS FORCING US TO WORK THROUGH THE HOLIDAYS!
IF ONLY THERE WAS SOME WAY TO REKINDLE THE MAGIC OF CHRISTMAS IN HIS STONY OLD HEART.
HMMM, THERE MIGHT BE AT THAT.

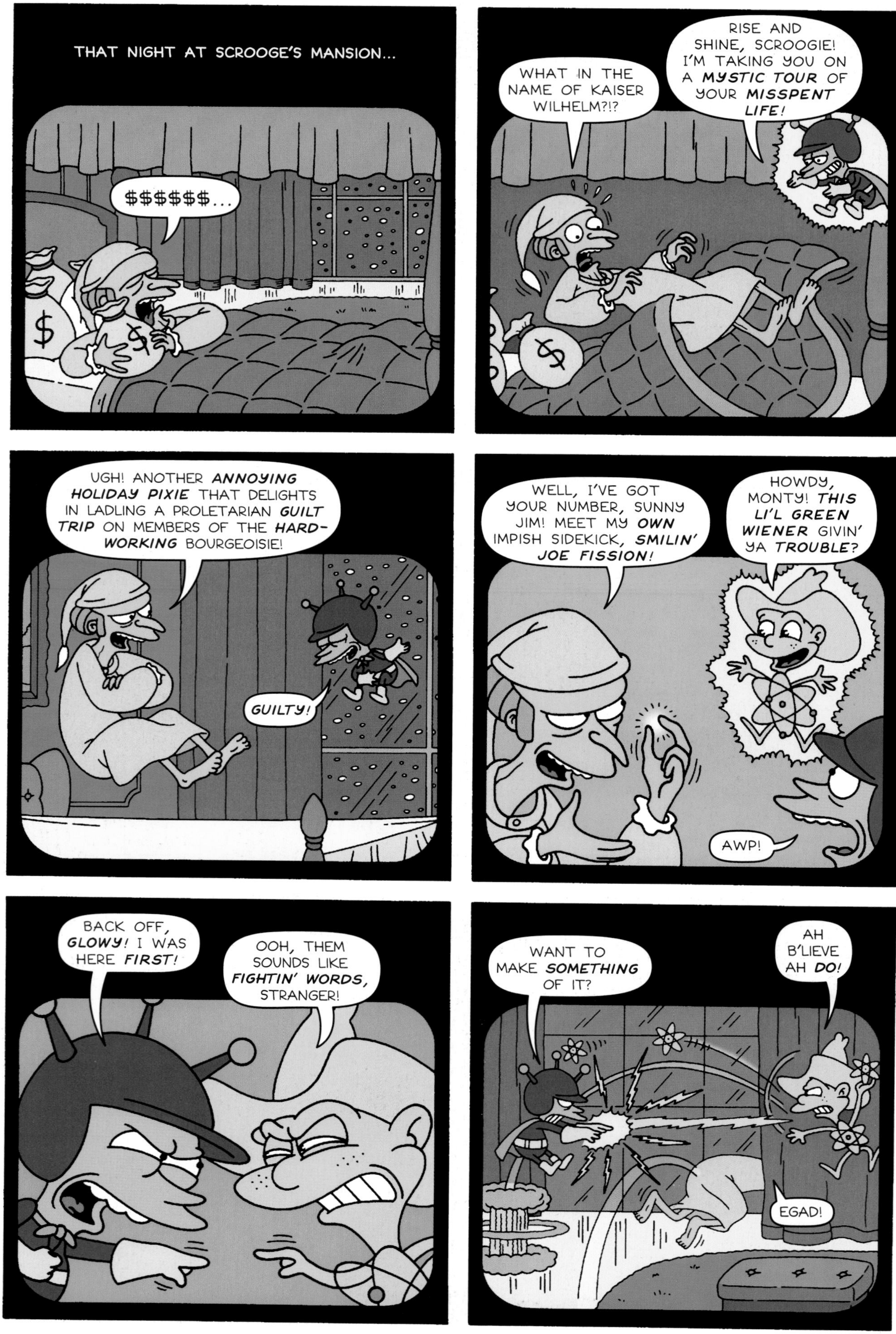

THAT NIGHT AT SCROOGE'S MANSION...
$$$$$$...
WHAT IN THE NAME OF KAISER WILHELM?!?
RISE AND SHINE, SCROOGIE! I'M TAKING YOU ON A MYSTIC TOUR OF YOUR MISSPENT LIFE!
UGH! ANOTHER ANNOYING HOLIDAY PIXIE THAT DELIGHTS IN LADLING A PROLETARIAN GUILT TRIP ON MEMBERS OF THE HARD-WORKING BOURGEOISIE!
GUILTY!
WELL, I'VE GOT YOUR NUMBER, SUNNY JIM! MEET MY OWN IMPISH SIDEKICK, SMILIN' JOE FISSION!
HOWDY, MONTY! THIS LI'L GREEN WIENER GIVIN' YA TROUBLE?
AWP!
BACK OFF, GLOWY! I WAS HERE FIRST!
OOH, THEM SOUNDS LIKE FIGHTIN' WORDS, STRANGER!
WANT TO MAKE SOMETHING OF IT?
AH B'LIEVE AH DO!
EGAD!

"AND SO IT CAME TO PASS THAT THERE WAS *PEACE ON EARTH* THAT BRIGHT CHRISTMAS MORNING, BUT AT WHAT COST? *AT WHAT COST?!?*"

The End

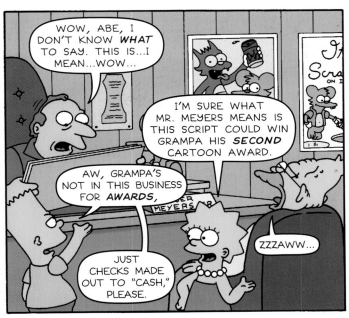

WOW, ABE, I DON'T KNOW *WHAT* TO SAY. THIS IS...I MEAN...WOW...

I'M SURE WHAT MR. MEYERS MEANS IS THIS SCRIPT COULD WIN GRAMPA HIS *SECOND* CARTOON AWARD.

AW, GRAMPA'S NOT IN THIS BUSINESS FOR *AWARDS*,

JUST CHECKS MADE OUT TO "CASH," PLEASE.

ZZZAWW...

COMES THE MIDDLE OF DECEMBER...

TONIGHT'S THE *BIG NIGHT!*

OUR CHRISTMAS SPECIAL'S ON!

THIS EVENING, WE ARE PLEASED TO PRESENT A *HOLIDAY EVENT* FOR THE WHOLE FAMILY...

...THE THIRTY-SIXTH ANNUAL SHOWING OF *"THE HAPPY LITTLE ELVES SAVE CHRISTMAS!"*

HEY!

WHERE'S *OUR* SPECIAL?

TYPICAL! THE NETWORKS COULDN'T STAND THE IDEA THAT KIDS MIGHT SEE SOME *QUALITY ENTERTAINMENT* FOR ONCE SO THEY STUCK THIS ON *AGAIN!*

HEY! KEEP IT DOWN! I HAVE *NO IDEA* WHAT I'M LOOKING AT...

...BUT THIS JUST MIGHT BE THE *BEST CARTOON* I EVER *WROTE!*

D'OH!

THE END

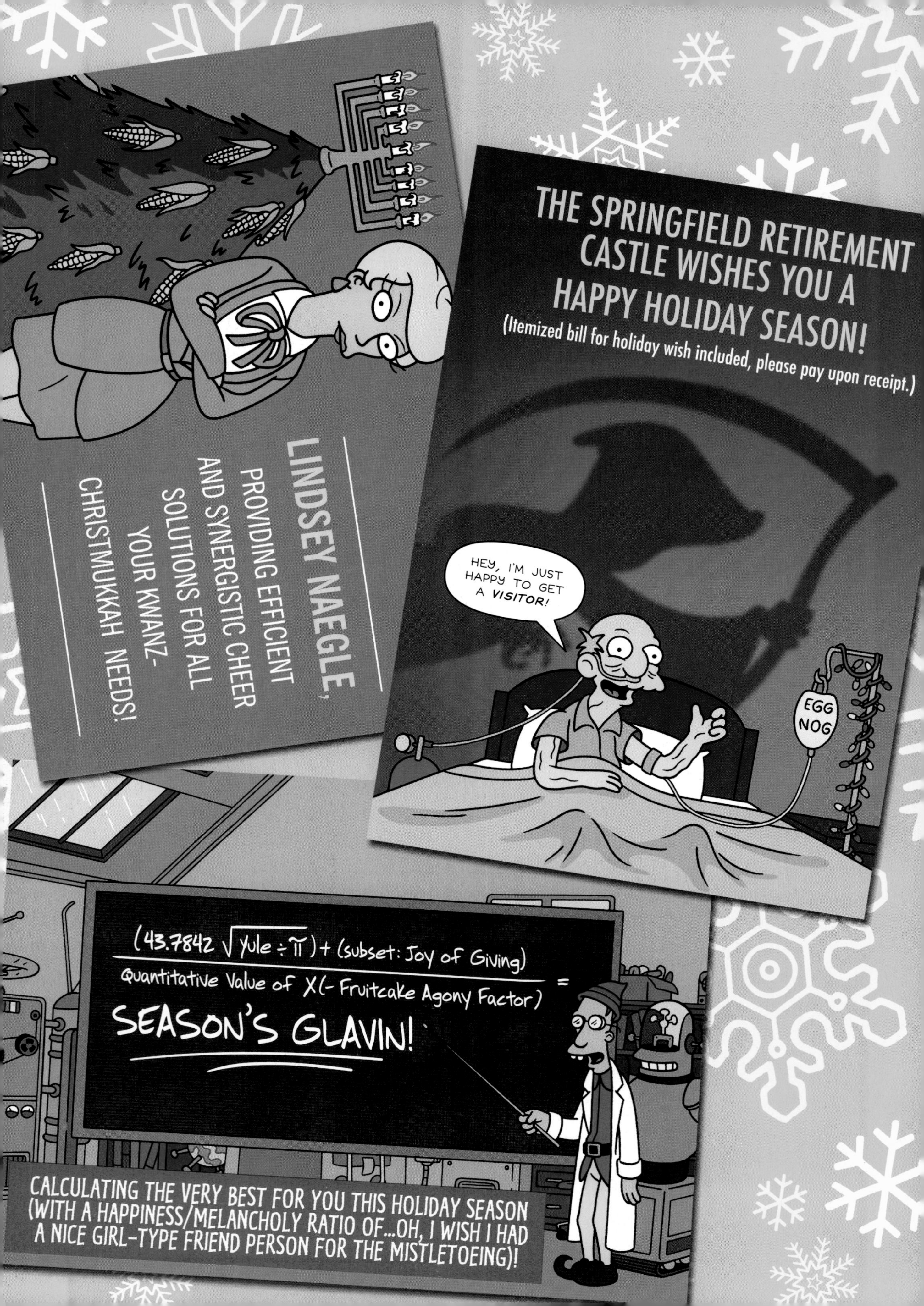
LINDSEY NAEGLE,
PROVIDING EFFICIENT
AND SYNERGISTIC CHEER
SOLUTIONS FOR ALL
YOUR KWANZ-
CHRISTMUKKAH NEEDS!
THE SPRINGFIELD RETIREMENT
CASTLE WISHES YOU A
HAPPY HOLIDAY SEASON!
(Itemized bill for holiday wish included, please pay upon receipt.)
HEY, I'M JUST HAPPY TO GET A VISITOR!
EGG NOG
(43.7842 √Yule ÷ π) + (subset: Joy of Giving)
Quantitative Value of X(- Fruitcake Agony Factor) =
SEASON'S GLAVIN!
CALCULATING THE VERY BEST FOR YOU THIS HOLIDAY SEASON
(WITH A HAPPINESS/MELANCHOLY RATIO OF...OH, I WISH I HAD
A NICE GIRL-TYPE FRIEND PERSON FOR THE MISTLETOEING)!

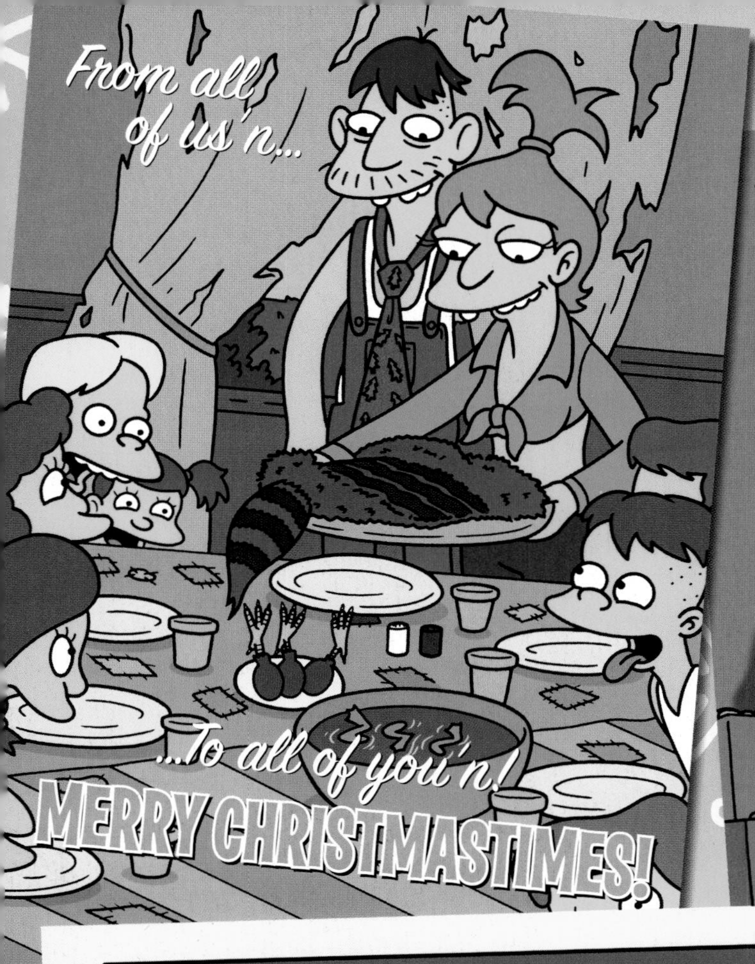
From all of us'n...
...To all of you'n!
MERRY CHRISTMASTIMES!

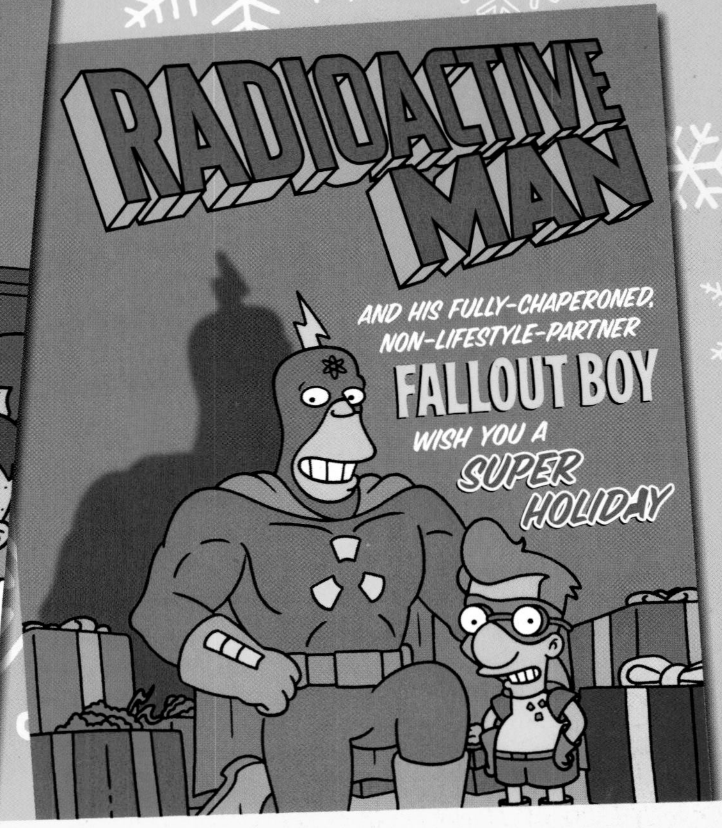
RADIOACTIVE MAN
AND HIS FULLY-CHAPERONED, NON-LIFESTYLE-PARTNER
FALLOUT BOY
WISH YOU A
SUPER HOLIDAY

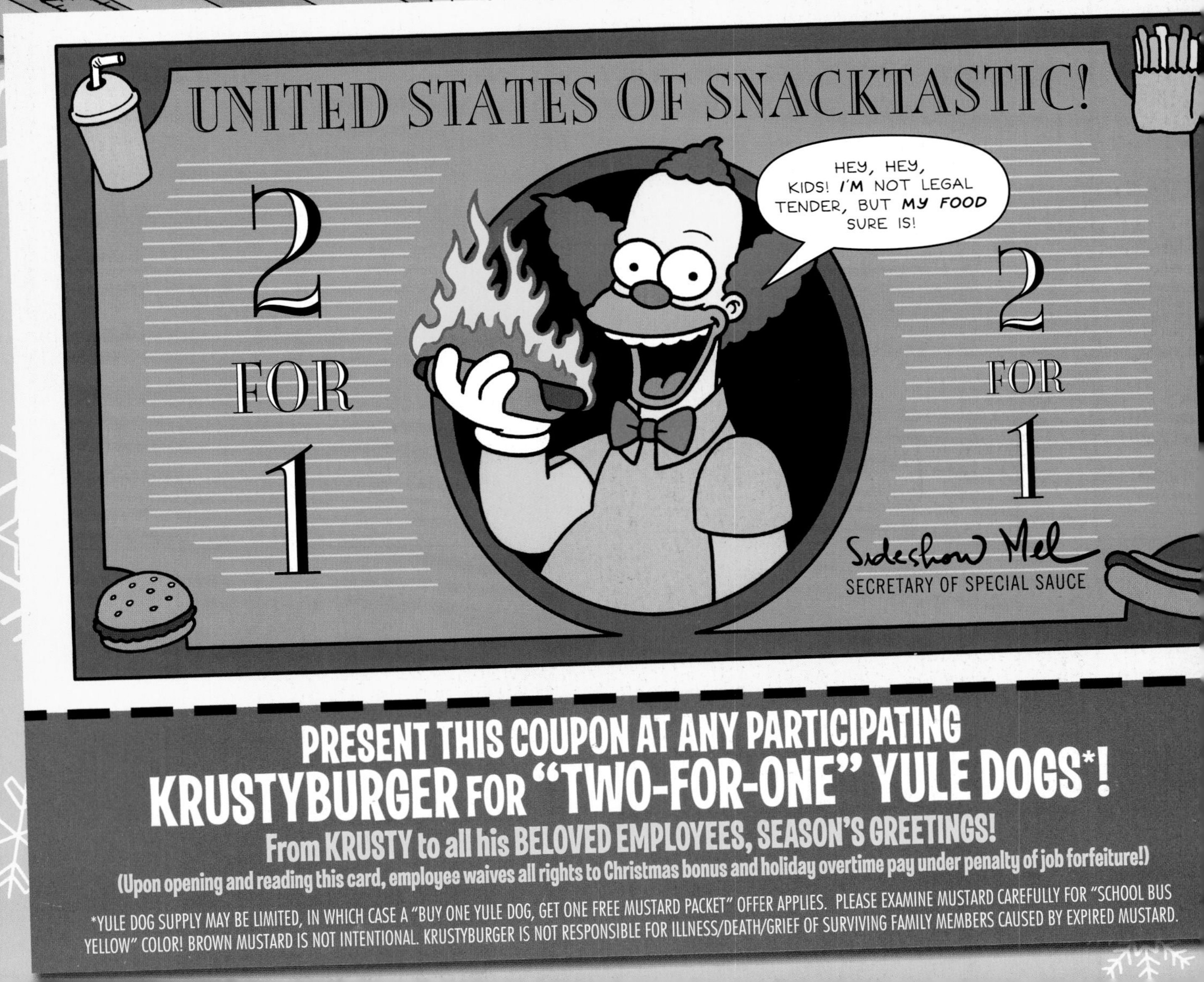
UNITED STATES OF SNACKTASTIC!
2 FOR 1
HEY, HEY, KIDS! I'M NOT LEGAL TENDER, BUT MY FOOD SURE IS!
2 FOR 1
Sideshow Mel
SECRETARY OF SPECIAL SAUCE
PRESENT THIS COUPON AT ANY PARTICIPATING
KRUSTYBURGER FOR "TWO-FOR-ONE" YULE DOGS*!
From KRUSTY to all his BELOVED EMPLOYEES, SEASON'S GREETINGS!
(Upon opening and reading this card, employee waives all rights to Christmas bonus and holiday overtime pay under penalty of job forfeiture!)
*YULE DOG SUPPLY MAY BE LIMITED, IN WHICH CASE A "BUY ONE YULE DOG, GET ONE FREE MUSTARD PACKET" OFFER APPLIES. PLEASE EXAMINE MUSTARD CAREFULLY FOR "SCHOOL BUS YELLOW" COLOR! BROWN MUSTARD IS NOT INTENTIONAL. KRUSTYBURGER IS NOT RESPONSIBLE FOR ILLNESS/DEATH/GRIEF OF SURVIVING FAMILY MEMBERS CAUSED BY EXPIRED MUSTARD.

WORST XMAS

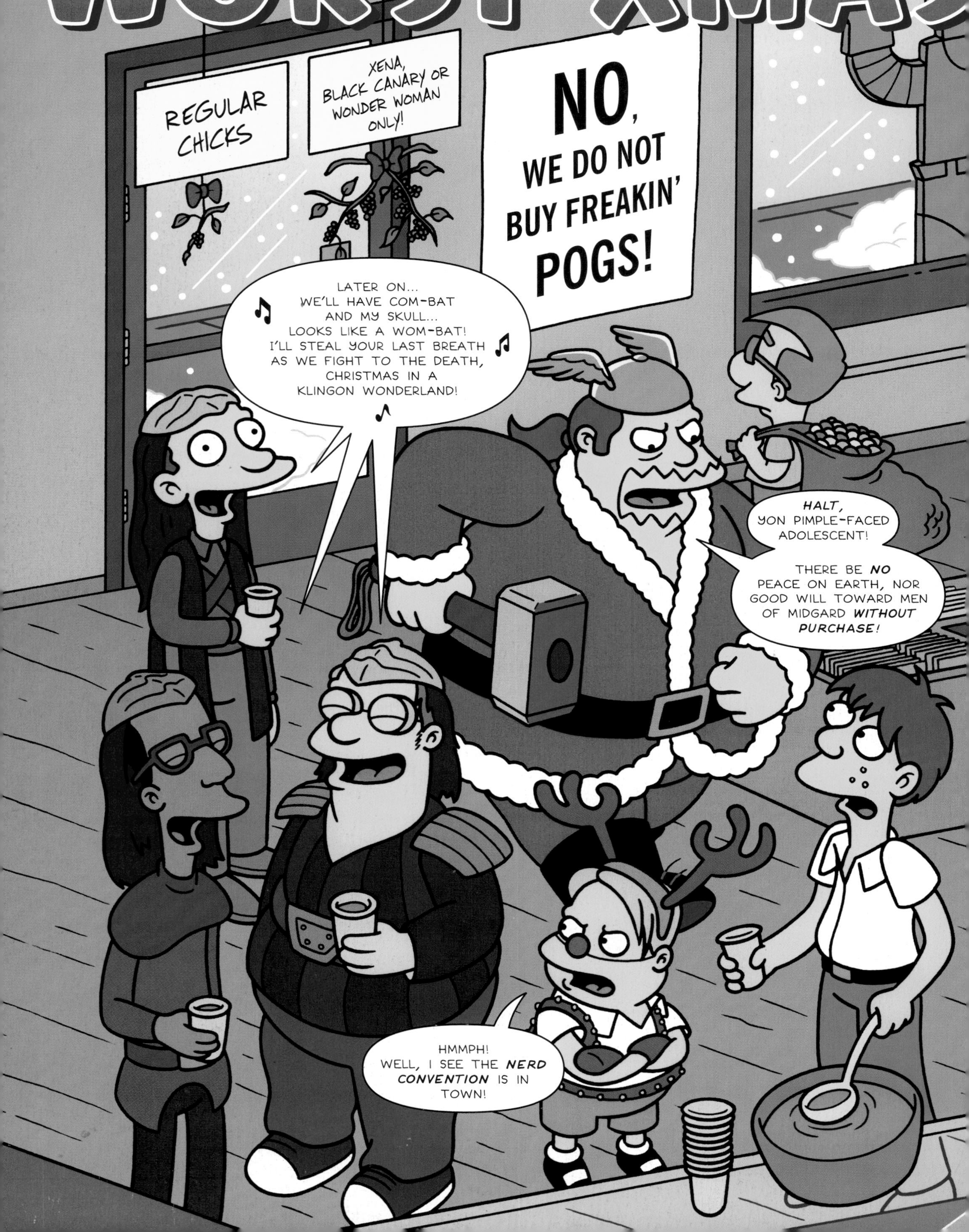
REGULAR CHICKS
XENA, BLACK CANARY OR WONDER WOMAN ONLY!
NO, WE DO NOT BUY FREAKIN' POGS!
LATER ON... WE'LL HAVE COM-BAT AND MY SKULL... LOOKS LIKE A WOM-BAT! I'LL STEAL YOUR LAST BREATH AS WE FIGHT TO THE DEATH, CHRISTMAS IN A KLINGON WONDERLAND!
HALT, YON PIMPLE-FACED ADOLESCENT!
THERE BE NO PEACE ON EARTH, NOR GOOD WILL TOWARD MEN OF MIDGARD WITHOUT PURCHASE!
HMMPH! WELL, I SEE THE NERD CONVENTION IS IN TOWN!

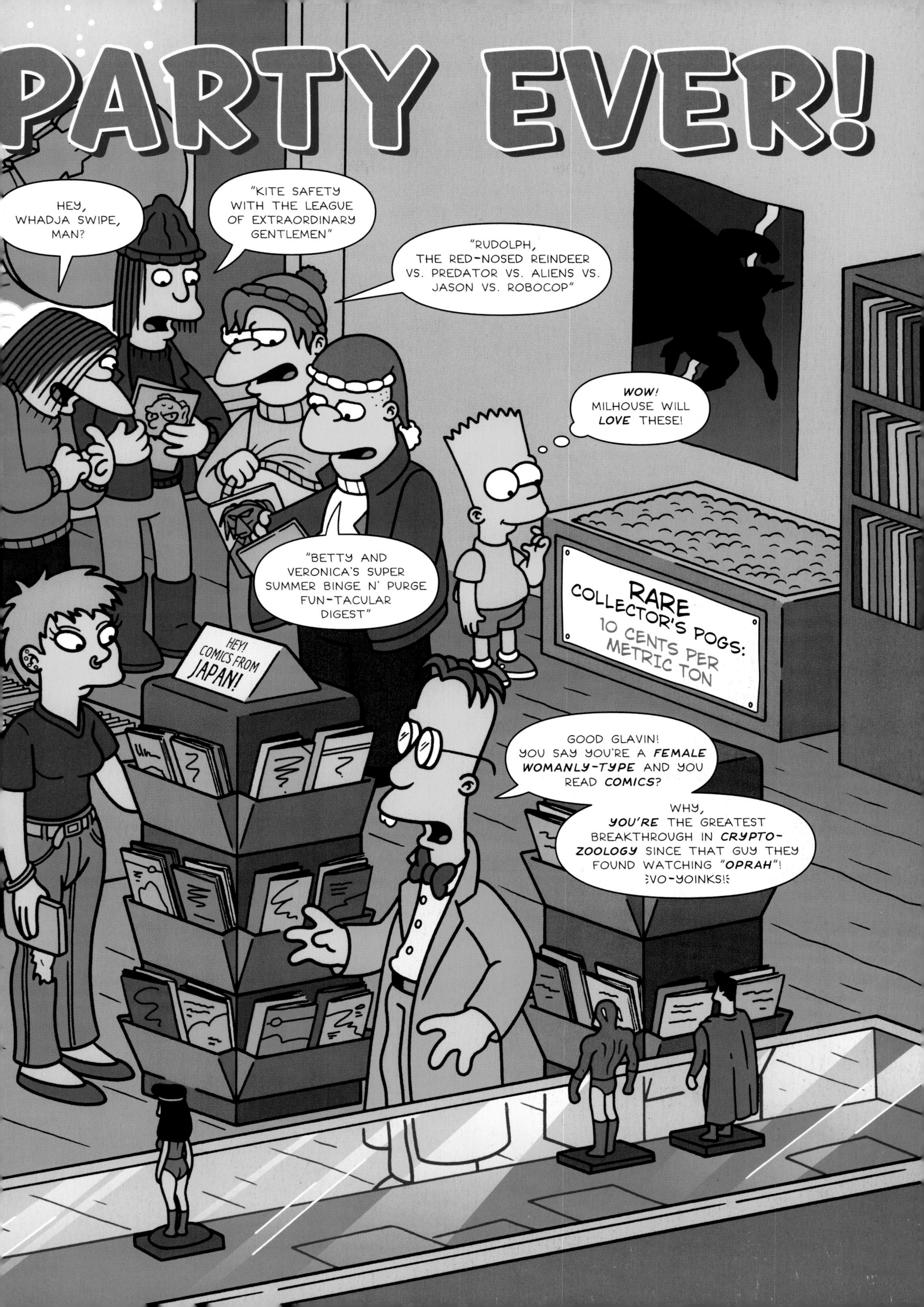
PARTY EVER!
HEY, WHADJA SWIPE, MAN?
"KITE SAFETY WITH THE LEAGUE OF EXTRAORDINARY GENTLEMEN"
"RUDOLPH, THE RED-NOSED REINDEER VS. PREDATOR VS. ALIENS VS. JASON VS. ROBOCOP"
WOW! MILHOUSE WILL LOVE THESE!
"BETTY AND VERONICA'S SUPER SUMMER BINGE N' PURGE FUN-TACULAR DIGEST"
HEY! COMICS FROM JAPAN!
RARE COLLECTOR'S POGS: 10 CENTS PER METRIC TON
GOOD GLAVIN! YOU SAY YOU'RE A FEMALE WOMANLY-TYPE AND YOU READ COMICS?
WHY, YOU'RE THE GREATEST BREAKTHROUGH IN CRYPTO-ZOOLOGY SINCE THAT GUY THEY FOUND WATCHING "OPRAH"! VO-YOINKS!

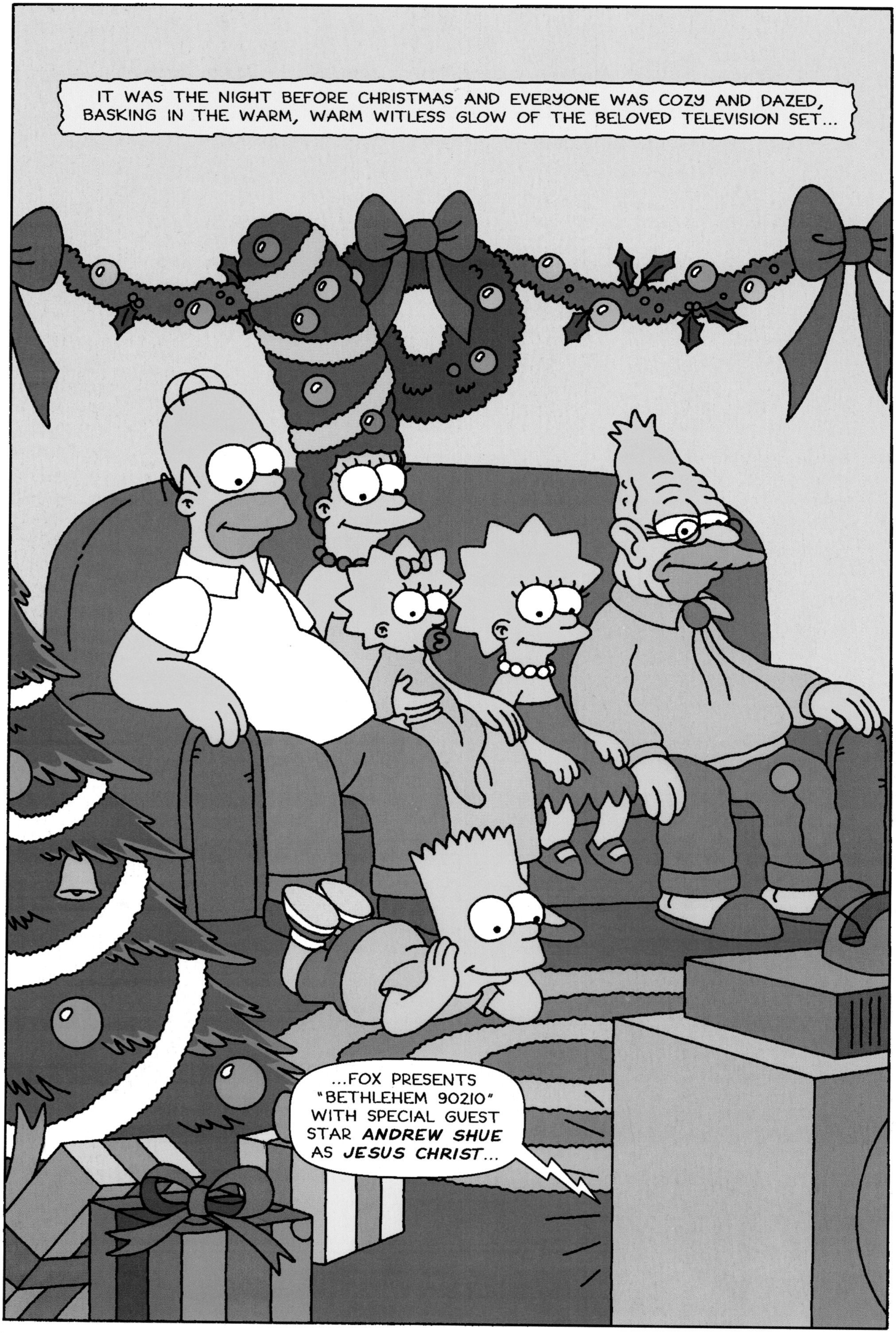
IT WAS THE NIGHT BEFORE CHRISTMAS AND EVERYONE WAS COZY AND DAZED, BASKING IN THE WARM, WARM WITLESS GLOW OF THE BELOVED TELEVISION SET...
...FOX PRESENTS "BETHLEHEM 90210" WITH SPECIAL GUEST STAR ANDREW SHUE AS JESUS CHRIST...

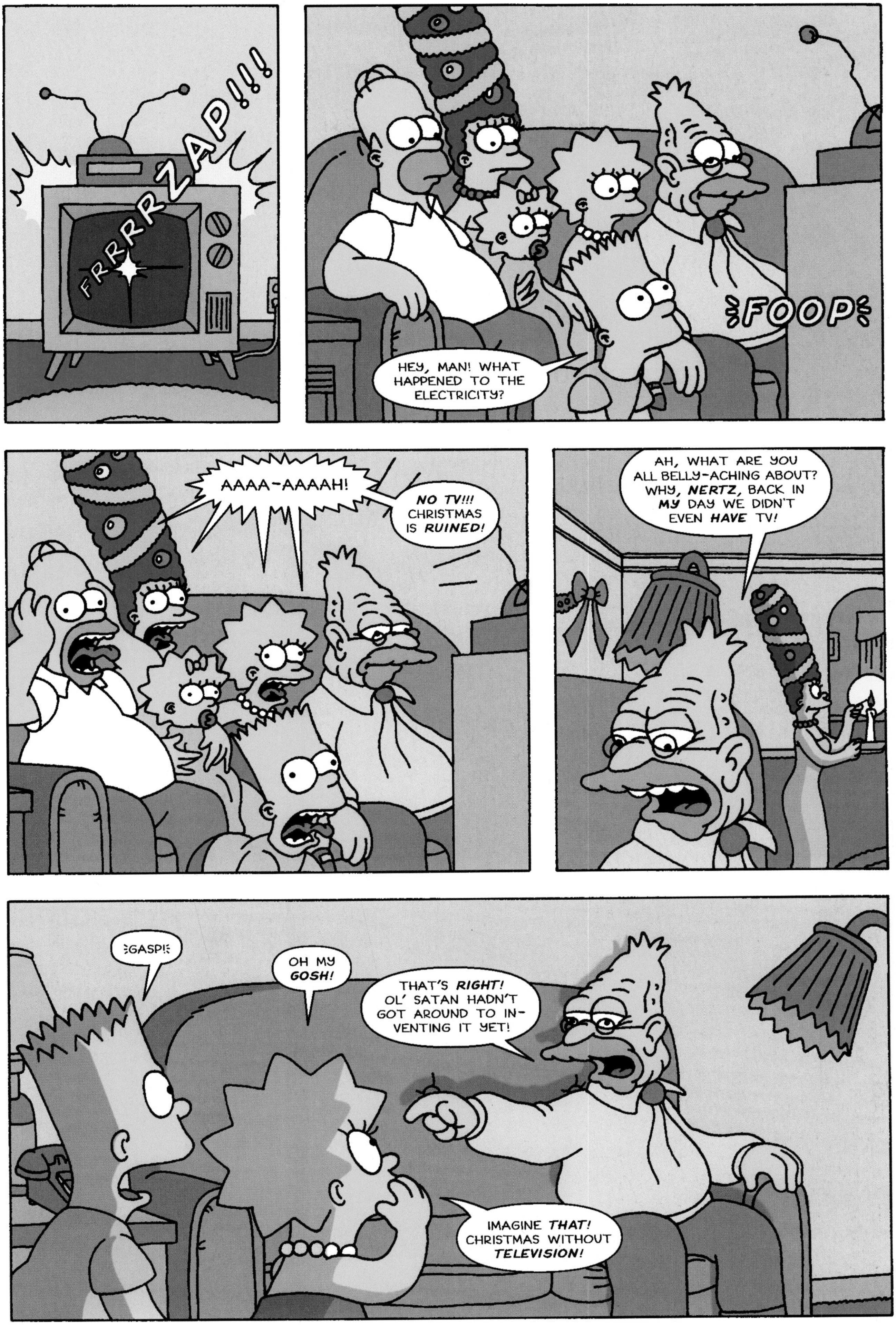
FRRRRZAP!!!!
FOOP
HEY, MAN! WHAT HAPPENED TO THE ELECTRICITY?
AAAA-AAAAH!
NO TV!!! CHRISTMAS IS RUINED!
AH, WHAT ARE YOU ALL BELLY-ACHING ABOUT? WHY, NERTZ, BACK IN MY DAY WE DIDN'T EVEN HAVE TV!
GASP!
OH MY GOSH!
THAT'S RIGHT! OL' SATAN HADN'T GOT AROUND TO IN-VENTING IT YET!
IMAGINE THAT! CHRISTMAS WITHOUT TELEVISION!

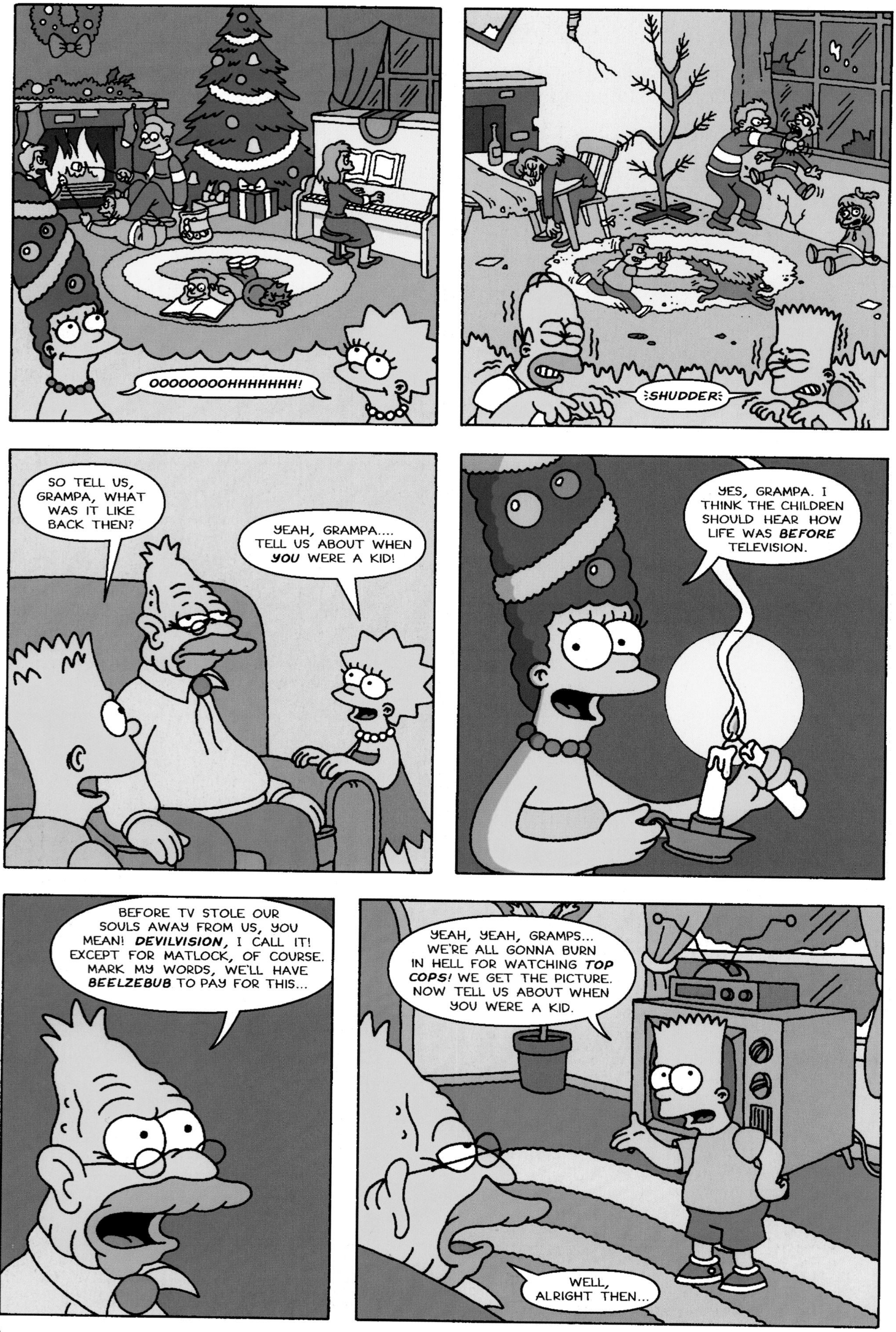

OOOOOOOOHHHHHHH!
SHUDDER
SO TELL US, GRAMPA, WHAT WAS IT LIKE BACK THEN?
YEAH, GRAMPA.... TELL US ABOUT WHEN YOU WERE A KID!
YES, GRAMPA. I THINK THE CHILDREN SHOULD HEAR HOW LIFE WAS BEFORE TELEVISION.
BEFORE TV STOLE OUR SOULS AWAY FROM US, YOU MEAN! DEVILVISION, I CALL IT! EXCEPT FOR MATLOCK, OF COURSE. MARK MY WORDS, WE'LL HAVE BEELZEBUB TO PAY FOR THIS...
YEAH, YEAH, GRAMPS... WE'RE ALL GONNA BURN IN HELL FOR WATCHING TOP COPS! WE GET THE PICTURE. NOW TELL US ABOUT WHEN YOU WERE A KID.
WELL, ALRIGHT THEN...

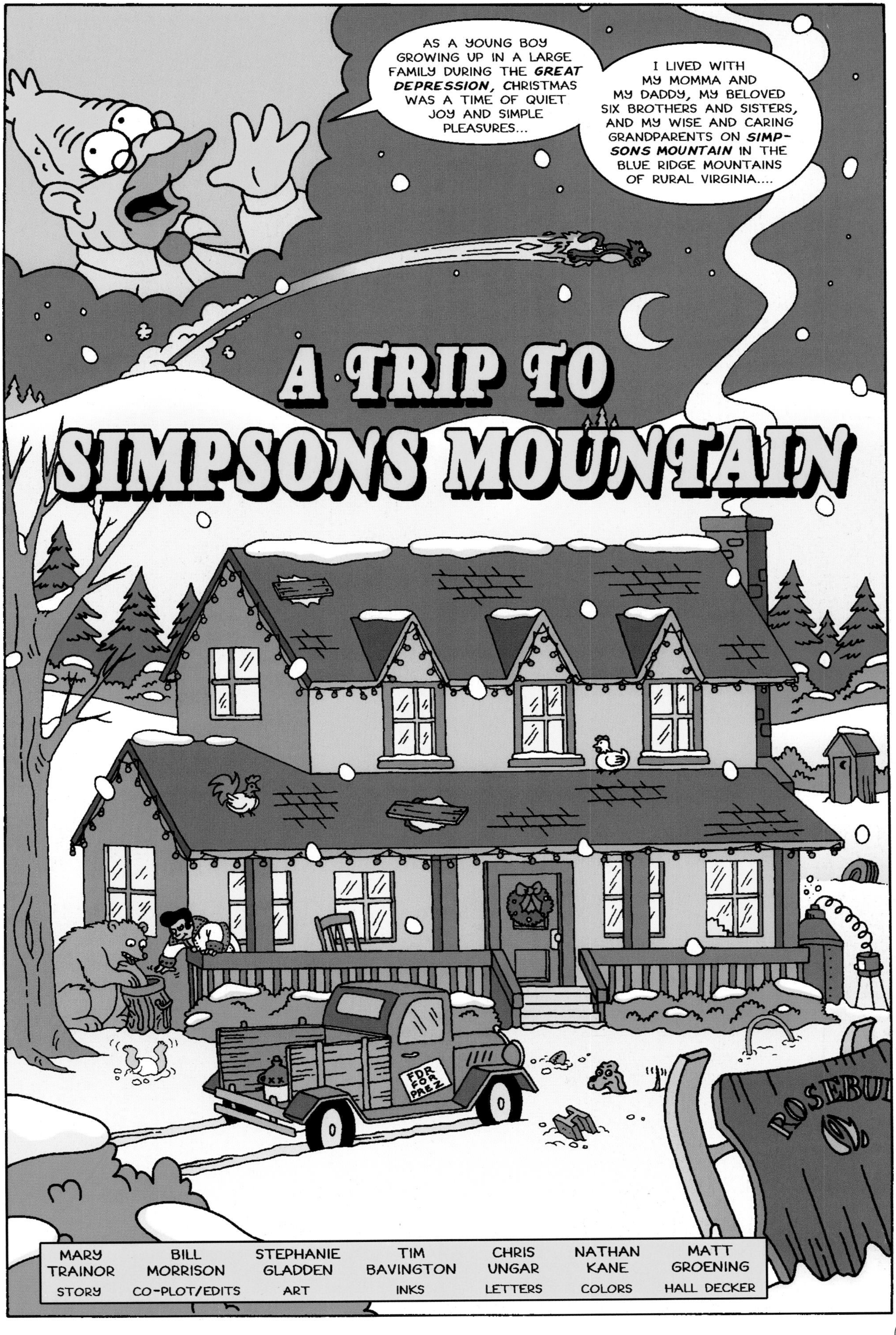
AS A YOUNG BOY GROWING UP IN A LARGE FAMILY DURING THE GREAT DEPRESSION, CHRISTMAS WAS A TIME OF QUIET JOY AND SIMPLE PLEASURES...
I LIVED WITH MY MOMMA AND MY DADDY, MY BELOVED SIX BROTHERS AND SISTERS, AND MY WISE AND CARING GRANDPARENTS ON SIMPSONS MOUNTAIN IN THE BLUE RIDGE MOUNTAINS OF RURAL VIRGINIA....
A TRIP TO SIMPSONS MOUNTAIN
FDR FOR PREZ
ROSEBU
MARY TRAINOR STORY
BILL MORRISON CO-PLOT/EDITS
STEPHANIE GLADDEN ART
TIM BAVINGTON INKS
CHRIS UNGAR LETTERS
NATHAN KANE COLORS
MATT GROENING HALL DECKER

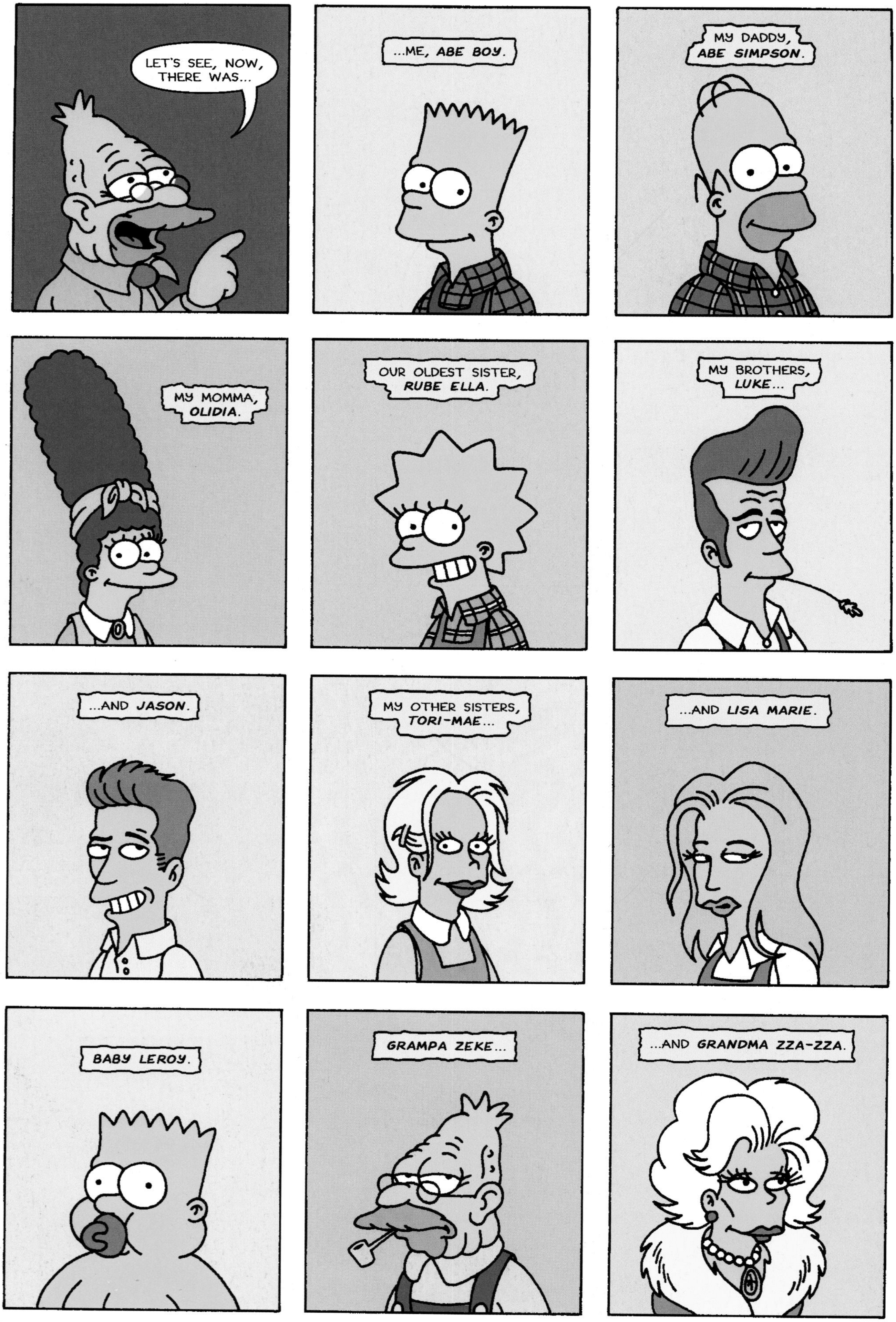
LET'S SEE, NOW, THERE WAS...
...ME, ABE BOY.
MY DADDY, ABE SIMPSON.
MY MOMMA, OLIDIA.
OUR OLDEST SISTER, RUBE ELLA.
MY BROTHERS, LUKE...
...AND JASON.
MY OTHER SISTERS, TORI-MAE...
...AND LISA MARIE.
BABY LEROY.
GRAMPA ZEKE...
...AND GRANDMA ZZA-ZZA.

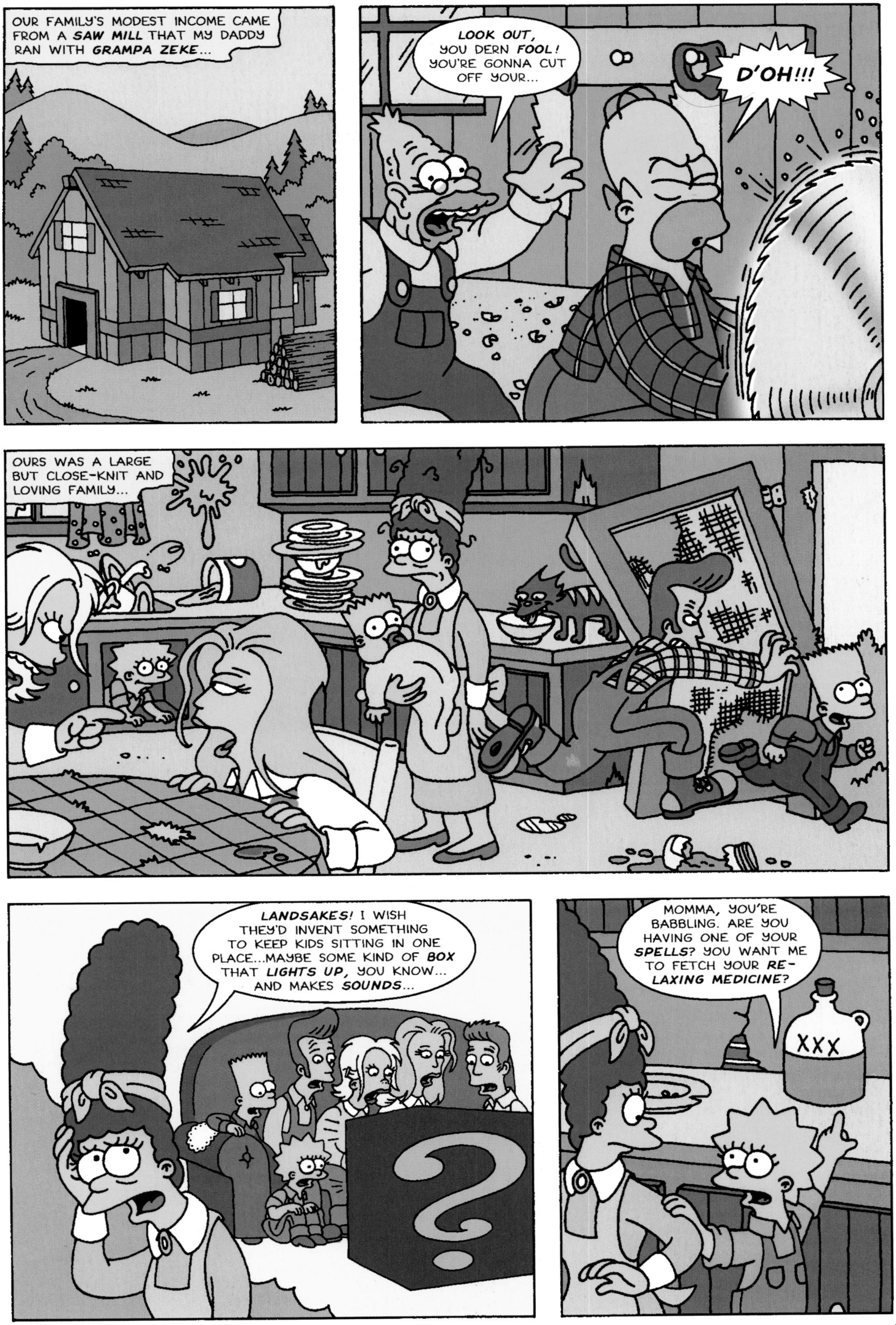
OUR FAMILY'S MODEST INCOME CAME FROM A **SAW MILL** THAT MY DADDY RAN WITH **GRAMPA ZEKE**...
LOOK OUT, YOU DERN **FOOL!** YOU'RE GONNA CUT OFF YOUR...
D'OH!!!
OURS WAS A LARGE BUT CLOSE-KNIT AND LOVING FAMILY...
LANDSAKES! I WISH THEY'D INVENT SOMETHING TO KEEP KIDS SITTING IN ONE PLACE...MAYBE SOME KIND OF **BOX** THAT **LIGHTS UP,** YOU KNOW... AND MAKES **SOUNDS**...
MOMMA, YOU'RE BABBLING. ARE YOU HAVING ONE OF YOUR **SPELLS?** YOU WANT ME TO FETCH YOUR **RE-LAXING MEDICINE?**
XXX

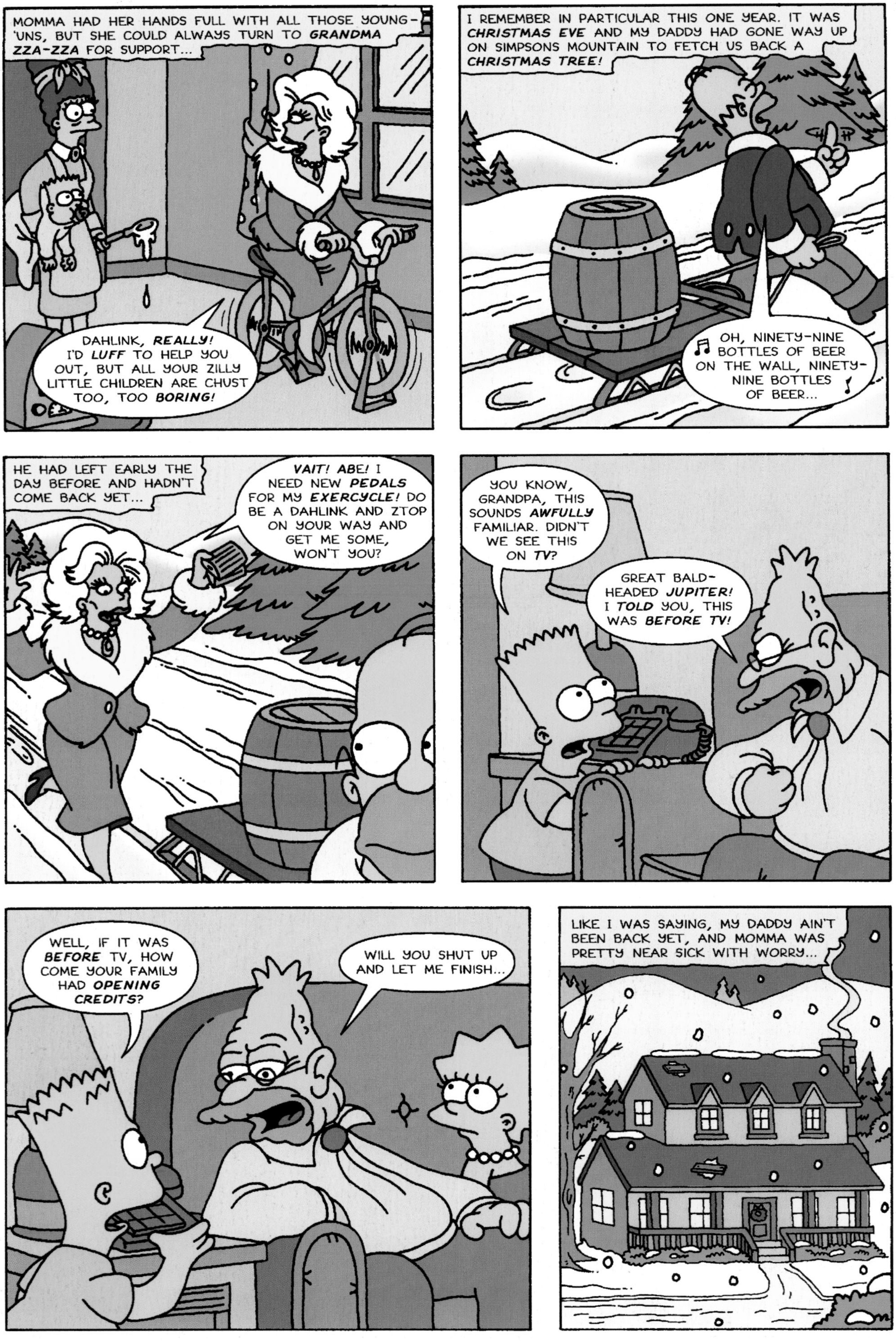
MOMMA HAD HER HANDS FULL WITH ALL THOSE YOUNG-'UNS, BUT SHE COULD ALWAYS TURN TO GRANDMA ZZA-ZZA FOR SUPPORT...
DAHLINK, REALLY! I'D LUFF TO HELP YOU OUT, BUT ALL YOUR ZILLY LITTLE CHILDREN ARE CHUST TOO, TOO BORING!
I REMEMBER IN PARTICULAR THIS ONE YEAR. IT WAS CHRISTMAS EVE AND MY DADDY HAD GONE WAY UP ON SIMPSONS MOUNTAIN TO FETCH US BACK A CHRISTMAS TREE!
OH, NINETY-NINE BOTTLES OF BEER ON THE WALL, NINETY-NINE BOTTLES OF BEER...
HE HAD LEFT EARLY THE DAY BEFORE AND HADN'T COME BACK YET...
VAIT! ABE! I NEED NEW PEDALS FOR MY EXERCYCLE! DO BE A DAHLINK AND ZTOP ON YOUR WAY AND GET ME SOME, WON'T YOU?
YOU KNOW, GRANDPA, THIS SOUNDS AWFULLY FAMILIAR. DIDN'T WE SEE THIS ON TV?
GREAT BALD-HEADED JUPITER! I TOLD YOU, THIS WAS BEFORE TV!
WELL, IF IT WAS BEFORE TV, HOW COME YOUR FAMILY HAD OPENING CREDITS?
WILL YOU SHUT UP AND LET ME FINISH...
LIKE I WAS SAYING, MY DADDY AIN'T BEEN BACK YET, AND MOMMA WAS PRETTY NEAR SICK WITH WORRY...

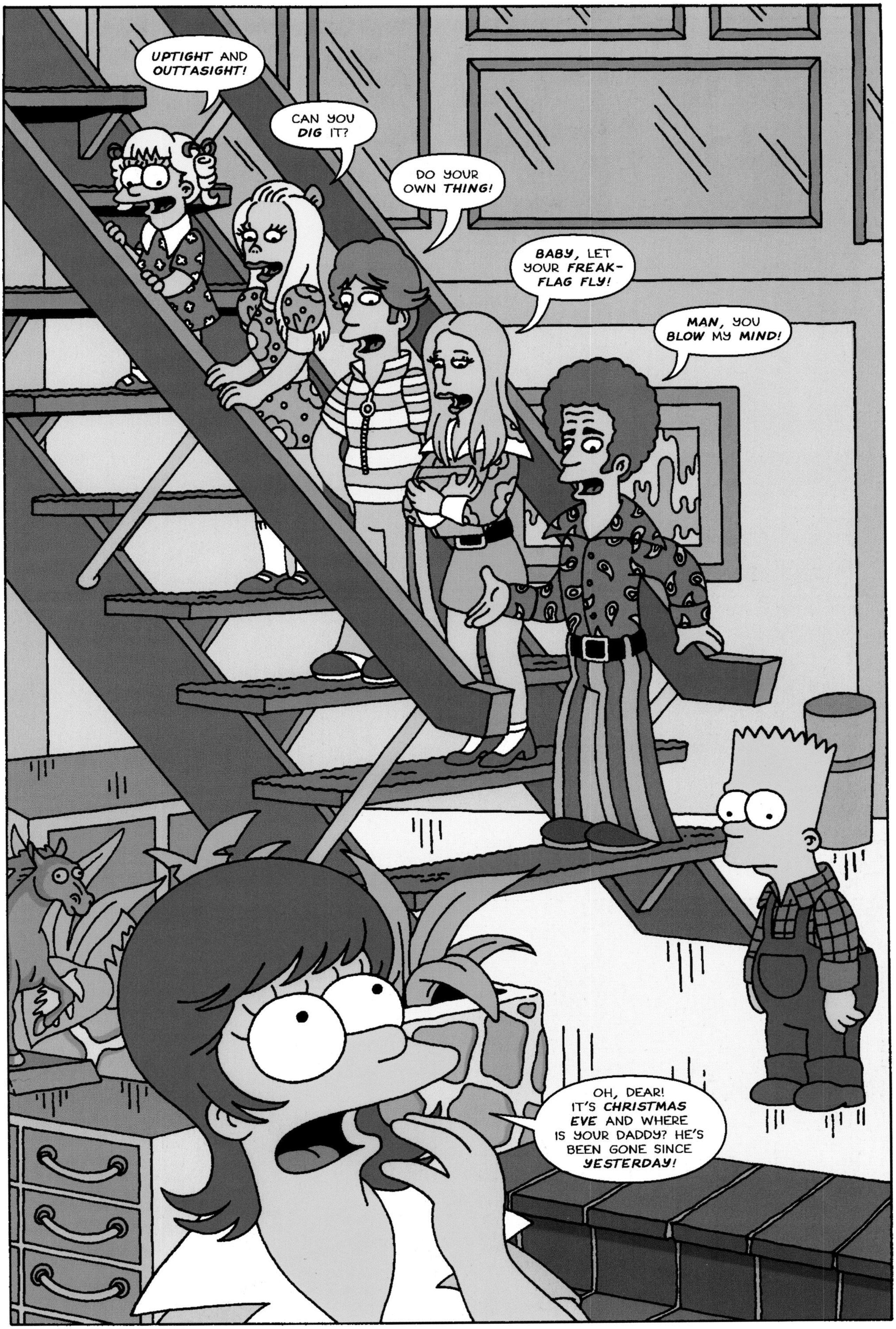
UPTIGHT AND OUTTASIGHT!
CAN YOU DIG IT?
DO YOUR OWN THING!
BABY, LET YOUR FREAK-FLAG FLY!
MAN, YOU BLOW MY MIND!
OH, DEAR! IT'S CHRISTMAS EVE AND WHERE IS YOUR DADDY? HE'S BEEN GONE SINCE YESTERDAY!

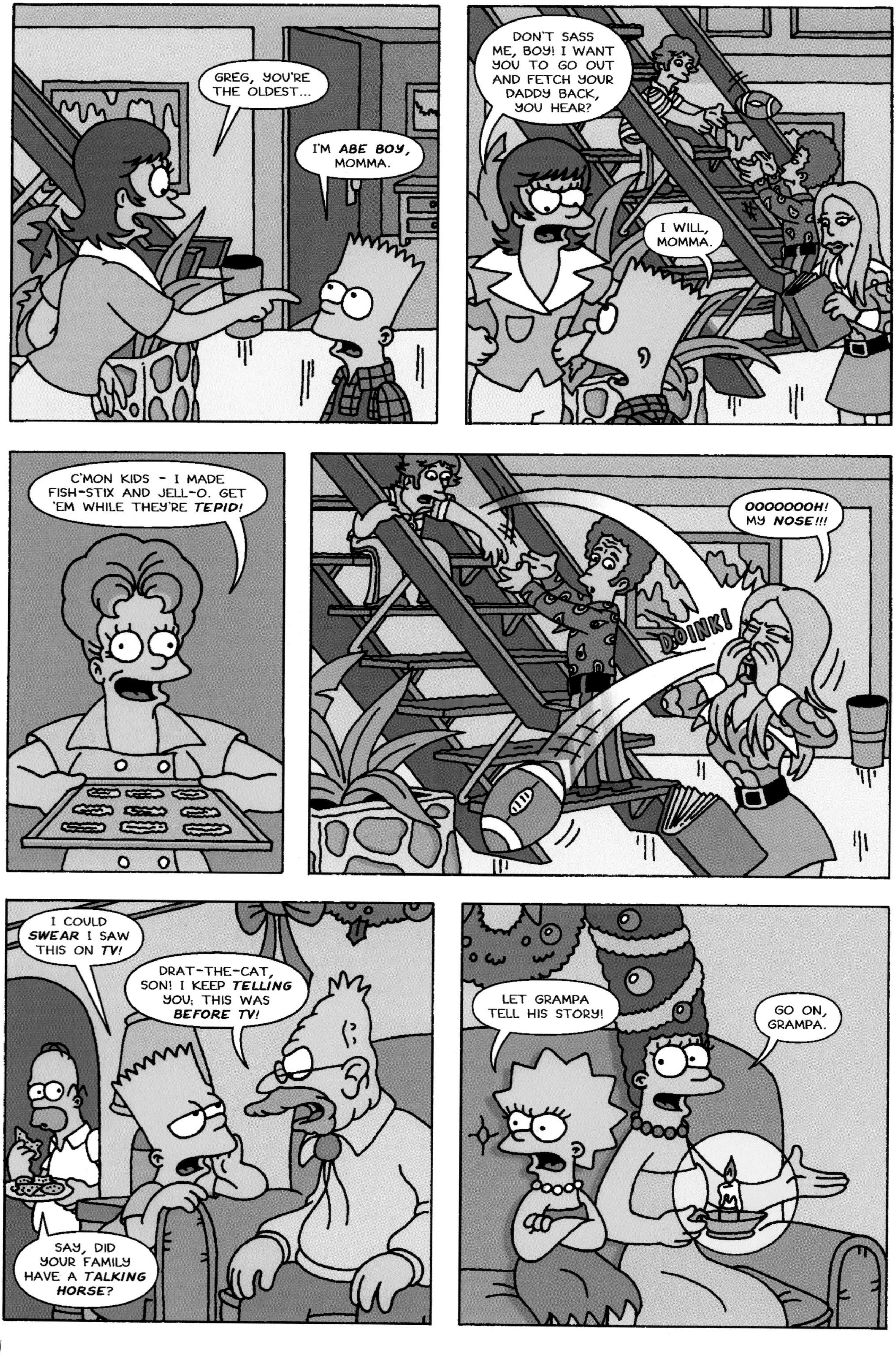
GREG, YOU'RE THE OLDEST...
I'M ABE BOY, MOMMA.
DON'T SASS ME, BOY! I WANT YOU TO GO OUT AND FETCH YOUR DADDY BACK, YOU HEAR?
I WILL, MOMMA.
C'MON KIDS - I MADE FISH-STIX AND JELL-O. GET 'EM WHILE THEY'RE TEPID!
OOOOOOOH! MY NOSE!!!
DOINK!
I COULD SWEAR I SAW THIS ON TV!
DRAT-THE-CAT, SON! I KEEP TELLING YOU; THIS WAS BEFORE TV!
SAY, DID YOUR FAMILY HAVE A TALKING HORSE?
LET GRAMPA TELL HIS STORY!
GO ON, GRAMPA.

AND SO, I SET OFF TO FIND MY DADDY. I PASSED THE HOME OF THE ECCENTRIC *BALDWIN SISTERS*...

TRUDGE TRUDGE TRUDGE TRUDGE

LOOK, IT'S THAT WHITE TRASH *ABE-BOY SIMPSON*. EVERY *CHRISTMAS EVE* HIS DADDY GOES OFF ON A BENDER AND *OLIDIA* SENDS THAT FOOL KID OUT LOOKING FOR HIM.

GOODNESS GRACIOUS. PEOPLE LIKE THAT GIVE *DRINKING* A BAD NAME.

YES, SISTER. THAT'S WHY WE MUST TAKE CARE TO SHARE OUR "RECIPE" WITH ONLY THE FINER FOLKS IN THIS TOWN...

...THE ONES WITH THE CHARM AND BREED-ING TO BE ALCOHOLICS...NOT MERE DRUNKARDS!

OH, AND LOOK, SISTER. HERE COMES OUR OWN *REVER-END REED*!

LET'S GET OUT THE GOOD CRYSTAL 8-OUNCE TUMBLERS, SHALL WE?

DURING *THE GREAT DEPRESSION*, MOMMA AND THE CHILDREN WERE SOMETIMES ABLE TO *SUPPLEMENT* OUR FAMILY'S MODEST *INCOME* BY TOURING THE COUNTRY *LIP-SYNCHING* INSIPID, *WHITE-BREAD* ROCK MUSIC.

PUTTA- PUTTA- PUT!

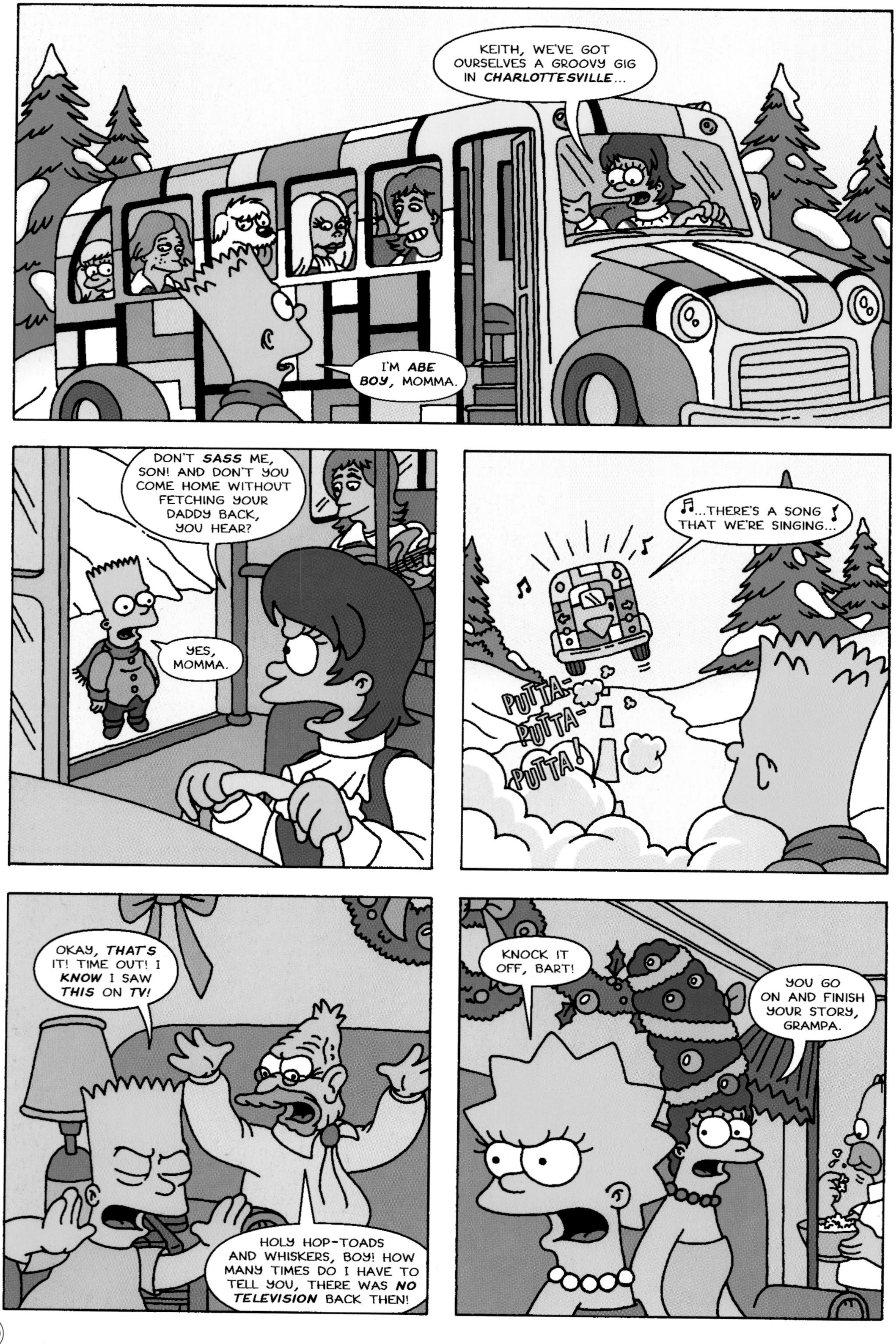
KEITH, WE'VE GOT OURSELVES A GROOVY GIG IN CHARLOTTESVILLE...
I'M ABE BOY, MOMMA.
DON'T SASS ME, SON! AND DON'T YOU COME HOME WITHOUT FETCHING YOUR DADDY BACK, YOU HEAR?
YES, MOMMA.
...THERE'S A SONG THAT WE'RE SINGING...
PUTTA-PUTTA-PUTTA!
OKAY, THAT'S IT! TIME OUT! I KNOW I SAW THIS ON TV!
HOLY HOP-TOADS AND WHISKERS, BOY! HOW MANY TIMES DO I HAVE TO TELL YOU, THERE WAS NO TELEVISION BACK THEN!
KNOCK IT OFF, BART!
YOU GO ON AND FINISH YOUR STORY, GRAMPA.

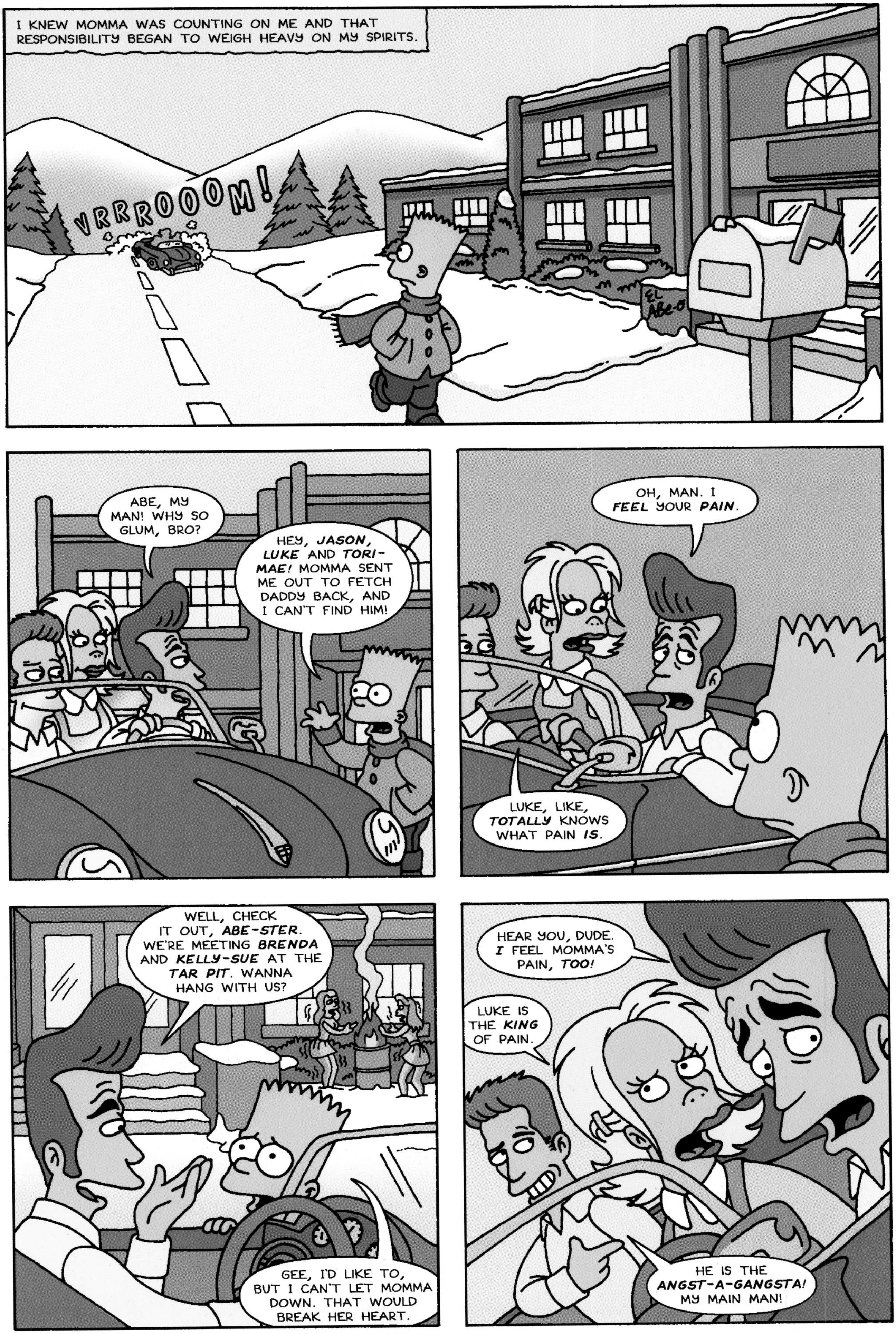
I KNEW MOMMA WAS COUNTING ON ME AND THAT RESPONSIBILITY BEGAN TO WEIGH HEAVY ON MY SPIRITS.
VRRROOOM!
ABE, MY MAN! WHY SO GLUM, BRO?
HEY, JASON, LUKE AND TORI-MAE! MOMMA SENT ME OUT TO FETCH DADDY BACK, AND I CAN'T FIND HIM!
OH, MAN. I FEEL YOUR PAIN.
LUKE, LIKE, TOTALLY KNOWS WHAT PAIN IS.
WELL, CHECK IT OUT, ABE-STER. WE'RE MEETING BRENDA AND KELLY-SUE AT THE TAR PIT. WANNA HANG WITH US?
GEE, I'D LIKE TO, BUT I CAN'T LET MOMMA DOWN. THAT WOULD BREAK HER HEART.
HEAR YOU, DUDE. I FEEL MOMMA'S PAIN, TOO!
LUKE IS THE KING OF PAIN.
HE IS THE ANGST-A-GANGSTA! MY MAIN MAN!

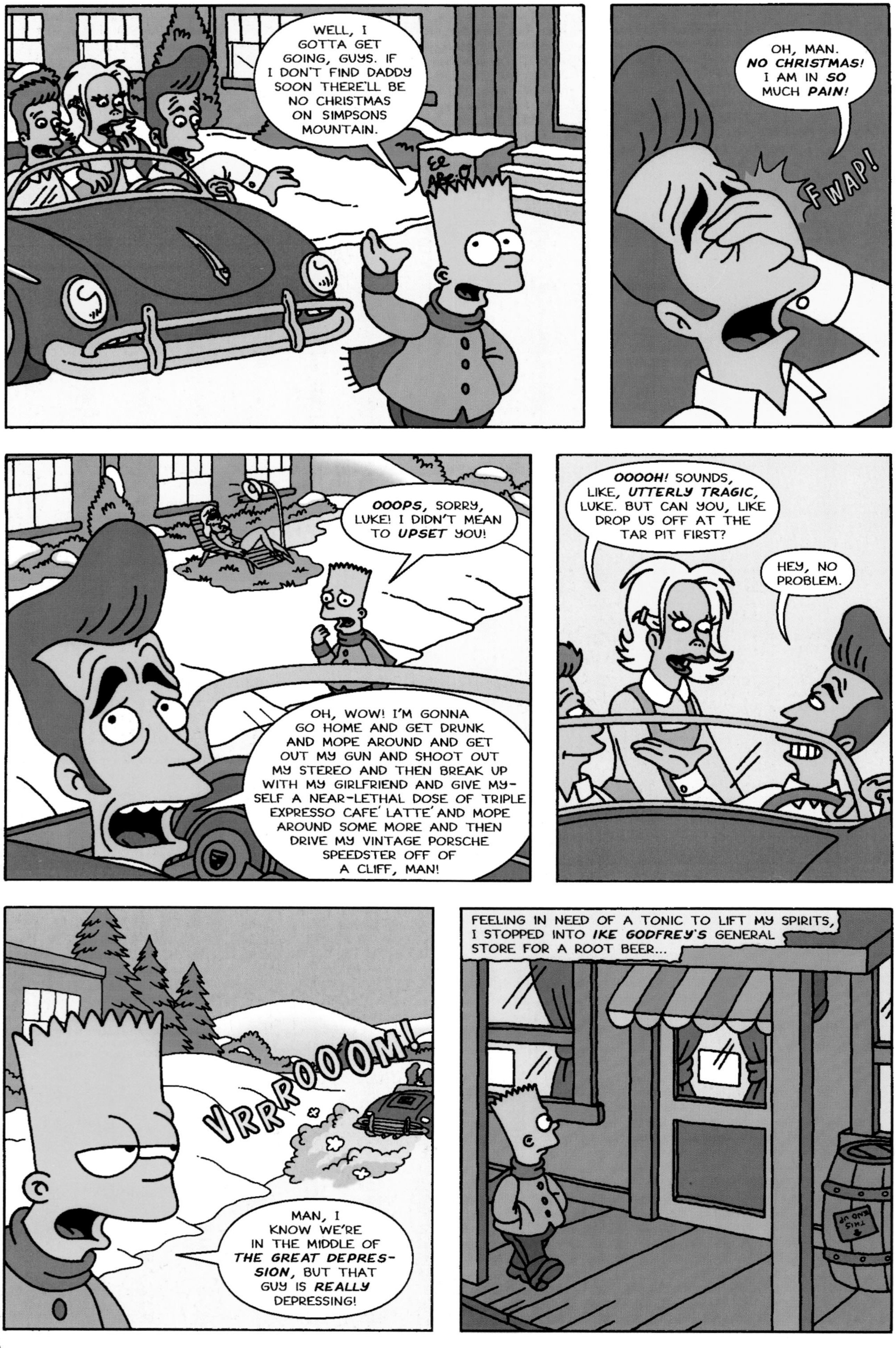
WELL, I GOTTA GET GOING, GUYS. IF I DON'T FIND DADDY SOON THERE'LL BE NO CHRISTMAS ON SIMPSONS MOUNTAIN.
OH, MAN. **NO CHRISTMAS!** I AM IN **SO** MUCH **PAIN!**
FWAP!
OOOPS, SORRY, LUKE! I DIDN'T MEAN TO **UPSET** YOU!
OH, WOW! I'M GONNA GO HOME AND GET DRUNK AND MOPE AROUND AND GET OUT MY GUN AND SHOOT OUT MY STEREO AND THEN BREAK UP WITH MY GIRLFRIEND AND GIVE MY-SELF A NEAR-LETHAL DOSE OF TRIPLE EXPRESSO CAFE' LATTE' AND MOPE AROUND SOME MORE AND THEN DRIVE MY VINTAGE PORSCHE SPEEDSTER OFF OF A CLIFF, MAN!
OOOOH! SOUNDS, LIKE, **UTTERLY TRAGIC,** LUKE. BUT CAN YOU, LIKE DROP US OFF AT THE TAR PIT FIRST?
HEY, NO PROBLEM.
VRRROOOOM!
MAN, I KNOW WE'RE IN THE MIDDLE OF **THE GREAT DEPRES-SION,** BUT THAT GUY IS **REALLY** DEPRESSING!
FEELING IN NEED OF A TONIC TO LIFT MY SPIRITS, I STOPPED INTO **IKE GODFREY'S** GENERAL STORE FOR A ROOT BEER...

UH, HELLO, IKE...BOY, YOU SURE HAVE *CHANGED* THE OLD PLACE!

YES. YES. YOU *BET!* I AM THOROUGHLY *MODERNIZED* NOW!

HI DIDDLY HO, BART!

MY NAME IS *ABE-BOY*, SIR.

NOW, NOW, SON. RESPECT YOUR ELDERS.

WOULD YOU CARE TO AVAIL YOURSELF OF OUR NEW SQUISHEE MACHINE?

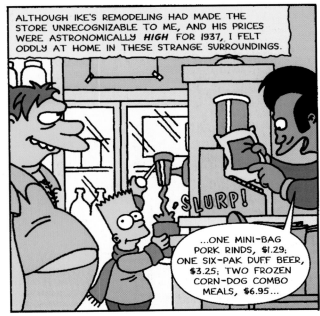

ALTHOUGH IKE'S REMODELING HAD MADE THE STORE UNRECOGNIZABLE TO ME, AND HIS PRICES WERE ASTRONOMICALLY *HIGH* FOR 1937, I FELT ODDLY AT HOME IN THESE STRANGE SURROUNDINGS.

SLURP!

...ONE MINI-BAG PORK RINDS, $1.29; ONE SIX-PAK DUFF BEER, $3.25; TWO FROZEN CORN-DOG COMBO MEALS, $6.95...

HAVE A NICE DAY!

?

THAT'S TOTALLY UNBELIEVABLE, GRAMPA. BUT AT *LEAST* IT DOESN'T SOUND LIKE SOMETHING I'VE SEEN ON *TV!*

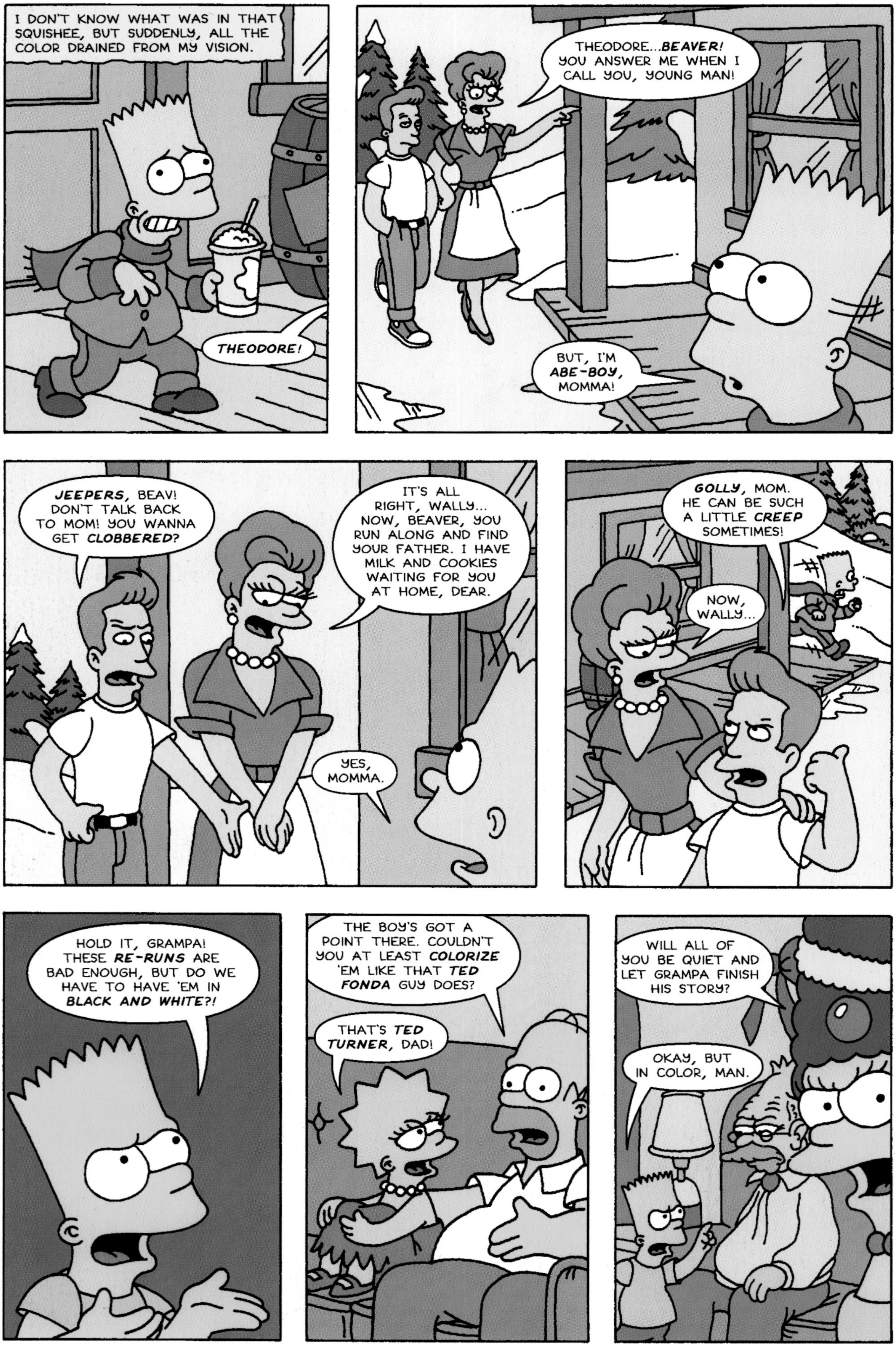
I DON'T KNOW WHAT WAS IN THAT SQUISHEE, BUT SUDDENLY, ALL THE COLOR DRAINED FROM MY VISION.
THEODORE!
THEODORE...BEAVER! YOU ANSWER ME WHEN I CALL YOU, YOUNG MAN!
BUT, I'M ABE-BOY, MOMMA!
JEEPERS, BEAV! DON'T TALK BACK TO MOM! YOU WANNA GET CLOBBERED?
IT'S ALL RIGHT, WALLY... NOW, BEAVER, YOU RUN ALONG AND FIND YOUR FATHER. I HAVE MILK AND COOKIES WAITING FOR YOU AT HOME, DEAR.
YES, MOMMA.
GOLLY, MOM. HE CAN BE SUCH A LITTLE CREEP SOMETIMES!
NOW, WALLY...
HOLD IT, GRAMPA! THESE RE-RUNS ARE BAD ENOUGH, BUT DO WE HAVE TO HAVE 'EM IN BLACK AND WHITE?!
THE BOY'S GOT A POINT THERE. COULDN'T YOU AT LEAST COLORIZE 'EM LIKE THAT TED FONDA GUY DOES?
THAT'S TED TURNER, DAD!
WILL ALL OF YOU BE QUIET AND LET GRAMPA FINISH HIS STORY?
OKAY, BUT IN COLOR, MAN.

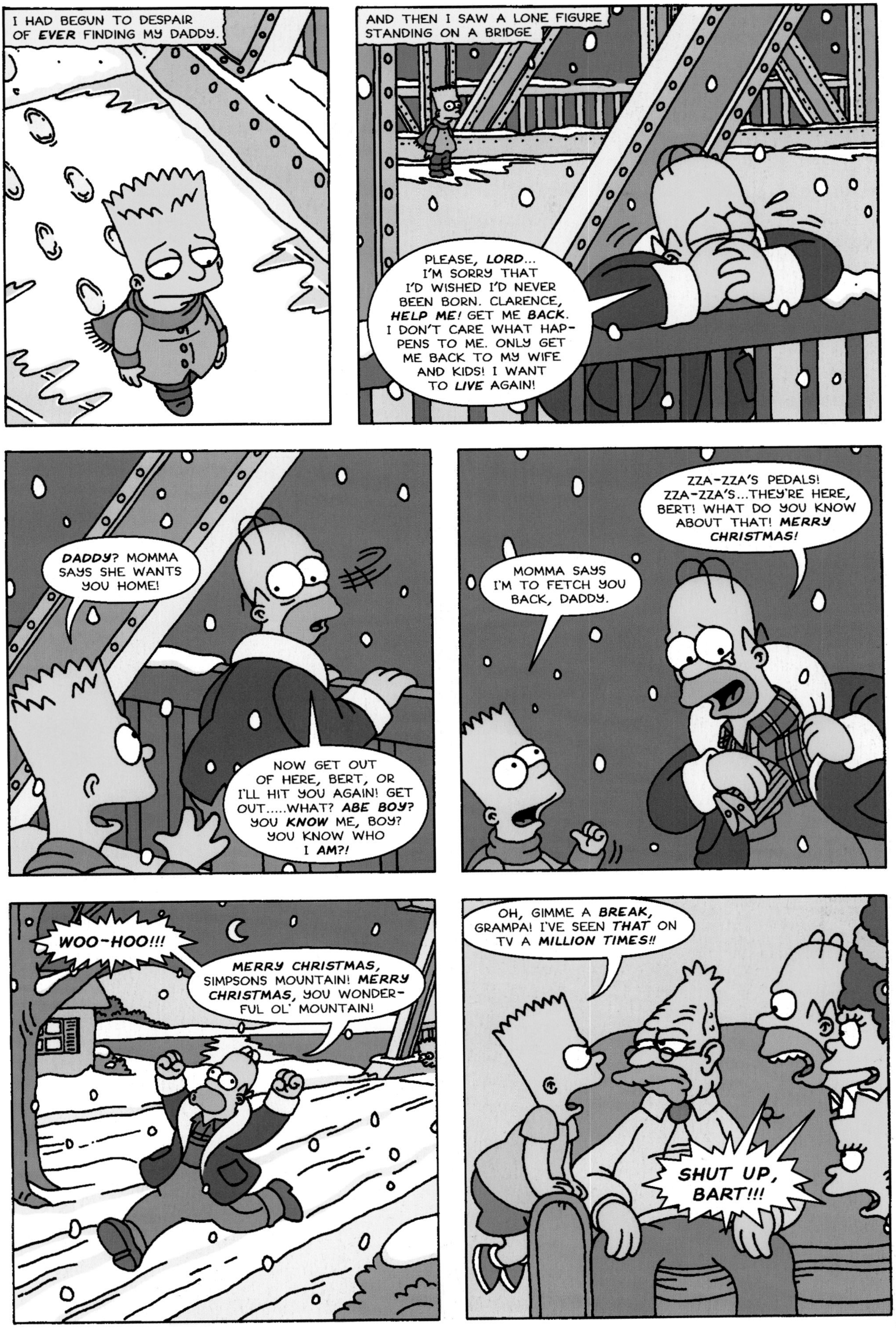
I HAD BEGUN TO DESPAIR OF **EVER** FINDING MY DADDY.
AND THEN I SAW A LONE FIGURE STANDING ON A BRIDGE
PLEASE, **LORD**... I'M SORRY THAT I'D WISHED I'D NEVER BEEN BORN. CLARENCE, **HELP ME!** GET ME **BACK**. I DON'T CARE WHAT HAPPENS TO ME. ONLY GET ME BACK TO MY WIFE AND KIDS! I WANT TO **LIVE** AGAIN!
DADDY? MOMMA SAYS SHE WANTS YOU HOME!
NOW GET OUT OF HERE, BERT, OR I'LL HIT YOU AGAIN! GET OUT.....WHAT? **ABE BOY?** YOU **KNOW** ME, BOY? YOU KNOW WHO I **AM?!**
MOMMA SAYS I'M TO FETCH YOU BACK, DADDY.
ZZA-ZZA'S PEDALS! ZZA-ZZA'S...THEY'RE HERE, BERT! WHAT DO YOU KNOW ABOUT THAT! **MERRY CHRISTMAS!**
WOO-HOO!!!
MERRY CHRISTMAS, SIMPSONS MOUNTAIN! **MERRY CHRISTMAS,** YOU WONDERFUL OL' MOUNTAIN!
OH, GIMME A **BREAK,** GRAMPA! I'VE SEEN **THAT** ON TV A **MILLION TIMES!!**
SHUT UP, BART!!!

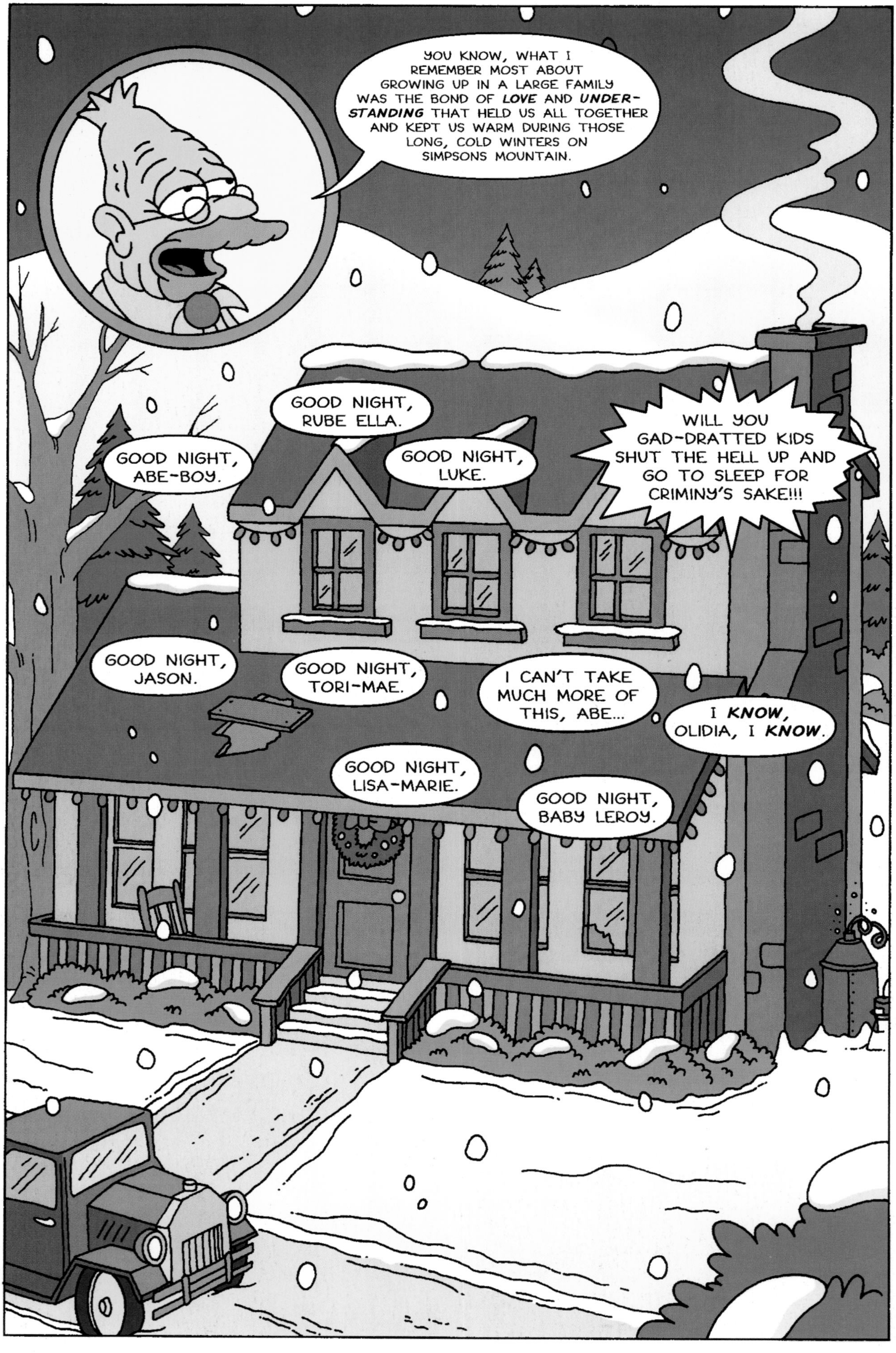
YOU KNOW, WHAT I REMEMBER MOST ABOUT GROWING UP IN A LARGE FAMILY WAS THE BOND OF ***LOVE*** AND ***UNDERSTANDING*** THAT HELD US ALL TOGETHER AND KEPT US WARM DURING THOSE LONG, COLD WINTERS ON SIMPSONS MOUNTAIN.
GOOD NIGHT, RUBE ELLA.
GOOD NIGHT, ABE-BOY.
GOOD NIGHT, LUKE.
WILL YOU GAD-DRATTED KIDS SHUT THE HELL UP AND GO TO SLEEP FOR CRIMINY'S SAKE!!!
GOOD NIGHT, JASON.
GOOD NIGHT, TORI-MAE.
I CAN'T TAKE MUCH MORE OF THIS, ABE...
I ***KNOW***, OLIDIA, I ***KNOW***.
GOOD NIGHT, LISA-MARIE.
GOOD NIGHT, BABY LEROY.

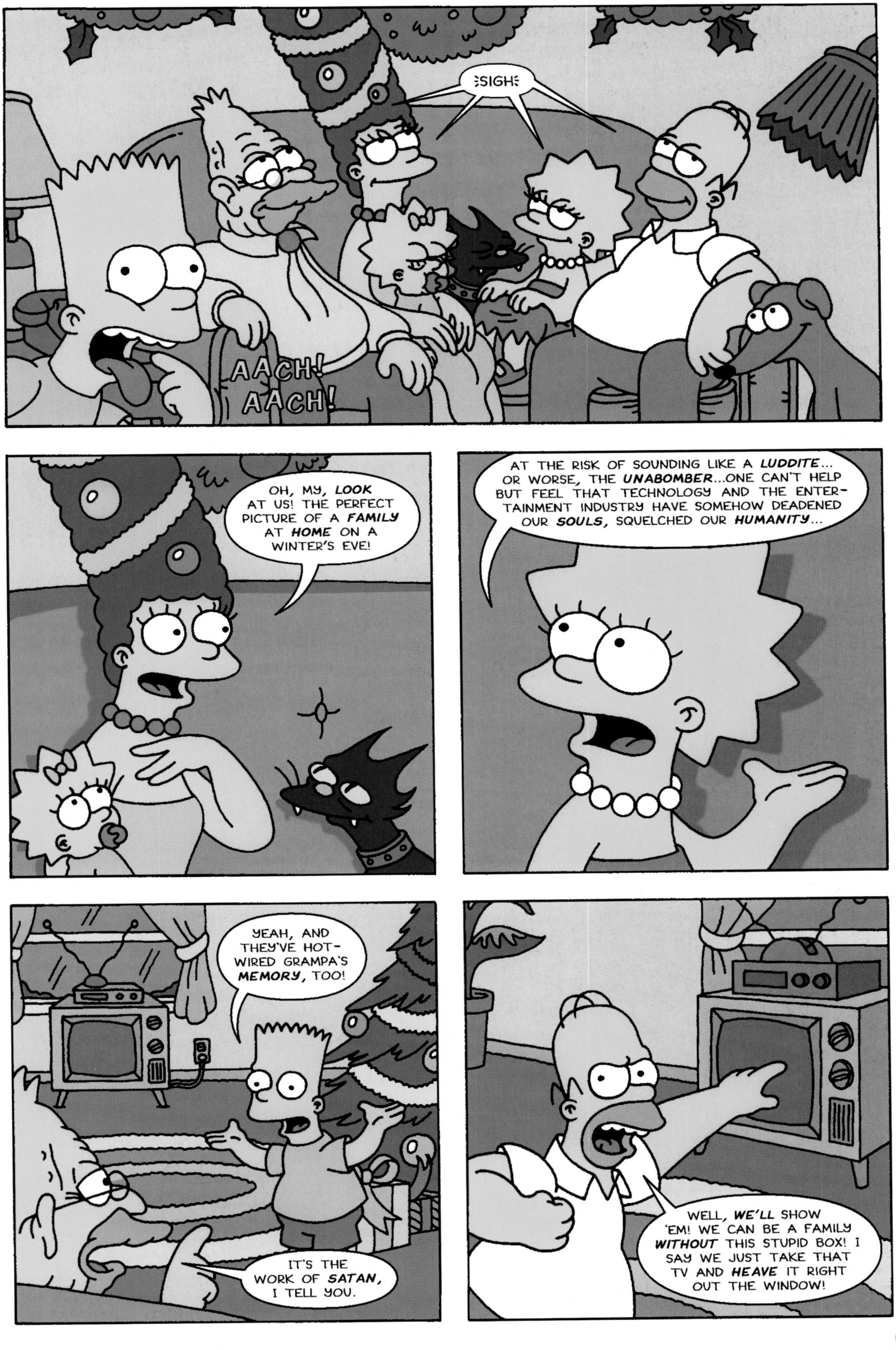

:SIGH:
AACH! AACH!
OH, MY, LOOK AT US! THE PERFECT PICTURE OF A FAMILY AT HOME ON A WINTER'S EVE!
AT THE RISK OF SOUNDING LIKE A LUDDITE... OR WORSE, THE UNABOMBER...ONE CAN'T HELP BUT FEEL THAT TECHNOLOGY AND THE ENTERTAINMENT INDUSTRY HAVE SOMEHOW DEADENED OUR SOULS, SQUELCHED OUR HUMANITY...
YEAH, AND THEY'VE HOT-WIRED GRAMPA'S MEMORY, TOO!
IT'S THE WORK OF SATAN, I TELL YOU.
WELL, WE'LL SHOW 'EM! WE CAN BE A FAMILY WITHOUT THIS STUPID BOX! I SAY WE JUST TAKE THAT TV AND HEAVE IT RIGHT OUT THE WINDOW!

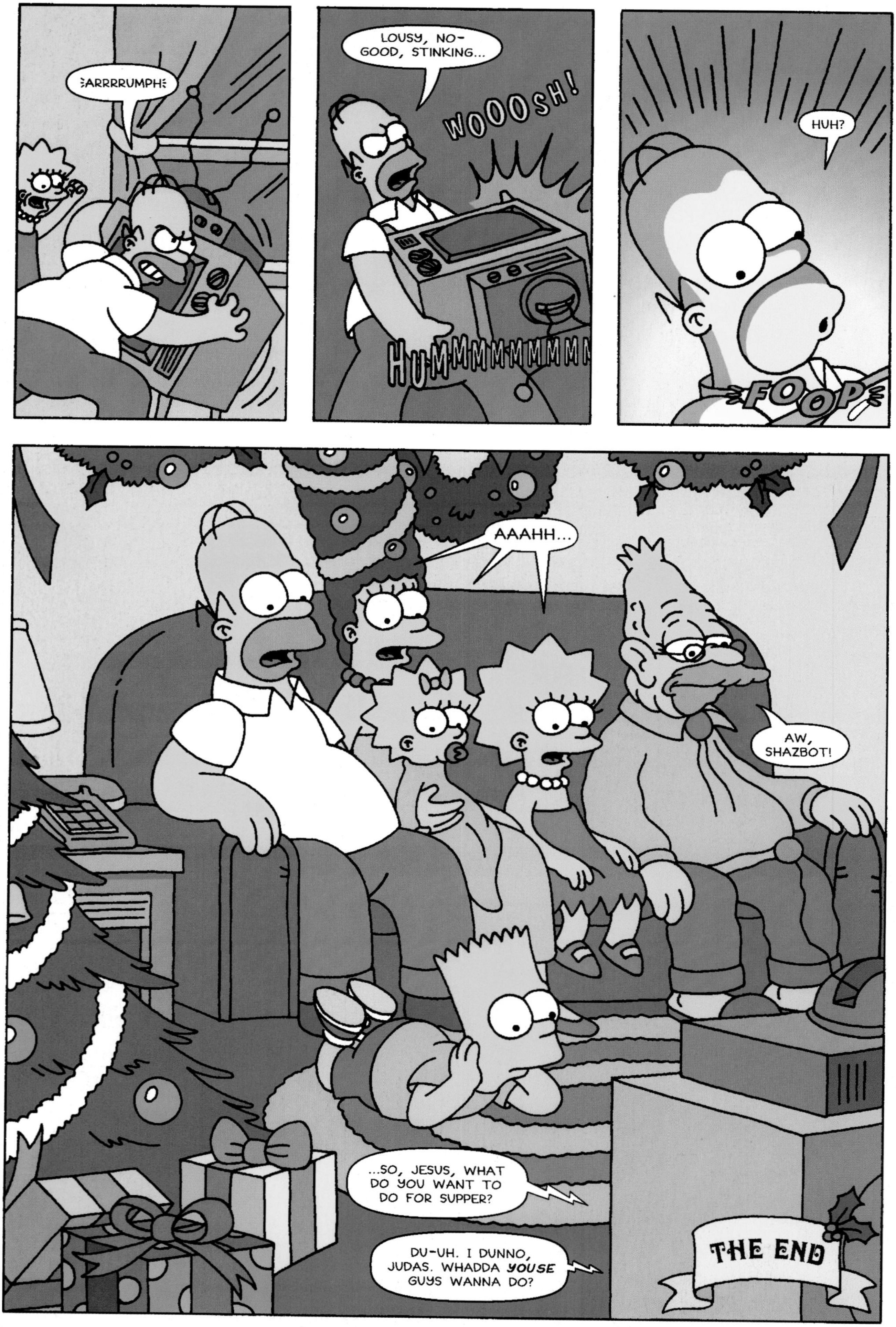
ARRRRUMPH
LOUSY, NO-GOOD, STINKING...
WOOOSH!
HUMMMMMMMMMM
HUH?
FOOP
AAAHH...
AW, SHAZBOT!
...SO, JESUS, WHAT DO YOU WANT TO DO FOR SUPPER?
DU-UH. I DUNNO, JUDAS. WHADDA YOUSE GUYS WANNA DO?
THE END

Bart Simpson in... CON-NUKAH!

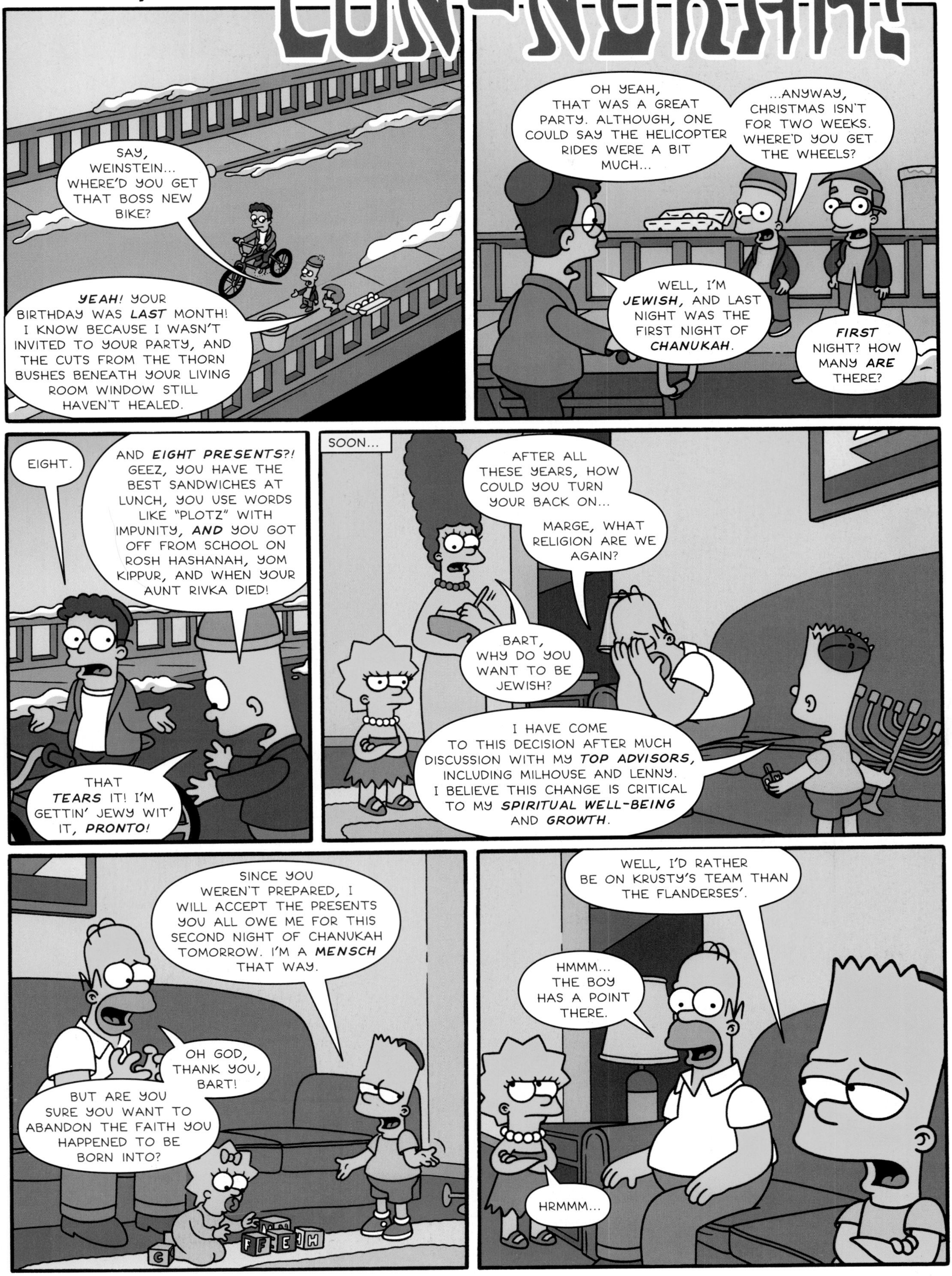
SAY, WEINSTEIN... WHERE'D YOU GET THAT BOSS NEW BIKE?
YEAH! YOUR BIRTHDAY WAS LAST MONTH! I KNOW BECAUSE I WASN'T INVITED TO YOUR PARTY, AND THE CUTS FROM THE THORN BUSHES BENEATH YOUR LIVING ROOM WINDOW STILL HAVEN'T HEALED.
OH YEAH, THAT WAS A GREAT PARTY. ALTHOUGH, ONE COULD SAY THE HELICOPTER RIDES WERE A BIT MUCH...
...ANYWAY, CHRISTMAS ISN'T FOR TWO WEEKS. WHERE'D YOU GET THE WHEELS?
WELL, I'M JEWISH, AND LAST NIGHT WAS THE FIRST NIGHT OF CHANUKAH.
FIRST NIGHT? HOW MANY ARE THERE?
EIGHT.
AND EIGHT PRESENTS?! GEEZ, YOU HAVE THE BEST SANDWICHES AT LUNCH, YOU USE WORDS LIKE "PLOTZ" WITH IMPUNITY, AND YOU GOT OFF FROM SCHOOL ON ROSH HASHANAH, YOM KIPPUR, AND WHEN YOUR AUNT RIVKA DIED!
THAT TEARS IT! I'M GETTIN' JEWY WIT' IT, PRONTO!
SOON...
AFTER ALL THESE YEARS, HOW COULD YOU TURN YOUR BACK ON...
MARGE, WHAT RELIGION ARE WE AGAIN?
BART, WHY DO YOU WANT TO BE JEWISH?
I HAVE COME TO THIS DECISION AFTER MUCH DISCUSSION WITH MY TOP ADVISORS, INCLUDING MILHOUSE AND LENNY. I BELIEVE THIS CHANGE IS CRITICAL TO MY SPIRITUAL WELL-BEING AND GROWTH.
SINCE YOU WEREN'T PREPARED, I WILL ACCEPT THE PRESENTS YOU ALL OWE ME FOR THIS SECOND NIGHT OF CHANUKAH TOMORROW. I'M A MENSCH THAT WAY.
OH GOD, THANK YOU, BART!
BUT ARE YOU SURE YOU WANT TO ABANDON THE FAITH YOU HAPPENED TO BE BORN INTO?
WELL, I'D RATHER BE ON KRUSTY'S TEAM THAN THE FLANDERSES'.
HMMM... THE BOY HAS A POINT THERE.
HRMMM...

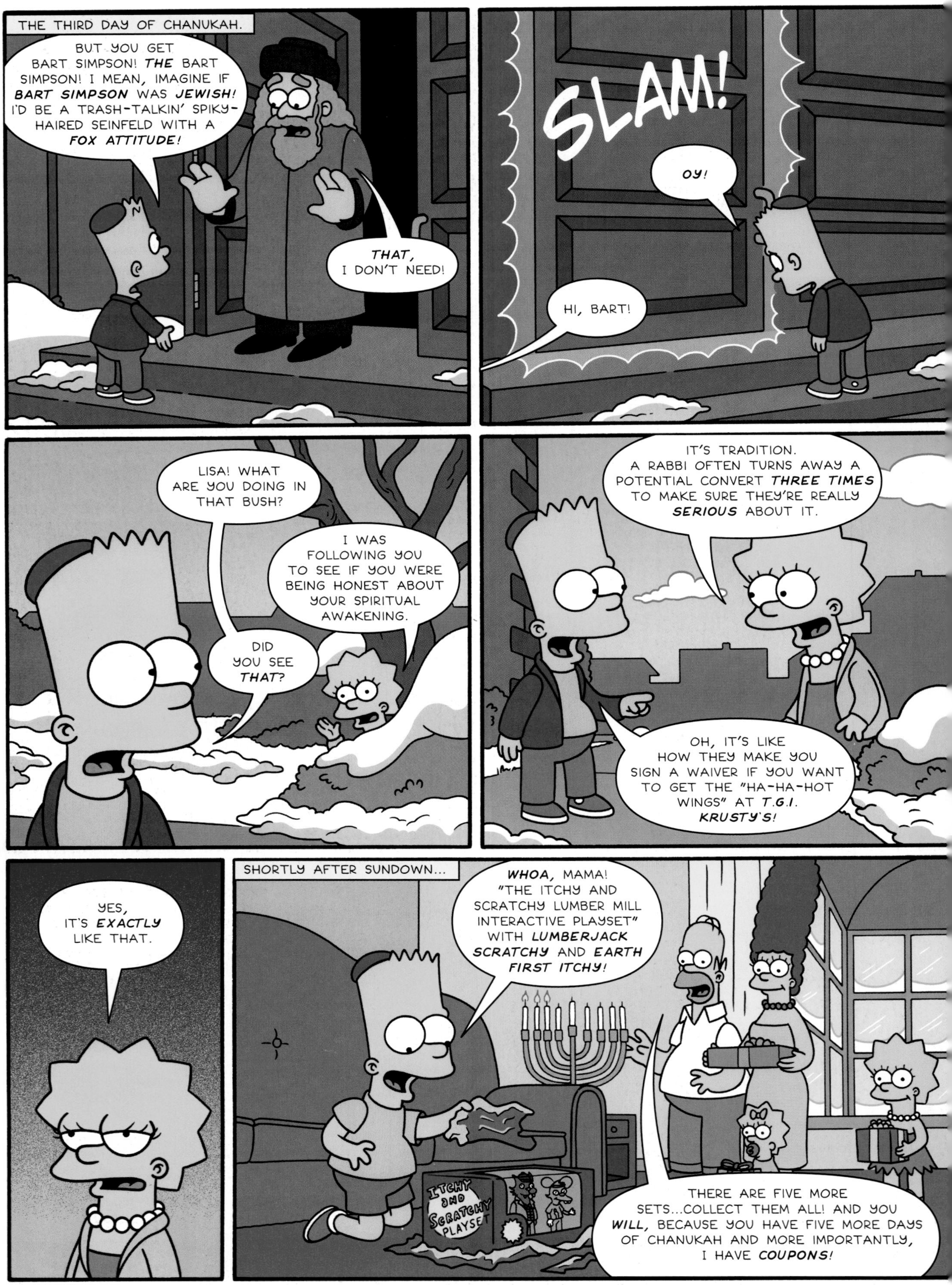
THE THIRD DAY OF CHANUKAH.
BUT YOU GET BART SIMPSON! THE BART SIMPSON! I MEAN, IMAGINE IF BART SIMPSON WAS JEWISH! I'D BE A TRASH-TALKIN' SPIKY-HAIRED SEINFELD WITH A FOX ATTITUDE!
THAT, I DON'T NEED!
SLAM!
OY!
HI, BART!
LISA! WHAT ARE YOU DOING IN THAT BUSH?
I WAS FOLLOWING YOU TO SEE IF YOU WERE BEING HONEST ABOUT YOUR SPIRITUAL AWAKENING.
DID YOU SEE THAT?
IT'S TRADITION. A RABBI OFTEN TURNS AWAY A POTENTIAL CONVERT THREE TIMES TO MAKE SURE THEY'RE REALLY SERIOUS ABOUT IT.
OH, IT'S LIKE HOW THEY MAKE YOU SIGN A WAIVER IF YOU WANT TO GET THE "HA-HA-HOT WINGS" AT T.G.I. KRUSTY'S!
YES, IT'S EXACTLY LIKE THAT.
SHORTLY AFTER SUNDOWN...
WHOA, MAMA! "THE ITCHY AND SCRATCHY LUMBER MILL INTERACTIVE PLAYSET" WITH LUMBERJACK SCRATCHY AND EARTH FIRST ITCHY!
ITCHY AND SCRATCHY PLAYSET
THERE ARE FIVE MORE SETS...COLLECT THEM ALL! AND YOU WILL, BECAUSE YOU HAVE FIVE MORE DAYS OF CHANUKAH AND MORE IMPORTANTLY, I HAVE COUPONS!

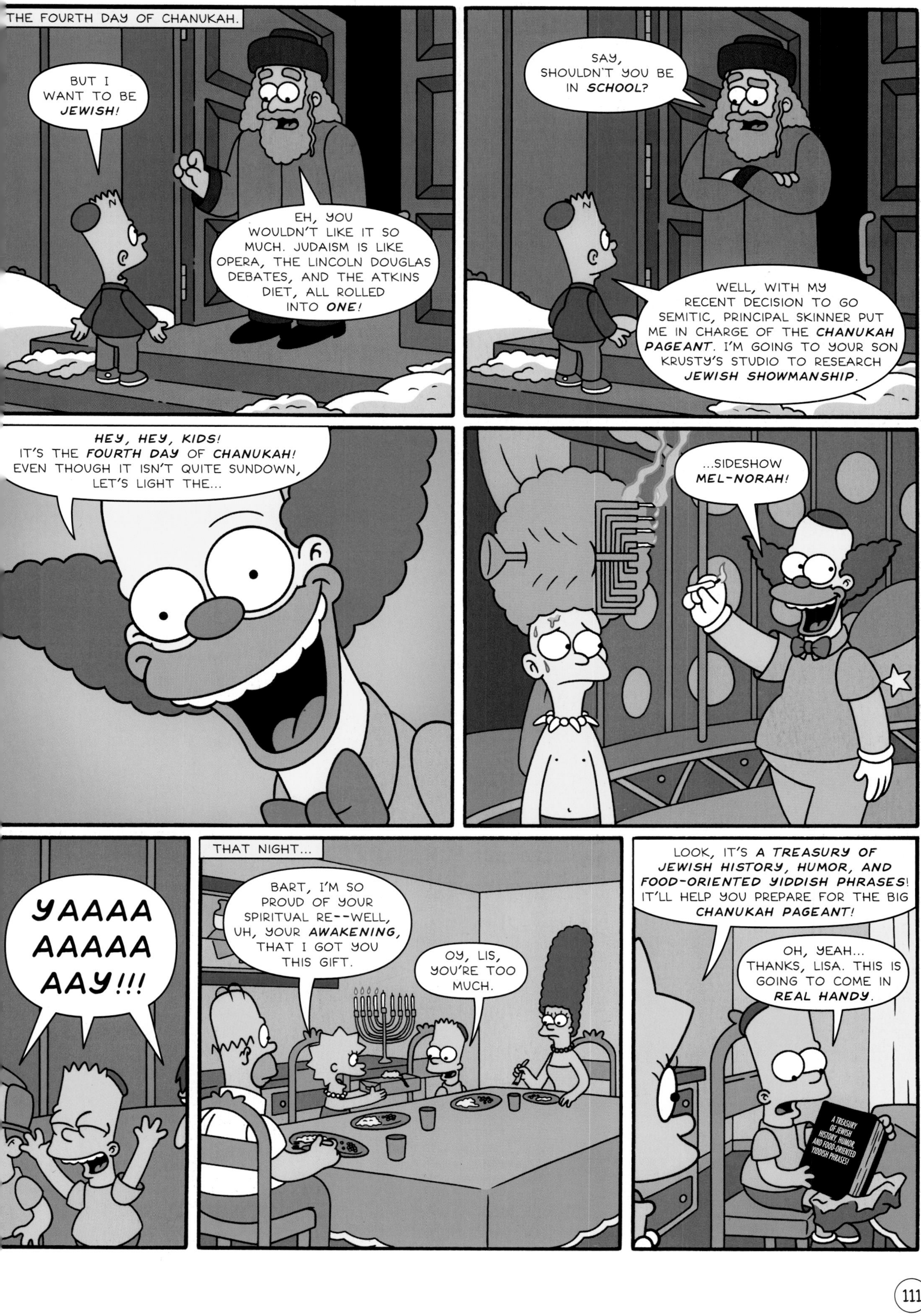
THE FOURTH DAY OF CHANUKAH.
BUT I WANT TO BE JEWISH!
EH, YOU WOULDN'T LIKE IT SO MUCH. JUDAISM IS LIKE OPERA, THE LINCOLN DOUGLAS DEBATES, AND THE ATKINS DIET, ALL ROLLED INTO ONE!
SAY, SHOULDN'T YOU BE IN SCHOOL?
WELL, WITH MY RECENT DECISION TO GO SEMITIC, PRINCIPAL SKINNER PUT ME IN CHARGE OF THE CHANUKAH PAGEANT. I'M GOING TO YOUR SON KRUSTY'S STUDIO TO RESEARCH JEWISH SHOWMANSHIP.
HEY, HEY, KIDS! IT'S THE FOURTH DAY OF CHANUKAH! EVEN THOUGH IT ISN'T QUITE SUNDOWN, LET'S LIGHT THE...
...SIDESHOW MEL-NORAH!
YAAAA AAAAA AAY!!!
THAT NIGHT...
BART, I'M SO PROUD OF YOUR SPIRITUAL RE--WELL, UH, YOUR AWAKENING, THAT I GOT YOU THIS GIFT.
OY, LIS, YOU'RE TOO MUCH.
LOOK, IT'S A TREASURY OF JEWISH HISTORY, HUMOR, AND FOOD-ORIENTED YIDDISH PHRASES! IT'LL HELP YOU PREPARE FOR THE BIG CHANUKAH PAGEANT!
OH, YEAH... THANKS, LISA. THIS IS GOING TO COME IN REAL HANDY.
A TREASURY OF JEWISH HISTORY, HUMOR, AND FOOD-ORIENTED YIDDISH PHRASES!

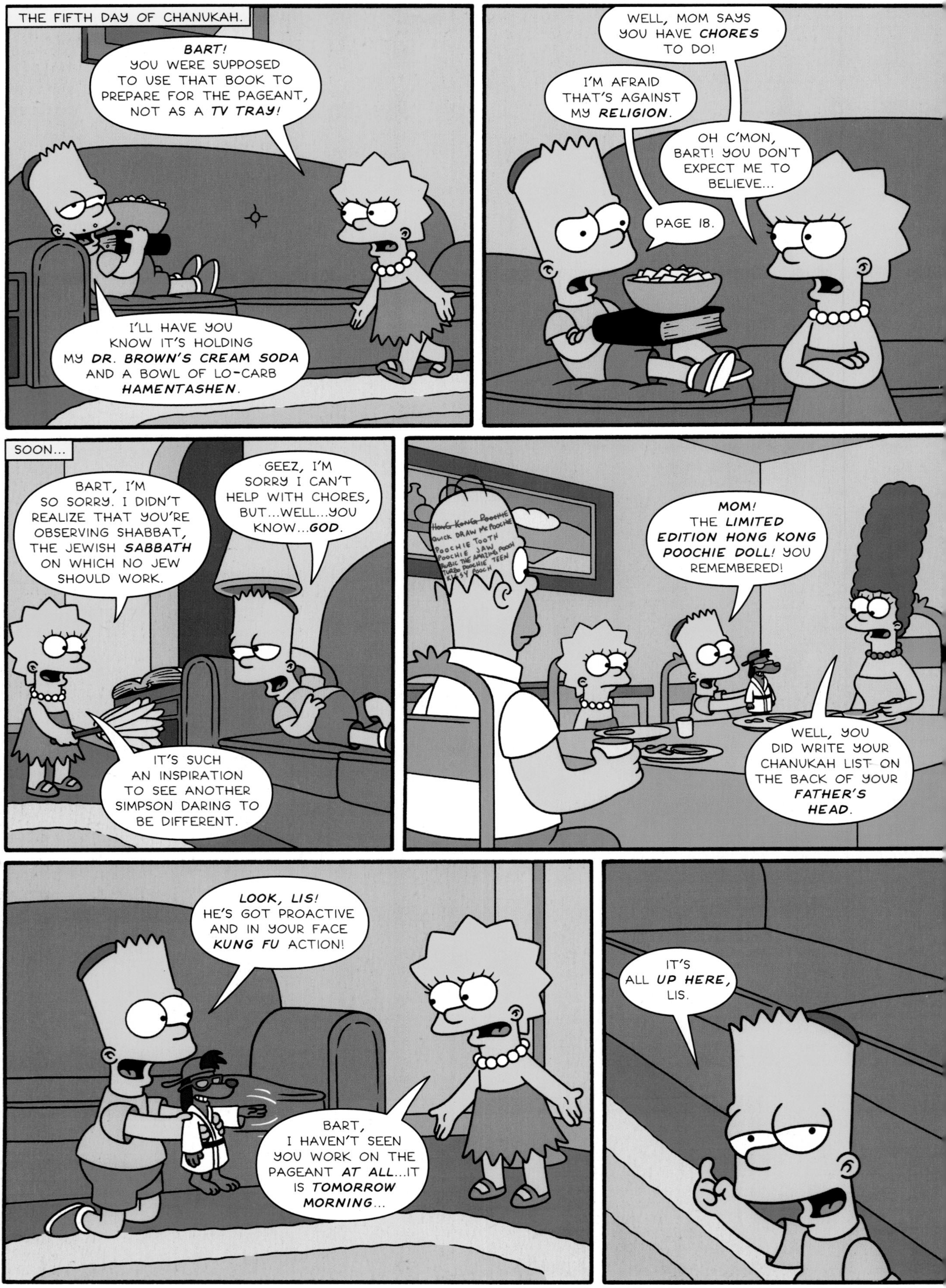
THE FIFTH DAY OF CHANUKAH.
BART! YOU WERE SUPPOSED TO USE THAT BOOK TO PREPARE FOR THE PAGEANT, NOT AS A TV TRAY!
I'LL HAVE YOU KNOW IT'S HOLDING MY DR. BROWN'S CREAM SODA AND A BOWL OF LO-CARB HAMENTASHEN.
WELL, MOM SAYS YOU HAVE CHORES TO DO!
I'M AFRAID THAT'S AGAINST MY RELIGION.
OH C'MON, BART! YOU DON'T EXPECT ME TO BELIEVE...
PAGE 18.
SOON...
BART, I'M SO SORRY. I DIDN'T REALIZE THAT YOU'RE OBSERVING SHABBAT, THE JEWISH SABBATH ON WHICH NO JEW SHOULD WORK.
GEEZ, I'M SORRY I CAN'T HELP WITH CHORES, BUT...WELL...YOU KNOW...GOD.
IT'S SUCH AN INSPIRATION TO SEE ANOTHER SIMPSON DARING TO BE DIFFERENT.
HONG KONG POOCHIE
QUICK DRAW MCPOOCHIE
POOCHIE TOOTH
POOCHIE JAW
RUBIC THE AMAZING POOCH
TURBO POOCHIE TEEN
KISSY POOCH
MOM! THE LIMITED EDITION HONG KONG POOCHIE DOLL! YOU REMEMBERED!
WELL, YOU DID WRITE YOUR CHANUKAH LIST ON THE BACK OF YOUR FATHER'S HEAD.
LOOK, LIS! HE'S GOT PROACTIVE AND IN YOUR FACE KUNG FU ACTION!
BART, I HAVEN'T SEEN YOU WORK ON THE PAGEANT AT ALL...IT IS TOMORROW MORNING...
IT'S ALL UP HERE, LIS.

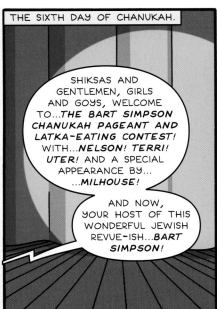

THE SIXTH DAY OF CHANUKAH.

SHIKSAS AND GENTLEMEN, GIRLS AND GOYS, WELCOME TO...*THE BART SIMPSON CHANUKAH PAGEANT AND LATKA-EATING CONTEST!* WITH...*NELSON! TERRI! UTER!* AND A SPECIAL APPEARANCE BY... ...*MILHOUSE!*

AND NOW, YOUR HOST OF THIS WONDERFUL JEWISH REVUE-ISH...*BART SIMPSON!*

HELLO, *SPRINGFIELD ELEMENTARY!* HERE'S THE HAPS ON CHANUKAH!

IT CAN BE SPELLED TWO DIFFERENT *WAYS*, IT LASTS EIGHT *DAYS*, AND AS FAR AS PRESENT-ORIENTED CELEBRATIONS GO, IT'S THE ONE THAT *PAYS*.

IT'S SO GREAT, YOU GET AT LEAST EIGHT!

IS BART GOING TO COVER ANY OF THE RICH HISTORY OF CHANUKAH? THE *MIRACLE OF THE OIL?* THE SCRAPPY FIGHTING OF *THE MACABEES?* THE GATEWAY TO GAMBLING THAT IS *THE DREIDEL?*

AND NOW, A MUSICAL NUMBER FROM ADAM SANDLER'S ANIMATED MASTERPIECE, *EIGHT CRAZY NIGHTS!*

THAT EVENING...

BART, I'M A LITTLE CONCERNED. CAN I ASK YOU SOMETHING?

SHOOT.

WHAT DOES JUDAISM *MEAN* TO YOU?

PRESENTS, EXTRA DAYS OFF FROM SCHOOL, AND REALLY GOOD *SMOKED FISH!*

I SHOULD'VE TAKEN A BREATH BEFORE ANSWERING THAT, HUH?

YOU WANT TO CONVERT FOR *TOYS AND HOLIDAYS?* THAT'S THE *WORST THING I'VE EVER HEARD!*

DON'T FORGET THE *LOX,* SISTER!

YOU'RE THE *SHALLOWEST* PERSON I'VE EVER MET... *INCLUDING MOE!*

TIME FOR *CHANUKAH!* LOOK, I MADE *GINGERBREAD RABBIS!*

I'M GOING TO SHOW THE SCHOOL WHAT *MISHEGAS* YOU'VE BEEN HANDING THEM!

MISHE-*WHAT* NOW?

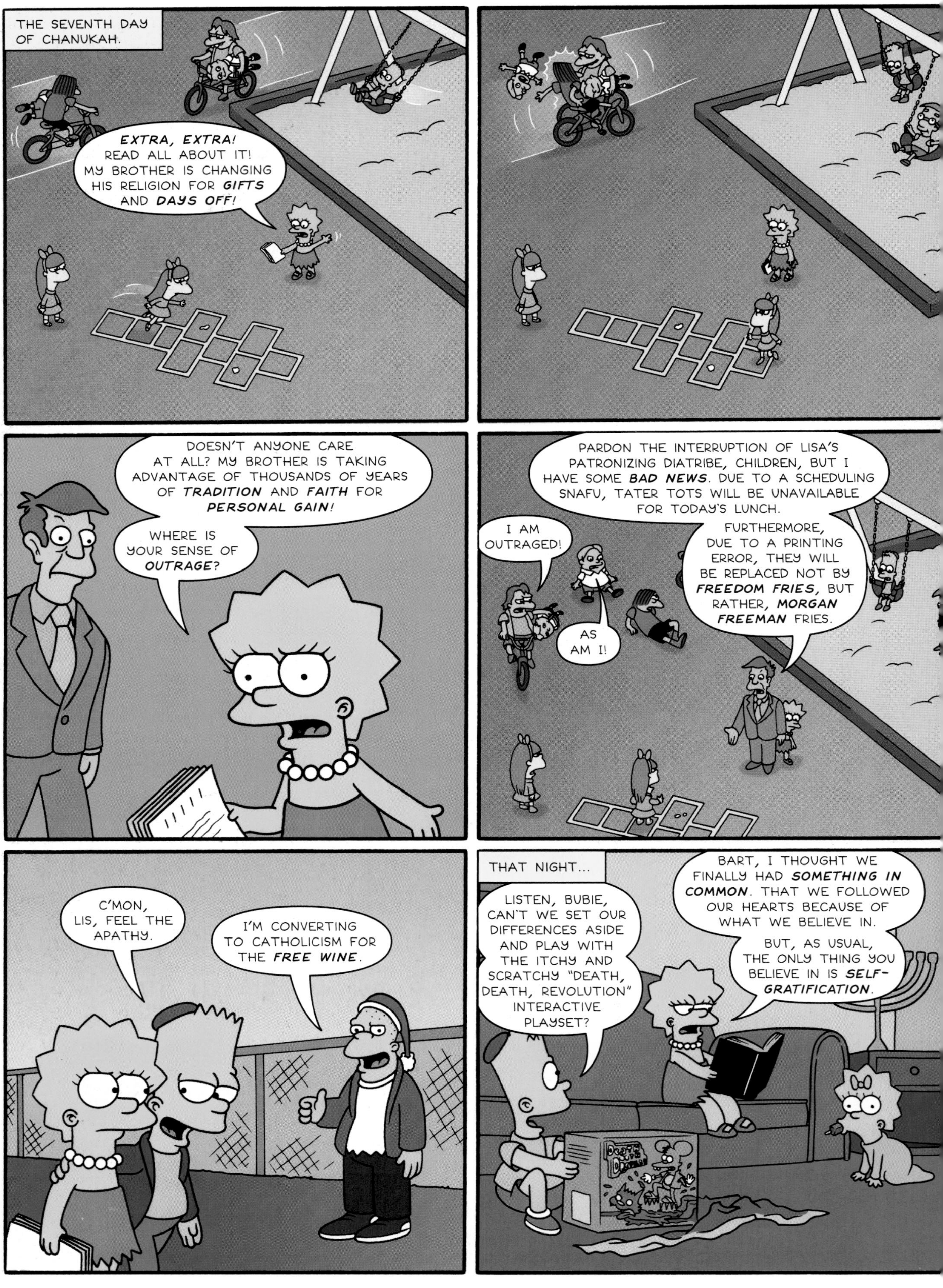
THE SEVENTH DAY OF CHANUKAH.
EXTRA, EXTRA! READ ALL ABOUT IT! MY BROTHER IS CHANGING HIS RELIGION FOR GIFTS AND DAYS OFF!
DOESN'T ANYONE CARE AT ALL? MY BROTHER IS TAKING ADVANTAGE OF THOUSANDS OF YEARS OF TRADITION AND FAITH FOR PERSONAL GAIN!
WHERE IS YOUR SENSE OF OUTRAGE?
PARDON THE INTERRUPTION OF LISA'S PATRONIZING DIATRIBE, CHILDREN, BUT I HAVE SOME BAD NEWS. DUE TO A SCHEDULING SNAFU, TATER TOTS WILL BE UNAVAILABLE FOR TODAY'S LUNCH.
FURTHERMORE, DUE TO A PRINTING ERROR, THEY WILL BE REPLACED NOT BY FREEDOM FRIES, BUT RATHER, MORGAN FREEMAN FRIES.
I AM OUTRAGED!
AS AM I!
C'MON, LIS, FEEL THE APATHY.
I'M CONVERTING TO CATHOLICISM FOR THE FREE WINE.
THAT NIGHT...
LISTEN, BUBIE, CAN'T WE SET OUR DIFFERENCES ASIDE AND PLAY WITH THE ITCHY AND SCRATCHY "DEATH, DEATH, REVOLUTION" INTERACTIVE PLAYSET?
BART, I THOUGHT WE FINALLY HAD SOMETHING IN COMMON. THAT WE FOLLOWED OUR HEARTS BECAUSE OF WHAT WE BELIEVE IN.
BUT, AS USUAL, THE ONLY THING YOU BELIEVE IN IS SELF-GRATIFICATION.

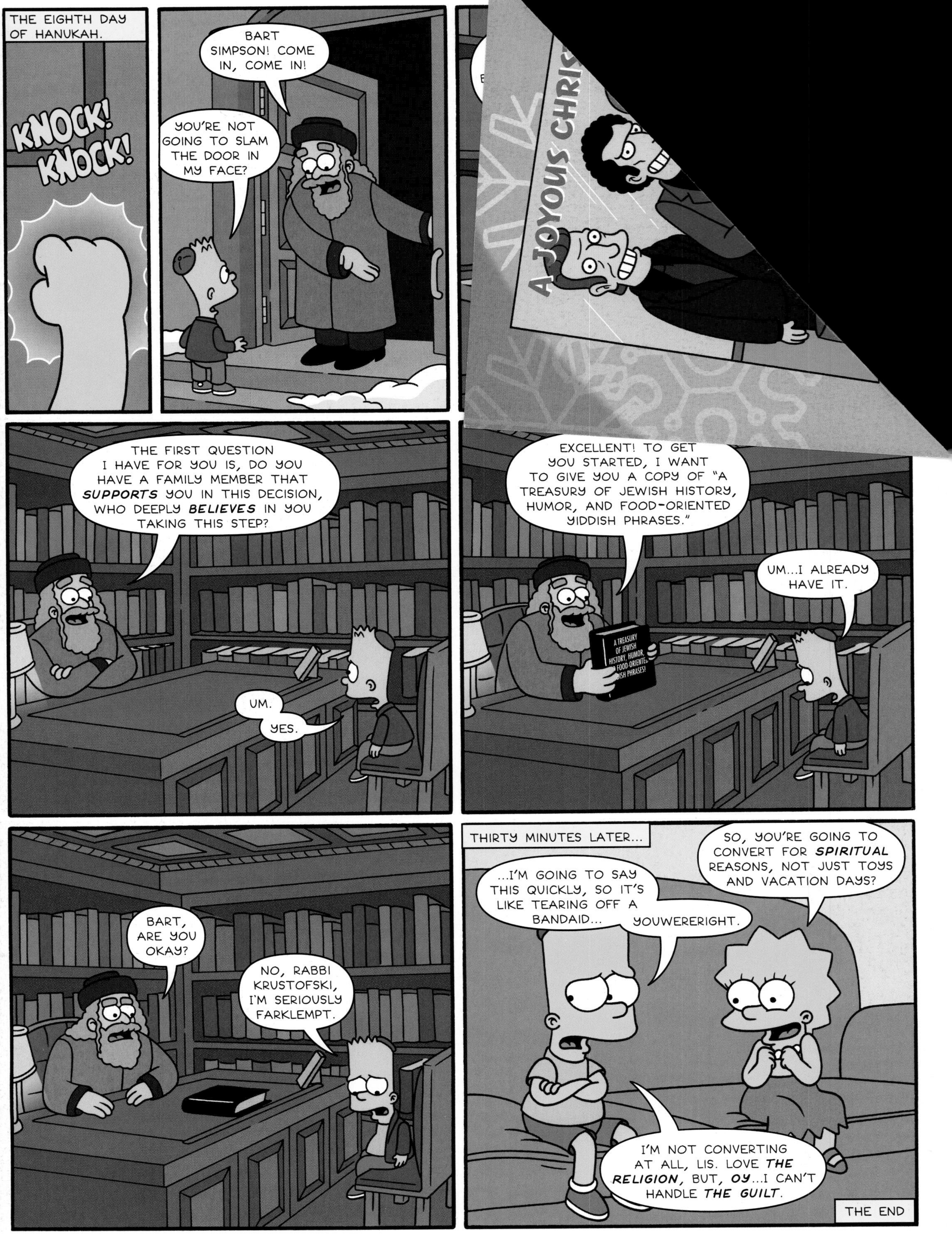
THE EIGHTH DAY OF HANUKAH.
KNOCK! KNOCK!
BART SIMPSON! COME IN, COME IN!
YOU'RE NOT GOING TO SLAM THE DOOR IN MY FACE?
THE FIRST QUESTION I HAVE FOR YOU IS, DO YOU HAVE A FAMILY MEMBER THAT SUPPORTS YOU IN THIS DECISION, WHO DEEPLY BELIEVES IN YOU TAKING THIS STEP?
UM.
YES.
EXCELLENT! TO GET YOU STARTED, I WANT TO GIVE YOU A COPY OF "A TREASURY OF JEWISH HISTORY, HUMOR, AND FOOD-ORIENTED YIDDISH PHRASES."
UM...I ALREADY HAVE IT.
BART, ARE YOU OKAY?
NO, RABBI KRUSTOFSKI, I'M SERIOUSLY FARKLEMPT.
THIRTY MINUTES LATER...
SO, YOU'RE GOING TO CONVERT FOR SPIRITUAL REASONS, NOT JUST TOYS AND VACATION DAYS?
...I'M GOING TO SAY THIS QUICKLY, SO IT'S LIKE TEARING OFF A BANDAID...
YOUWERERIGHT.
I'M NOT CONVERTING AT ALL, LIS. LOVE THE RELIGION, BUT, OY...I CAN'T HANDLE THE GUILT.
THE END

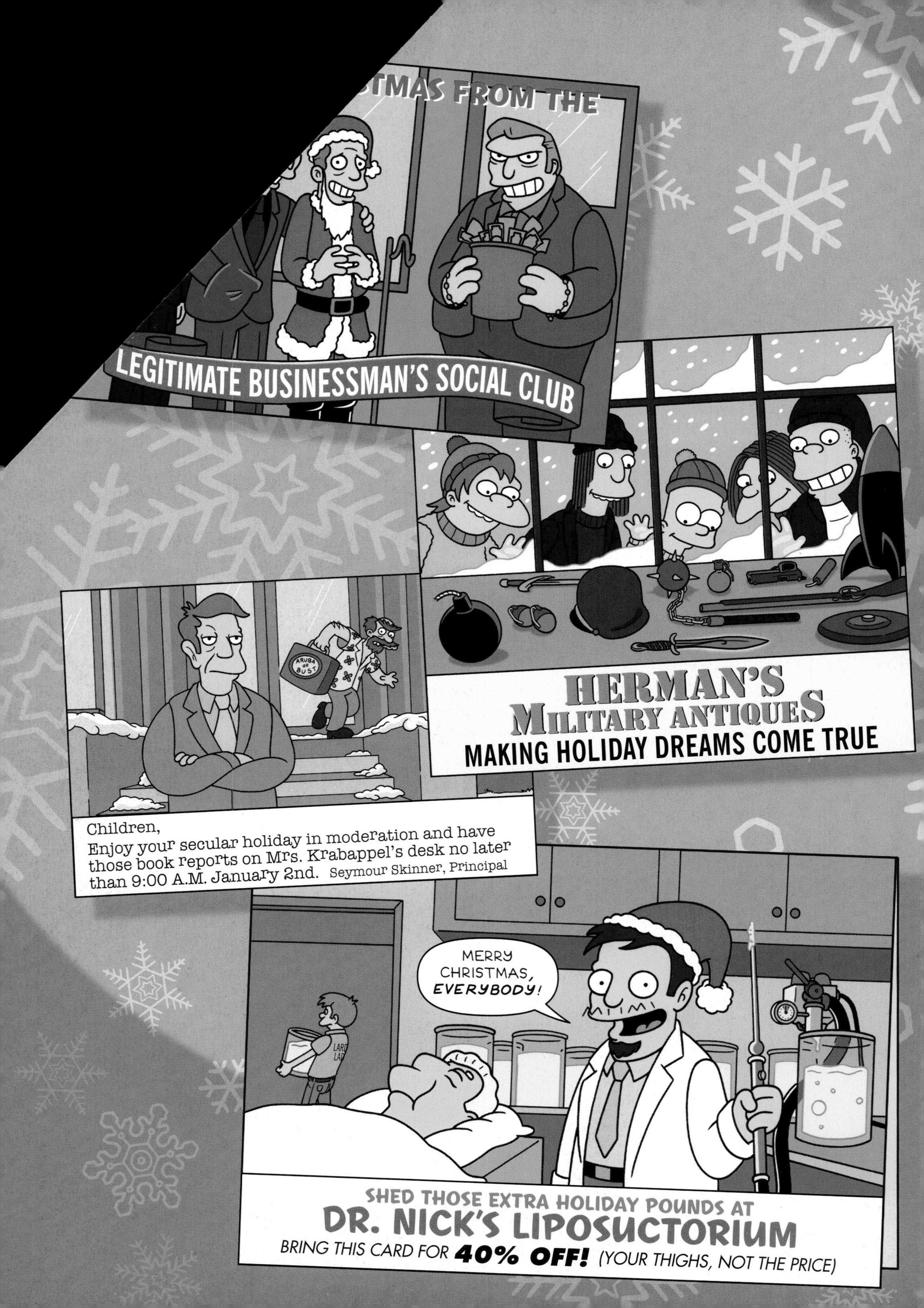

STMAS FROM THE
LEGITIMATE BUSINESSMAN'S SOCIAL CLUB
HERMAN'S
MILITARY ANTIQUES
MAKING HOLIDAY DREAMS COME TRUE
ARUBA OR BUST
Children,
Enjoy your secular holiday in moderation and have those book reports on Mrs. Krabappel's desk no later than 9:00 A.M. January 2nd. Seymour Skinner, Principal
MERRY CHRISTMAS, *EVERYBODY!*
LARD LAD
SHED THOSE EXTRA HOLIDAY POUNDS AT
DR. NICK'S LIPOSUCTORIUM
BRING THIS CARD FOR **40% OFF!** (YOUR THIGHS, NOT THE PRICE)

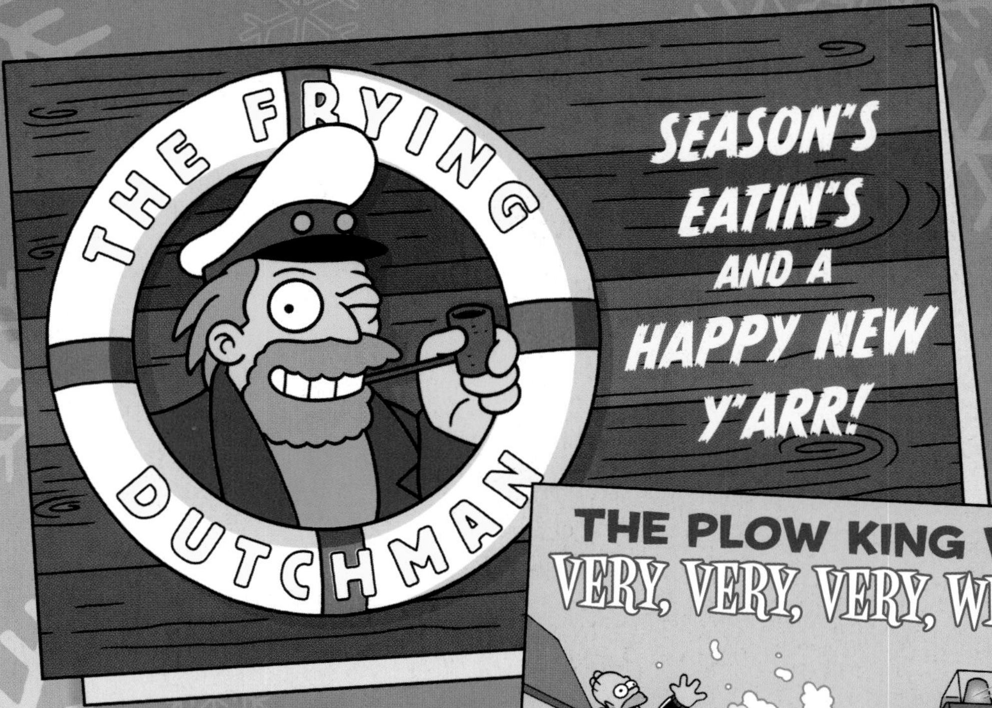
THE FRYING DUTCHMAN
SEASON'S EATIN'S AND A HAPPY NEW Y'ARR!

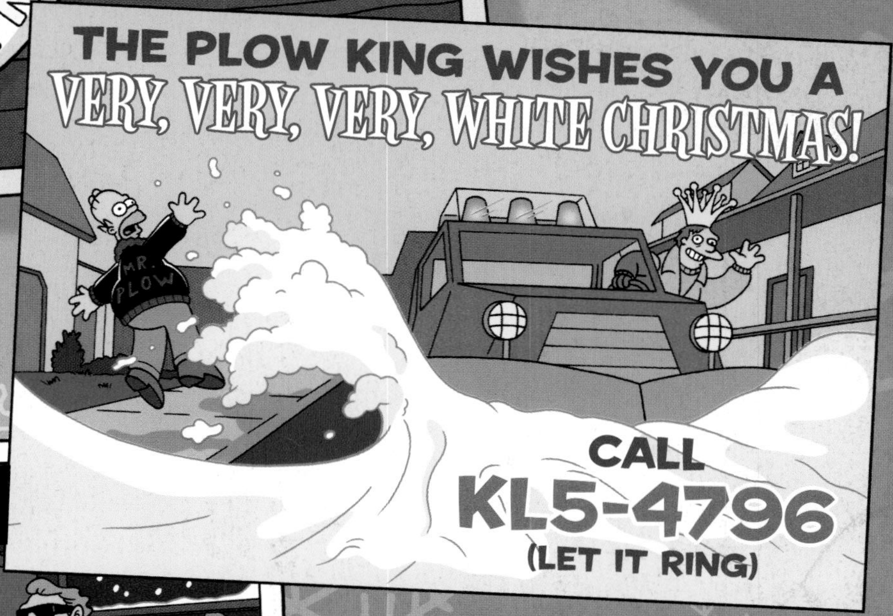
THE PLOW KING WISHES YOU A
VERY, VERY, VERY, WHITE CHRISTMAS!
MR. PLOW
CALL
KL5-4796
(LET IT RING)

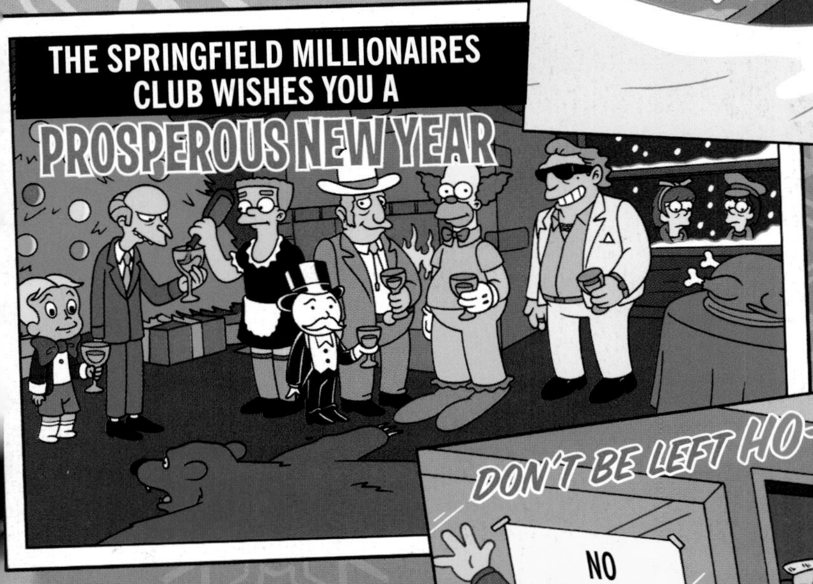
THE SPRINGFIELD MILLIONAIRES CLUB WISHES YOU A
PROSPEROUS NEW YEAR

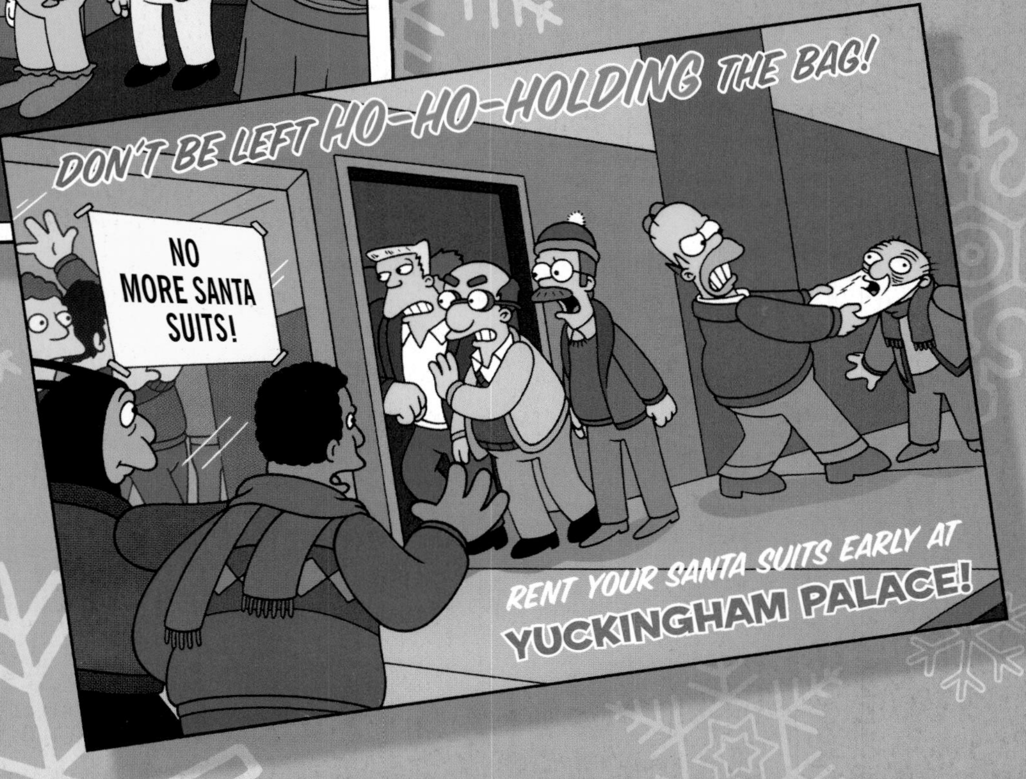
DON'T BE LEFT HO-HO-HOLDING THE BAG!
NO MORE SANTA SUITS!
RENT YOUR SANTA SUITS EARLY AT
YUCKINGHAM PALACE!

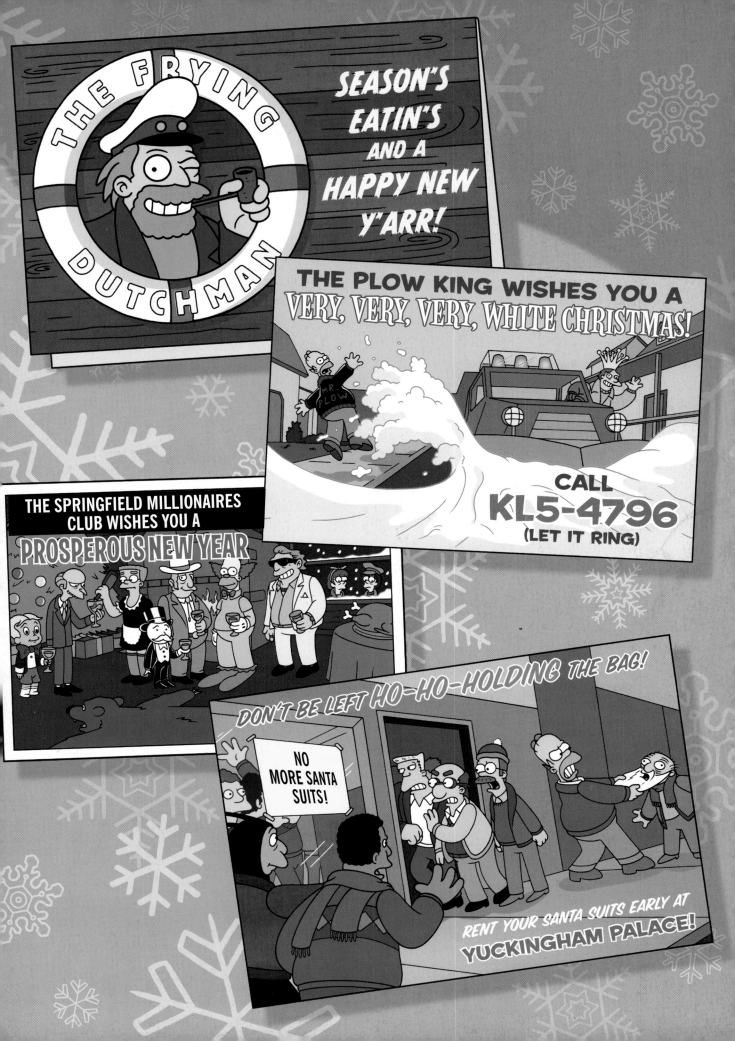

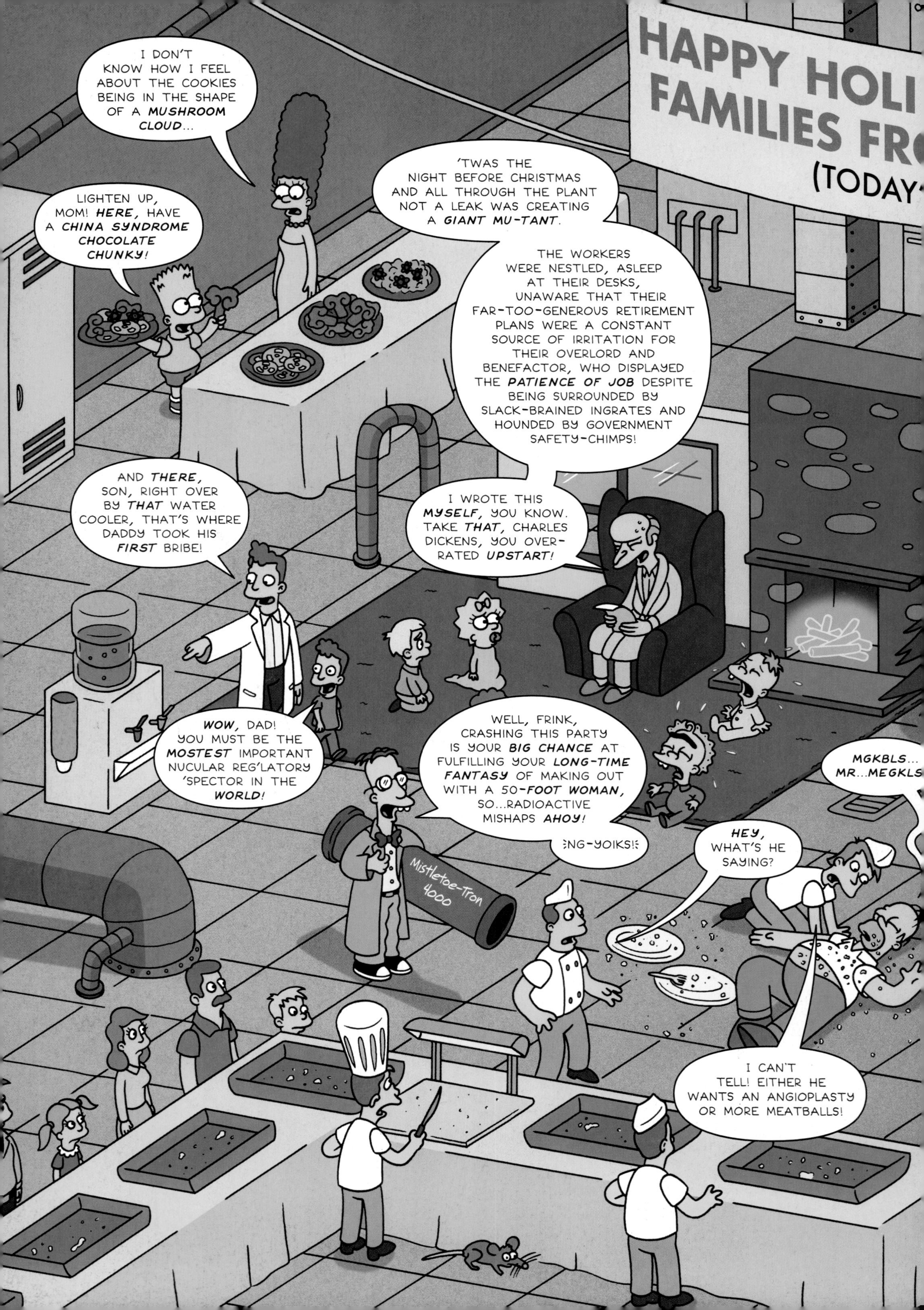
HAPPY HOLI
FAMILIES FR
(TODAY
I DON'T KNOW HOW I FEEL ABOUT THE COOKIES BEING IN THE SHAPE OF A MUSHROOM CLOUD...
LIGHTEN UP, MOM! HERE, HAVE A CHINA SYNDROME CHOCOLATE CHUNKY!
'TWAS THE NIGHT BEFORE CHRISTMAS AND ALL THROUGH THE PLANT NOT A LEAK WAS CREATING A GIANT MU-TANT.
THE WORKERS WERE NESTLED, ASLEEP AT THEIR DESKS, UNAWARE THAT THEIR FAR-TOO-GENEROUS RETIREMENT PLANS WERE A CONSTANT SOURCE OF IRRITATION FOR THEIR OVERLORD AND BENEFACTOR, WHO DISPLAYED THE PATIENCE OF JOB DESPITE BEING SURROUNDED BY SLACK-BRAINED INGRATES AND HOUNDED BY GOVERNMENT SAFETY-CHIMPS!
I WROTE THIS MYSELF, YOU KNOW. TAKE THAT, CHARLES DICKENS, YOU OVER-RATED UPSTART!
AND THERE, SON, RIGHT OVER BY THAT WATER COOLER, THAT'S WHERE DADDY TOOK HIS FIRST BRIBE!
WOW, DAD! YOU MUST BE THE MOSTEST IMPORTANT NUCULAR REG'LATORY 'SPECTOR IN THE WORLD!
WELL, FRINK, CRASHING THIS PARTY IS YOUR BIG CHANCE AT FULFILLING YOUR LONG-TIME FANTASY OF MAKING OUT WITH A 50-FOOT WOMAN, SO...RADIOACTIVE MISHAPS AHOY!
NG-YOIKS!
Mistletoe-Tron 4000
MGKBLS... MR...MEGKLS
HEY, WHAT'S HE SAYING?
I CAN'T TELL! EITHER HE WANTS AN ANGIOPLASTY OR MORE MEATBALLS!

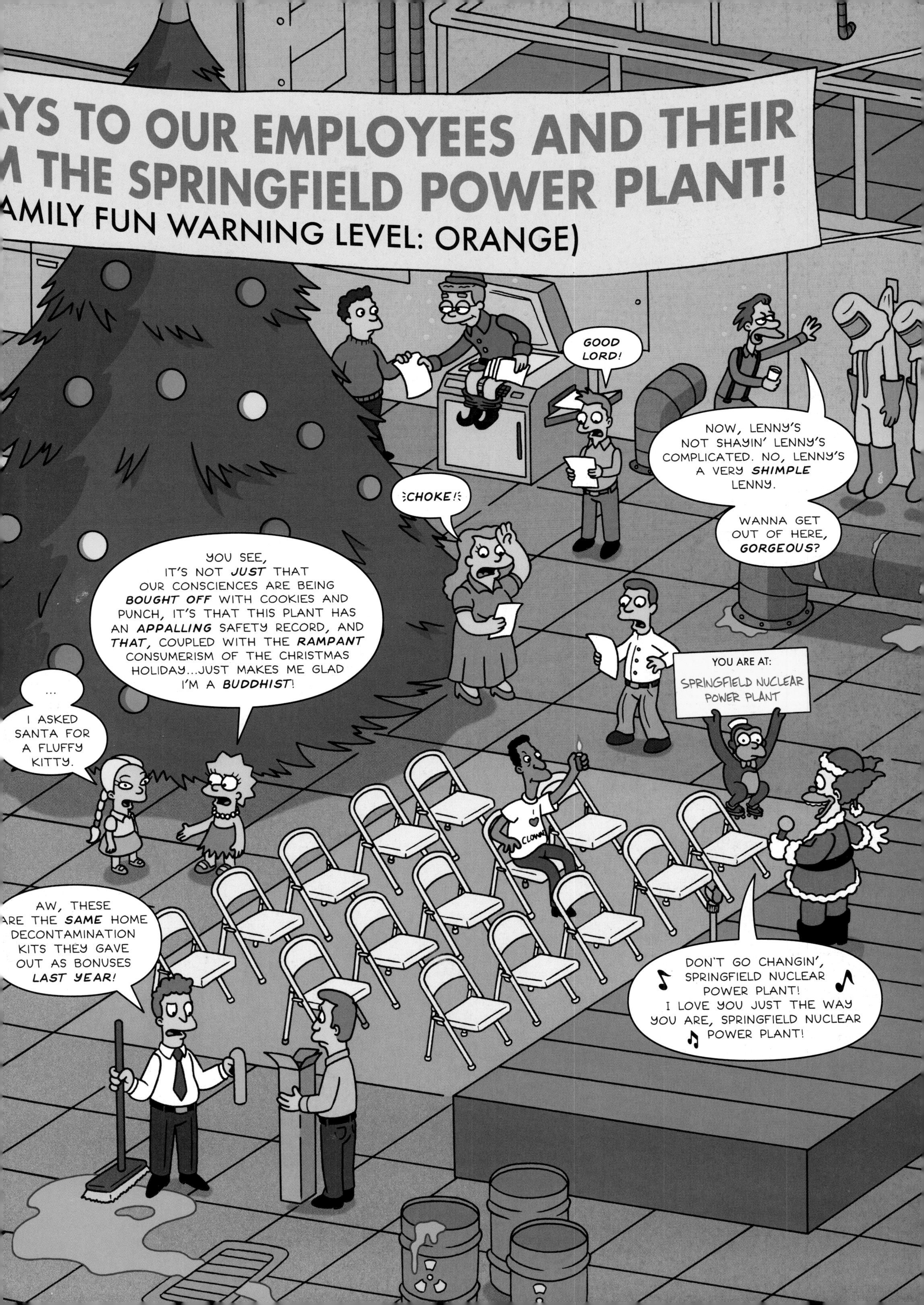
AYS TO OUR EMPLOYEES AND THEIR
M THE SPRINGFIELD POWER PLANT!
AMILY FUN WARNING LEVEL: ORANGE)
GOOD LORD!
NOW, LENNY'S NOT SHAYIN' LENNY'S COMPLICATED. NO, LENNY'S A VERY SHIMPLE LENNY.
WANNA GET OUT OF HERE, GORGEOUS?
CHOKE!
YOU SEE, IT'S NOT JUST THAT OUR CONSCIENCES ARE BEING BOUGHT OFF WITH COOKIES AND PUNCH, IT'S THAT THIS PLANT HAS AN APPALLING SAFETY RECORD, AND THAT, COUPLED WITH THE RAMPANT CONSUMERISM OF THE CHRISTMAS HOLIDAY...JUST MAKES ME GLAD I'M A BUDDHIST!
...
I ASKED SANTA FOR A FLUFFY KITTY.
YOU ARE AT:
SPRINGFIELD NUCLEAR POWER PLANT
AW, THESE ARE THE SAME HOME DECONTAMINATION KITS THEY GAVE OUT AS BONUSES LAST YEAR!
DON'T GO CHANGIN', SPRINGFIELD NUCLEAR POWER PLANT! I LOVE YOU JUST THE WAY YOU ARE, SPRINGFIELD NUCLEAR POWER PLANT!

CHRISTMAS IS MY FAVORITE "MAS" OF ALL! HERE'S WHAT HAPPENED TO ME ON THAT DAY!

my CHRISTMAS DAY

by Ralph Wiggum

I woke up early and Mom undid my **snoozy belts**.

Then, I went downstairs and opened **candy socks!**

Doctor Hiccup says I have to wear a helmet to make my head shaped right. Now I have a **red** one for **church!**

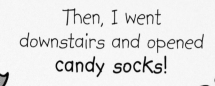

Mom got me a new T-shirt with **words** on it!

I'M ALLERGIC TO ALMOST EVERYTHING

I was so happy, I set the **Christmas Goose** free to go find its **head and neck!**

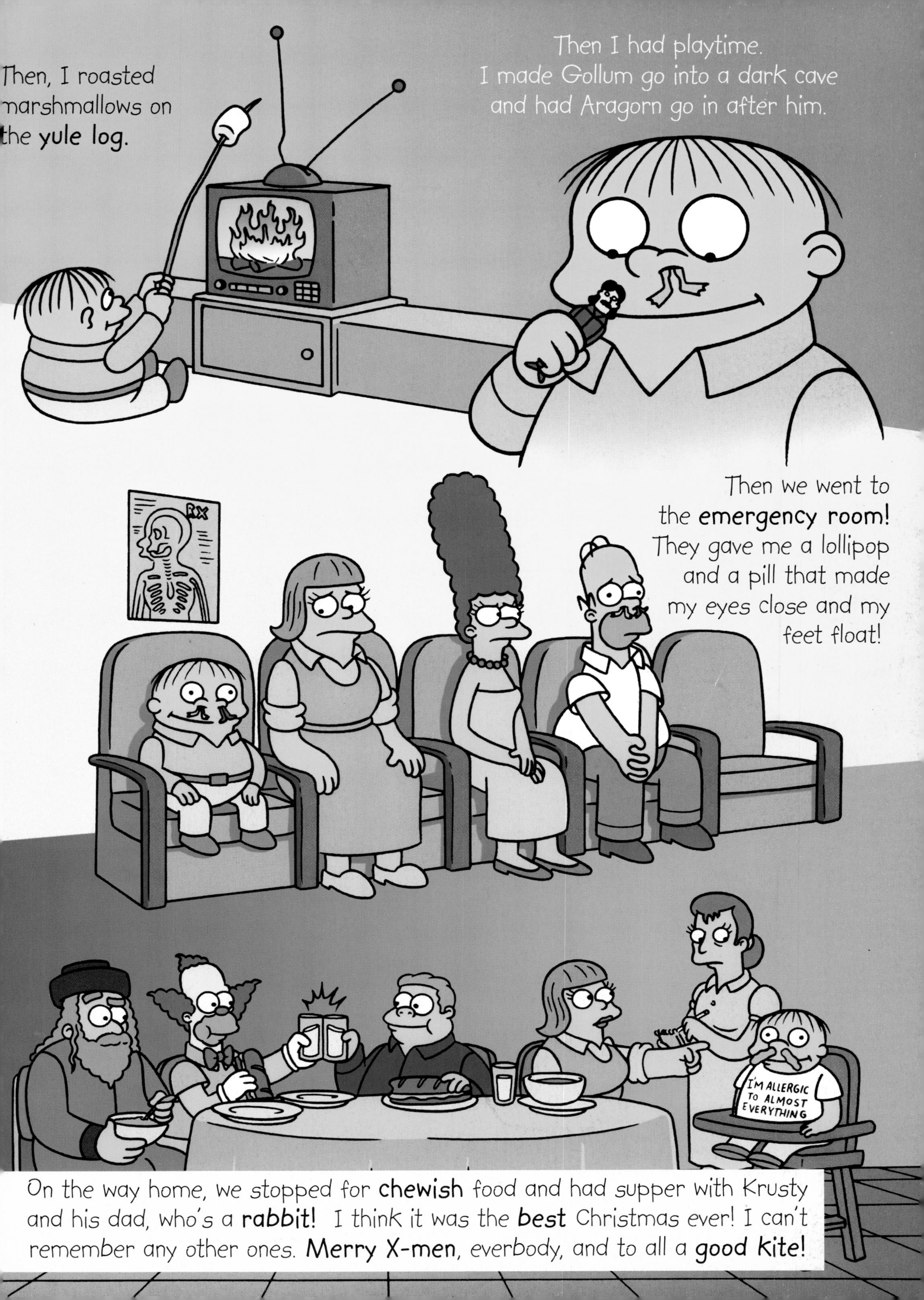
Then, I roasted marshmallows on the **yule log**.
Then I had playtime. I made Gollum go into a dark cave and had Aragorn go in after him.
Then we went to the **emergency room!** They gave me a lollipop and a pill that made my eyes close and my feet float!
RX
I'M ALLERGIC TO ALMOST EVERYTHING
On the way home, we stopped for **chewish** food and had supper with Krusty and his dad, who's a **rabbit!** I think it was the **best** Christmas ever! I can't remember any other ones. **Merry X-men**, everbody, and to all a **good kite!**

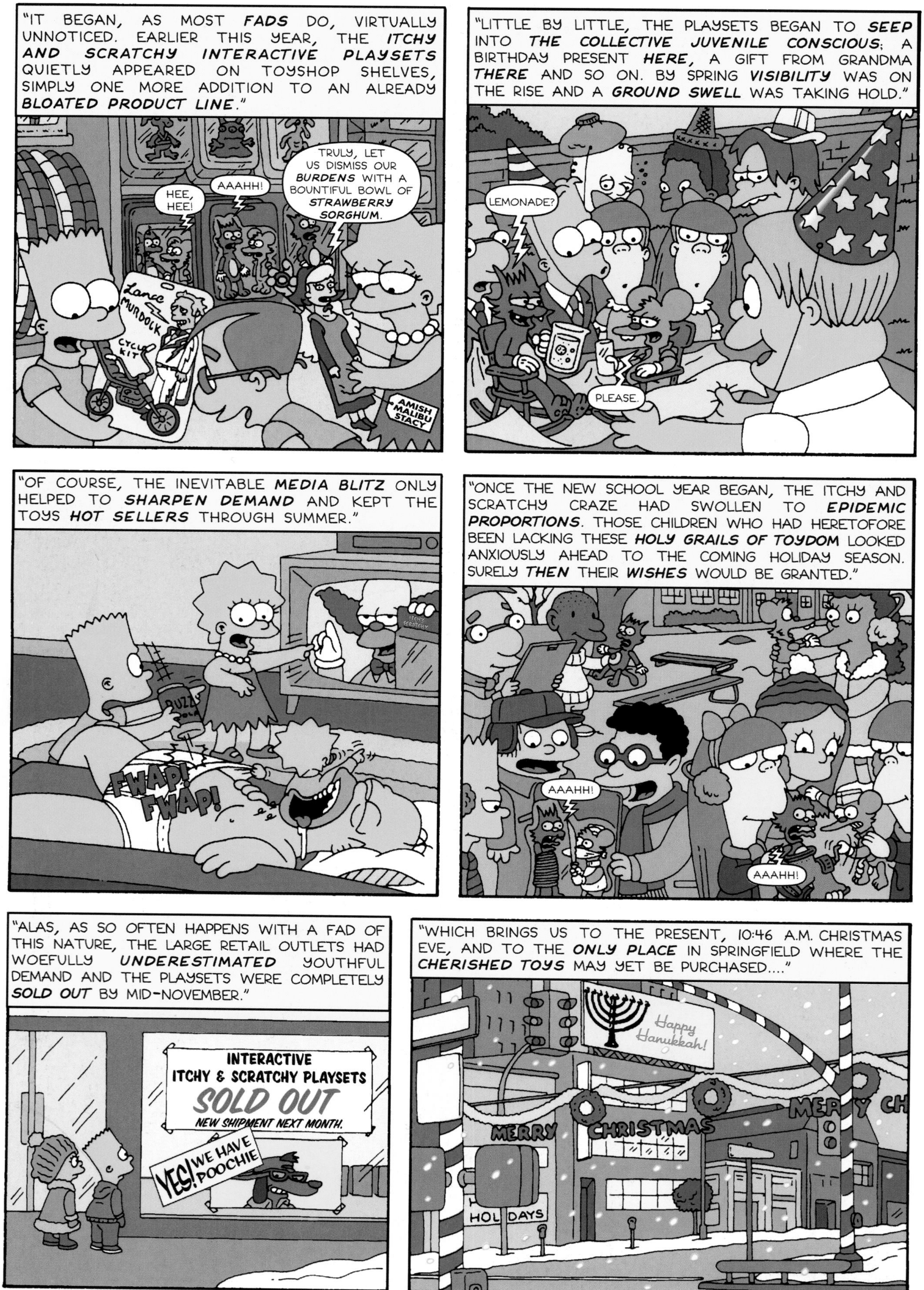
"IT BEGAN, AS MOST FADS DO, VIRTUALLY UNNOTICED. EARLIER THIS YEAR, THE ITCHY AND SCRATCHY INTERACTIVE PLAYSETS QUIETLY APPEARED ON TOYSHOP SHELVES, SIMPLY ONE MORE ADDITION TO AN ALREADY BLOATED PRODUCT LINE."
HEE, HEE!
AAAHH!
TRULY, LET US DISMISS OUR BURDENS WITH A BOUNTIFUL BOWL OF STRAWBERRY SORGHUM.
Lance MURDOCK CYCLE KIT
AMISH MALIBU STACY
"LITTLE BY LITTLE, THE PLAYSETS BEGAN TO SEEP INTO THE COLLECTIVE JUVENILE CONSCIOUS; A BIRTHDAY PRESENT HERE, A GIFT FROM GRANDMA THERE AND SO ON. BY SPRING VISIBILITY WAS ON THE RISE AND A GROUND SWELL WAS TAKING HOLD."
LEMONADE?
PLEASE.
"OF COURSE, THE INEVITABLE MEDIA BLITZ ONLY HELPED TO SHARPEN DEMAND AND KEPT THE TOYS HOT SELLERS THROUGH SUMMER."
BUZZ COLA
FWAP! FWAP!
"ONCE THE NEW SCHOOL YEAR BEGAN, THE ITCHY AND SCRATCHY CRAZE HAD SWOLLEN TO EPIDEMIC PROPORTIONS. THOSE CHILDREN WHO HAD HERETOFORE BEEN LACKING THESE HOLY GRAILS OF TOYDOM LOOKED ANXIOUSLY AHEAD TO THE COMING HOLIDAY SEASON. SURELY THEN THEIR WISHES WOULD BE GRANTED."
AAAHH!
AAAHH!
"ALAS, AS SO OFTEN HAPPENS WITH A FAD OF THIS NATURE, THE LARGE RETAIL OUTLETS HAD WOEFULLY UNDERESTIMATED YOUTHFUL DEMAND AND THE PLAYSETS WERE COMPLETELY SOLD OUT BY MID-NOVEMBER."
INTERACTIVE ITCHY & SCRATCHY PLAYSETS SOLD OUT
NEW SHIPMENT NEXT MONTH.
YES! WE HAVE POOCHIE
"WHICH BRINGS US TO THE PRESENT, 10:46 A.M. CHRISTMAS EVE, AND TO THE ONLY PLACE IN SPRINGFIELD WHERE THE CHERISHED TOYS MAY YET BE PURCHASED...."
Happy Hanukkah!
MERRY CHRISTMAS
HOLIDAYS

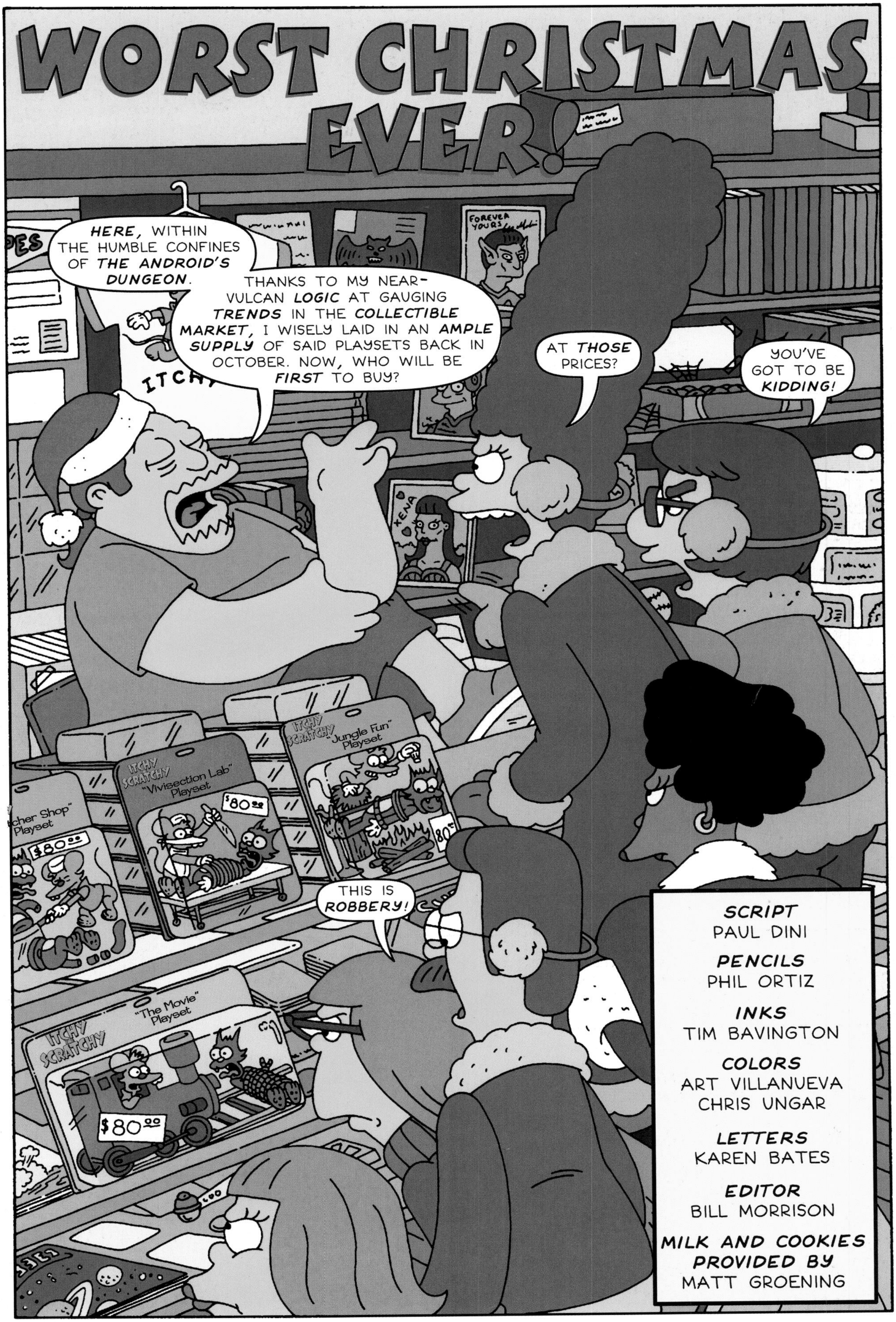
WORST CHRISTMAS EVER!
HERE, WITHIN THE HUMBLE CONFINES OF THE ANDROID'S DUNGEON.
THANKS TO MY NEAR-VULCAN LOGIC AT GAUGING TRENDS IN THE COLLECTIBLE MARKET, I WISELY LAID IN AN AMPLE SUPPLY OF SAID PLAYSETS BACK IN OCTOBER. NOW, WHO WILL BE FIRST TO BUY?
AT THOSE PRICES?
YOU'VE GOT TO BE KIDDING!
THIS IS ROBBERY!
FOREVER YOURS
XENA
ITCHY SCRATCHY "Vivisection Lab" Playset
$80.00
ITCHY SCRATCHY "Jungle Fun" Playset
"The Movie" Playset
ITCHY SCRATCHY
SCRIPT
PAUL DINI
PENCILS
PHIL ORTIZ
INKS
TIM BAVINGTON
COLORS
ART VILLANUEVA
CHRIS UNGAR
LETTERS
KAREN BATES
EDITOR
BILL MORRISON
MILK AND COOKIES PROVIDED BY
MATT GROENING

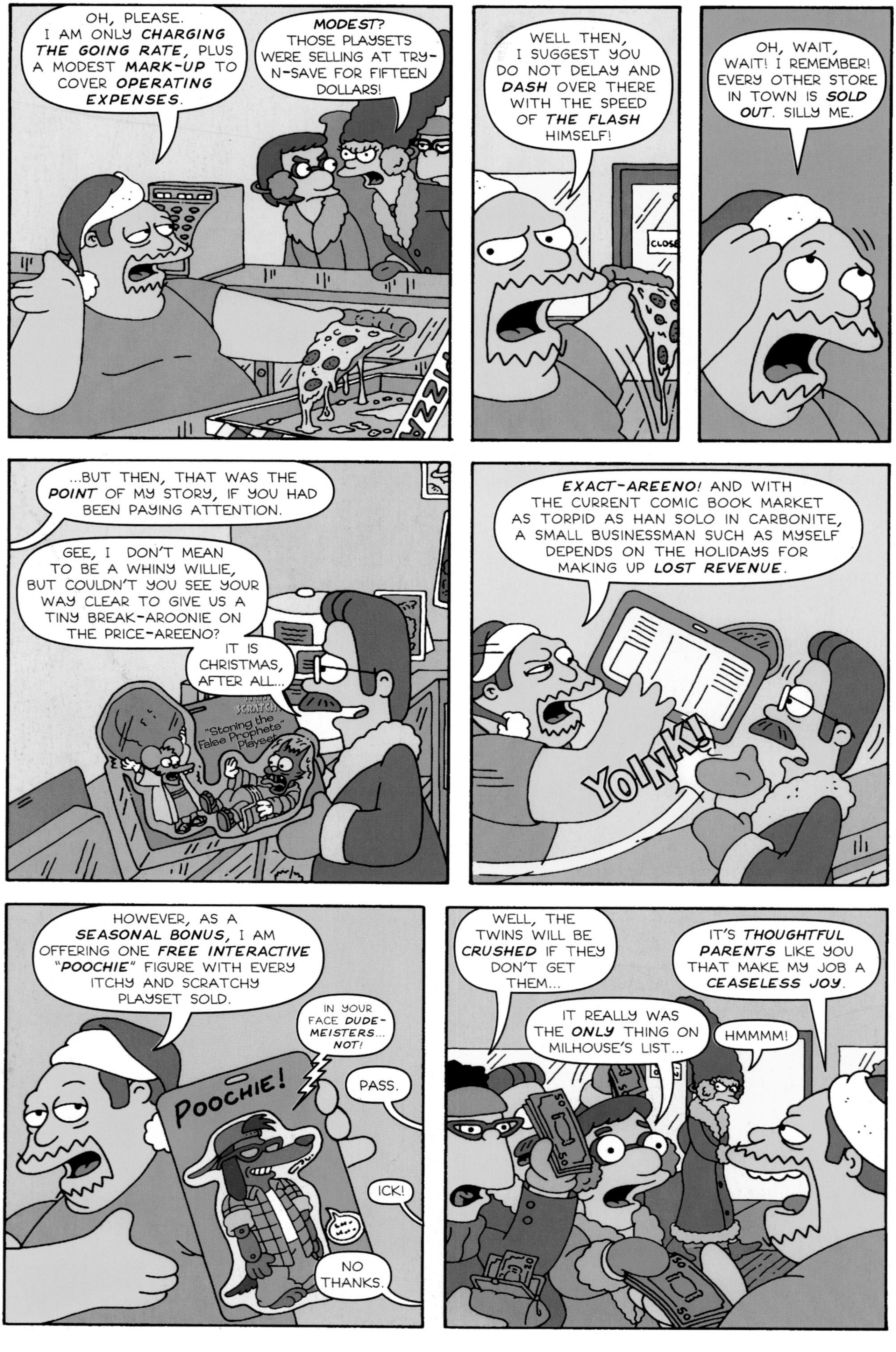
OH, PLEASE. I AM ONLY CHARGING THE GOING RATE, PLUS A MODEST MARK-UP TO COVER OPERATING EXPENSES.
MODEST? THOSE PLAYSETS WERE SELLING AT TRY-N-SAVE FOR FIFTEEN DOLLARS!
WELL THEN, I SUGGEST YOU DO NOT DELAY AND DASH OVER THERE WITH THE SPEED OF THE FLASH HIMSELF!
OH, WAIT, WAIT! I REMEMBER! EVERY OTHER STORE IN TOWN IS SOLD OUT. SILLY ME.
...BUT THEN, THAT WAS THE POINT OF MY STORY, IF YOU HAD BEEN PAYING ATTENTION.
GEE, I DON'T MEAN TO BE A WHINY WILLIE, BUT COULDN'T YOU SEE YOUR WAY CLEAR TO GIVE US A TINY BREAK-AROONIE ON THE PRICE-AREENO?
IT IS CHRISTMAS, AFTER ALL...
"Stoning the False Prophets" Playset
EXACT-AREENO! AND WITH THE CURRENT COMIC BOOK MARKET AS TORPID AS HAN SOLO IN CARBONITE, A SMALL BUSINESSMAN SUCH AS MYSELF DEPENDS ON THE HOLIDAYS FOR MAKING UP LOST REVENUE.
YOINK!
HOWEVER, AS A SEASONAL BONUS, I AM OFFERING ONE FREE INTERACTIVE "POOCHIE" FIGURE WITH EVERY ITCHY AND SCRATCHY PLAYSET SOLD.
POOCHIE!
IN YOUR FACE DUDE-MEISTERS... NOT!
PASS.
ICK!
NO THANKS.
WELL, THE TWINS WILL BE CRUSHED IF THEY DON'T GET THEM...
IT REALLY WAS THE ONLY THING ON MILHOUSE'S LIST...
HMMMM!
IT'S THOUGHTFUL PARENTS LIKE YOU THAT MAKE MY JOB A CEASELESS JOY.

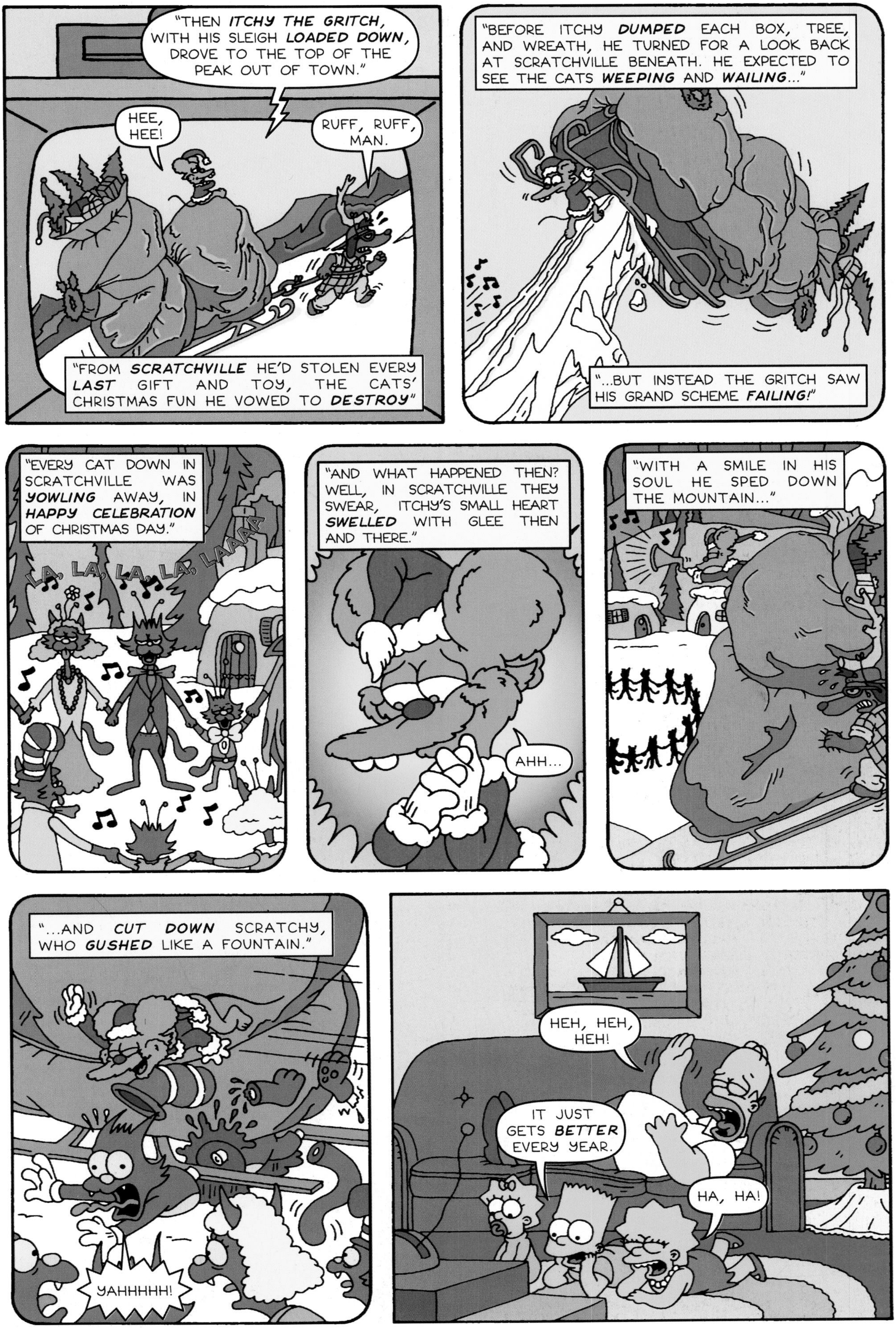
"THEN ITCHY THE GRITCH, WITH HIS SLEIGH LOADED DOWN, DROVE TO THE TOP OF THE PEAK OUT OF TOWN."
HEE, HEE!
RUFF, RUFF, MAN.
"FROM SCRATCHVILLE HE'D STOLEN EVERY LAST GIFT AND TOY, THE CATS' CHRISTMAS FUN HE VOWED TO DESTROY"
"BEFORE ITCHY DUMPED EACH BOX, TREE, AND WREATH, HE TURNED FOR A LOOK BACK AT SCRATCHVILLE BENEATH. HE EXPECTED TO SEE THE CATS WEEPING AND WAILING..."
"...BUT INSTEAD THE GRITCH SAW HIS GRAND SCHEME FAILING!"
"EVERY CAT DOWN IN SCRATCHVILLE WAS YOWLING AWAY, IN HAPPY CELEBRATION OF CHRISTMAS DAY."
LA, LA, LA, LA, LAAAA
"AND WHAT HAPPENED THEN? WELL, IN SCRATCHVILLE THEY SWEAR, ITCHY'S SMALL HEART SWELLED WITH GLEE THEN AND THERE."
AHH...
"WITH A SMILE IN HIS SOUL HE SPED DOWN THE MOUNTAIN..."
"...AND CUT DOWN SCRATCHY, WHO GUSHED LIKE A FOUNTAIN."
YAHHHHH!
HEH, HEH, HEH!
IT JUST GETS BETTER EVERY YEAR.
HA, HA!

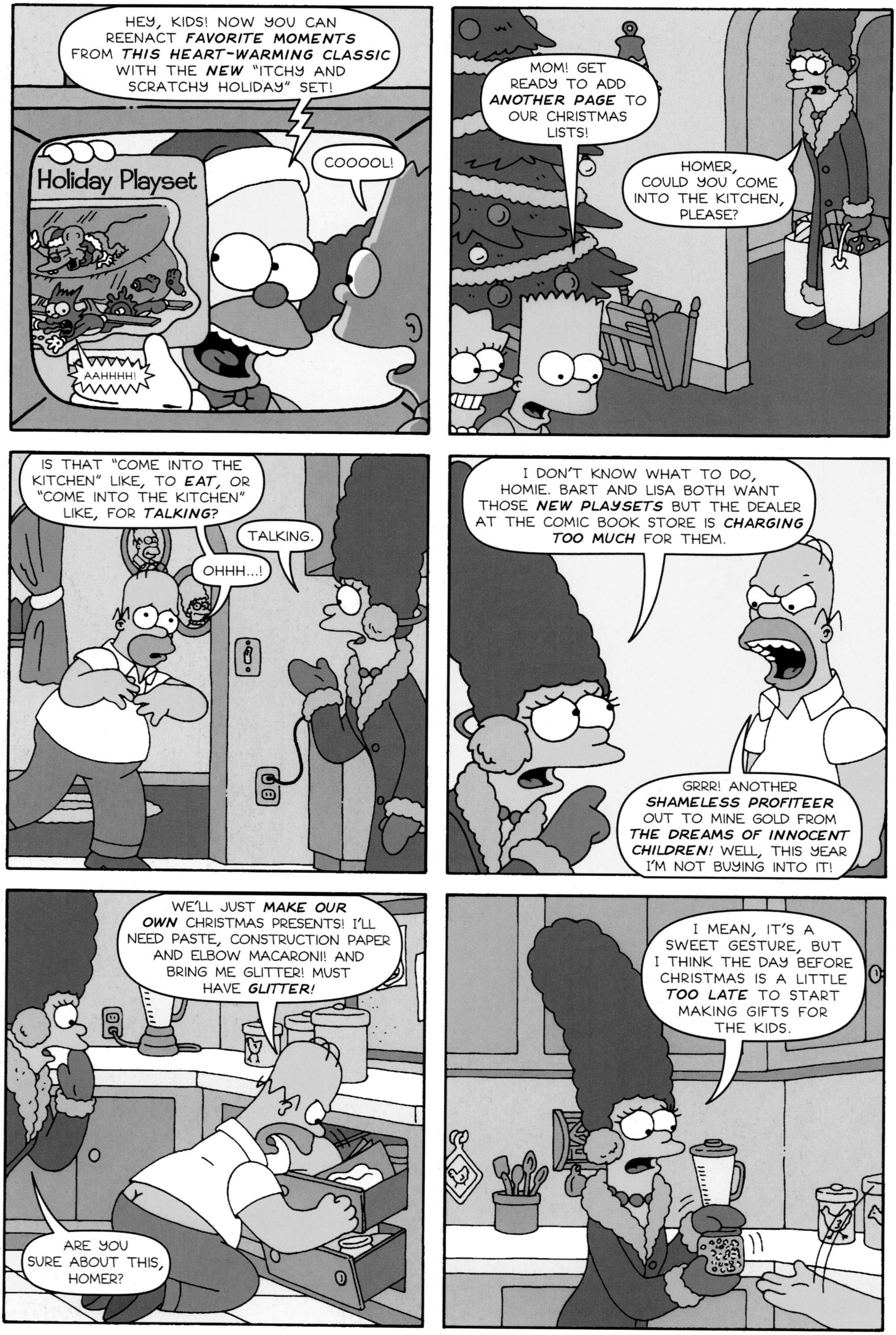
HEY, KIDS! NOW YOU CAN REENACT FAVORITE MOMENTS FROM THIS HEART-WARMING CLASSIC WITH THE NEW "ITCHY AND SCRATCHY HOLIDAY" SET!
Holiday Playset
AAHHHH!
COOOOL!
MOM! GET READY TO ADD ANOTHER PAGE TO OUR CHRISTMAS LISTS!
HOMER, COULD YOU COME INTO THE KITCHEN, PLEASE?
IS THAT "COME INTO THE KITCHEN" LIKE, TO EAT, OR "COME INTO THE KITCHEN" LIKE, FOR TALKING?
TALKING.
OHHH...!
I DON'T KNOW WHAT TO DO, HOMIE. BART AND LISA BOTH WANT THOSE NEW PLAYSETS BUT THE DEALER AT THE COMIC BOOK STORE IS CHARGING TOO MUCH FOR THEM.
GRRR! ANOTHER SHAMELESS PROFITEER OUT TO MINE GOLD FROM THE DREAMS OF INNOCENT CHILDREN! WELL, THIS YEAR I'M NOT BUYING INTO IT!
WE'LL JUST MAKE OUR OWN CHRISTMAS PRESENTS! I'LL NEED PASTE, CONSTRUCTION PAPER AND ELBOW MACARONI! AND BRING ME GLITTER! MUST HAVE GLITTER!
ARE YOU SURE ABOUT THIS, HOMER?
I MEAN, IT'S A SWEET GESTURE, BUT I THINK THE DAY BEFORE CHRISTMAS IS A LITTLE TOO LATE TO START MAKING GIFTS FOR THE KIDS.

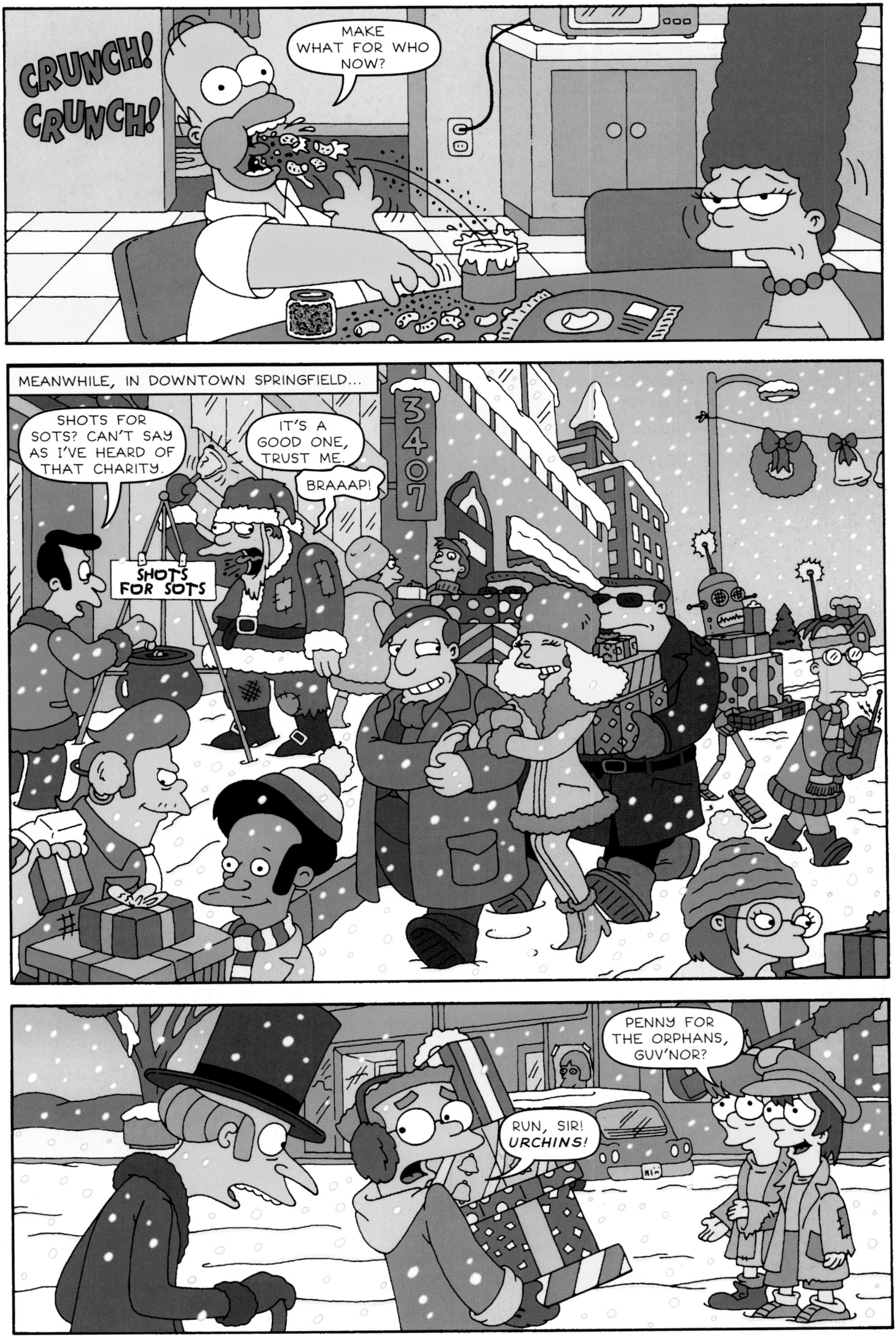
CRUNCH! CRUNCH!
MAKE WHAT FOR WHO NOW?
MEANWHILE, IN DOWNTOWN SPRINGFIELD...
SHOTS FOR SOTS? CAN'T SAY AS I'VE HEARD OF THAT CHARITY.
IT'S A GOOD ONE, TRUST ME.
BRAAAP!
SHOTS FOR SOTS
3407
PENNY FOR THE ORPHANS, GUV'NOR?
RUN, SIR! *URCHINS!*

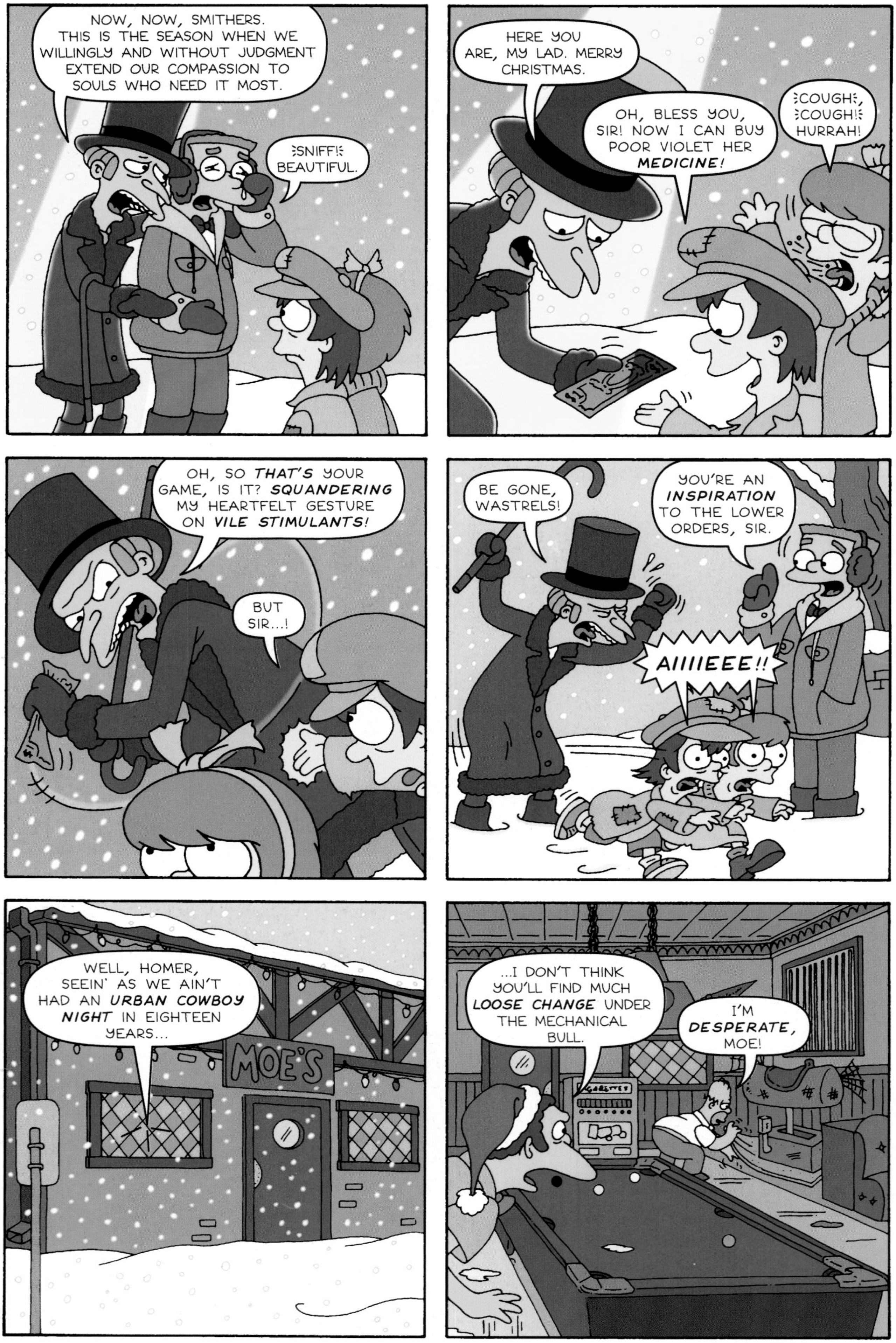
NOW, NOW, SMITHERS. THIS IS THE SEASON WHEN WE WILLINGLY AND WITHOUT JUDGMENT EXTEND OUR COMPASSION TO SOULS WHO NEED IT MOST.
SNIFF! BEAUTIFUL.
HERE YOU ARE, MY LAD. MERRY CHRISTMAS.
OH, BLESS YOU, SIR! NOW I CAN BUY POOR VIOLET HER MEDICINE!
COUGH, COUGH! HURRAH!
OH, SO THAT'S YOUR GAME, IS IT? SQUANDERING MY HEARTFELT GESTURE ON VILE STIMULANTS!
BUT SIR...!
BE GONE, WASTRELS!
YOU'RE AN INSPIRATION TO THE LOWER ORDERS, SIR.
AIIIIEEE!!
WELL, HOMER, SEEIN' AS WE AIN'T HAD AN URBAN COWBOY NIGHT IN EIGHTEEN YEARS...
MOE'S
...I DON'T THINK YOU'LL FIND MUCH LOOSE CHANGE UNDER THE MECHANICAL BULL.
I'M DESPERATE, MOE!

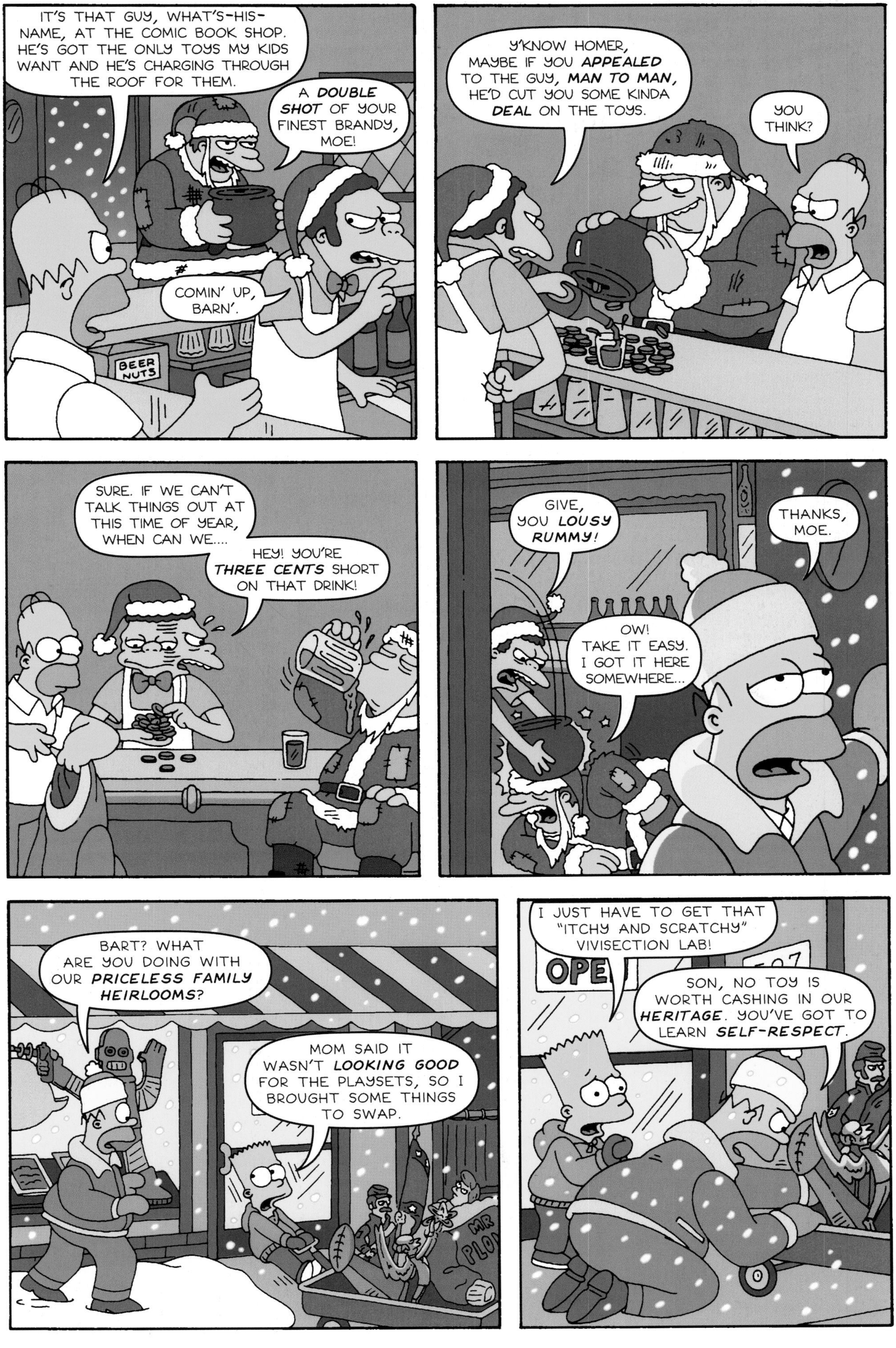
IT'S THAT GUY, WHAT'S-HIS-NAME, AT THE COMIC BOOK SHOP. HE'S GOT THE ONLY TOYS MY KIDS WANT AND HE'S CHARGING THROUGH THE ROOF FOR THEM.
A DOUBLE SHOT OF YOUR FINEST BRANDY, MOE!
COMIN' UP, BARN'.
BEER NUTS
Y'KNOW HOMER, MAYBE IF YOU APPEALED TO THE GUY, MAN TO MAN, HE'D CUT YOU SOME KINDA DEAL ON THE TOYS.
YOU THINK?
SURE. IF WE CAN'T TALK THINGS OUT AT THIS TIME OF YEAR, WHEN CAN WE....
HEY! YOU'RE THREE CENTS SHORT ON THAT DRINK!
GIVE, YOU LOUSY RUMMY!
THANKS, MOE.
OW! TAKE IT EASY. I GOT IT HERE SOMEWHERE...
BART? WHAT ARE YOU DOING WITH OUR PRICELESS FAMILY HEIRLOOMS?
MOM SAID IT WASN'T LOOKING GOOD FOR THE PLAYSETS, SO I BROUGHT SOME THINGS TO SWAP.
I JUST HAVE TO GET THAT "ITCHY AND SCRATCHY" VIVISECTION LAB!
SON, NO TOY IS WORTH CASHING IN OUR HERITAGE. YOU'VE GOT TO LEARN SELF-RESPECT.

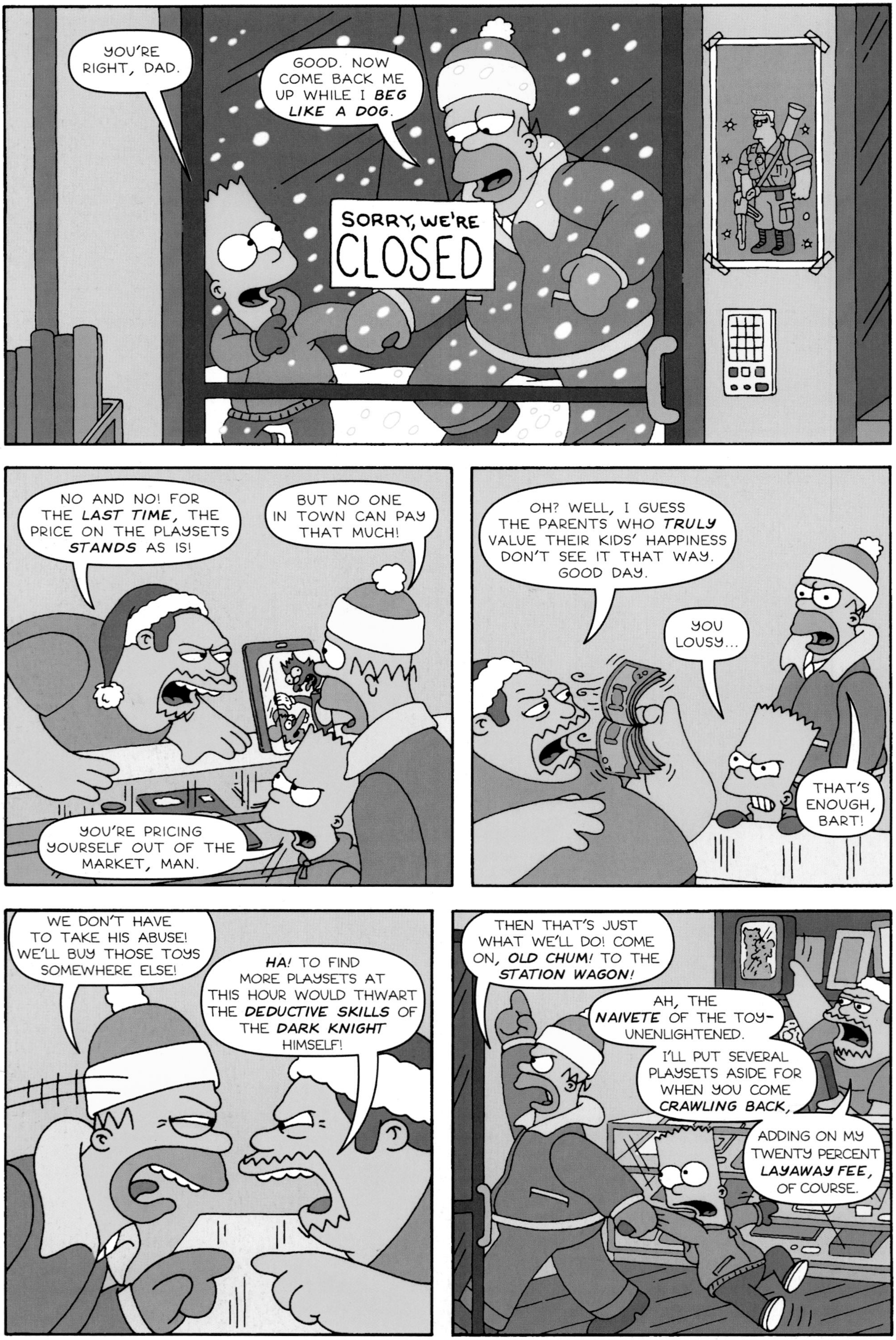
YOU'RE RIGHT, DAD.
GOOD. NOW COME BACK ME UP WHILE I *BEG LIKE A DOG*.
SORRY, WE'RE CLOSED
NO AND NO! FOR THE *LAST TIME*, THE PRICE ON THE PLAYSETS *STANDS* AS IS!
BUT NO ONE IN TOWN CAN PAY THAT MUCH!
YOU'RE PRICING YOURSELF OUT OF THE MARKET, MAN.
OH? WELL, I GUESS THE PARENTS WHO *TRULY* VALUE THEIR KIDS' HAPPINESS DON'T SEE IT THAT WAY. GOOD DAY.
YOU LOUSY...
THAT'S ENOUGH, BART!
WE DON'T HAVE TO TAKE HIS ABUSE! WE'LL BUY THOSE TOYS SOMEWHERE ELSE!
HA! TO FIND MORE PLAYSETS AT THIS HOUR WOULD THWART THE *DEDUCTIVE SKILLS* OF THE *DARK KNIGHT* HIMSELF!
THEN THAT'S JUST WHAT WE'LL DO! COME ON, *OLD CHUM!* TO THE *STATION WAGON!*
AH, THE *NAIVETE* OF THE TOY-UNENLIGHTENED.
I'LL PUT SEVERAL PLAYSETS ASIDE FOR WHEN YOU COME *CRAWLING BACK*,
ADDING ON MY TWENTY PERCENT *LAYAWAY FEE*, OF COURSE.

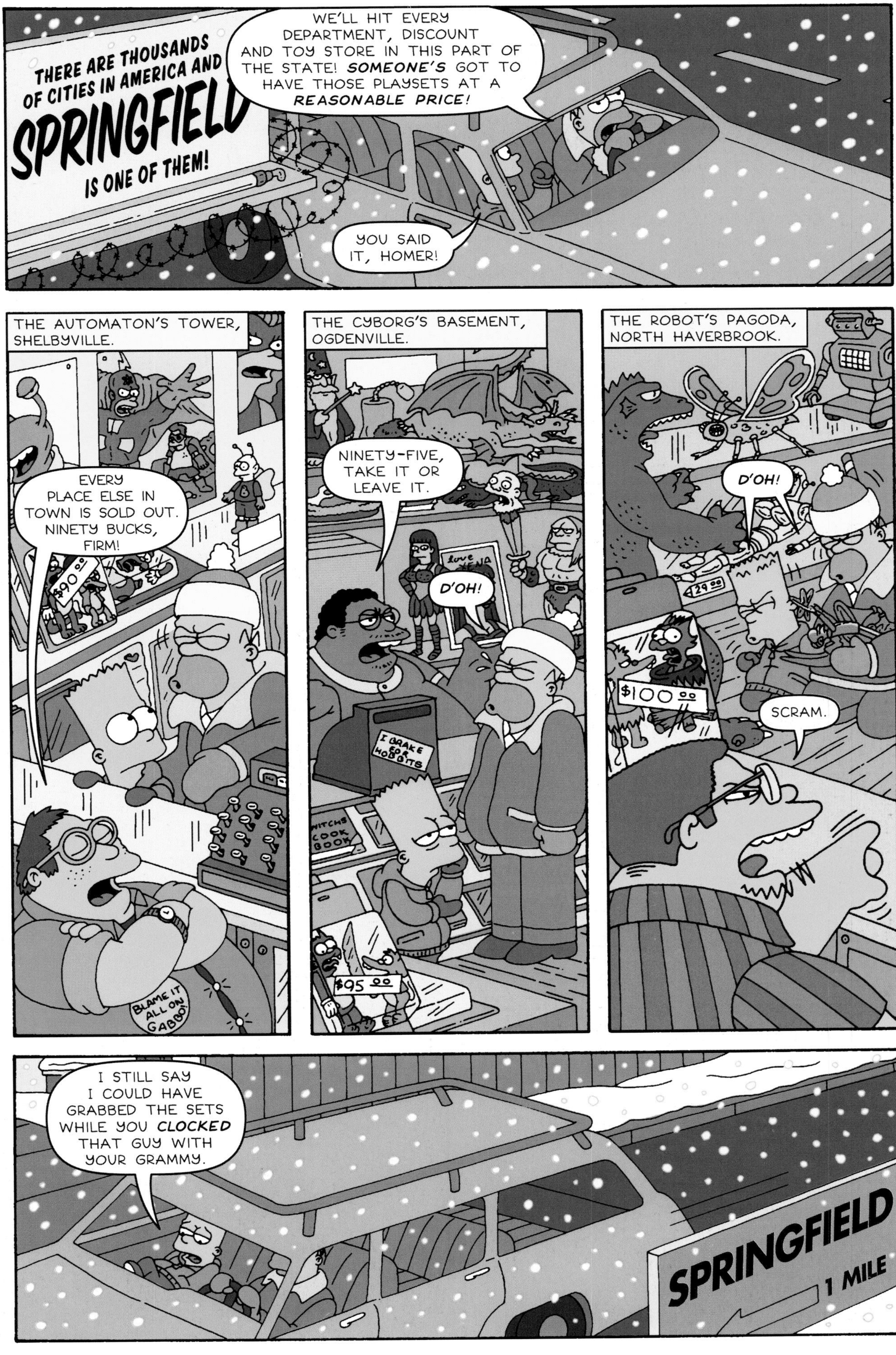
THERE ARE THOUSANDS OF CITIES IN AMERICA AND SPRINGFIELD IS ONE OF THEM!
WE'LL HIT EVERY DEPARTMENT, DISCOUNT AND TOY STORE IN THIS PART OF THE STATE! SOMEONE'S GOT TO HAVE THOSE PLAYSETS AT A REASONABLE PRICE!
YOU SAID IT, HOMER!
THE AUTOMATON'S TOWER, SHELBYVILLE.
EVERY PLACE ELSE IN TOWN IS SOLD OUT. NINETY BUCKS, FIRM!
$90.00
BLAME IT ALL ON GABBO
THE CYBORG'S BASEMENT, OGDENVILLE.
NINETY-FIVE, TAKE IT OR LEAVE IT.
D'OH!
I BRAKE FOR HOBBITS
WITCHS COOK BOOK
$95.00
THE ROBOT'S PAGODA, NORTH HAVERBROOK.
D'OH!
$29.00
$100.00
SCRAM.
I STILL SAY I COULD HAVE GRABBED THE SETS WHILE YOU CLOCKED THAT GUY WITH YOUR GRAMMY.
SPRINGFIELD 1 MILE

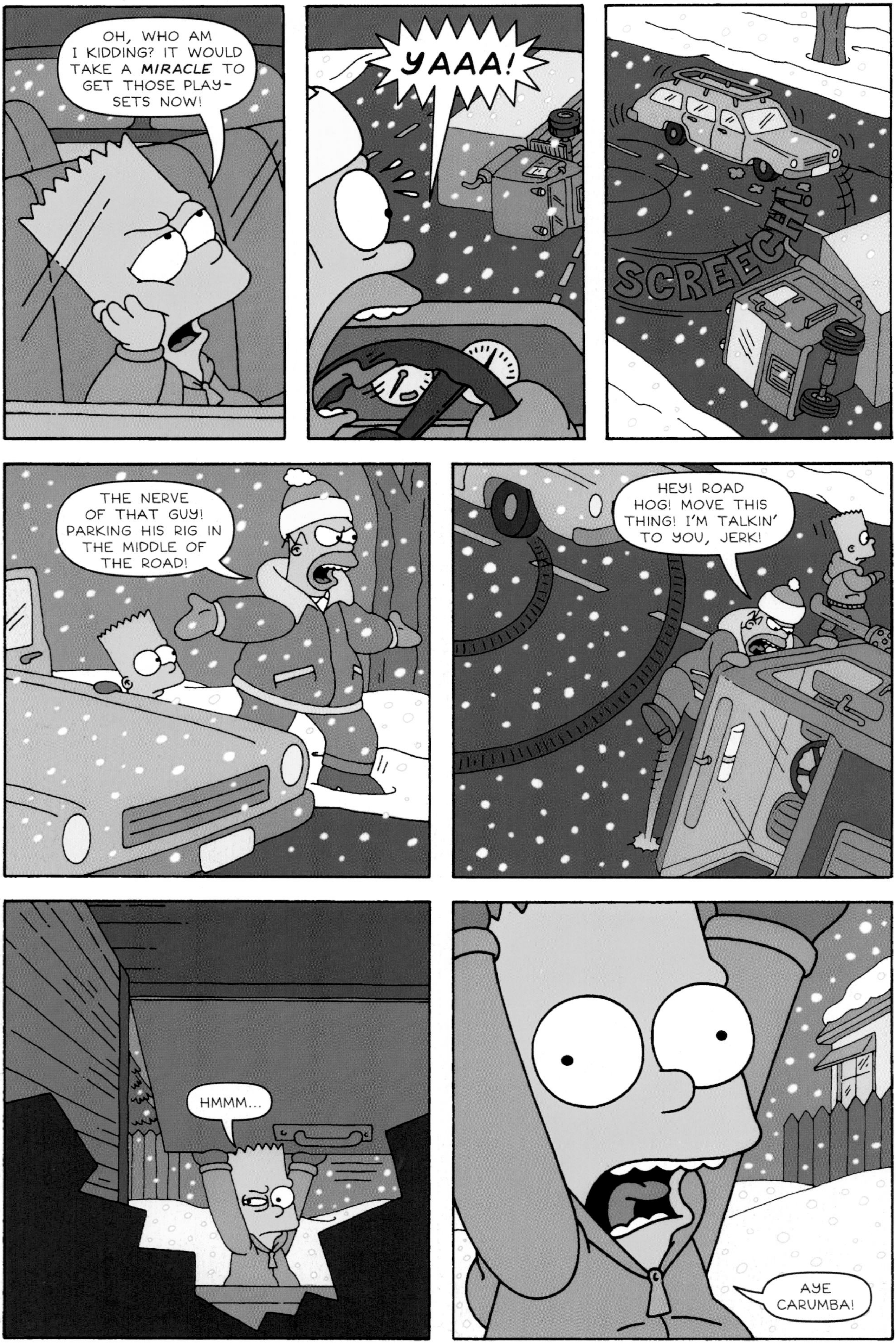

OH, WHO AM I KIDDING? IT WOULD TAKE A MIRACLE TO GET THOSE PLAY-SETS NOW!
YAAA!
SCREECH!
THE NERVE OF THAT GUY! PARKING HIS RIG IN THE MIDDLE OF THE ROAD!
HEY! ROAD HOG! MOVE THIS THING! I'M TALKIN' TO YOU, JERK!
HMMM...
AYE CARUMBA!

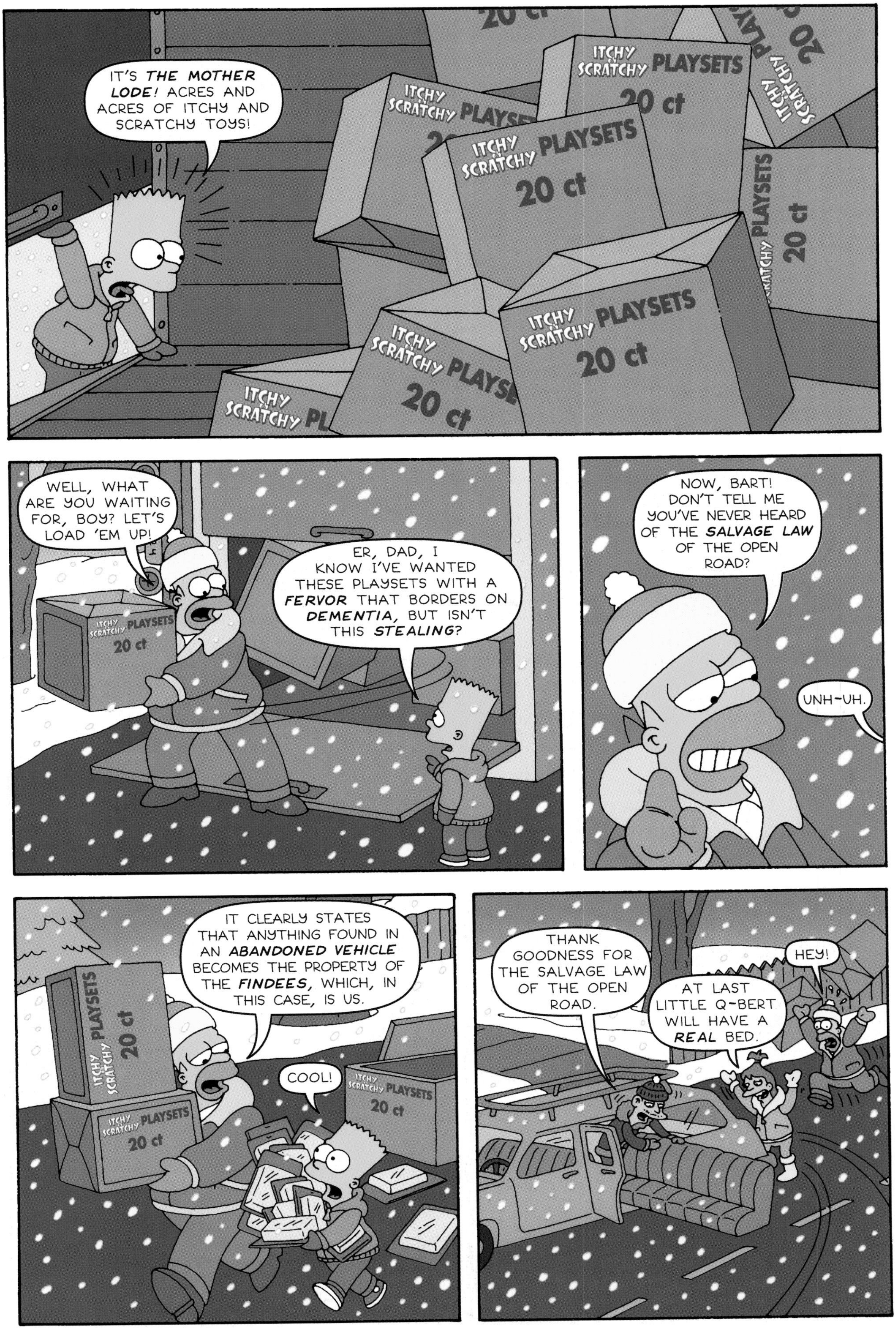

IT'S THE MOTHER LODE! ACRES AND ACRES OF ITCHY AND SCRATCHY TOYS!
ITCHY & SCRATCHY PLAYSETS 20 ct
WELL, WHAT ARE YOU WAITING FOR, BOY? LET'S LOAD 'EM UP!
ER, DAD, I KNOW I'VE WANTED THESE PLAYSETS WITH A FERVOR THAT BORDERS ON DEMENTIA, BUT ISN'T THIS STEALING?
NOW, BART! DON'T TELL ME YOU'VE NEVER HEARD OF THE SALVAGE LAW OF THE OPEN ROAD?
UNH-UH.
IT CLEARLY STATES THAT ANYTHING FOUND IN AN ABANDONED VEHICLE BECOMES THE PROPERTY OF THE FINDEES, WHICH, IN THIS CASE, IS US.
COOL!
THANK GOODNESS FOR THE SALVAGE LAW OF THE OPEN ROAD.
AT LAST LITTLE Q-BERT WILL HAVE A REAL BED.
HEY!

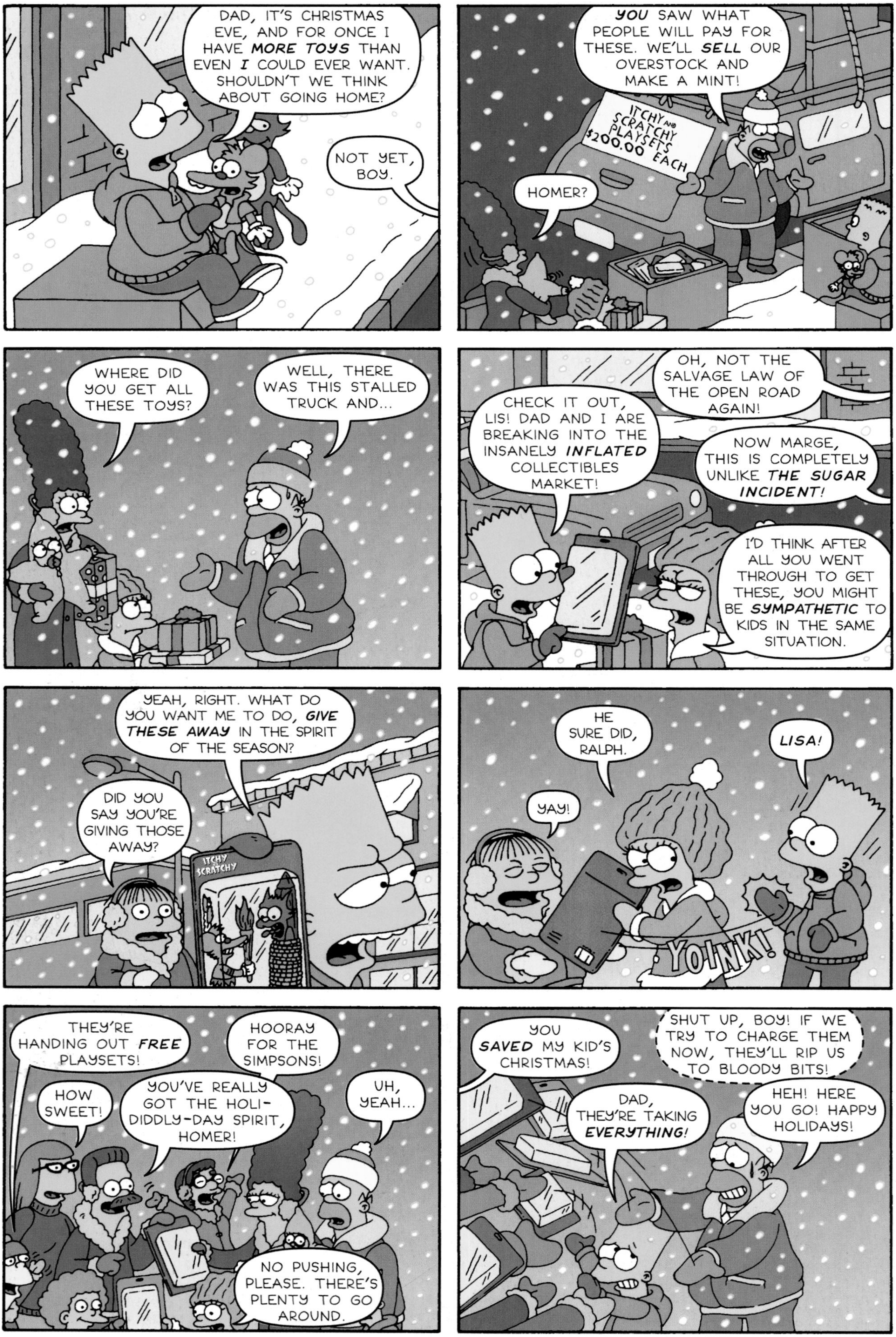
DAD, IT'S CHRISTMAS EVE, AND FOR ONCE I HAVE MORE TOYS THAN EVEN I COULD EVER WANT. SHOULDN'T WE THINK ABOUT GOING HOME?
NOT YET, BOY.
YOU SAW WHAT PEOPLE WILL PAY FOR THESE. WE'LL SELL OUR OVERSTOCK AND MAKE A MINT!
ITCHY AND SCRATCHY PLAYSETS $200.00 EACH
HOMER?
WHERE DID YOU GET ALL THESE TOYS?
WELL, THERE WAS THIS STALLED TRUCK AND...
OH, NOT THE SALVAGE LAW OF THE OPEN ROAD AGAIN!
CHECK IT OUT, LIS! DAD AND I ARE BREAKING INTO THE INSANELY INFLATED COLLECTIBLES MARKET!
NOW MARGE, THIS IS COMPLETELY UNLIKE THE SUGAR INCIDENT!
I'D THINK AFTER ALL YOU WENT THROUGH TO GET THESE, YOU MIGHT BE SYMPATHETIC TO KIDS IN THE SAME SITUATION.
YEAH, RIGHT. WHAT DO YOU WANT ME TO DO, GIVE THESE AWAY IN THE SPIRIT OF THE SEASON?
DID YOU SAY YOU'RE GIVING THOSE AWAY?
ITCHY SCRATCHY
HE SURE DID, RALPH.
LISA!
YAY!
YOINK!
THEY'RE HANDING OUT FREE PLAYSETS!
HOORAY FOR THE SIMPSONS!
HOW SWEET!
YOU'VE REALLY GOT THE HOLI-DIDDLY-DAY SPIRIT, HOMER!
UH, YEAH...
NO PUSHING, PLEASE. THERE'S PLENTY TO GO AROUND.
YOU SAVED MY KID'S CHRISTMAS!
SHUT UP, BOY! IF WE TRY TO CHARGE THEM NOW, THEY'LL RIP US TO BLOODY BITS!
DAD, THEY'RE TAKING EVERYTHING!
HEH! HERE YOU GO! HAPPY HOLIDAYS!

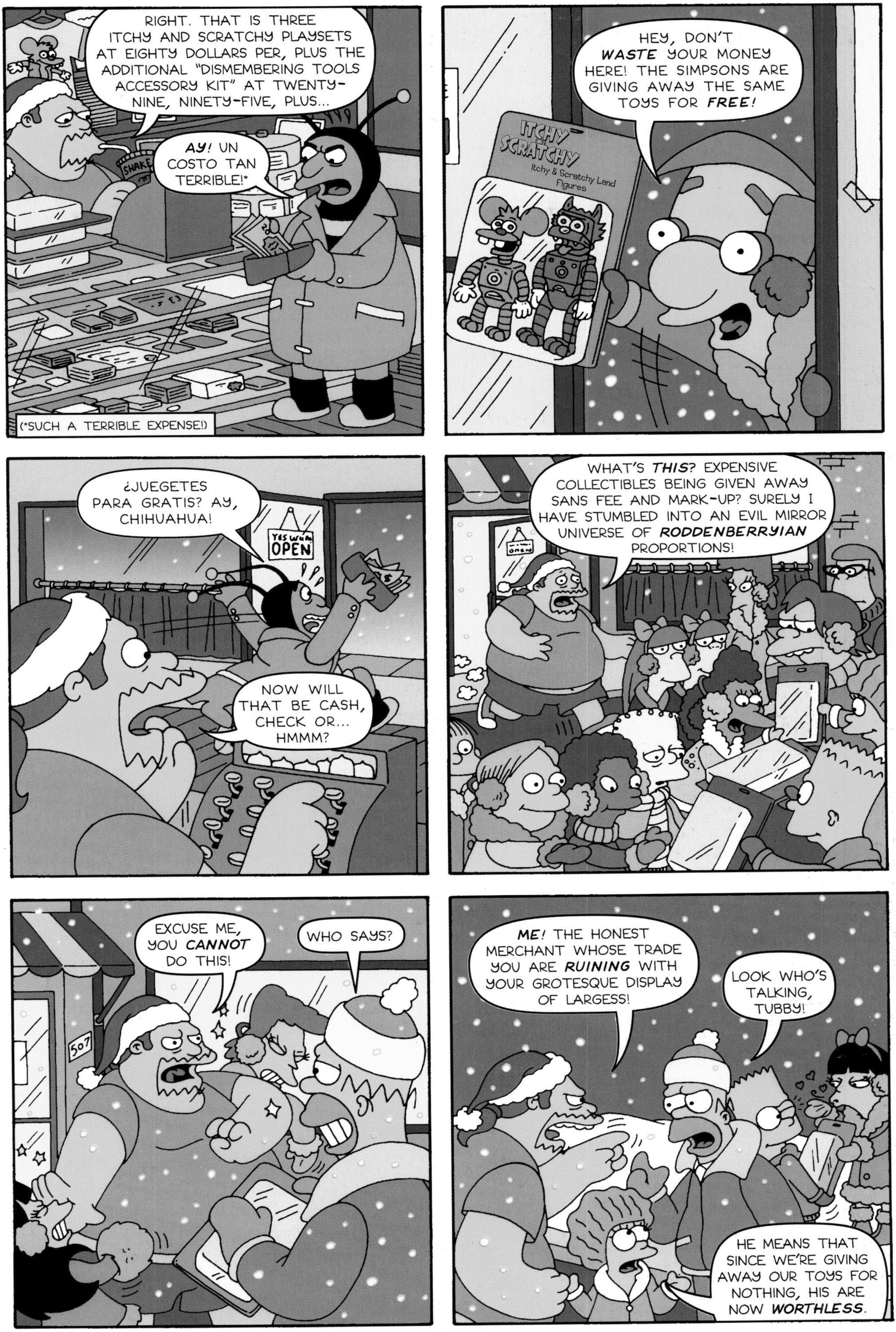
RIGHT. THAT IS THREE ITCHY AND SCRATCHY PLAYSETS AT EIGHTY DOLLARS PER, PLUS THE ADDITIONAL "DISMEMBERING TOOLS ACCESSORY KIT" AT TWENTY-NINE, NINETY-FIVE, PLUS...
SHAKE
AY! UN COSTO TAN TERRIBLE!*
(*SUCH A TERRIBLE EXPENSE!)
HEY, DON'T WASTE YOUR MONEY HERE! THE SIMPSONS ARE GIVING AWAY THE SAME TOYS FOR FREE!
ITCHY & SCRATCHY
Itchy & Scratchy Land Figures
¿JUEGETES PARA GRATIS? AY, CHIHUAHUA!
YES WE'RE OPEN
NOW WILL THAT BE CASH, CHECK OR... HMMM?
WHAT'S THIS? EXPENSIVE COLLECTIBLES BEING GIVEN AWAY SANS FEE AND MARK-UP? SURELY I HAVE STUMBLED INTO AN EVIL MIRROR UNIVERSE OF RODDENBERRYIAN PROPORTIONS!
EXCUSE ME, YOU CANNOT DO THIS!
WHO SAYS?
507
ME! THE HONEST MERCHANT WHOSE TRADE YOU ARE RUINING WITH YOUR GROTESQUE DISPLAY OF LARGESS!
LOOK WHO'S TALKING, TUBBY!
HE MEANS THAT SINCE WE'RE GIVING AWAY OUR TOYS FOR NOTHING, HIS ARE NOW WORTHLESS.

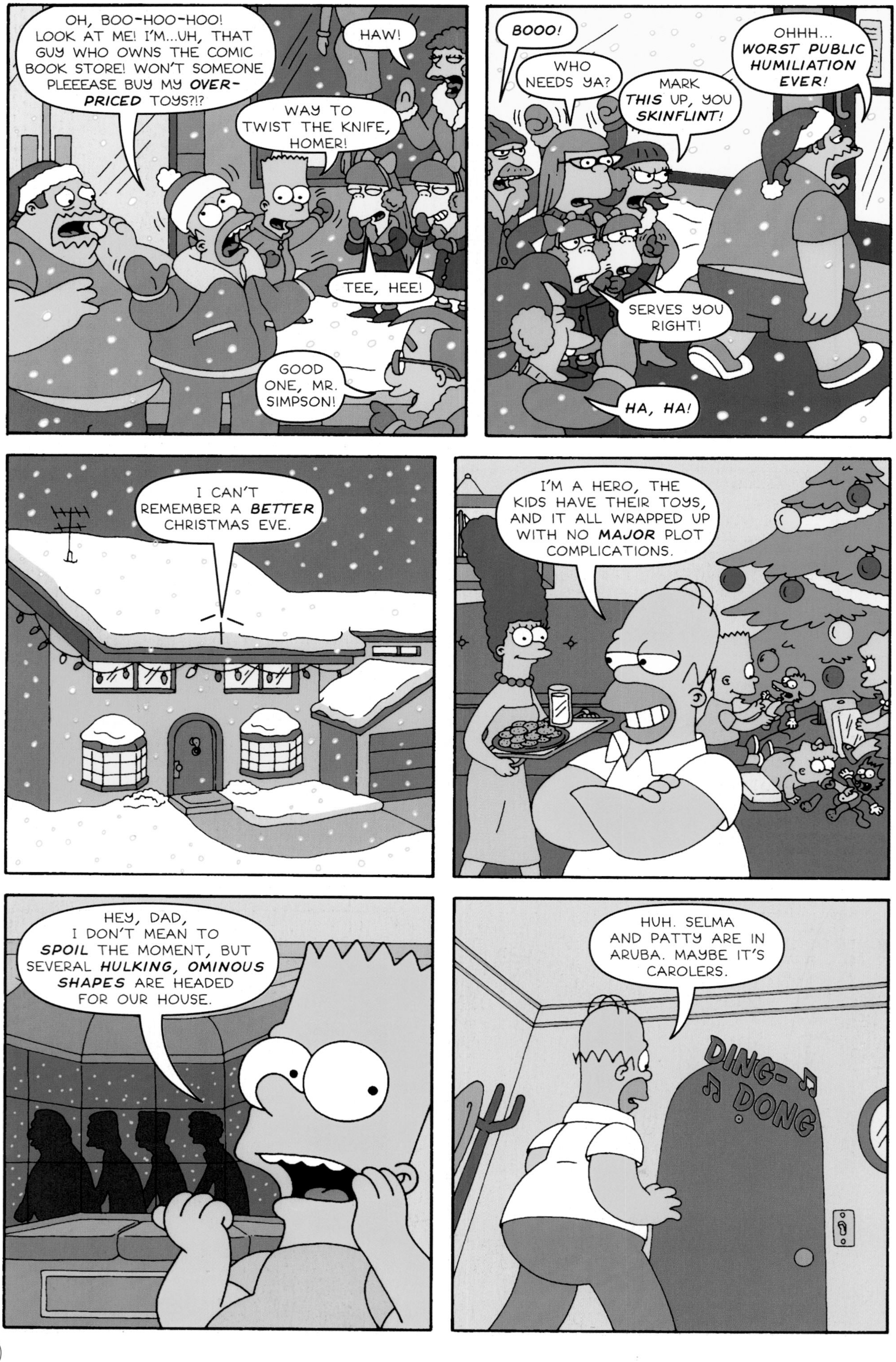
OH, BOO-HOO-HOO! LOOK AT ME! I'M...UH, THAT GUY WHO OWNS THE COMIC BOOK STORE! WON'T SOMEONE PLEEEASE BUY MY **OVER-PRICED** TOYS?!?
HAW!
WAY TO TWIST THE KNIFE, HOMER!
TEE, HEE!
GOOD ONE, MR. SIMPSON!
BOOO!
WHO NEEDS YA?
MARK **THIS** UP, YOU **SKINFLINT!**
OHHH... **WORST PUBLIC HUMILIATION EVER!**
SERVES YOU RIGHT!
HA, HA!
I CAN'T REMEMBER A **BETTER** CHRISTMAS EVE.
I'M A HERO, THE KIDS HAVE THEIR TOYS, AND IT ALL WRAPPED UP WITH NO **MAJOR** PLOT COMPLICATIONS.
HEY, DAD, I DON'T MEAN TO **SPOIL** THE MOMENT, BUT SEVERAL **HULKING, OMINOUS SHAPES** ARE HEADED FOR OUR HOUSE.
HUH. SELMA AND PATTY ARE IN ARUBA. MAYBE IT'S CAROLERS.
DING-DONG

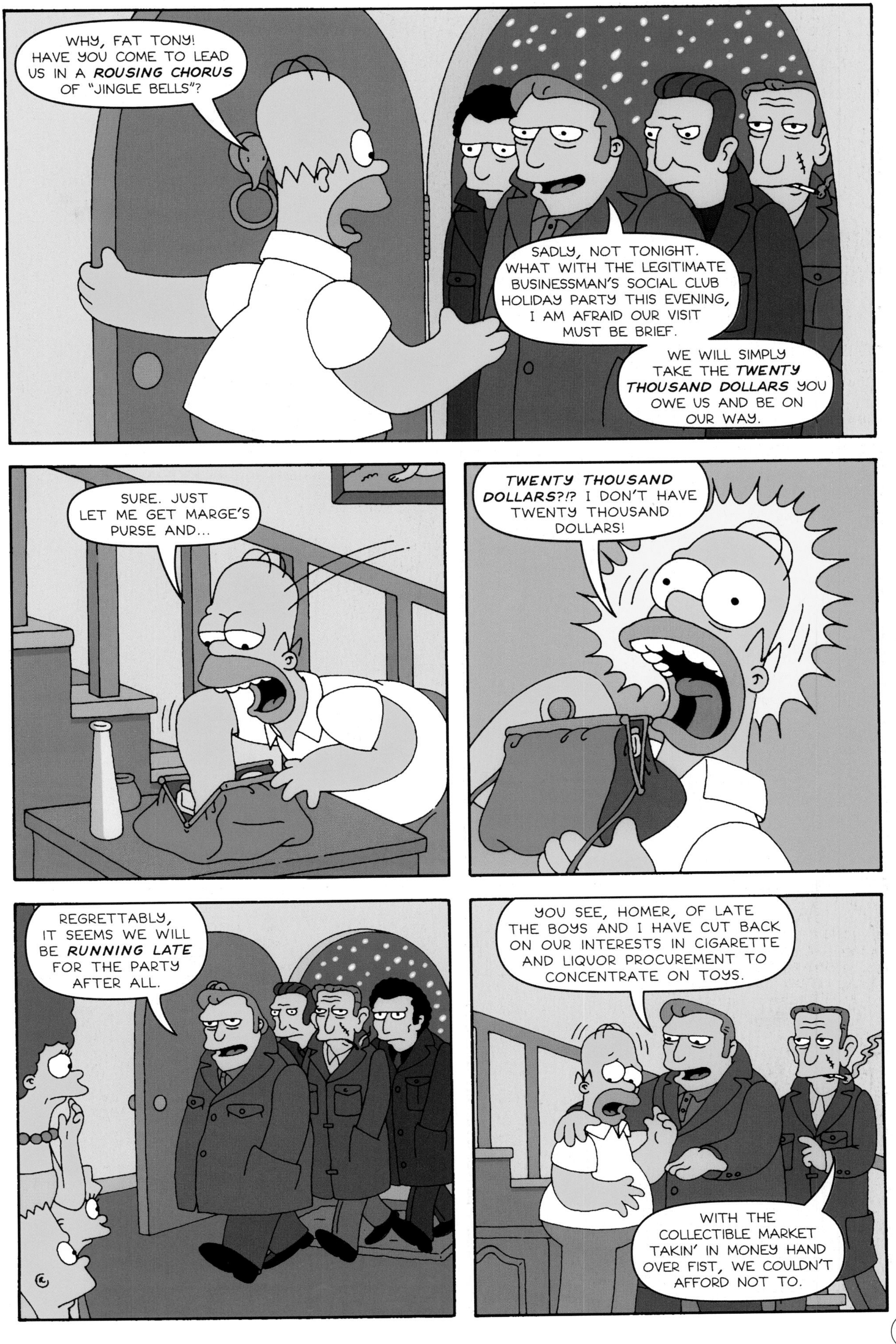
WHY, FAT TONY! HAVE YOU COME TO LEAD US IN A **ROUSING CHORUS** OF "JINGLE BELLS"?
SADLY, NOT TONIGHT. WHAT WITH THE LEGITIMATE BUSINESSMAN'S SOCIAL CLUB HOLIDAY PARTY THIS EVENING, I AM AFRAID OUR VISIT MUST BE BRIEF.
WE WILL SIMPLY TAKE THE **TWENTY THOUSAND DOLLARS** YOU OWE US AND BE ON OUR WAY.
SURE. JUST LET ME GET MARGE'S PURSE AND...
TWENTY THOUSAND DOLLARS?!? I DON'T HAVE TWENTY THOUSAND DOLLARS!
REGRETTABLY, IT SEEMS WE WILL BE **RUNNING LATE** FOR THE PARTY AFTER ALL.
YOU SEE, HOMER, OF LATE THE BOYS AND I HAVE CUT BACK ON OUR INTERESTS IN CIGARETTE AND LIQUOR PROCUREMENT TO CONCENTRATE ON TOYS.
WITH THE COLLECTIBLE MARKET TAKIN' IN MONEY HAND OVER FIST, WE COULDN'T AFFORD NOT TO.

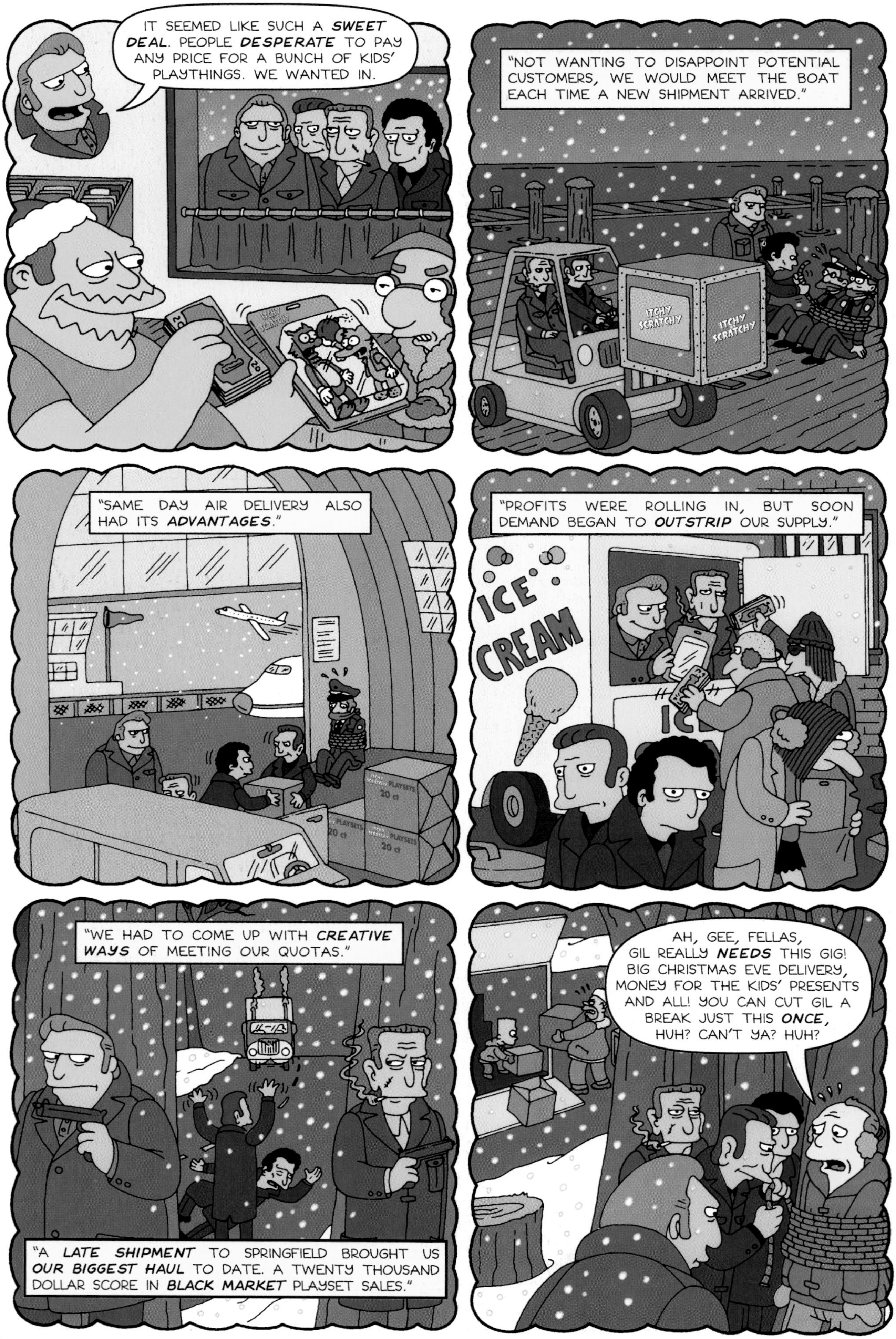
IT SEEMED LIKE SUCH A SWEET DEAL. PEOPLE DESPERATE TO PAY ANY PRICE FOR A BUNCH OF KIDS' PLAYTHINGS. WE WANTED IN.
"NOT WANTING TO DISAPPOINT POTENTIAL CUSTOMERS, WE WOULD MEET THE BOAT EACH TIME A NEW SHIPMENT ARRIVED."
ITCHY SCRATCHY
ITCHY SCRATCHY
"SAME DAY AIR DELIVERY ALSO HAD ITS ADVANTAGES."
PLAYSETS 20 ct
"PROFITS WERE ROLLING IN, BUT SOON DEMAND BEGAN TO OUTSTRIP OUR SUPPLY."
ICE CREAM
"WE HAD TO COME UP WITH CREATIVE WAYS OF MEETING OUR QUOTAS."
"A LATE SHIPMENT TO SPRINGFIELD BROUGHT US OUR BIGGEST HAUL TO DATE. A TWENTY THOUSAND DOLLAR SCORE IN BLACK MARKET PLAYSET SALES."
AH, GEE, FELLAS, GIL REALLY NEEDS THIS GIG! BIG CHRISTMAS EVE DELIVERY, MONEY FOR THE KIDS' PRESENTS AND ALL! YOU CAN CUT GIL A BREAK JUST THIS ONCE, HUH? CAN'T YA? HUH?

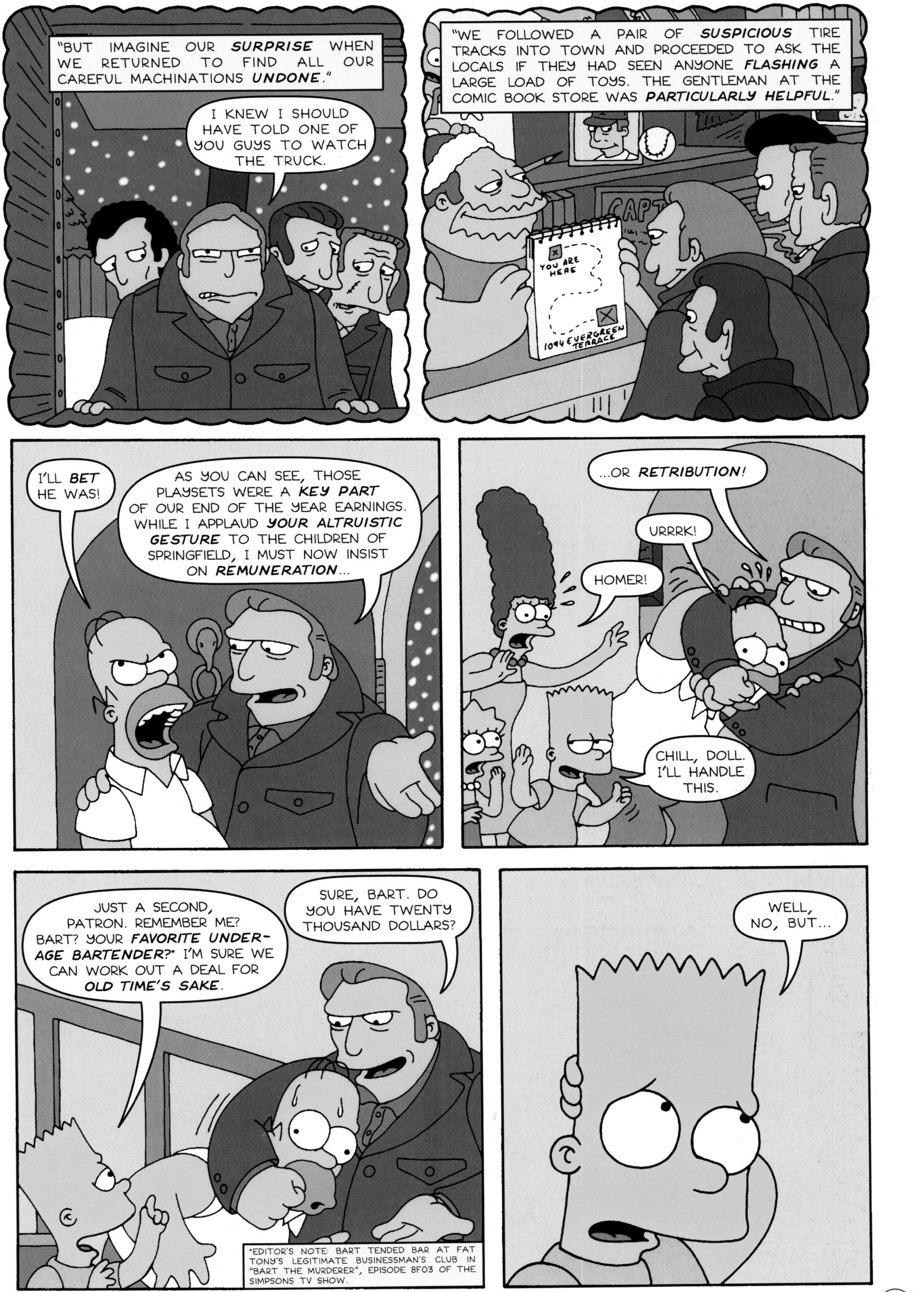
"BUT IMAGINE OUR SURPRISE WHEN WE RETURNED TO FIND ALL OUR CAREFUL MACHINATIONS UNDONE."
I KNEW I SHOULD HAVE TOLD ONE OF YOU GUYS TO WATCH THE TRUCK.
"WE FOLLOWED A PAIR OF SUSPICIOUS TIRE TRACKS INTO TOWN AND PROCEEDED TO ASK THE LOCALS IF THEY HAD SEEN ANYONE FLASHING A LARGE LOAD OF TOYS. THE GENTLEMAN AT THE COMIC BOOK STORE WAS PARTICULARLY HELPFUL."
YOU ARE HERE
1094 EVERGREEN TERRACE
I'LL BET HE WAS!
AS YOU CAN SEE, THOSE PLAYSETS WERE A KEY PART OF OUR END OF THE YEAR EARNINGS. WHILE I APPLAUD YOUR ALTRUISTIC GESTURE TO THE CHILDREN OF SPRINGFIELD, I MUST NOW INSIST ON REMUNERATION...
...OR RETRIBUTION!
URRRK!
HOMER!
CHILL, DOLL. I'LL HANDLE THIS.
JUST A SECOND, PATRON. REMEMBER ME? BART? YOUR FAVORITE UNDER-AGE BARTENDER?* I'M SURE WE CAN WORK OUT A DEAL FOR OLD TIME'S SAKE.
SURE, BART. DO YOU HAVE TWENTY THOUSAND DOLLARS?
WELL, NO, BUT...

*EDITOR'S NOTE: BART TENDED BAR AT FAT TONY'S LEGITIMATE BUSINESSMAN'S CLUB IN "BART THE MURDERER", EPISODE 8F03 OF THE SIMPSONS TV SHOW.

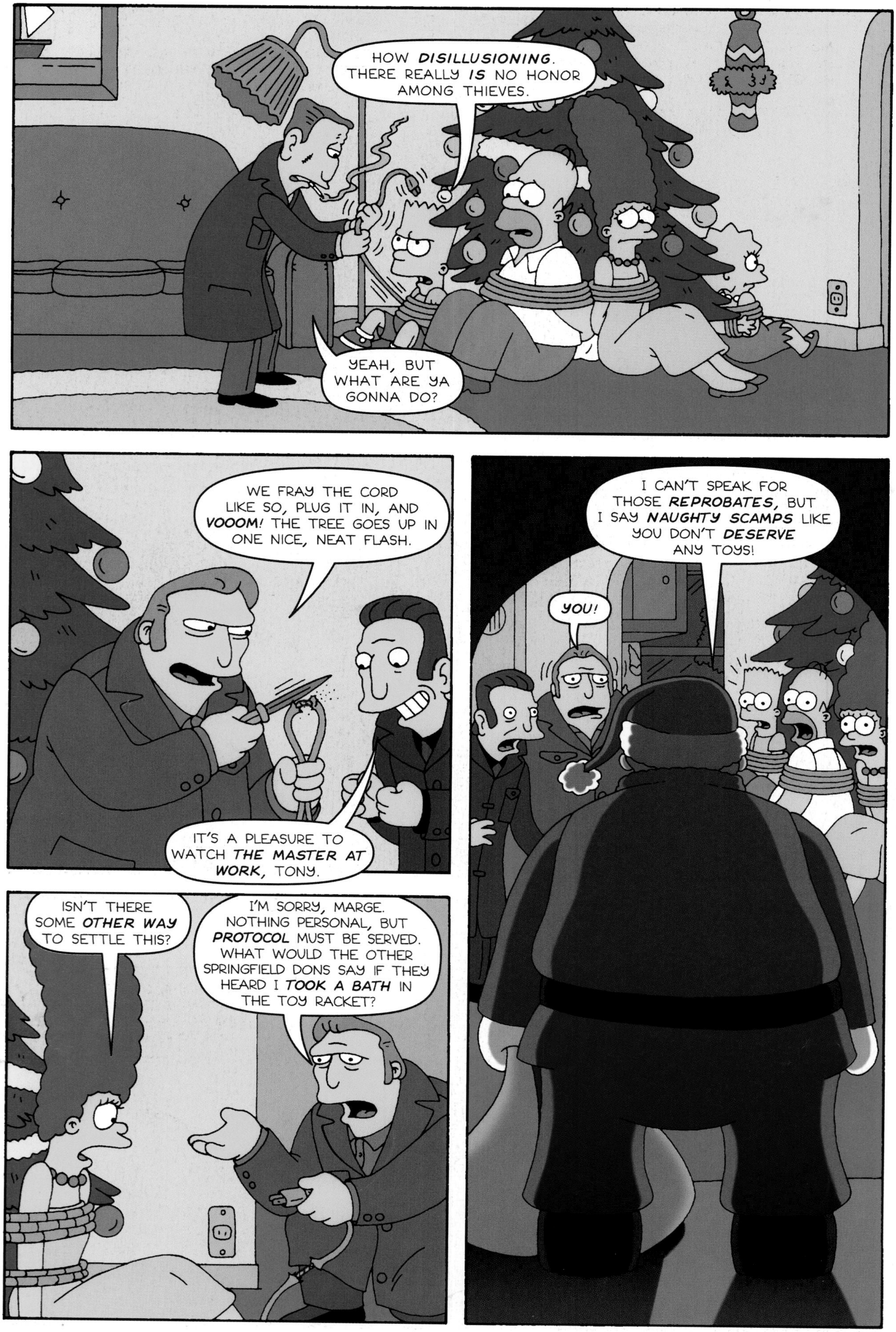
HOW **DISILLUSIONING**. THERE REALLY **IS** NO HONOR AMONG THIEVES.
YEAH, BUT WHAT ARE YA GONNA DO?
WE FRAY THE CORD LIKE SO, PLUG IT IN, AND ***VOOOM!*** THE TREE GOES UP IN ONE NICE, NEAT FLASH.
IT'S A PLEASURE TO WATCH ***THE MASTER AT WORK,*** TONY.
ISN'T THERE SOME ***OTHER WAY*** TO SETTLE THIS?
I'M SORRY, MARGE. NOTHING PERSONAL, BUT ***PROTOCOL*** MUST BE SERVED. WHAT WOULD THE OTHER SPRINGFIELD DONS SAY IF THEY HEARD I ***TOOK A BATH*** IN THE TOY RACKET?
I CAN'T SPEAK FOR THOSE ***REPROBATES,*** BUT I SAY ***NAUGHTY SCAMPS*** LIKE YOU DON'T ***DESERVE*** ANY TOYS!
YOU!

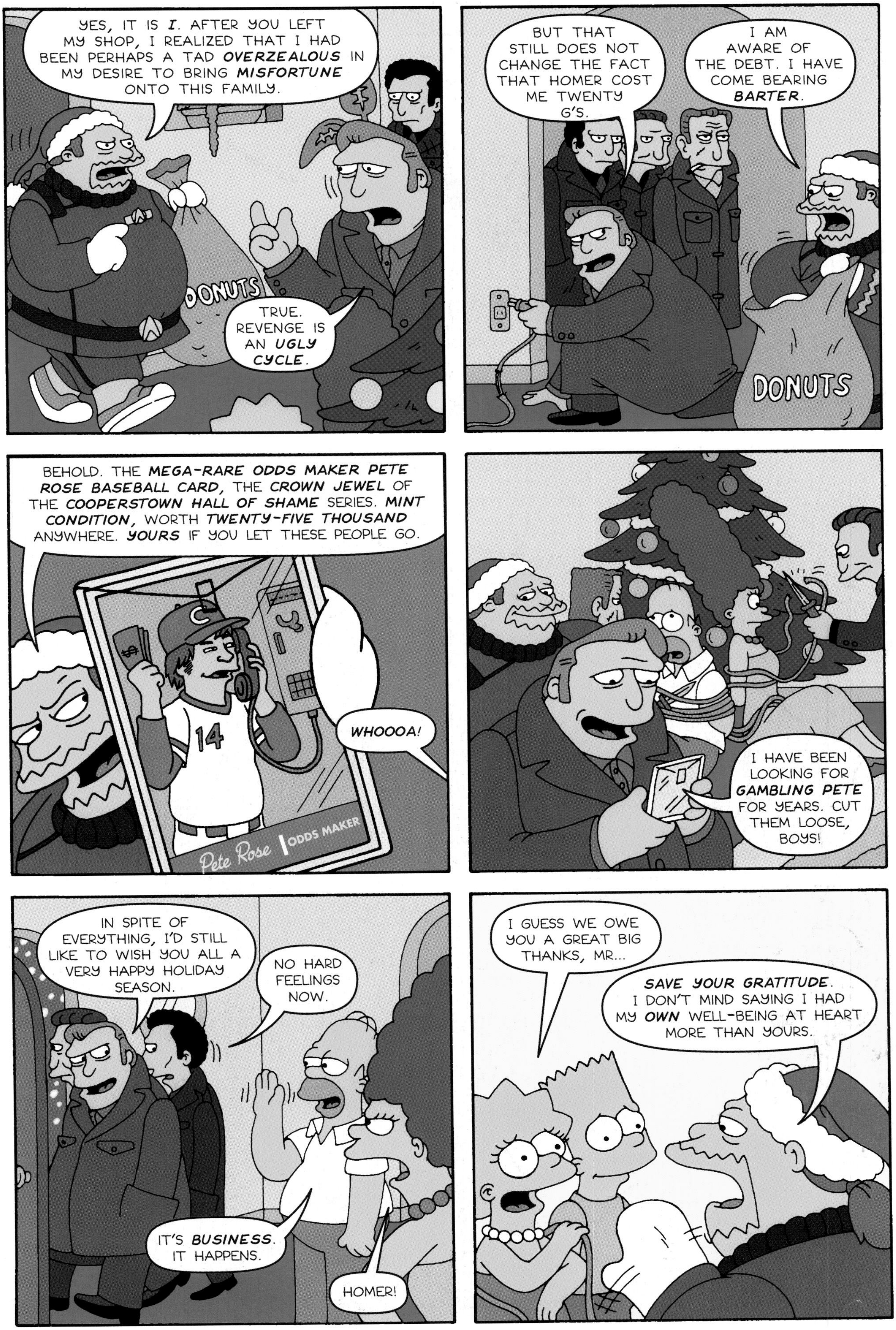

YES, IT IS I. AFTER YOU LEFT MY SHOP, I REALIZED THAT I HAD BEEN PERHAPS A TAD OVERZEALOUS IN MY DESIRE TO BRING MISFORTUNE ONTO THIS FAMILY.
DONUTS
TRUE. REVENGE IS AN UGLY CYCLE.
BUT THAT STILL DOES NOT CHANGE THE FACT THAT HOMER COST ME TWENTY G'S.
I AM AWARE OF THE DEBT. I HAVE COME BEARING BARTER.
DONUTS
BEHOLD. THE MEGA-RARE ODDS MAKER PETE ROSE BASEBALL CARD, THE CROWN JEWEL OF THE COOPERSTOWN HALL OF SHAME SERIES. MINT CONDITION, WORTH TWENTY-FIVE THOUSAND ANYWHERE. YOURS IF YOU LET THESE PEOPLE GO.
14
Pete Rose
ODDS MAKER
WHOOOA!
I HAVE BEEN LOOKING FOR GAMBLING PETE FOR YEARS. CUT THEM LOOSE, BOYS!
IN SPITE OF EVERYTHING, I'D STILL LIKE TO WISH YOU ALL A VERY HAPPY HOLIDAY SEASON.
NO HARD FEELINGS NOW.
IT'S BUSINESS. IT HAPPENS.
HOMER!
I GUESS WE OWE YOU A GREAT BIG THANKS, MR...
SAVE YOUR GRATITUDE. I DON'T MIND SAYING I HAD MY OWN WELL-BEING AT HEART MORE THAN YOURS.

THE TOY GIVE-AWAY THIS AFTERNOON TURNED YOU SIMPSONS, HOWEVER BRIEFLY, INTO *LOCAL HEROES*. IF IT CAME OUT THAT I HAD AIDED THE GANGSTERS, I WOULD HAVE BEEN FURTHER *VILIFIED* BY THE COMMUNITY, AND MY STORE *SHUNNED* LIKE A TREK FAN AT A B5 CONVENTION.

THAT IS *COLD*.

BUT PEOPLE HAVE *SHORT MEMORIES*, AND I AM *CONFIDENT* YOUR GOOD DEED WILL SOON BE *FORGOTTEN*. THEN I MAY ONCE AGAIN CHARGE AS I PLEASE FOR WHATEVER *FLASH IN THE PAN* TOY THAT NEXT SPARKS THE PUBLIC'S FANCY.

OOOH! NEW *FUNZO*!

HEY KIDS! NOW I'M MORE FUNZO THAN EVER! TEE-HEE!

MUST HAVE!

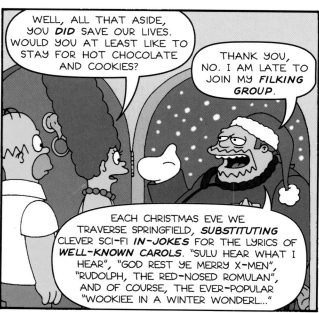

WELL, ALL THAT ASIDE, YOU *DID* SAVE OUR LIVES. WOULD YOU AT LEAST LIKE TO STAY FOR HOT CHOCOLATE AND COOKIES?

THANK YOU, NO. I AM LATE TO JOIN MY *FILKING GROUP*.

EACH CHRISTMAS EVE WE TRAVERSE SPRINGFIELD, *SUBSTITUTING* CLEVER SCI-FI *IN-JOKES* FOR THE LYRICS OF *WELL-KNOWN CAROLS*. "SULU HEAR WHAT I HEAR", "GOD REST YE MERRY X-MEN", "RUDOLPH, THE RED-NOSED ROMULAN", AND OF COURSE, THE EVER-POPULAR "WOOKIEE IN A WINTER WONDERL..."

UGGGGHHHHH!

SLAM!

ALL THINGS CONSIDERED, LIS', I'D SAY THIS WAS ONE OF OUR *BETTER* CHRISTMAS EVES. WE *MADE OUT LIKE BANDITS* AND NO ONE GOT *KILLED*.

YESSS, BUT I STILL HAVE THIS *NAGGING FEELING* THAT SOMETHING IS GOING UNRESOLVED.

COME ON, FELLAS, ENOUGH'S ENOUGH! GIL *NEEDS A BREAK* HERE, OKAY? FELLAS? YOU WOULDN'T LET OL' GIL DOWN, WOULD YA? *FELLAS*?

THE END